El Birdos

ALSO BY DOUG FELDMANN
AND FROM McFARLAND

*September Streak: The 1935 Chicago Cubs
Chase the Pennant* (2003)

*Fleeter Than Birds: The 1985 St. Louis Cardinals
and Small Ball's Last Hurrah* (2002)

*Dizzy and the Gas House Gang: The 1934 St. Louis Cardinals
and Depression-Era Baseball* (2000)

El Birdos

The 1967 and 1968
St. Louis Cardinals

Doug Feldmann

McFarland & Company, Inc., Publishers
Jefferson, North Carolina, and London

LIBRARY OF CONGRESS CATALOGUING-IN-PUBLICATION DATA

Feldmann, Doug, 1970–
    El Birdos : the 1967 and 1968 St. Louis Cardinals / Doug
Feldmann.
        p.   cm.
    Includes bibliographical references and index.

    ISBN-13: 978-0-7864-2965-3
    (softcover : 50# alkaline paper) ∞

    1. St. Louis Cardinals (Baseball team)— History.
I. Title.
GV875.S3F455   2007
796.357'640977866 — dc22   2007005327

British Library cataloguing data are available

Cover photograph: Pitcher Bob Gibson (St. Louis
Mercantile Library, University of Missouri St. Louis)

Manufactured in the United States of America

McFarland & Company, Inc., Publishers
  Box 611, Jefferson, North Carolina 28640
    www.mcfarlandpub.com

To the people of Clinton County, Illinois

the home of Ski,
the Clinton County League,
the pork tenderloin sandwich at the Knotty Pine,
and unwavering Cardinals loyalty

Acknowledgments

The author wishes to thank Bob Broeg, Ed Wilks, and Neal Russo of the *St. Louis Post-Dispatch* for their colorful accounts of the Cardinals' games from 1967 and 1968, as well as Jeff Ecker and Norm Richards of the St. Louis-Bob Broeg Chapter of the Society for American Baseball Research.

Bob, you live on in our hearts.

Table of Contents

Prologue

By faith the walls of Jericho fell, after the people had marched around them for seven days.

— Hebrews 11:30

The sun was shining through the 96 tiny arches atop the circular furnace for the last time. Even though it was early October, the rays belted down upon the grass in typical St. Louis summertime fashion, as if it was a special order from God to make all things appropriate on this most important day. And just as the great horns announced the arrival of the gladiators into the Roman coliseum, the Yamaha organ of Ernie Hays proclaimed that the revered modern spectacle was about to begin, complete with its own special ballad.

> *Meet me in St. Louie, Louie*
> *Meet me at the fair*
> *Don't tell me the lights are shining*
> *Any place but there*
> *We will dance the Hoochie-Koochie*
> *I will be your tootsie-wootsie*
> *If you'll meet me in St. Louie, Louie*
> *Meet me at the fair*

Next, the masses witnessed the fulfillment of a local celebrity's final wish. Jack Buck, who had been the radio announcer for St. Louis Cardinals baseball games since the 1950s, had passed away in 2002. In a video message to the crowd before this particular contest, his son Joe — who, because of his own prominence in broadcasting was away for a national telecast of a football game — shared his late father's regrets for not being able to be present in St. Louis on this day. Joe, however, asked that the crowd honor his father with

1

one of Jack's favorite ballpark moments—everyone singing the "Star-Spangled Banner" *a cappella*. In a stirring moment, 50,000 voices were unified to celebrate the song that Mr. Buck loved the most.

When the post-song cheering had ended, all the damp eyes shifted downward to the playing field and fixed on an 82-year-old man named Albert Schoendienst, known locally as "Red," the man who had also perhaps accumulated the greatest pension in the history of the western world. It was Schoendienst's 56th year with the Cardinals (and 61st in professional baseball overall) as a player, coach, manager, or executive, counting two different periods from when he was signed in 1942 until his trade to the New York Giants in 1956, and his return to the organization in 1961 until the present day. As Schoendienst walked towards home plate with a baseball glove in hand, he waved to the crowd that was greeting him with one of the most frenzied standing ovations ever heard at Busch Stadium. Next came a 66-year-old man named Mike Shannon, who like Schoendienst was wearing an unbuttoned white Cardinals jersey, but was uniquely accessorized with his usual all-black attire underneath. Shannon strode tall to the pitching mound, and flapped his arms back to let one fly towards his former manager. He one-hopped the ceremonial pitch, and the ball skipped past Schoendienst to the screen as the crowd laughed in supportive amusement. At that point, Red must have been wondering what calamity could have potentially befallen his experiment to make Shannon—an outfielder for most of his professional baseball life—a third baseman at the start of the 1967 season.

The pre-game ceremonies concluded and the game commenced, as the thousands had before in the old ballpark. At the start of the sixth inning, a man named Osborne Earl Smith suddenly appeared, strolling through the wagon gate from the right field wall, and began touring the warning track of the entire park in an open convertible, much akin to a great ancient warrior making a final encore appearance to the sands of the coliseum. Stopping at the right field corner where his lap had begun, Mr. Smith peeled off the number "1" that had been affixed to the outfield wall—it had been the uniform number he wore for the Cardinals—and thus revealed a "0," informing the whole world that this was now an official game on October 2, 2005—and no such regular-season game would ever again be played in Busch Stadium.

Thus, the nearing end of old Busch Stadium — in actuality, the second ballpark to bear the name — and the opening of the new one in 2006 was designed to ignite a rebirth of the downtown area of St. Louis; such a rebirth had also been sought in the early 1960s. It was another time of profound change in the city, an epoch in which St. Louis transformed the downtown into a revitalized economic and cultural engine of the region. The Cardinals, too, restored some of the glory of their past, beating the mighty Yankees in a seven-game series in 1964, and constructing an impressive new stadium in

1966. The new Cardinals home became the hub of regional life, just as its predecessor, Sportsman's Park (renamed the first Busch Stadium in 1953), and the rest of "Grand North Grand" had attracted people as the magnet of the community through the first half of the twentieth century. With the new Busch, the downtown area prospered to achieve a greater degree of stability than Grand Avenue, as the latter has experienced pronounced decay near the hallowed ballpark corners that meet at Sullivan, Spring, and Dodier Streets. But such is the pathway of life — for cities, for people, and even for ballparks. When one segment of existence is no longer palatable, useful, or even sustainable, we attempt to reach a peaceable agreement with our pasts, while planning to cement a new pledge to our futures.

So at 4:33 P.M., central time, Cardinals pitcher Jason Isringhausen — himself a visitor at Busch many times as a boy, growing up in nearby Piasa, Illinois—fired a strike past a swinging Chris Denorfia of the Cincinnati Reds, bringing down the final regular-season curtain on one of the storied venues of baseball's past half-century. The attendees did not want to leave, so parading out afterwards were over a hundred more former Cardinals players, joining Schoendienst, Shannon, and Smith. After an hour and a half, the ceremonies came to a close in the only way possible in St. Louis—with the Budweiser Clydesdales stomping through the wagon gate in the outfield while the organist Hays appropriately performed "Here Comes the King" for one last glorious time.

Concrete and seats and scoreboard placards were not removed by the fans as souvenirs as they left the stadium, for playoff games would still be held on the premises in the coming weeks. But for most of us, this game — a Cardinals win, though the 7–5 score seems incidental — was our goodbye. Having just walked down the grandstand ramp onto the corner of Seventh and Walnut for the last time, I was among the thousands who must have felt the same strange mix of sadness and comfort. Busch Stadium appeared on the earth five years before I did, but as far as I was concerned, it had been at that intersection forever, and would always be there.

I then wandered down Clark Avenue with my friend Jason. We recapped our favorite Busch moments in our ten-minute walk back to his car. He drove me to my flight at Lambert, even though it was a bit out of his way en route to his home in Chicago. We sat quietly during the ride. I then started rambling internally about my childhood — visiting relatives in Carlyle ... lunch at Father Jerome's ... Clinton County League games ... Cards-Cubs in the evening ... hot nights at Busch ... pizza afterwards at the Knotty Pine in Breese.

Because of the construction of the new stadium, we had to take a detour down South 14th Street to Gravois, taking us to Jefferson and out to U.S. 40 towards the airport. Going northbound on Jefferson, one has a magnificent view of downtown looking back east. Just before we turned west onto Route

40, we noticed the stadium sneaking one last peek at us. Within two months Busch, its tiny arches, and our material connection to the 1960s renaissance of the city and its team had been broken. But before that stadium had even celebrated its first birthday back in the latter half of the 1960s, its dirt and grass would be christened by a team that would excite the city for the remainder of the decade, a team that became known as "El Birdos"—a colorful nickname applied by one of its most colorful characters.

1. Seventh and Walnut

This is still a good-looking park. But the new stadium will be better for the fans. It's not like we're going to another state or another city. We're going next door. I look at it as progress.

— Red Schoendienst, 1965

In more ways than one, it seemed like Mr. Solomon Joseph Hemus *just couldn't win* as the manager of the St. Louis Cardinals. Coming up through the ranks as a product of the organization, he had made the major leagues as a player in 1949 and wound up tying for the National League lead in runs scored in 1952 with 105, equaling the mark of his more famous teammate, Stan Musial. Hemus remained with the team until being traded to the Philadelphia Phillies in 1956, but returned to the Cardinals at the end of the 1959 season at the age of 36 to take over as player-manager. Most importantly to the St. Louis fans and media, it seemed like he just could not win consistently on the field, always the ultimate barometer of success in sports at any level past high school. In all fairness to Hemus, this is true only in the most literal sense — as his three-year tenure at the Cardinals' helm (1959–1961) netted him a final record of 190 wins and 192 losses, just mathematically poor enough for his detractors to label him as a loser. On a more personal front, Solly just could not win the support of the Cardinals fan base either, as he wound up being the symbolic capstone of the dark decade of the 1950s for the ball club. When Hemus had taken over at the start of the 1959 season, he had inherited a team that was 72–82 the year before under Fred Hutchinson, who himself had been relieved with ten games remaining in the schedule and replaced by former Chicago Cubs third baseman Stan Hack. Hutchinson had been the team's fifth manager of the 1950s when he led them to a second place finish in 1957, their highest placement in the decade. But Hemus could do no better, as many of his moves left Cardinals fans — and poor Solly himself — scratching their heads.

5

While the Cardinals came up short in every year of the '50s in their pursuit of a championship, the individual dominance of their greatest star,
Musial, hardly faded. Musial, the man from Donora, Pennsylvania, who batted like he was "peeking around the corner," would make the All-Star team
in every year of the decade, capturing his fourth, fifth, sixth, and seventh batting titles among other laurels in the ten-year stretch. By the time Hemus
assumed command in 1959, however, age had begun to take its toll on Musial,
and the slugger had been gradually shifting his defensive duties to first base.
It was a position that he never liked ("It's scary to be that close to the batter," Musial once said), an experiment that started way back in 1946 when he
returned to the Cardinals after a stint in the Navy at the end of World War
II, four years after his rookie campaign. He had been signed to the Cardinals
as a left-handed pitcher in 1938, but shortly before an imminent release from
the organization after some bad outings off the mound, his powerful batting
stroke provided a long career in terrorizing pitchers around the National
League.

But now, the glory days of "Stan the Man" appeared to be passing him
by, and he apparently found no sympathy in his ex-teammate who was now
his on-field boss. Musial's average would fall to .255 in just 115 games in 1959,
the first time in his career that his batting mark had gone under .310 for a
season. But more appalling than Musial's statistical fade was the fact that
Hemus benched him for an entire month during the 1960 season, something
that seemed senseless to the rest of the players and to most members of the
media. Many were attributing Musial's fade not to age, but to his adjustment
to a new pitch introduced into the baseball dictum called the slider, a new
combination of the fastball and curveball. By July 1961, however, Hemus was
let go — and in his place went Johnny Keane, a man who was serving on
Hemus's staff as a coach. Leaving the premises bitterly, Hemus felt as if he
had been backstabbed by Keane and Keane's friend, Cardinals general manager Bing Devine. Devine had been the Cardinals' general manager since 1957,
coming back to St. Louis after a six-year stint as the general manager of the
club's minor league team at Rochester, New York. Like Keane, he was really
a Cardinals man through and through. His work with the organization went
back to the 1930s, and he formerly had played baseball at Washington University in St. Louis.

With the sourness of Hemus behind them, the players became more
relaxed under the leadership of Keane. Musial was able to finish his career
with a flourish, his average leaping up to .330 in 1962 at the age of 41. It was
that year that President John F. Kennedy, aged 45, said to Stan, "A couple of
years ago they told me I was too young to be president and you were too old
to be playing baseball. But we fooled *them*." It had been, in part, the product of a newfound workout regimen offered to Musial by Walter Eberhardt,

who had taught biomechanics at St. Louis University. Buoyed by an emotional announcement of his impending retirement at a picnic given by Cardinals owner and beer magnate August A. Busch Jr. during late August of 1963, Musial would lead the Cardinals on one final, brilliant charge, helping the team go 19–1 during a stretch in September that year which almost garnered them the pennant. When he hit a home run on September 10, 1963, he did so in honor of his first grandchild, recently born; when he got two hits in his last game on September 29 at old Busch Stadium, he amazingly had finished his career with 1,815 hits in the home park, and 1,815 hits on the road. Consistency was his trademark as much as anything, however, for he never had a prolonged slump — Musial batted at least .323 during every month on the baseball calendar for his career. He had first mentioned his possible retirement to Devine in early August, as the two were having breakfast in Milwaukee.

Playing under Keane for his final two seasons was a peaceful way for Musial to bow out with dignity; but it also set the foundation for one of the greatest decades in Cardinals history. Keane had a nondescript career as a professional player himself, all of it in the minor leagues. He had been hit in the head by a pitched ball in the Texas League in 1935, effectively ending his playing career at the age of 23. For six years he studied to become a Catholic priest, a devotion he relinquished to give a life in baseball one more attempt. Unlike Hemus, he cut the Cardinals players loose and let them play without too much restriction — at least on the field. He did not drink, and discontinued poker games among the players as he saw gambling as a destructive vice. It was in consideration of the younger players on the team that he discouraged it, just as he discouraged players from living in parts of the city that had too many "social distractions."

While no new pennants had yet flown over the old St. Louis ballpark on the corner of Grand and Dodier by the early 1960s, enthusiasm on the part of the new owner had never faltered, as Keane was cemented as the leader of choice on the field for the ball club. Busch had bought the team in 1953 for nearly $4 million from a group headed by a local man named Fred Saigh. In strange turn of events, Saigh would soon be sent to prison for income tax evasion, but was loyally able to shift some deals beforehand that prevented a group from Milwaukee from buying the team and moving it to that city. The brewery's purchase of the ball club helped Budweiser — Busch's signature product — to soon pass Schlitz as the number-one selling beer in America. And soon after, the ball field called Sportsman's Park was renamed Busch Stadium (this after league officials discouraged — and then had to forbid — Mr. Busch from going with his original choice, Budweiser Park). The Cardinals, though vastly more successful, had been the tenants to the old St. Louis Browns, the club that owned the park. It was the only field in the major leagues that was in constant use, with never a day off in the summer for ground crews to tend to it. With the city's other club out of the way (as the Browns were off to Baltimore in 1954 to become the Orioles), Busch immediately embarked on an aggressive overhaul of the stadium, upgrading the locker rooms and parts of the grandstand. Nonetheless, his ultimate dream was a shining new downtown stadium. And in 1963, buildings on a 30-acre tract of land near the Mississippi River were razed in St. Louis' old Chinatown neighborhood to make the dream a reality. The Equitable Life Insurance Company was solicited for a $33 million loan, two-thirds of which the newly formed Civic Center Redevelopment Corporation of St. Louis asked the city to generate with the corporation complementing the other third. Busch put up $5 million of his own money as a down payment on the project, and the balance soon followed. Ground was broken on May 24, 1964, as city leaders hailed the shoveling as the signal of a new era in St. Louis.

When the project had started, life in St. Louis for Gussie Busch revolved around beer and baseball, a marriage growing in love with each passing season. He would always tell guests at his frequent parties to grab another "On-heuser product"; at his personal card games that he loved so much, Busch would actually fine employees for asking for a beer instead of a "Bud." He had become very accustomed to either telling people what to do, or buying what he needed. He soon found out, however, that such strong-arming techniques did not work in the world of professional baseball — in some cases, simply because many of the owners were just as wealthy as he. Once, he had wanted to buy star shortstop Ernie Banks from the Chicago Cubs for $500,000, a deal which Cubs owner Phil Wrigley refused. When Busch was stunned that it did not transpire as he wished, his scouts plainly told him, "Mr. Busch, Mr. Wrigley needs half a million about as much as you do."

As 1964 rolled around, perhaps the lone misfortune about the baseball season in St. Louis was Musial had retired a year too soon, missing out on one more championship as Keane and the Cardinals won 28 of their last 39 games and took the World Series title over the New York Yankees. It was, however, one last flag for old Busch Stadium, with the new park to be ready sometime in 1966. The Yankees had recovered from an erratic '63 campaign which saw their inept play lead to them nearly being outdrawn at the gate by the new team in town, the Mets, who in their second year of existence fell only 200,000 attendees behind the Yankees. Like the final glory for old Busch Stadium, the 1964 American League pennant was the last gasp for the great Yankees teams from the Golden Era of baseball, considered to begin with the years of the Great Depression, through World War II, and lasting throughout the 1950s. Among the fading stars of the Bronx was the immortal Mickey Mantle, who at 32 was already struggling with the body of a player much older. A carousing lifestyle coupled with relentless play in the field had left that body broken. Why didn't he take better care of himself, his friends and teammates asked. "All of the men in my family die before they're 40," Mantle regularly answered, and usually plainly and stoically. Convinced that he would not live much longer, he decided to live life to the fullest every day.

In the midst of the championship for the Cardinals, it was what happened immediately following the 1964 World Series in October — and a cloak-and-dagger, clandestine move by Busch back in August of that year — that would profoundly alter the course of the ball club for the remainder of the 1960s.

In August of '64, former Cardinals shortstop and major league manager Leo Durocher was being secretly pursued by Busch to replace Keane at the end of the season. This action was sought by Busch after he felt that Keane and Devine had been keeping some of the day-to-day operations of the ball club a secret from him. Cardinals radio broadcaster Harry Caray, in fact, admitted that Busch had asked him to summon Durocher to a business breakfast at Busch's residence in August to discuss a contract for 1965, and Durocher had been spotted around St. Louis by several eyewitnesses for days beforehand. Upon gaining knowledge that Devine was privately chastising the move, Busch had him fired immediately, and most figured that it was just a matter of days before Keane would be handed his walking papers as well.

With the ensuing charge of the Cardinals to the world title, however, Busch altered himself in mid–personnel move. He made what he thought to be the right public-relations function and gave Keane a vote of confidence, as well as the offer of a new contract, as the men met the press on October 17, two days after the final World Series game against the Yankees. In a shocking twist, however, Keane stunningly announced that he was not only resigning as manager of the Cardinals, but would also accept the same post with the Yankees, the team he had just defeated for the championship. In doing so, Keane ended his four-decade relationship with the Cardinals organization. Nikita Khrushchev had stepped down as premier of the Soviet Union on the same day, and China had exploded its first hydrogen bomb within twenty-four hours as well; but the sportswriters were calling it an even draw in comparison with the local detonation that the manager had unleashed. Naturally, Busch was furious; for years within his brewery, he had never allowed matters of personnel to be shaped to anything but his own liking, let alone to have one of his employees pull the carpet out from under him. But now it had actually happened, a sly move on the part of Keane that culminated as his own personal retaliation for Busch having fired his friend, Devine, back in August. Perhaps the most ironic and sweetest nectar of all for Keane was the fact that he was secretly finalizing his deal with the Yankees *while Busch was simultaneously making plans to relieve him*. It was the end of 31 years in the St. Louis organization for him, but he figured that the time was right. "Johnny Keane is a person with a lot of character," Cardinals pitcher Bob Gibson told the press in his manager's defense moments before the announcement was made, but just as the rumors were beginning to fly. "He never took anything from anybody. If he thought he was right and you were wrong about a certain thing, he was not going to tell you different, no matter who you happened to be. I wish him luck in whatever he does."

In later years, Gibson reflected more on the first manager to make a positive impact in his major league career. "I was going to miss John. But you get used to these things. I think you can get used to almost anything. I think you could probably get used to dying if you did it more than once."

A hint of trouble had begun for Devine a couple of years earlier, when like Durocher, another storied name from baseball's past had resurfaced with an office in St. Louis once again. While wishing to exercise as much control over the ball club as he could, Colonel Busch still realized that he did not have the baseball knowledge necessary to handle the direct operations. As a result, he had many of his assistants whispering in his ear, and this is where he learned of Devine's supposed secrets that were being kept. The same assistants had another idea for Busch — that the shrewdest man the game had ever seen was available to help with personnel matters, and what was more, the man had once worked for the Cardinals. The man's name was Wesley Branch Rickey, an Ohio man of temperance who long ago had been a .239 hitter in 343 big league at-bats and who, like Hemus, had actually been a career sub-.500 manager himself with the Cardinals and the Browns. Rickey, in fact, had a record 13 stolen bases charged against him when he caught a game for the Yankees in 1907. But no front office executive in the game had ever been more respected, be it in the brilliance of his transactions or in the foresight of his ideas. He was already the club president and business manager when he also became the field manager of the Cardinals in 1919, a move that was executed at the time to save money — something that would become a Rickey trademark in the following decades. He left the playing field in 1925 in order to concentrate on his duties as the general manager, a post he would have with the Cardinals for the next 17 years. After crafting monumental moves with the Brooklyn Dodgers, Rickey left in 1950 to become the executive vice president and general manager of the Pittsburgh Pirates, a position he would hold for five years after selling his stock in the Dodgers, valued at over a million dollars. In 1959, he was given the title of president of the new Continental League, a maverick plan that folded a year later without a game ever being played. Upon arriving in St. Louis on October 29, 1962, to work for the Cardinals for the second time in his life, Rickey told Busch words that he wanted to hear when he was hired: "I could be doing a better job than Devine with players that cost half as much." Busch was tired of losing, and his conviction for a winner was now coupled with his persistence as a businessman. The yes-men around him convinced Busch that hiring Rickey — and giving Rickey the power to make any deals he saw fit — would return the Cardinals to glory. He was given the title of senior consultant for player development, and asked to confer with the general manager on a regular basis.

The Rickey impact on baseball had reached far and wide, and with the exception of his racial integration of the major leagues in 1947 with the entrance of Jackie Robinson to the Dodgers, none of his experiments had a further-reaching effect than his implementation of the farm system years earlier. Young men would be identified and trained in the Cardinals way of baseball, and as such, the organization would be able to "grow its own" talent, a phrase that stemmed from a food-saving slogan made popular during World War II. The farm system — estimated at one point to contain 32 teams and over 600 players under contract with the St. Louis organization — would allow the Cardinals to compete with the more economically-advantaged teams in the East. Its fruits were seen in the 1940s, as the Cardinals won four pennants and three World Series titles as Rickey was moving on to work for the Dodgers. As a mainstay of the organization's philosophy, no team in baseball history had been built on speed, defense, and toughness more prominently than the Cardinals. Their type of player was said to be epitomized by Johnny Martin, better known as "Pepper," a thick-muscled outfielder-turned-third baseman from the late 1920s and '30s who readily admitted to being a hobo in the days before the Great Depression. Martin came from Oklahoma, possessing a sinewy body and a perpetual mouthful of tobacco. He offered running speed, quick wrists with the bat, and a powerful throwing arm over which he had no control. Coaches throughout his career were afraid to use him as a pitcher in trepidation of Martin killing a batter by hitting him in the head. Simply put, he was a "tough guy," as one Cardinals scout described him. He had trouble catching balls in the infield and the outfield, but made up for his hard hands with an equally-resistant chest — off which he played many a line drive. As Rickey's farm system continued to flourish through Martin's heyday with Durocher, Dizzy Dean, Joe Medwick, and the rest of Frankie Frisch's Gas House Gang in the 1930s, scouts combed the oil fields, corn farms, and other patches of isolated back-forties along side roads to uncover the agrarian talent that was in such abundant supply in the American Heartland. All boys in the South and West wanted to play for the Cardinals; the kingdoms of New York, Pittsburgh, and even Chicago seemed to be worlds away. These young players were to be taught that "Cardinal Way" of baseball, and those without the raw desire shown by the patriarch Martin were quickly given a bus ticket back home. Rickey was so impressed with his idea of the farm system, in fact, that in 1951 he testified before Congress that it had saved baseball during the Depression, and as such, it should now be exempt from monopoly lawsuits.

Consequently, Devine naturally had felt uncomfortable with the presence of Rickey — a sacred cow not only in St. Louis and with the Cardinals, but within the sport itself — as both men struggled for ultimate power in the decisions made about players. Rickey wanted the power as much or more than Devine did, and he made it clear to Devine that he wasn't brought on board to merely be a $65,000-a-year advisor — rather, that he intended to run the show. Two years later, Devine would be ultimately replaced by Bob Howsam, with Rickey staying on as advisor. Devine believed that Caray had much to do with his demise, perceiving that the broadcaster had undermined him in Caray's private meetings with Busch. While the insistence of Devine and Keane to make deals for players usually won out, Rickey made his feelings felt in no uncertain terms. When catcher Bob Uecker was traded to the Cardinals from the Milwaukee Braves for outfielder Gary Kolb, he met Rickey in the locker room. "Mr. Rickey, I'm Bob Uecker, and I've just joined your club," offering to shake his hand.

"Yes, I know," Rickey responded. "And I didn't want you. I wouldn't trade one Gary Kolb for a hundred Bob Ueckers." And Uecker would be out the door less than two years later, traded to the Philadelphia Phillies.

Rickey perhaps had cause for arrogance, for it was estimated by writer Jules Tygiel that nearly half of the big-league ballplayers by the early 1960s had been nurtured through the farm systems that Rickey had once established. That being the case, players over the decades had always felt powerless in their salary negotiations with him. Durocher called him "the cheapest, the shrewdest, and the most hardhearted of men ... if you went into Rickey's office to talk salary, and you left four hours later taking a dime less than what you wanted coming in, he would consider that a victory." And as Cardinals outfielder Enos Slaughter added, "He'd go to the safe to get you a nickel's change." When a young player was preparing to negotiate a contract with Rickey, he reportedly got the following advice from a veteran: "Don't drink the night before, keep your mouth shut, and your hands in your pockets." At one point during the Depression, Rickey had asked Durocher (as well as other members of the Cardinals) to take as much as a 40 percent cut in salary — all while Rickey would not budge in lowering his own $40,000 annual rate, with Internal Revenue Service figures later placing his income at over $49,000 for 1934, making him the highest-paid man in baseball. His fiscal conservatism during his early years in the game, however, was applauded by most; the organization had been so poor in Rickey's first stay through the 1920s, in fact, that he had to borrow one of his wife's fine oriental rugs to use at the Cardinals' offices to impress an important visitor that was arriving.

Rickey proved to be the most frugal of men during his first years as a front office executive, and it was clear that his procedure had not changed in his later years. His attitude about money could be traced back to his college days at Ohio Wesleyan, when his mother — whom he had promised that he would never be at a ballgame on a Sunday — would send him a dollar every month to assist with his expenses. Every month, young Branch would send the dollar back to her. Later, he would use the same discipline to attain a law degree from the University of Michigan.

Things changed quickly for him after the Cardinals' World Series triumph in 1964. On October 19 — two days after Keane made his stunning announcement to Busch and the media — Rickey was fired from his post by Busch. One year later, the 84-year-old Rickey was being honored with his induction in to the Missouri Sports Hall of Fame in the small town of Columbus. Shortly into his talk, he staggered and mumbled into the microphone, "I don't believe I'm going to be able to speak any longer." He suffered a heart attack, collapsing over the podium before the stunned audience. He died three weeks later while in intensive care at Boone County Memorial Hospital in Missouri.

With the embarrassment of the Keane situation, Busch knew that he needed to hire a new manager that would represent a good public image. Howsam had suggested Charley Metro, currently a scout for the Chicago White Sox and who had managed under Howsam in the minor leagues at Denver. But there was a more local, recognizable choice that Busch wanted; he found his man in Albert "Red" Schoendienst, a man who was part of Cardinals lore from the glorious decade of the 1940s. Busch wasted no time in acting, as Schoendienst was hired on the 20th, the day after Rickey was let go.

Schoendienst was born on February 2, 1923, in Germantown, Illinois, part of Clinton County that sits approximately 40 miles to the east of St. Louis. In addition to the area's love for baseball, Schoendienst took an interest in the other two primary pastimes of the region as well, fishing and hunting (although the latter would have to wait until his teenage years, when he was finally able to afford a gun). He would later liken the walking trips to the nearby community of New Baden for fishing to "a daily death march," but nonetheless usually enjoyed a good pull of "catfish, and an occasional bass" for his efforts with the pole. His father, Joseph, was a coal miner who supplemented the family income by also painting bridges and working as a prison guard. Together with his Irish wife, Mary (truly a minority in the quasi–Deutschland that made up the county), Joseph had six sons and one daughter, with all of the boys possessing red hair and the girl blonde. The other area boys from around Clinton County, traveling over to Germantown to play ball from the nearby hamlets of Beckemeyer, Aviston, Bartelso, and Breese, soon made Albert bat left-handed in their sandlot games — for he was too good for everyone else from the right side. "Growing up in Germantown," Schoendienst told one writer, "I could find a ballgame and play everyday." At the age of 16 in 1939, after leaving school two years earlier ("I just up and quit," Schoendienst said frankly), he went to work for the Civilian Conservation Corps, one of the many Depression-era government work programs set up by the Roosevelt administration. While working on a job hedging posts, a stray nail shot up and hit him in the eye. The doctors wanted to remove the eye, but the young Albert refused. Finally, another physician found a way to save it, although it would cause Schoendienst tremendous pain for the rest of his life, and occasionally he would cover it with a patch. Red would say that the only temporary relief he could muster for the condition was "rapid blinking."

Three years after the accident in June 1942 — in the middle of one of the greatest Cardinals summers ever — he was shooting pool one day with boyhood friend Joe Linnemann in a Germantown hall as the two listened to the St. Louis ballgame on the radio. They soon came up with the idea to hitchhike a ride to the city for a tryout with the Cardinals. Strolling along U.S. Route 50 to the west, they found the driver of a milk truck that obliged. The boys were as excited as could be. "The best part of this," Schoendienst told Linnemann on the trip into St. Louis, "is that we'll get to see the Cardinals play Brooklyn for free!" Schoendienst — who had only twenty-five cents in his pocket for the trip — slept on a park bench the first night in the city in order to save his funds, while Joe found other accommodations. The following afternoon, four hundred young ballplayers showed their stuff at Sportsman's Park for the club, but only two walked out of the stadium with contracts — Linemann and a catcher from the Italian neighborhood of St. Louis (known locally as "The Hill") named Joe Garagiola. Schoendienst went back to Germantown terribly depressed, but better news was already on its way. The Cardinals' top scout, Joe Mathes, had missed the tryout with out-of-town business. When he returned and found out that Schoendienst was not offered a contract, he berated the rest of his scouting staff and personally went across the river to seek out the player. Mathes drove straight to the Schoendienst home in Germantown, and signed Albert at the kitchen table for the salary of $75 a month. He was sent to his first professional assignment at Union City, Tennessee, and shortly after getting hits in each of his first eight professional at-bats he was promoted to Rochester of the International League. The manager of the Rochester team was none other than the former Gas Houser Pepper Martin, who was in the middle of yelling at his inept squad in the locker room when Schoendienst arrived. Partly because of being in the midst of his anger, Martin mistook Schoendienst for a lost kid. "We don't need any bat boys!" Martin yelled, as he slammed the clubhouse door in Red's face. After a couple of more tries at the door, however, Schoendienst was able to convince Martin that he was indeed a Cardinals farmhand, sent to play in the infield for him. Albert proved his mettle to the salty old

Pepper, ending the 1943 season as the second-youngest batting champion in the history of the International League with a .337 average at the age of 20, second only to Wee Willie Keeler in 1892. He indeed looked younger than he was, especially as he was wearing baseball spikes that were two sizes too big for him. One umpire, in fact, had nicknamed him "Snowshoes" because his cleats flopped as he ran. Missing nearly the entire next year for his service in the army, Schoendienst was released from military duty on New Year's Day in 1945 because of his eye problem. Unfortunately, something even more frightening had surfaced from his army physical, as scant signs of tuberculosis had been detected in his system. It was something that would impact him more profoundly years down the road.

Still, he did not let anything sidetrack his drive to the major leagues. With the Cardinals having all-league shortstop Marty Marion in place, they looked to utilize the talents of Schoendienst elsewhere. They put him in left field for his rookie year of 1945, and he hit .278 in his first big-league season with 26 stolen bases (which led the circuit) at the age of 22. Manager Eddie Dyer had visualized using Red as a "super-sub," being able to fill in at any position. When Marion got hurt, Schoendienst sparkled at shortstop; when Whitey Kurowski went down, Red filled in admirably for him at third. Soon, Dyer began to understand that the kid was not going to be a reserve forever. The club's other second basemen, Emil Verban and Lou Klein, were shipped off to Philadelphia and the Mexican League respectively. Second base wasn't Red's favorite position, but it now offered him a spot in the starting lineup. It would be a perfect fit, as he made the All-Star team for the first time and found a home as a keystoner for the next fifteen years. He helped the Cardinals to a World Series victory over the Boston Red Sox in 1946, as he had resumed his switch-hitting (something he had previously abandoned) with such remarkable balance that an impressed Red Sox manager Joe Cronin was prompted to say, "It's weird — it's like having a hitter look at himself in a full-length mirror." The main reason that Schoendienst wanted to switch-hit was his ongoing problem with his eye — he claimed that he could not see a curveball from a right-handed pitcher while batting from the right side.

One evening in 1947, Schoendienst was on a St. Louis streetcar traveling up Grand Avenue after he had been at a dinner party on the city's south side. He got into a conversation with a pretty girl sitting nearby, and before long, the gal would become his bride. A city girl all her life, Mary Eileen O'Reilly was an Irish lass and Fontbonne College graduate who would soon be introduced to the rural quaintness of Germantown and Clinton County. When their wedding day finally arrived, they honeymooned afterwards with her watching Red play third base in a game at Sportsman's Park. After a line drive nearly took his head off, she suggested that Dyer remove Red from the perilous position and keep him at second permanently.

By 1956, Red had been an All-Star nine times, and had led the league in at-bats, doubles, sacrifice bunts, and stolen bases in various years. An unexpected bombshell suddenly hit him on June 14, 1956, however, as he was traded from his beloved Cardinals to the New York Giants along with three other players for Whitey Lockman, Alvin Dark, and two others. A life-long resident of the St. Louis metro area, he was sad to leave. "Stan [Musial] said it was his saddest day in baseball," Schoendienst once wrote. "I thought I could still play, and I didn't want to have to uproot Mary and the rest of the family and move to New York. St. Louis was home, and that's where we wanted to be." Mary was pregnant with their third child, making matters more complex. The trade — made by Cardinals general manager Frank Lane — was so unpopular with St. Louis fans that Busch afterwards stripped Lane of his unilateral power to make trades (Lane also had a plan in the works to send Musial to the Phillies for pitcher Robin Roberts; fortunately for Cardinals fans, that move never came to fruition). Nonetheless, Red fought through the change to make only four errors in 606 chances at second base for the entire season, which penciled out to a .993 fielding percentage (an all-time record for the position until Bobby Grich would break it with a .997 mark in 1985). Almost one year later to the day of the trade he was dealt again — back to the Midwest, but this time to the Milwaukee Braves. Disappointed with having to move once again, he nonetheless responded with a league-leading 200 hits while finishing third (behind Musial and Hank Aaron) for MVP honors. But in 1958, Schoendienst received even more staggering news than being traded, as he was diagnosed with full-blown tuberculosis in November — over ten years after it had first been detected by army doctors, and just after the birth of his and Mary's fourth child, son Kevin. Doctors were convinced that he would never play again, but Schoendienst — after missing all of 1959 — fought back to play in 68 games in 1960 at the age of 37.

At that point Schoendienst was released by the Braves, but good news followed as he was picked up once again by the Cardinals and Devine, who had replaced Lane not long after Lane had made his infamous deal with New York. Red knew that he would be only a sparingly-used reserve in St. Louis, but his heart was warmed in returning to his "home country," for he had even turned down a more lucrative offer to play every day with the American League expansion team in Los Angeles, the Angels. But Schoendienst was most grateful to be reunited with his old friend, Musial, who at the age of 40 was beginning to view the end of his own career. Schoendienst and Musial had first been temporary roommates in spring training at St. Petersburg, Florida, in 1946. Later in the season, when Max Lanier — the Cardinals left-hander who won 17 games in their world championship year of 1944 — was rooming with Schoendienst, he left him a note one morning without saying goodbye. It read, "Keep hitting those line drives, Red — Signed, Max." For on May 23rd Lanier, along with former Cardinals catcher Mickey Owen and a handful of other major leaguers, had jumped to the rogue Mexican League in search of higher pay. Musial, at that point, went to the Cardinals' traveling secretary Leo Ward and asked to be permanently roomed with Schoendienst. Decades later, when asked by an interested person how they chose to decorate their room, the modest Musial answered in the closest tone he ever approached to bragging. "I guess we filled that room with hits," he said, laughing. After 1946, neither one wanted another roommate ever again.

Lanier had won all six of his starts to that date, as the Cardinals were tied with the Brooklyn Dodgers atop the National League standings. A total of 23 players had been raided from major league rosters by Mexican League promoter Jorge Pasquel, who offered large salaries but no long-term promises to the expatriates. Before the end of the 1940s, however, the Mexican League was itself in arrears for funds, and the exiled players found playing and coaching jobs in Canada before returning to the front offices of their former bosses in New York, Chicago, Cincinnati, St. Louis, and other places with their hats in their hands, asking for one more chance to play in the States.

Before the 1962 season, Schoendienst was left unprotected by the Cardinals in the next expansion draft, as the New York Mets and Houston Colt .45s were entering the National League. It was not the Cardinals' intention to let him go, but they figured they could easily pass Red through without being claimed, which in turn would save a roster spot for a younger player. Both expansion teams expressed a casual interest, but fortunately in the end, Red was permitted to remain a Cardinal. After tying the National League record with 22 pinch-hits that season, Schoendienst would finish his playing career with the Cardinals the following year in 1963, appearing only five times as a pinch hitter before being named a coach at the roster cut-down deadline in the middle of May. It had long been the idea of Busch, Keane, and Devine to offer Red a coaching job with the team as a back-up plan in case he did not make the roster coming out of spring training, but five weeks into the season, all knew that the time was now right. "I hoped to manage someday, here or somewhere," Schoendienst would recall years later. "But I was perfectly happy coaching for Johnny Keane. He was, in every sense, a good man." The thoughtful Keane was the type of manager that Red wanted to be. And over the years, among the most common praise that Schoendienst's players would shower on him was his stoicism — his ability to get neither too high in victory, nor too low in defeat.

When Schoendienst was hired as the manager to replace Keane, Musial was elated. "I think he's going to be such an effective, relaxed manager, he'll last a long time." While they were teammates and roommates in St. Louis, it was always Schoendienst — not Musial, to the surprise of some Cardinals fans — who had displayed the aspirations to be a major league manager. "I knew he wanted to manage," Stan continued. "He was an instinctive player, he'd played for many different managers, and he always got along with the men he played for and with." And twenty years after hanging out in the pool halls of Clinton County, the man who helped Red launch his professional baseball career was still at his side as well. In the mid–1960s, Linnemann and Schoendienst were in business together, operating a nursing home in Germantown.

The transition in leadership was not as smooth as some would have liked, as the Cardinals went from first place to seventh place in 1965 with a record of 80–81, as the batting averages of every starting position player but one had declined. While the Cardinals were getting their bearings under the new skipper, there was a new era dawning in baseball in the mid–1960s as the sport was becoming part of the collective bargaining process found in other sectors of the labor market. Soon coming was a nervous tension with the start of the 1966 season, as on March 5, player representatives of the newly-formed Major League Baseball Players Association elected Marvin Miller as their executive director. The players association was certainly employing an experienced hand, as Miller had formerly been the assistant to the president of the United Steelworkers, and was now replacing Wisconsin judge Robert Cannon as the executive administrator of the players organization. There appeared to be an initial peace between the owners and players, as in August of '65, a deal was reached in which the owners agreed to increase their contributions to the players' pension funds by 55 percent from the ever-expanding pool of revenue from All-Star Game and World Series television broadcasts. Some seeds of bitterness were sown as well, however, when it was discovered that some of the money was also being used to pay Miller's salary, which some believed to be beyond his contracted rate. To combat the rise of the players' union, the owners hastily constructed their own Player Relations Committee. Almost immediately upon taking the job, Miller went to war with Cronin, now the president of the American League. Cronin was frustrated with Miller's attitude, as Cronin felt that the owners' concessions to the players was "enough, but never enough" while negotiations appeared to be spiraling downwards.

Suddenly the legal world had seemed to invade the game of baseball. Soon another Wisconsin magistrate — State Circuit Court judge Elmer W. Roller — decreed that the Braves must either stay in Milwaukee or the National League should guarantee an expansion franchise to the city for the 1966 season. Since the latter was a practical impossibility, the move was seen to force the hand of the Braves franchise. The Braves would begin the season in Atlanta anyway, and the protracted courtroom fight would be waged until July, when the Wisconsin Supreme Court ruled that the state was powerless in trying to keep the team in the state. The final blow was struck by the United States

Supreme Court five months later, as a 4–3 decision to deny review of the State of Wisconsin's suit to have the case heard in federal court. It is the last hurdle for the Braves to clear in taking up permanent residence in Atlanta, and yet another affirmation of the federal protection of baseball from antitrust laws. The Braves would play their first game in Dixie on April 12, 1966, a 3–2 loss to the Pittsburgh Pirates. A week and a half earlier, the Braves nearly pulled another coup that could have landed them the top college pitching prospect of the decade. On April 3, it was announced that Tom Seaver, the fire-balling hurler from the University of Southern California, had signed with the New York Mets for a bonus of $50,000. This was only the end of a saga involving the pitcher, however, a series of events which could have had Seaver landing with any of several teams. The Braves' top farm club at Richmond, Virginia, had signed Seaver for $40,000 in February of '66, a month after the Braves had selected him in the amateur draft. It was supposed to be Seaver's senior year at USC; but since he had turned professional, he was not allowed to pitch in college again, even though his Richmond contract was voided by the commissioner's office as it had been signed after USC's season had already begun (and the misstep by the Richmond club forbade the Braves from negotiating with Seaver for at least three years). A special draft was held for Seaver's rights, and three teams equaled Richmond's offer — the Mets, the Philadelphia Phillies, and the Cleveland Indians. The Mets' name was drawn out of a hat, and they were given the rights to sign the promising pitcher.

The Cardinals and the City of St. Louis had been trying to lay their own groundwork for future success as well. Plans were being made for a dazzling new scene in downtown St. Louis — not only in baseball circles, but also in civic development. In 1965, St. Louis mayor A. J. Cervantes bought the Spanish Pavilion, which served as Spain's exhibit hall at the 1964 World's Fair in New York, and had it moved to St. Louis to celebrate the city's Spanish colonial heritage. The display would last only a few years, as a hotel was ultimately built over the top of it. Nonetheless, it was the genesis of a new beginning for the downtown area which had been deteriorating for a considerable number of years. The overall plan involved the renovation of historical buildings that were salvageable, in addition to finding plots for new construction. "This is a pilot area," Cervantes announced, understanding the far-reaching implications of what would occur. "If it works here, we hope to continue it in other parts of downtown and the city. I think it is a new concept in the rebuilding of cities." Aside from the new stadium, planning for a grand memorial to westward expansion had been underway since the mid–1930s, primarily fueled by a local businessman named Luther Ely Smith. The riverfront area was a priority to civic leaders for reconstruction long before Cervantes came to power, as after railroads had rendered steamboat travel on the Mississippi River obsolete, the riverfront area of St. Louis had rapidly deteriorated, even to the point of holding one of the biggest Hoovervilles of the Great Depression. With Smith providing the financial support, an architectural contest was announced on May 30, 1947, for the development of a plan of a monument for the site. A prize of $125,000 was offered to the winner. One hundred and seventy-two entries were submitted, and Number 144 was chosen — a skyward-reaching arch design of Eero Saarinen and his design firm in Bloomfield Hills, Michigan. (Saarinen, in fact, had beaten out another design that had been sent in by his father; when a congratulatory telegram arrived at their home, all family members and friends mistakenly assumed it was for the older Saarinen.) Construction would not begin until the early 1960s, when 1,000 tons of stainless steel would be brought by train car from the Pittsburgh–Des Moines Steel Company of Pennsylvania for the outer shell of the arch. In addition, more steel was utilized inside the structure for support of the arch's legs, and the equivalent concrete for a six-story building was laid underground for its foundation. The final piece (or keystone) which held the pressure of the legs together was put into place on October 28, 1965. It was four years after Saarinen's death, and fourteen years after the passing of Smith, as more than 10,000 onlookers cheered from the streets below. To this day, the Gateway Arch remains the tallest monument in the United States, a perfect 630 feet at its apex and an equal 630 feet wide at its base.

Two weeks after the new stadium would host its first ballgame in May of 1966, Vice President Hubert Humphrey and Secretary of the Interior Stewart Udall would be on hand to dedicate the arch, and its infamous clanky rides to the top for the general public would begin on July 23, 1967. The cultural heart of St. Louis had long been found on North Grand Avenue, where sat not only the old Busch Stadium but the Fox Theatre, Powell Symphony Hall, and St. Louis University, among other gems; now, the new focus was downtown. By 1974, the Gateway Arch would be ranked by travel professionals as the fourth-most visited destination in the world, trailing only Lenin's tomb and the two amusement parks that had been opened by Walt Disney in California and Florida.

By the time May 8, 1966, rolled around, the Cardinals were struggling with a record of 8–13 and an eighth-place standing in the National League. The San Francisco Giants were in town for the last series at the old ballpark, beginning on May 6. They had just finished a series at home against the Dodgers, and in the opener of that series on May 4, their long-time superstar, Willie Mays, set a National League record with his 512th home run off Claude Osteen. The shot allowed Mays to pass Mel Ott on the career home run list; three months later, Mays would have more homers than any right-handed hitter ever, hitting his 534th to pass Jimmie Foxx and place himself second only to the great Babe Ruth. Mays had been a fixture in center field for the Giants since 1951, when their manager, Durocher, got him from the club's Minneapolis farm team where the 20-year-old had been hitting .477 since the beginning of the season. With the Cardinals off to a slow start for the season, the new stadium offered hope for the players as well as the city, as a fresh excitement had propelled St. Louis into a state of euphoria. At 3:15 P.M. Central Time on the 8th of May — just about the moment that American League slugger Frank Robinson was hitting the only ball ever to travel out of Memorial Stadium in Baltimore — Alex Johnson grounded into a double play to end the game as San Francisco pulled out a 10–5 win over the Cardinals which kept the Giants in first place in the National League. Almost immediately after the contest was over, the ground crew dug up home plate at the old yard, took it to a waiting helicopter that was stationed behind second base, and the chopper fluttered off to the east to deliver the plate to the new ballpark downtown as nearly 18,000 in attendance watch with mixed emotions. The Giants and Cardinals remained on the field for a few nostalgic moments, and then headed to the locker rooms in the old structure for the last time.

The shift from old to new was emblematic of the tumultuous decade of the 1960s, a time that, when mentioned in contemporary living as "The Sixties," evokes an everlasting array of images as diverse and disturbing as can be imagined. It was an era that enveloped and transformed an entire planet, complete with actions and personalities that would change the world forever. By May of 1966, a confusing war in a corner of Southeast Asia ignited a large portion of this transformation. It soon became known to Americans simply as Vietnam, a war which was decades in the making, having basically started with Japan's transfer of Vietnamese power to Ho Chi Minh's provisional government after World War II in 1945. It was now in its third year of official U.S. involvement, while some had claimed that clandestine American raids had been occurring in the region since the late 1950s. After being armed by the Soviet Union and China since the early '50s, the Communist sympathizers in the northern part of the country, comprising a faction known as the *Vietminh*, carried out attacks on French troops after France had declared possession of the region from Great Britain. Soon a full-scale struggle was launched for control of the entire country, and by the time the 1966 baseball season had begun, nearly a quarter of a million American troops were involved in the conflict.

Citizens in the United States in the mid–1960s were already politically weary from the numbing events of earlier in the decade, with the ever-growing war at the forefront of this exhaustion. As always in times of social crisis, the people looked for items in the traditional American cultural landscape that provided stability. And as always, baseball was among them. The 1960s had already seen its share of tragedy, including a staredown of nuclear proportions between Kennedy and Khrushchev, a failed invasion of Cuba by

Kennedy-organized and U.S.-supported Cuban expatriates in 1962 (known as the Bay of Pigs) and the assassination of Kennedy in 1963, among other watershed events. Thus, many citizens again looked to the start of the major league baseball season as part of the comfortable cycle of the calendar, a perennial source of peace that could always be depended upon. As would be recalled by President Bill Clinton decades later, professional baseball in the 1960s served the public with cultural reminders of true togetherness, as a black shortstop could flip the ball to a Hispanic second baseman, who in turn could throw the ball to a white first baseman to complete a double play — the ultimate product of cooperation and teamwork in the game. Thus, with the 1966 season still relatively fresh in May, the good citizens of St. Louis looked forward to a bright future with their sparkling new ballpark.

As the players were dressing after the game in the decrepit locker rooms of old Busch for the last time on May 8, a note was sent inside to both the visitor and the home areas that summoned one of the players from each team. A trade had been struck between the two organizations, catching the Giants just as they were ready to leave for the airport. The Cardinals had sent them their former bonus-baby left-handed pitcher Ray Sadecki, a twenty-game winner at the age of 23 in the Cards' championship year of '64. In return, St. Louis had received Orlando Cepeda, the slugging first baseman who had been a six-time All-Star. Sadecki's brother Mike was sitting next to Ray in front of his locker when the news came.

"Who do I cheer for now?" he asked the pitcher.

"The Giants!" Ray said, in getting one final laugh out of his now-former Cardinal teammates. "*We'll* beat those bums, just like *we* did today!"

Both players were stunned by the move, but Cepeda appeared to be more pleased than Sadecki. Cepeda had not been entirely happy in San Francisco, as he could not seem to get along with managers Alvin Dark and Herman Franks. In one example, Cepeda was not pleased with their forbidding the first baseman from bringing his stereo into the locker room. Also, Dark had tried using him in the outfield, another idea that Cepeda did not like. "I was tired of playing different spots in San Francisco," he would say. Cepeda also felt that he had been shortchanged in terms of salary in San Francisco. "I hit 36 home runs and had 114 RBIs and we won the pennant [in 1962], but they still wanted to cut my pay," he claimed. "I could have had better years, but I had to fight Dark *and* the other teams' pitchers. The Giants said that I wouldn't sacrifice myself, but I had played third base and the outfield and didn't complain.

"In 1966, my pay was cut [from being injured], so I asked Franks to let me play so that I could get my money back," he continued. "I told coach Hank Sauer that I wanted to work hard and become the best left fielder in the league. Then Franks said that Willie McCovey was breaking his back for him — that was the same as saying I wasn't doing anything for him. He told me that I couldn't play on the club because there were outfielders like Len Gabrielson and Don Landrum. But when I was traded to the Cardinals, Red Schoendienst told me that I had a job and that all he wanted was one hundred percent effort. I told Red I would give him 125 percent."

McCovey was ready to take over full-time duties at first base for the Giants after Cepeda had undergone knee surgery in December of 1964, so a deal of some manner had been imminent. Cepeda had experienced a childhood disease that left him bowlegged, contributing further to the stress on his knee in later years. There were some, not the least of whom was Cardinals' team physician Dr. I.C. Middleman, who were concerned about Cepeda's durability before having the deal consummated. "After I got permission to examine Cepeda's bad knee — and before we agreed to the trade of Ray Sadecki — I called our trainer, Bob Bauman," Middleman said. "Bauman thought that the knee was at an appropriate stage of recovery." Despite his troubles with the joint, Cepeda was certainly still in the midst of his offensive prime, having earlier won the National League Rookie of the Year honors with the Giants in 1958, three years after originally signing with them at the age of 17. Also in the 1958 season, he homered three times in three days on two separate occasions. He was then the runner-up to Robinson (then a member of the Cincinnati Reds) in the 1961 National League MVP voting, when Cepeda had led the league in home runs (46) and RBIs (142). Wes Westrum, the manager of the New York Mets, knew that the Cardinals were not only getting a quality player, but more importantly, they were getting one who could be a difference-maker in the standings. "When Cepeda first came up, I said he'd be a great one," Westrum proclaimed, pointing out that he was a rookie coach for the Giants in 1958 — the same year that Orlando was a rookie player. "He doesn't give in a bit at the plate, no matter who's pitching. He goes in on the ball all the time. He's always been a very aggressive hitter; he's the type of hitter who can carry a ball club for quite a while. I'd say that he could easily be the difference of ten victories over a full season."

Cepeda's father, Pedro, was an accomplished player in the Caribbean and had been called "The Bull" and "The Babe Ruth of Puerto Rico." Consequently, Orlando was nicknamed "Baby Bull" as the cherished offspring. Pedro was perhaps most famous in Puerto Rico for attacking a heckling fan in the stands, a spectacle in which he charged all the way from second base to the seats behind first base after hitting a double — at the age of 44. He was placed in handcuffs by police and taken out of the stadium. Later, he would become involved in Orlando's development as a player — so involved, in fact, that he marched out into the middle of one of Orlando's games to criticize him about a poor play he had made. In another instance, after Orlando had failed to get a hit in his first two times at bat in a championship game, his father leaned over the grandstand to give him some more advice. "If you don't get a hit the next time," the youngster remembered his father saying, "don't even come home after the game."

His older brother, Pedro, Jr., became an accountant, as the parents wished for at least one of their sons to attend college. "The Bull" had passed away by the mid–1950s, just after Orlando had signed his first professional contract for $500 and had reported to Salem, Virginia, in the Appalachian League. He was reminded often by his mother to not be like the old man. "Keep your cool — remember your father," she would say.

A good idea, in considering that Cepeda was famous in the players' circles for the large warclub he used. He typically waved a 36-ounce bat, one of the heaviest in the major leagues. On occasion, when he was feeling especially strong, he would grab a stick that weighed as much as 40 ounces. And always on the cutting edge of being "hip," as Cepeda liked to put it, he might well have been the creator of the "high-five," as noted by one St. Louis writer. "Cepeda picked up a little hip himself during his San Francisco days, and that is where he picked up the hip handshake, which consists of just touching palms instead of shaking hands after a home run. 'I started it in San Francisco,' he said, 'and now it's spreading all over the National League.'"

Just days before the new Busch Stadium opened, the last remnants of memories from the championship season of 1964 had closed in New York. On May 7 the general manager of the Yankees, Ralph Houk, fired Johnny Keane and appointed himself as the field manager. Keane's club had a miserable record of 4–16 to start the year, and the change sparked life into the Bronx Bombers as they went 13–4 in their next 17 games under Houk. Keane meanwhile — who had pulled what the press considered a masterful bait-and-switch on Gussie Busch just seven months earlier — would never be the same psychologically or physically. On January 6, 1967, he would die of a heart attack in Houston, perhaps wondering if he should have ever left St. Louis.

After losing three straight to San Francisco, the Cardinals shut out the Cubs in Chicago on May 10 before heading home to open the new ballpark two nights later against the Atlanta Braves. Legendary *St. Louis Post-Dispatch* sportswriter Bob Broeg cautioned readers in his May 11 article against expecting everything to be immediately perfect in the new building. "When the stadium opens tomorrow night, the key word must be patience," he advised. "Just as families often move into new homes before property is landscaped and other minor things are ready, new stadiums are opened before the last nut is bolted. Access roads are never ready on time, such as the upcoming traffic relieving stretch over the railroad yards from Twentieth Street, to link up the stadium directly with the Daniel Boone Expressway west and the unfinished Poplar Street Bridge east.

"A capital ship of the Navy takes a shakedown cruise. A giant jet of the sky undergoes a test flight. Even a great pitcher must warm up." Added umpire Bill Jackowski, assigned to work the opening series, "After all, everything has bugs in it at first — even an electric toothbrush."

At a private party given by Busch for old sportswriters and former Cardinals players at the ballpark the night before it opened, Broeg's predecessor as the *Post-Dispatch* beat writer for the Cardinals, J. Roy Stockton, had these words for the brewery king when Stockton went to the microphone. "I had a reputation for being mean, when I was only trying to be honest," he began, in review of his many comments about the beer man over the years in his articles for the *Post-Dispatch*. "But there never was a man, no citizen of the city, who has done more for the city than you, Gussie Busch."

The land that held the actual structure took up twelve acres in downtown St. Louis, and was 130 feet tall from the playing field to the top of the stadium where the 96 miniature arches surrounded the brim and peeked down at the customers below, looming just beyond the last row of chairs. "Sitting in the top row of seats gives one the feeling of looking almost straight down to the distant playing field," marveled writer Frank Leeming of the *Post-Dispatch* upon his first trek up to the fourth tier, giving fans an "inside look" 24 hours before the first pitch. "Several persons, particularly elderly ones, may experience a sensation of vertigo when they climb to their seats and turn around to face the field for the first time." One of the first customers would suggest that escalators would have been a nice idea by the architect. The designers had indeed consulted everyone else — or so it seemed, as even a "home run expert" was retained by the planners. His name was Robert Kingsley, who described himself as "a consultant on home run dimensions for Busch Stadium and other major league parks." Kingsley submitted his proposal for the distance of the outfield wall from home plate in the new stadium, predicting that the Cardinals and the visiting teams would combine for approximately 135 home runs over the course of a season. "My projection of 135 home runs a year at St. Louis was based on a major league team with average home-run hitting potential and average pitching potential," Kingsley explained simply. "I used the same standards everywhere for recommending fence distances and heights." Kingsley had worked for the federal government as a mapmaker at the Pentagon before becoming a "home run engineer as a hobby," as he put it. In advising Dodger Stadium builders in Los Angeles, he predicted there would be 170 home runs in its first season in 1962; there were 172 in actuality. Also for 1962, he forecasted 200 for the inaugural campaign of D.C. (later RFK) Stadium in Washington; 193 were hit.

Busch Stadium would be staffed in its first season by 320 ushers, which was over 100 more than had ever been used — even for World Series games — at the old ballpark on Grand Avenue.

CURTAIN TIME — LOOK OUT, ARCH!

Read the headline of the *Post-Dispatch* sports section on May 12. The full official name of the park was the awkward title of Civic Center Busch Memorial Stadium. Almost 50,000 fans—the largest crowd believed to ever have watched a sporting event in Missouri, and officially the largest to have seen a professional sporting contest in St. Louis—lined up outside three hours before game time in eager anticipation of the eight o'clock contest. They were issued certificates that cited them as "First-Nighters," snuggling in for a first pitch that was thrown in 55-degree weather which would drop another five degrees before the game was over. It was indeed the "coldest May in memory," as Broeg wrote, but it didn't deter the enthusiasm. The festivities began two hours earlier, as three live bands strummed away as the excitement began to build. Once inside the massive new ballpark, the fans could not believe their eyes. "This is the most beautiful thing I have ever seen," said one woman from Affton, Missouri. "They couldn't have found a better place for this stadium." Only small disappointments surfaced, such as the absence of hot dogs at the concession stands (as the gas lines for cooking had not been hooked up), as cold ham and cheese sandwiches were served instead. The refrigeration system was not functioning properly either, as vendors hurriedly tried to ice down their beers in a manual fashion. Chunks of sod were coming up in the outfield as the game started, and the immature grass behind home plate had been hastily spray-painted an off-green.

Getting the umpires ready for the opener at the new ballpark was a local high school kid named Jerry Gibson, his job known simply as the "umpires' boy." As he did before every game, Gibson would assist the umpires in shining their shoes, keeping the umpires' lockers neat, and helping them rub the gloss off the baseballs to be used in the game. Six weeks later, he would be promoted in becoming the Cardinals' regular batboy. Gibson would go on to chronicle his efforts in a 1970 book entitled *Big League Batboy*, which gave the public a new perspective into the job. Gibson had been making $3.50 a day as the umpires' boy in 1966 (plus a dollar a day in tips from each of the four umpires), when suddenly the Cardinals' regular batboy told the boss that he could not keep up with the duties and complete his studies at a local junior college. Upon getting the batboy job, Gibson upped his wage to $6.50 a day and $10 for double headers (in addition — despite not spending the entire season with the club as batboy — he would receive $211 in tips from the Cardinals players at the end of the 1966 schedule). Gibson lived a few blocks away from the old ballpark on Agnes Street, and as any boy would, thought he had the best job in the world.

By the time the new stadium was opening, Cardinals' outfielder Lou Brock was on a pace to strike out 218 times for 1966, which would have shattered the single-season record of 175 set by Dave Nicholson. Having enough of Brock's lack of recent contact at the plate, Schoendienst benched him for the opening night game and instead inserted Johnson — who took the final swing in the old ballpark — into the lineup.

It was a surreal scene for the home folks, as the Cardinals ran out to their positions in their home white uniforms while strolling onto unfamiliar pastures. Pitcher Ray Washburn fired the first pitch at the Braves' Felipe Alou, a ball that missed the strike zone low and outside. Catcher Tim McCarver turned and gave the ball to home plate umpire John Kibler. Kibler turned and walked it over to National League president Warren Giles, who placed it in his pocket for safe transport to the National Baseball Hall of Fame and Museum in Cooperstown, New York.

After Alou was put out, Gary Geiger strutted to the plate for the Braves. Geiger, only recently acquired by Atlanta after spending eight years in the American League, had a large contingent of supporters in the stands from his nearby home of Murphysboro, Illinois. He put himself in the Busch Stadium record books as he laced a sharp single to the outfield for the ballpark's first safety. Next up was Hank Aaron, whom Washburn promptly struck out. Native St. Louisan Mike Shannon recorded the first hit for the Cardinals on the riverfront in the bottom half.

Over the course of the game, many of the fans were disappointed by a perceived lack of animation on the two large scoreboards in the outfield. The $1.5 million electronic placards, constructed by the Fair Play Scoreboard Company of Des Moines and the General Indicator Corporation of Pardeeville, Wisconsin, had been advertised as comparable to the fabulous displays seen in the Houston Astrodome — the so-called "Eighth Wonder of the World," which had introduced the planet to indoor professional baseball when it opened thirteen months earlier; its scoreboard was not appreciated by many. "The Houston scoreboard," complained one writer, "much to the disgust of baseball men across the country, takes an active part in the game, waging psychological warfare against the foe and actually entering into the game. Baseball always has had an understanding that such facilities will remain neutral when play is in progress." Aside from the one found in the Astrodome, the new Busch Stadium scoreboard would be the only one in the major leagues with multi-colored displays, pumping enough electricity with its 35,000 lights to illuminate 450 homes, or the equivalent of the electric power used by a town of 2,000 people. The board in right field was supposed to have read, "LET'S SEE THE DOME MATCH THIS," as the helicopter carrying the American flag made its way into the stadium, but it malfunctioned.

Outside, bar owners near the new ballpark — looking forward to increased sales in the future — could not gauge things from the opening night, as business was called "uneven" because of the long three-and-a-half hour game.

Brock, benched at the start of the game, delivered a pinch-hit single with the bases loaded in the twelfth inning off Braves pitcher Phil Niekro—in his final season as a reliever before beginning a long career as a starter—to send the crowd home happy with a 4–3 Cardinals win. Moments later, fans would encounter one of the first modern traffic snarls to hit downtown St. Louis.

On July 12, the new stadium would host its first (and only) All-Star Game. In the middle of one of the hottest summers in St. Louis since the Great Depression, fans and players withstood 105-degree heat—reaching as high as 113 on the field—as the hometown hero McCarver scored the winning run for the National League on a tenth-inning single by Maury Wills of the Dodgers. Nearly 150 people in attendance at the game had to be treated for heat exhaustion. It was here where Casey Stengel uttered his famous words about the circular, still-air stadium: "It sure holds the heat well."

Come August, when three professional sports would come together on the schedule, it would be the job of stadium superintendent Barney Rodgers to transform the multi-purpose facility for use for football and soccer as well. "They told me this would be the most interesting summer of life," Rodgers said with nervous anticipation. "I can hardly wait to find out." Each time Rodgers and his small crew of eight helpers would change the field to a different sport, it would cost $1,000—normally picked up by the club to which sport the field was changing, be it the baseball Cardinals, the Cardinals of the National Football League, or the local professional soccer team, the Stars. Some had feared an overuse of the $20,000 turf, with memories of the scorched grass of Sportsman's Park still in their heads. Rodgers nonetheless remained confident that the carefully-selected grass would hold up. "The Civic Center Redevelopment Corporation could have found cheaper grass closer to home," he pointed out, "but we went to Arkansas and hauled back the toughest Zoysia we could find." In the midst of considering protection of the nice new turf, someone had proposed to Rodgers that the football Cardinals establish a separate practice field somewhere near downtown. "I've looked around the riverfront here, but I haven't found an area that hasn't already been earmarked for something else," he informed. "We could solve all our problems, though, if we could find one." Rodgers had begun working on baseball fields twenty years earlier, when doctors had told him that his serious liver ailment had been caused by poor air quality at the office job in which he had been working.

The Cardinals would remain erratic for the rest of 1966, but they were encouraged by the revitalized excitement of the downtown atmosphere. For the new surroundings had even helped lead to some progress in the standings—an 83–79 record for 1966, good for sixth place in the National League. And while still in the second division, it was an improvement over the previous year. "Things are coming along," Schoendienst said in optimistic anticipation of 1967. "The league had better watch out for us."

2. The Omaha Express

They're young, but they've all had a lot of experience. This club could explode.
— Stan Musial

Looking to return to championship form, the entire Cardinals organization received a boost early in the year when Musial was named to the Cardinals' general manager post on January 23, 1967. He had replaced Bob Howsam, who in turn had replaced Devine, with Devine being named president of the New York Mets in November 1966. It had been over three years since Musial had retired as a player, ending his playing days as the greatest Cardinal of them all, amassing more hits than anyone in National League history during his twenty-two full seasons with St. Louis between 1941 and 1963. He was quietly offered the job first in 1964, but had turned it down. "When I retired as a player," he remembered, "Gussie Busch would have given me anything I wanted, but I didn't want to be general manager then because I didn't think I was ready for the job." As Musial got word that the job was now his in early 1967, he phoned his mother back in Pennsylvania.

"Now I guess you can go back to playing baseball," his mother concluded.

"No, Mother," he replied, "I don't think I'll let my new authority carry me that far."

The hiring of Musial was applauded by the entire team, which according to pitcher Bob Gibson "indicated right off the bat that we would again be a player-oriented organization, as we had been with Bing Devine and Johnny Keane running the show." It also served as a promising reunion for Musial and his longtime friend Schoendienst, as the two were roommates for all or parts of 13 years with the Cardinals. As teammates, they took turns driving each other to the ballpark each day (mostly it was Red doing the driving, as—incredibly, by today's superstar standards—Musial did not own an automobile for several years). What would be the first unpleasant task he would encounter? the press asked him.

"That will be to tell my first veteran ballplayer that he has been released," he said.

In the middle of February, he took a moment to reflect upon his first few weeks on the job. "I like it," Musial said. "I had too much free time [before becoming general manager], but not now. I'm learning as I go, about dealing with rules and regulations and [player trade] options, waivers, and other points of technical baseball law, but it's all very interesting." He had yet to go through a full round of contract negotiations with players, but felt he would be well received when the moment happened. "I've been there myself, and they [the players] know it," Musial said of the pressured feeling of having a pen and typed-out paper lying between him and the general manager. "I'm going to start off being fair and try, as a result, to minimize this business of bouncing contracts back and forth unsigned."

His good friend Schoendienst was 44 years old entering the 1967 season, and was working under his third-straight one-year contract with the team. It was representative of a personal philosophical underpinning to which he adhered, a carry-over from his days a player when the mere idea of expecting a multi-year contract was absurd. It was an era when a player, no matter who it was, had to make his spot on the roster every year—especially when dealing with the penny-pinching administration of the Cardinals, which Hall of Fame pitcher Dizzy Dean once referred to as "that cheap bunch in St. Louis." But as Red returned to manage the Cardinals, he still had the mindset that baseball should be as simple and wholesome as his rearing in Clinton County—an honest day's wages for an honest day's work. Like Musial, Broeg was most optimistic about Schoendienst leading the Cards heading into '67. "At 44, freckle-faced, green-eyed Red Schoendienst still retains his resemblance to the barefoot rascal who roamed the Mississippi River in the ageless writing of Samuel Clemens," Broeg penned, in comparison of the skipper's country-traipsing background to Mark Twain's Huck Finn. "If the baseball Cardinals he's now leading to a pennant seem to be having fun at their work, it's the reflection of the relaxed approach of a manager who leads with loose reins." Schoendienst had made it a point to not try and regulate the players' personal habits, so long as they didn't interfere with their performance on the field. Cepeda, for one, appreciated the philosophy. "Red let you play ball," the first baseman would confirm years later. "Give him 100 percent and he was right behind you. He was a great manager who deserves to be in the Hall of Fame. He figured that we were professional ballplayers, and that we know what to do. He let us play, and didn't bother anybody."

When Tim McCarver was asked what he thought of Schoendienst, he said simply and respectfully, "He treats us like men."

An article for *Sports Illustrated* summarized his managing strategy, which was nearly as simple. "[Schoendienst says to] utilize speed to its best advantage, play the best players most often — and stick with them during hard times — and keep the ones who do not play reasonably happy. Like most managers, he will occasionally build a doghouse, but he always keeps the backdoor to it open; you got yourself in, now get yourself out."

Six days after Musial was hired, Rickey was elected to the Hall of Fame by special vote, two years after his death. He had been a pillar of the sport for nearly sixty years, the greatest craftsman of talent the game had ever seen. People were again reminded that, because of his efforts — first in establishing the foundation of the farm system decades earlier, and with his more recent assistance during his second stay with the ball club's front office — the Cardinals looked indeed ready to return to championship form. But in addition to "traditional" prospects cultivated by the farm system, the Cardinals since the 1950s had been looking to embrace a newly-discovered pool of talent in the black player, a vault that Rickey had opened just a few years earlier in Brooklyn. Team executives in St. Louis saw an opportunity to tap a new resource, and in accordance with their history of scouring for talent anywhere, they wanted to be in the front of the line. It was also an opportunity for the city to enhance its social image, for some outside the Midwest looked at St. Louis as being a Southern town with slowly-evolving ideas on racial matters. The Chase Park Plaza Hotel in St. Louis, as one example, was the last among the inns in the National League cities to allow black players to stay on the premises. Busch wanted this mindset changed, and shortly after he purchased the team in 1953, the Cardinals signed their first black player in May for $3,000, a 23-year-old student at Fresno State College by the name of Len Tucker who had been noticed by Cardinals scout Ken Penner. Tucker proceeded to overwhelm each minor league in which he played for the next ten years, from Peoria, Illinois, to Saskatoon, Canada, to Modesto, California. He never got the call to the Cardinals, however, while in 1954, a first baseman by the name of Tom Alston became the first black player in Cardinals history. Alston had come at quite a price — the Cardinals sent $100,000, as well as veteran Dick Sisler, to the San Diego club in the Pacific Coast League for rights to his services.

By 1959 — twelve years after Jackie Robinson had broken the major league color barrier with the Dodgers — African-Americans George Crowe, Bill White, and a 20-year-old outfielder named Curt Flood were making significant contributions to the Cardinals. And by the mid-1960s, it could be argued that the National League held most of the young black talent in the game, with the greater talent pool making the circuit more of a speed game than that of the American League. While Crowe and White were products of the vaunted Cardinals farm system, Flood had been obtained in a trade from the Cincinnati Reds. And while no man had impacted the game on the field more than Robinson, no individual player would impact the game as much off it than Flood, mostly well beyond his playing days.

Flood only stood 5'9", but in a description more often applied to a football or basketball player, he seemed to play much bigger than he was. He was born in Houston in 1938, but his family moved to Oakland the following year. Growing up in a tough ghetto section of the city, he was forced by his boyhood friends to continuously play catcher in sandlot games, as he was considered too small to do anything else. "I could hit, though," Flood would say quickly in his defense with a smile. "I knew that when we chose up sides, I wasn't the last kid who was picked." Just the chance to play was something he relished in the poverty-stricken neighborhood where his family lived. "We were poor," he admitted to Ed Wilks of the *St. Louis Post-Dispatch*. "I don't mean we starved; we didn't. We were just poor. Dad was a laborer, and he worked in a hospital, too. He did very menial jobs. There were six of us in the family, and we lived in a two-family house — upstairs. We didn't miss a lot of things, but we didn't have a lot of things, either." Flood was helped along by a teacher at his school, George Powles, who served as an extra father-figure to Flood and who also coached Flood's American Legion baseball team, which had Frank Robinson on its roster a few years earlier. "We were always over at his house," Flood said of Powles, "nine, ten of us at a time. He wanted to make sure he knew what we were doing, and where we were. And he wanted to be sure that we were getting enough to eat." Frank Robinson's success— culminating as a signee of the Reds in 1953 — helped Flood get $4,000 in agreeing to a contract with the Cincinnati ball club three years later (in 1955, Jesse Gonder was also signed by the Reds from Flood's neighborhood; in 1956, another of Flood's teammates in the Oakland school system — Vada Pinson — was signed by the Reds as well, and like Flood would become a major league All-Star). Flood was subsequently sent to High Point of the Carolina League where he won the batting title, hitting .340 to go along with 29 home runs and 128 runs batted in. Back when a move from the Carolina League to the South Atlantic League was a promotion (unlike today, in which the former is considered "High-A" ball and the latter "Low-A"), his next stop was in Savannah in 1957, where he successfully made a transition to third base. He was playing in the midst of a Georgia law that forbade him from dressing in the same area of the locker room as his white teammates. Flood had been a shortstop throughout his high school career — and a switch hitter, a trait that he wished he had never relinquished. "I wish I never had stopped," he mentioned about batting left-handed. "I don't know why, but I just started concentrating on batting right-handed."

During the 1957 season in Cincinnati, Don Hoak had emerged as the permanent third baseman for the club in hitting .293 and 19 home runs after coming to the Reds in a trade with the Cubs. So after securing his first major league hit that autumn (after taking one unsuccessful at-bat in the big leagues the previous season), Flood knew that greater things on the diamond would have to be found in another city, and the organization obliged.

At the winter meetings, Devine and field manager Hutchinson sat down to negotiate some possible trades with Gabe Paul and Birdie Tebbetts of the Reds, and on December 5, 1957, they struck a deal. Flood was acquired by St. Louis in a trade which, at first, the Cardinals' executives were unsure of making. But at the last minute, Devine — seeking to make his first deal as the general manager — urged Hutchinson to go through with it. Devine visualized Flood as ultimately becoming a great center fielder with his speed. The move was actually *mandated* by Gussie Busch — one of the few baseball decisions that Busch ever made, as he left almost all other personnel choices to his staff. "It was the only time the president of the club overruled everyone else," Busch would jokingly remember years later about his directive of putting Flood in center field. It was the beginning of a strong personal fondness that the CEO would have for this particular player, only to have that relationship crumble by the end of the 1960s in a business dispute. But in rising through the St. Louis system a decade earlier, Flood spent less than a month at the Cardinals' Triple-A affiliate at Omaha, as the organization had seen all it needed to. It was plain to all who observed his skills that this abundantly-talented ballplayer was certainly, sooner or later, going to be the center fielder in St. Louis. Helping towards this pursuit was the fact that working with Flood every day was a man named Terry Moore, who was the best center fielder the city of St. Louis had ever seen before the names Flood, McGee, and Edmonds entered Cardinals lore. But also at the outset of his big league career, Flood struggled mightily at the plate. In his first three seasons with the Redbirds, Flood saw his average consistently drop, from .261 to .255 to .237 by the end of the 1960 campaign. "I don't remember much from my first spring training with the Cardinals," Flood recalled as an example, "because I was scared to death." In addition, he had spent most of his first few years with the Cardinals as more of a utility player at all positions than as a pure center fielder. But just as the promising young pitcher Gibson and several others had felt inhibited in the circumstances that season of 1960, relief was quickly on the way.

When Keane took over as the manager 80 games into the 1961 season, one of the first things he did was to tell Flood, "You're my everyday center fielder, and that's where you're going to stay." With a renewed sense of confidence, Flood finished the year with a sparkling .322 mark with the ease of knowing that he would not be pulled from the lineup after a bad day, as

Curt Flood readies himself for the regular season in an exhibition game in Florida.
(***St. Louis Globe-Democrat*** / Archives of the St. Louis Mercantile Library)

had tended to be the case with Keane's predecessor, Hemus. He was learning his limitations at the plate, and more importantly, learning how to utilize the skills he did possess. "Curt hit a lot of home runs in the minors," Bill White once said in a television interview. "In the big leagues, he was ten feet short [of the fence with his hits] until he met George Crowe." Crowe, a black man, was considered a leader on the club for both the white and black players. He retired from the Cardinals at age 40 in 1961, but served as a veritable extra coach on the field for the club during his final stay. Three years later, in the midst of helping lead the Cardinals to their '64 world championship, Flood had led the National League in hits with 211, part of his first All-Star appearance and his second Gold Glove season. When he took over the club the following year, Schoendienst knew exactly where he wanted Flood in his lineup. "He did everything you wanted a second-place hitter to do," Red recalled later, "handling the bat well and being able to hit to the opposite field. He understood the game very well and knew what he needed to do in every situation. If he saw the third baseman playing way back of the bag, he knew to lay the ball down. I didn't have to give him a sign."

Heading into 1967, Flood was maintaining a streak of miscue-free defense in the outfield that had never been seen in league records. It started in late 1965, and during the 1966 schedule, he went 159 straight games—which included 396 chances—without an error, a National League record for one season. Now finally comfortable in his role as a player, he was able to share his talents in other facets of life as well. Flood was a gifted artist and in his spare time could be found doodling with colored pencils, a piece of charcoal, or one of any other number of instruments. He had been paid as much as $500 for one of his previous works, and was reputed by some team members to have made as much as $15,000 on his artwork in the past two years alone. "I paint temperamentally," Flood explained. "I might get up at six o'clock in the morning and paint, or I might paint at night after a ballgame. The mood just has to hit me. I can't force it." He had once presented Busch with a portrait the outfielder drew of the beer magnate, which Flood had sketched from a black-and-white photograph, his usual model instead of a live one. Busch was so impressed with the 15- by 19-inch drawing that he wanted to secure Flood's services to make portraits of each of Busch's children. "They take about two or three weeks to finish," Flood explained. "I work two or three hours a day on them. It's one of the few ways I've found to relax."

Having possessed several youngsters at key positions on the team in 1964, most had expected the Cardinals to take their lumps in the World Series against the seasoned Yankees. Learning from the veterans like White, third baseman Ken Boyer, shortstop Dick Groat, second baseman Julian Javier, and pitcher Barney Schultz, however, the promising neophytes who were filling the other positions absorbed the precious knowledge that the veterans offered. Originally, Rickey had fought the deal that brought Groat to the Cardinals from the Pirates for prospects Julio Gotay and Don Cardwell, transgressing his theory that you never trade a younger player for an older one. With the glory of the experience behind them, the young Cardinals of the early sixties headed into the late sixties as battle-tested veterans, sowing their own leadership roles from disappointing seasons in 1965 and 1966 in an effort to advance the team to the top of the standings once again. "We're satisfied with our young veteran club," Musial said as 1967 approached. "They're young, but they've all had a lot of experience. This club could explode."

One of those leaders that developed over the course of the decade was a player that his teammates lovingly called "Buckethead," and he played a position where a leader is always needed on any baseball team. To further demonstrate his assertiveness, he also served as the Cardinals' player representative in the newly-formed Players Association. In addition, he was also one of the fastest catchers in the major leagues. Indeed, Tim McCarver displayed his qualities in many unique ways on and off the field.

Scouted by one of the greatest catchers ever in former Yankee Bill Dickey,

McCarver had broken in for eight games with the Cardinals in 1959 at the age of 17 after a stellar high school career in baseball and football during his high school days as the son of a police lieutenant in Memphis, turning down football scholarships from major universities such as Notre Dame and Tennessee to sign with the Cardinals. He received a bonus of $75,000 that year from the St. Louis baseball club, a somewhat high figure for that era which caused some resentment among some of the other players in the organization. He soon proved his mettle, though, after hitting .340 at Keokuk and .360 back home in Memphis in minor league play. While McCarver didn't possess tremendous physical attributes, he utilized his speed well and made a decent throw to second base. "He doesn't have a shotgun arm," noted Cardinals coach Joe Schultz as the young backstop progressed through the system, "but he has more than made up for it by learning to get rid of the ball as quickly as anyone in the game." The catcher's position in St. Louis became all his in 1963 at the age of 21; a year later, he found himself hitting the game-winning home run in the fifth game of the World Series, hitting .478 for the entire set as the Cardinals triumphed. At this point, it was clear that he had firmly taken the leadership reins of the club, and it was proven in spring training of 1965 when he angrily confronted a cocky rookie left-handed pitcher named Steve Carlton about who was supposed to be calling the pitches. By the end of the 1966 season, the All-Star hero McCarver had led the league in triples with 13 (the first time a catcher had ever led the National or American League in the category), as he took immediate advantage of the vast alleyways of the new Busch Stadium. "The ball died in right field in the old park," McCarver pointed out, "but it sure carried in the new stadium." Although he now called St. Louis home, McCarver kept up his connections down the river in Memphis. He and friend John Grisanti opened a restaurant near downtown, where every Cardinals game was witnessed either via television or radio. And, each time the hometown's favorite son got a base hit, a bell would be rung behind the bar in celebration.

Another of the youngsters to grow up in a hurry in the fall of 1964 was Mike Shannon, who at the age of 24 that year had just completed his first substantive season in the major leagues as the Cardinals' right fielder. Shannon had been hitting .278 at the Jacksonville minor league team that summer, and had previously experienced brief stints with the big league club in '62 and '63 (for 10 and 32 games respectively). While mostly playing center field for most of his minor league career, Shannon took advantage of an opportunity when Charlie James, another native St. Louisan, had gone down with an injury. After starring at quarterback for Christian Brothers High School in St. Louis, Shannon — like McCarver — had offers from coast to coast to play football in college. Choosing to stay close to home, Shannon went on to play for a season on the freshman team at the University of Missouri. Intending to stay at Mizzou to attain a degree in psychology, he instead left after one year when he was signed by the Cardinals in 1958 after a tryout at Busch Stadium and was given a $50,000 bonus.

Shortly after arriving in professional baseball, Shannon had gained the nickname "Moon Man"—in part because of a "floating" act he performed while avoiding a high-and-tight pitch once in the minors, but also because of the unpredictability of his stories that he would spontaneously share with anyone passing by the room.

Throughout their history, the Cardinals had always clung to the simplest philosophies for success. One of the tenets of quality baseball to which they adhered was the maintenance of excellent defense up the middle. Along with McCarver and Flood, further solidifying the middle of the field was the double play combination of Javier and shortstop Dal Maxvill. While Maxvill was still undergoing his internship at short under Groat during the championship season of 1964, Javier was already yet another veteran available to guide the younger players on the squad, having been originally signed for only $500 to the Pittsburgh Pirates' minor league system in 1956 out of the Dominican Republic. After minor league stops in the Pirates organization that included Brunswick (GA), Jamestown (NY), Clinton (IA), Douglas (AZ), Lincoln (NE), and Columbus (OH), Javier arrived to the Cardinals in a trade involving pitcher Wilmer "Vinegar Bend" Mizell on May 27, 1960. Javier immediately took over as the Cardinals' keystoner as a 23-year-old rookie that year, and gained the nickname of "The Phantom" with his remarkable ability to avoid the charging runner on a double play. "Look at my long fingers," Javier once told a reporter, showing off some of his physical advantages for using a baseball glove. "I could have played the piano." He instantly established himself as a team player, leading the National League in sacrifices that season with 15. His skills were recognized nationally three years later, as he was awarded his first All-Star appearance in 1963. The entire Cardinals infield was recognized, in fact, as Groat, Boyer, and White would join him. When the season was concluded, Javier (along with Cepeda) took part in the first (and last) Hispanic Major League All-Star Game at the Polo Grounds in New York on October 12, 1963, as the Nationals beat the Americans 5–2. Unfortunately, Javier would miss the majority of the '64 World Series with an injury. Still in a generous mood, however, he gave the Cardinals' clubhouse boy his old car when St. Louis had clinched the National League pennant, just as Javier had promised him a few months earlier. A broken finger from being hit by a Vern Law pitch on June 17, 1965, put Javier on the shelf for seven weeks that season as well, and he felt the effects carry over into 1966 as he batted a career-low .228 while keeping his defensive play at a high level. For even throughout his batting struggles, Devine defended as him the best defensive second baseman in Cardinals history—better than Frankie Frisch, Rogers Hornsby, or Schoendienst. A similarly-impressed Broeg agreed. "He ranges like Frisch and Schoendienst for ground balls, roams for pop flies with the skill of the old Flash [Frisch] and the Redhead, pivots quickly with the strong arm of Hornsby and Frisch, and runs on the straightaway with almost the fastest of them."

Javier was instrumental in starting a Little League in his hometown area of San Francisco de Macoris in the Dominican Republic, long since the days when Javier and his boyhood friends had to play baseball with bats made of rough wood they had stripped from guava trees. Playing high school ball with the Alou brothers, Javier regularly displayed himself as the fastest player in town. He also took up smoking at an early age, as he witnessed both of his grandmothers regularly puffing on cigars. "They are strong cigars, too," Javier confirmed, "and many older women in my country smoke them." The smoking of cigars is regularly followed, Julian noted, by Dominican beers that contained 14 percent alcohol.

After contributing to the development of youth baseball in the Dominican Republic, Javier next turned to his brother, Edmundo, helping him pay for medical school even with the relatively-modest earnings that most ballplayers were still earning in the 1960s.

By 1960, the young Maxvill had been considered a top infield prospect and had garnered interest from several major league clubs, but there was only one place that he wanted to play. Growing up just across the river from St. Louis in the industrial town of Granite City, Illinois, Maxvill had been offered baseball scholarships by the University of Missouri and Northwestern University. But he wanted to stay close to home, as well as enroll in a top-notch engineering program. He chose Washington University in St. Louis, returning home in the summers to work in the Granite City steel mills, cleaning oil out of the furnaces. "I didn't know what a jackhammer looked like," Maxvill recalled, "but I told them I had used one before because I wanted to pick up the overtime pay. The jackhammer weighed at least 50 pounds. I had to operate it inside a furnace. My job was to break up the concrete in the furnace. I never worked so hard in all my life." It was quite a job indeed for the skinny young man whose Cardinals teammates would later name "Bonesy." After batting .350 for WV, he tried out for some other clubs and netted a couple of offers, which included $4,000 from Pittsburgh and $2,000 from the Washington Senators. When the Pirates discovered that Maxvill had let the Senators know how much Pittsburgh was offering, both organizations were insulted and pulled their offers as Maxvill wound up with nothing. Then suddenly, the shortstop at the Cardinals' minor league team in Winnipeg broke his leg, and an able substitute was needed. Devine, as the WV graduate himself, knew whom to call. Maxvill put his name on the dotted line with the Redbirds for a mere $1,000, to be doubled if he was able to finish the season with the team in Canada. He did so, and was promoted to Tulsa in 1961 where he hit .348 and played a brilliant shortstop, which preceded a call-up to the Cardinals the following season at the age of 23.

After the Cardinals acquired Groat, Maxvill spent much of the '63 and '64 seasons on the bench. When he was demoted to the minor leagues at Jacksonville, he refused to report and considered using his engineering talents in another career. His wife, Diane, talked him out of it, but his troubles continued as a disagreement with Jacksonville manager Harry Walker led to Maxvill being sent to another farm club at Indianapolis. When Indianapolis didn't want him, he was sold once again, this time to a minor league team in Salt Lake City. He was enduring a six-hour layover in a Chicago airport when Maxvill, very depressed, speculated on his future. "My spirits were really down and I kept walking past the ticket counter, thinking about buying a ticket to St. Louis and forgetting baseball," he continued. "I was sweating at the airport. There was no air conditioning. Finally, at 1:30 in the morning, I called Diane and she talked me into giving baseball one more try." By 1966, Maxvill finally worked himself back to the point of being the Cardinals' starting shortstop.

Unlike Maxvill, Javier, McCarver, and several of the others, baseball was not always the first love of Lou Brock as a child. But soon, the acoustic qualities of the game caught hold of him. "I was always fascinated by the sound of a ball off a bat," he revealed. "To this day, to me, there is no greater sound than a bat hitting a baseball in an open field or park." Born in El Dorado, Arkansas, on June 18, 1939, Brock's family moved to Collinston, Louisiana, where he learned about the travails of poverty. "When I was a kid, I thought that was the way that everyone lived," he said. "I didn't know there was such a thing as a steady job. I thought everyone had a steady job for a day or two and then got another one." When he was in the fourth grade, little Lou once sent a spitball flying past the ear of a classmate. As a penalty, the teacher sent him to the library to write a report on the topic of baseball, and specifically on four players named Jackie Robinson, Joe DiMaggio, Don Newcombe, and Stan Musial. Brock, intrigued by what he learned, decided to give the game a try, and soon he could not be kept from the field. His mother had forbidden him to play ball on Sundays, but Lou and the other local boys snuck away from church to do so anyway, sprinting to a nearby empty lot, stripping off their Sunday shirts and knocking the ball around in their best-dressed trousers. "Our white shirts and ties would be intact when we got home," Brock recalled, "but our pants would be ripped to shreds." Using sports as a way to pass the time, Brock was mostly used as a pitcher through his high school playing days, although he batted .536 as a senior. Hitchhiking all the way to Baton Rouge for 160 miles, he went on to play baseball and major in mathematics on an academic scholarship at Southern University after graduating fourth in a class of 105 at his high school near Collinston. Despite his aspirations to become an architect, he lost the academic scholarship after one year, and while trying to earn one through the baseball route, he worked as a janitor and landscaper to make ends meet for his tuition in the interim. Unfortunately, his first year at college was tough on the field too, as he set a Southern record by striking out in 15 consecutive at-bats at one point. He came of age in his sophomore season, nearly equaling his senior-year high school mark with a .520 average (best in the Southwest Athletic Conference) and was later chosen to represent the United States in the Pan-American Games in 1959. After his junior campaign, he got on a bus—with all the money he had to his name—to go to St. Louis for a tryout that was supposedly confirmed with the Cardinals. When he arrived in the city, however, he found that no one was expecting him. With less than $10 left, he made his way to Chicago, staying with a friend and hoping to catch on with either the Cubs or White Sox as he washed dishes to support himself in the meantime. It was 1960, and after a couple of workouts, the Cubs gave him $12,000 to sign — almost half of which he cashed at a local bank and stuffed in his pockets for the bus ride back to Baton Rouge. He spent one season in the minors, playing Class C ball at St. Cloud, Minnesota, in 1961 as he led the circuit in nearly every offensive category, including batting average (.361), hits, doubles, and runs scored, as well as adding fourteen homers and 82 RBIs. He did so well, in fact, that he was called up to the majors before the season was over. The next year as a regular with the Cubs, he hit one of only four homers to ever land in the center field bleachers at the Polo Grounds in New York. It was the first time that people in the big leagues began to notice the unusual strength he possessed in his body that was not quite six feet tall and weighed only 170 pounds. But for the most part, he struggled on the north side of Chicago—at least with himself—and was not happy in blue pinstripes, his batting average leveling out at a mediocre .258 for the 1963 season as he stole 24 bases but was also thrown out twelve times. He made only eight errors in 140 games, but his obvious discomfort in the outfield led to most of his catches being of the circus variety. His theatrics in the pasture led a writer for the *Chicago Daily News* that year to offer, "If you have watched all the Cub home games thus far you probably had come to the conclusion that Lou Brock is the worst outfielder in baseball history. He really isn't, but he hasn't done much to prove it."

Then suddenly in the middle of the '64 season, one of the more meteoric personnel shifts occurred in the history of the National League. Cardinals pitcher Ernie Broglio was ironically convinced that St. Louis was "one talented young outfielder away from challenging for the World Series." On June 15, he found himself and Brock as the principals in a six-player deal that sent Broglio to the Cubs and that young outfielder to the Redbirds. The Cardinals had just fallen under the .500 mark for the season, and Devine knew that a deal had to be made to jump-start the club; he subsequently contacted John Holland, his counterpart at the Cubs. At first, Bob Gibson thought it was the worst trade of which he had ever heard, as did Bill White; both were not pleased with the Cardinals giving up a proven, established pitcher in Broglio, who had won 18 games for St. Louis the previous summer. There was such a furor in the clubhouse, in fact, that Keane had to call a team meeting to settle things down. "Maury Wills is a good runner, but he can't run with this kid," the manager told the St. Louis papers about the new player, whom Keane had been watching for over a year. Ernie Banks had been Brock's roommate with the Cubs, and he would be most sorry to see Brock leave the Windy City.

Back in his rookie year of 1962, Brock had spent all of his 106 games with the Cubs in center field. In 1963, he was abruptly moved to right field for all of his 140 games, which is where he spent all but one of his games with the Cubs in 1964 as well before being traded. In finishing the '64 season with the Cardinals, however, he spent 99 out of 102 games in left field. The right field sun is murderous to those who play that position at Wrigley Field, and Brock was relieved with his new position and new city in St. Louis. "In Chicago, I wasn't too successful," Brock recalled to a writer after his playing days were over, "and in the back of my mind, I knew there was a chance that any day I'd be sent to the minor leagues. When it turned out that I was instead going to St. Louis, that gave me a new sense of purpose. It was a fresh start, a change of scenery; and I felt like I was leaving all my troubles behind." On the offensive side, Keane almost immediately gave Brock the green light to basically run at will. "It took just a few games for us to realize that we did the right thing," the manager would say later about the monumental trade. "Lou was sparkling right from the start. And he learned so quickly; within a month, he was as much of a base-stealing threat as any player in the league."

Two years later, Broglio would be released by the Cubs at the age of 30, while Brock's baseball story was only beginning. On July 5, 1966, the Cubs sent Broglio — posting a record of 2–6 for the season to that date for Chicago — to their Pacific Coast League farm club at Tacoma, Washington, and he was never recalled to the major leagues again.

It was that season that Brock led the majors in stolen bases for the first time with 74, proving what a terror Keane had unleashed on the league, and what the Cubs had left behind. As soon as he got on base, taking second almost became an obsession for Brock. "First base is nowhere," he once told a writer. "And most times, it is useless to stay there. On the other hand, second base is probably the safest place on the field. When I steal second, I practically eliminate the double play, and I can score on almost any ball hit past the infield. Third? The ball club doesn't want me to steal third unless the situation is critical." Surprisingly, he also did not normally check the third base coach for signs the way most base runners do. "I don't have time," he said. "I'm involved with my own strategy.

"I don't steal the base as much as I *take* it," he continued. "To me, the word 'steal' contains the element of surprise, and I don't surprise anyone when I head for second base. The other clubs would be surprised if I *didn't*." Brock once claimed that he could read the catcher's sign without seeing the catcher's fingers; for a bone moves on top of the forearm when the middle finger is wiggled, which would suggest at least a "two" sign being given — that is, some type of off-speed pitch. He also had a library of movies of the pick-off moves of many National League pitchers, volumes that he compiled at his own expense.

It was while Brock was a rookie with the Cubs that he discovered the length to second base was 13 steps — and he would count out those 13 steps a million more times.

*   *   *   *

Growing up in the rough neighborhoods of Omaha, Nebraska, Bob Gibson was sickly as a child and once nearly died after getting an infection. As an infant, he spent a year in the hospital, battling illnesses ranging from asthma to rickets to a rheumatic heart. His father, nicknamed "Pack," worked odd jobs around Omaha and had passed away shortly before Bob was born in 1935, as Mrs. Gibson supported Robert and his six siblings by working at a laundry. Sometimes going without enough to eat, the family considered it a special treat when they could enjoy fried chicken on a Saturday night. Bob's two older brothers, Richard and Josh, had gone away to fight in World War II; upon their return, Josh (whose real name was Leroy) became the steadying male influence in young Bob's life. It became Josh's aim in life to get Bob out of the Omaha ghetto (the dwelling at which young Bob had his ear bitten by a rat, causing further illness), and it was decided that the vehicle to drive him to safety would be sports, to be provided by the personal coaching and prodding of Josh himself. Josh ran the athletics program at the YMCA on the north side of Omaha, seeing it as his own direct way to improve his surroundings. A move to a new public housing unit in Omaha, named Logan Fontelle, finally afforded the family the opportunity to have working utilities for the first time in their lives. With not much else to do during the day, Bob ran through the nearby fields and lots, often inventing games with his friends. "Robert just wouldn't sit still," his mother remembered. "Josh used to offer him dimes if he would stay in one place for five minutes, but he couldn't do it." Nonetheless, Josh's impact on his little brother was indeed profound. When Josh was especially hard on him, Bob went home crying to his mother.

"Robert, don't play with him anymore," she would say. Then turning to

Josh, she would add, "You leave my baby alone. He's tired. If he don't want to play, he don't have to." But Bob would go back and play with Josh again anyway.

"He was the one who got me going," Bob said of Josh. "When he came back from the war about 1945, when I was ten, he took particular interest in me. He made me work a little harder because he expected me to do better than the other kids. He spent money out of his own pocket for equipment for the boys in the neighborhood. He got us uniforms any way that he could. They weren't new; they came from other teams that had sponsors, and no two of our uniforms had the same sponsor's name on them."

Bob had wanted to play football in high school, but was told by the coaches that he was too small. He ran track instead, as he was able to high-jump his own height — six feet, one inch. As for one of the two other sports that interested him, Gibson noted that most blacks in Omaha had mostly played softball in that day — not baseball — but that idea had completely changed with Robinson's integration of the National League in 1947. Three years later, Gibson — at the age of 15 — was leading the first all-black team to win a Nebraska state American Legion baseball championship, in addition to setting the Omaha indoor record for the high jump at five feet, eleven inches while elevating to his six-foot-one mark outdoors.

Three years later in 1953, Indiana University had just won its second national championship in basketball when Bob had graduated from high school. Basketball was his first love, and he sincerely believed it would be his ticket to college. "The most spectacular is Gibson," the *Omaha World-Herald* newspaper trumpeted when announcing its all-city high school basketball team that year. "He's the boy with springs in his toes and basketball magic in his fingertips." He sent off his college application to Indiana, wishing to play for the Hoosiers, but was denied.

Gibson was tempted to sign with the Negro Leagues for baseball and make a little money, but Josh insisted that he attend college. With less than two months before the start of the fall semester and offers running short, Josh made a few phone calls and Bob found himself at Creighton University in Omaha, a school that was near the Logan Fontelle neighborhood. Shortly before he enrolled, however, his mother had moved to another part of the city as part of an ill-fated relationship she had established with a friend. Bob nonetheless made the necessary longer trek to school, and became the first black man to play on the baseball and basketball teams, and would ultimately become the first black inducted into the Creighton Sports Hall of Fame. He planned (indifferently) to major in sociology, looking to become a social worker or a high school athletic director if a career as an athlete didn't work out.

"Something dealing with people," Gibson would later tell a reporter about his alternate work plans at the time.

The reporter then asked him, "Do you like dealing with people?"
Gibson responded, "I did then. I don't now."

In reality, though, Gibson had little interest in academics. "I went to college on a basketball scholarship and I went to play basketball," he admitted in his first autobiography, *From Ghetto to Glory*. "Not to study. Not to work. Not to improve my mind. Not to earn a degree. Not to prepare for my future. I went to play basketball. That was the only thing that interested me." Nonetheless, he stayed at Creighton four years, leaving just a few credits short of a degree.

And despite having pitched very little for the baseball team at Creighton, pro clubs saw mound potential in the switch-hitting outfielder and catcher. He would soon leave behind those qualities, including the switch-hitting, after the Cardinals had hold of him for a while. "That's some arm," Keane said when he saw Gibson throw a baseball for the first time. "Let's sign him and start him off as a pitcher. I'll guarantee you if he doesn't make it as a pitcher, he'll sure as hell make it as an outfielder." Later, after beginning his career with the major league club, Gibson was seen taking some ground balls by Frankie Frisch. With the smoothness and athleticism that Gibson displayed, Frisch was convinced that Gibson could have become one of the better infielders in the league.

The Cardinals got him for $4,000 as Gibson stayed right at home in Omaha to pitch for the minor league team there under Keane's managership in 1957. He played with the Harlem Globetrotters basketball team in the off-season, making an extra $4,000 to supplement his monthly baseball salary that ended with the close of the summer. The Globetrotters' representative, Parnell Woods, had been impressed with Gibson's play when the 'Trotters had played a game against Gibson and some local college all-stars in Omaha, and he asked the native son to sign. Gibson inked a contract with Woods and got married the same week. But while he tried to enjoy his time with the famous hardwood team, Gibson preferred a more direct, realistic, in-your-face kind of basketball. "I'd rather play the game seriously, but it was only one season," Gibson thought back, "then Bing Devine told me to give it up. He felt I shouldn't divide myself between two sports. It was all right with me. The only reason I did it was because it was a winter job and I made good money." But despite keeping himself in shape year-round, one of his detractors was his first major league manager, Hemus. "He'll never make a big league pitcher," the manager snarled. "He throws everything at the same speed." Nonetheless, he was invited to spring training with the big league club in 1958 with a shot at making the roster. Gibson was startled to find, however, that the living arrangements at the Cardinals' spring training complex at St. Petersburg, Florida, were segregated. He recalled a black woman who ran a boarding house on the outskirts of St. Petersburg where the black play-

Bob Gibson's intimidating follow-through — it terrorized hitters in the 1960s and beyond. (*St. Louis Globe-Democrat* / Archives of the St. Louis Mercantile Library)

ers lived, "who charged us $49 a week for a room and a couple of meals a day. It was a shame ... and a disappointment." Gibson felt she had overcharged the players since she knew they had no other choice for accommodations.

Later, in 1961, Bill White had gone against the concept of the whites-only team breakfast while the club was training in St. Petersburg, and hosted a mixed meal. Soon after, a friend of the Busch family bought two hotels in St. Petersburg that were adjoined, and blocked out the rooms for two months so that all of the players could stay together for the first time. "A major highway ran right by the motel," wrote David Halberstam, "and there, in an otherwise segregated Florida, locals and tourists alike could see the rarest of sights: white and black children swimming in the motel pool together, and white and black players, with their wives, at desegregated cookouts." It was noted that Musial — at the end of his playing career, and already having been afforded his earned luxury of staying in a private residence during spring training — chose to stay with the team in appreciation of the new-found togetherness. With the welcoming new surroundings, Gibson decided to bring his wife and daughters down for a family vacation. As they stopped along the way, however, they met restaurants and hotels that would not serve them.

Gibson made his major league debut on April 15, 1959, coming in relief against Dodgers great Don Drysdale; nine years later, the two men would have a longer and more pronounced duel on the mound. Gibson — soon to become known to his teammates as "Hoot"—permitted a home run to the first batter he faced, Jim Baxes, which was the first of Baxes' career in what would be his only major league season at the age of 30. Bouncing back and forth between the minor leagues and the Cardinals' bullpen for the next two years, the pitcher then posted a 6–11 record with the Cardinals in his first year as a starter in 1961, as he struggled with his control in leading the league in walks with 119. It was a symptom of the notion that he was, perhaps, trying to throw *too* hard. "When I was up with the Cardinals in 1959 and 1960, I didn't get to pitch often," Gibson once told a St. Louis writer. "So when I did get into a game, I'd try to strike everybody out, because I thought I had to if I wanted to get another chance soon." He immediately felt more comfortable when Keane was given the managerial job, as Gibson soared to his first All-Star Game appearance in 1962 while logging a league-best five shutouts despite having his season cut short with a broken ankle suffered during batting practice. The same strategy that Keane used with Flood — assuring him that, despite any mistakes he might make, he would be in the lineup regularly — also worked in motivating Gibson. "The first day Keane took over," Gibson said, "He walked up to me in the clubhouse, handed me the ball, and simply said, 'Here, you pitch.' He pitched me in the rotation every fourth day, and from then on I knew I could pitch in the majors." He became even more dominant a year later, sporting an 18–9 record as the strike zone was raised from the belt buckle of the batter to the "letters," a general area across the batter's chest.

He took amazing care of his body — he did not smoke, a habit discouraged from his rearing back in Omaha (which was corrected when Josh caught Bob utilizing a makeshift pipe when the younger Gibson was twelve. As an adult, he frequently removed himself from situations where another person was smoking). And as a general rule in conserving energy, Gibson did not like to waste pitches. If he got an 0–2 count on a batter, he would go for a corner of the plate and try to get the batter out — but not necessarily on a strikeout — on the next pitch. He would also throw at a batter who tried to get on base by bunting for a hit — seeing such a technique as an insult — in addition to the other situations of defending a teammate who was hit, retaliating for a home run hit against him, as well as others. No player was above getting brushed back by a pitch, no matter how esteemed. After Duke Snider hit his 370th home run off him on April 17, 1961, Gibson broke Snider's elbow on a pitch in Snider's next at-bat, and Snider would never be the same player again, retiring three years later. "Hitters were the enemy," Gibson simply explained, "and the inside pitch was my warhead." Snider would have his comeuppance in 1964 before hanging them up, however, as he homered off Gibson one last time while playing for the Giants. He was the chief ruler in an era of baseball where the pitchers— not the umpires— patrolled the game, and patrolled it effectively. "Gibson utilized every edge he had as a pitcher," said the man who knew him best — his catcher, McCarver. "Others, including [Sandy] Koufax and [Don] Drysdale and Nolan Ryan, threw a little harder, but Gibson had expert control of the fastball and it moved so much that I rarely caught it squarely in the pocket of the mitt. When Gibson threw the fastball, I could actually feel the heat of the pitch through the glove and the skin into my bone.... I never saw anyone as compelled to win as Bob Gibson was." The movement on Gibson's pitches was so sharp, in fact, that often McCarver and the other Cardinals catchers could not handle them. On June 7, 1966, at Pittsburgh, as one such example, Gibson tied a record with four strikeouts in one inning — the extra one coming on the dropped-third-strike variety.

Though never able to focus on anything but his beloved craft of pitching, Gibson tried to relax with hobbies such as constructing model cars, and the mantle at home included several pieces of his work, including a 1937 Ford, a 1939 Ford, and a 1941 Lincoln. He was also an avid bridge player, and was as fiercely competitive in his card games as he was on the mound. He never spoke to anyone while sitting at the card table, let alone to opponents on the field; Gibson was deathly afraid of making friends with players on the other teams, something he considered most inappropriate. "A lot of players on other teams tried to get him to talk to them, when they would be standing around the cage during batting practice, but Gibson wouldn't do it," Schoendienst recalled. "He never said anything to anybody. He just went out and played." But while many people thought that Gibson's sullen stare towards the plate was meant to intimidate the hitter, it was actually the result of a minor vision problem, for he often had to squint to see McCarver's signs.

Steve Carlton had gotten his feet wet as a major leaguer — along with his aforementioned baptism of the pecking order from McCarver — as a 20-year-old in 1965. After receiving nine starts in his second season of '66, he appeared ready to assume the role of a solid number-two hurler behind Gibson in the rotation, even though there were many scouts around the National League who thought he did not throw hard enough. Carlton had been born a few days before Christmas in 1944, after his father, Joe, had settled in the Miami area to work as an airline mechanic and had met his wife, Ann. His tall, thin build made basketball a natural sport for Steve — but he gave it up his senior year of high school to focus on baseball. "I've been a pitcher, nothing else, since I was twelve years old in Little League," he said to the writers upon his arrival in St. Louis. "Until I left high school, though, I only played baseball in season — despite the nice weather in Miami." Carlton signed with the Cardinals through their scout Chase Riddle in 1963 for $5,000 after completing a semester at Dade Junior College near Miami. In addition to Riddle, Carlton was also scouted by Howie Pollet, the Cardinals' pitching coach in 1963 and a great lefthander himself for the Redbirds in years gone by. "The Cardinals weren't originally going to sign Carlton," Pollet remembered, "until I told George Silvey, the scouting director, that I'd take $5,000 out of my own pocket to get him. At the tryout we had for him, he impressed me with his sneaky fastball, and he had a curve good enough to take a $5,000 gamble on him." The young lefty put his name on the dotted line, and a year later, Carlton met his future wife, Beverly — a Canadian gal — while pitching in the Northern League. He was then brought up to the Cardinals at the end of '64 season at the age of 19, although he did not get into a game that season. "I was awed, in a daze," he remembered. "But I remember the day I joined the team at Cincinnati. Bob Gibson pitched, won, and hit three doubles." With his tender years, the organization decided he needed more seasoning in the minors, and Carlton was sent to Tulsa for much of the next two years. "Carlton's role with the 1967 Redbirds is not definite," Broeg would write in March. "The early indications are that the lanky lefthander is likely to be used in long relief or as a spot starter."

Nearly as highly-considered as Gibson and Carlton as a young pitcher in the early 1960s was Washburn. He had helped lead Whitworth College into the NAIA World Series in 1960 — a tournament in which Washburn ironically had dominated Brock's Southern University team — and was subsequently given a $50,000 bonus for signing with the Cardinals after graduating. Washburn reached the big leagues in 1961, debuting as a 23-year-old before becoming a regular member of the staff the following season. Nonetheless, by 1967, he was simply hoping to return to his old form. Since tearing a shoulder muscle early in the 1963 season, Washburn had been unable to put together a full season; when he did pitch, he seemed to tire quickly, logging only nine complete games in 63 starts over the previous four seasons, dating back to the injury. He had shown revived promise in spring training of 1966, as a 1.45 ERA in Florida translated into an improved regular season record of 11–9. "I'd like to think I could win 20 games, but I think I will win at least 17," Washburn surmised. "I have to do this for us to have a real good year."

The fourth candidate for the Cardinals' starting rotation in 1967 would be a battle between southpaws Al Jackson and Larry Jaster. Jackson held the upper hand on experience, winning 13 games for the Cards in '66 (along with 15 defeats) in coming over from the New York Mets in a trade. Jaster, who

As a young lefthander in the Cardinals' starting rotation, Steve Carlton showed promise of becoming one of the game's dominant pitchers. (*St. Louis Globe-Democrat* / Archives of the St. Louis Mercantile Library)

was signed by St. Louis in 1962 after a brief stay at Michigan State University, offered more raw potential. In 1965 he was called up late in the season, and responded with three complete-game wins. In 1966, he would shut out the Dodgers five straight times (a major league record against one team for a season) as Los Angeles went on to the pennant. Those five shutouts against the Dodgers alone would tie him for the league lead, a collection that saw the

Dodgers bat .157 in the five games, accumulating 24 hits in the 45 innings, all singles. With that success behind him, Jaster felt physically ready to enter the rigors of a regular spot on the starting staff. "I'm thick through the chest and slow to loosen up, partly because I did weight-lifting as a kid," Jaster said in describing his 6'3", 210-pound frame. "But if I can get my curve and changeup over better, I think I can help more than I did before and beat other clubs more often. I'd like to start 30 ballgames, which would indicate I was pitching well, and at least do as well, percentage-wise, but have a few more victories than last year." He gained the nickname of "Creeper" from the other players on the Cardinals team, as he was able to lurch around the locker room very quietly despite his tall stature. Jaster's younger brother, Danny — also a left-handed pitcher — would pitch in 1967 for the Cardinals' minor league team in Arkansas.

A fifth candidate for starting duty was Dick Hughes, who was 29 years old but had yet to see the major leagues. Hughes grew up in the Mid-South where his family made a living on their 550-acre cattle ranch near Stephens, Arkansas, on the Louisiana border. He attended the University of Arkansas for a couple of years on a scholarship, and then married his hometown sweetheart before plunging into the minor leagues. He had originally gone to a Cardinals' tryout in 1958 after an especially uncomfortable train ride for several hours. "I had a roomette on the train — I was really living," recalled Hughes, laughing. "The roomette was as big as a large bed, and I had to prop my legs up against the wall. I got ten-dollar-a-day expense money, and after the three days I went back home with twenty of the thirty dollars." When Musial telephoned the Hughes homestead soon after to offer him a $1,500 bonus to sign, Dick had been outside spreading fertilizer on the family turf. Out of breath from sprinting from the field to the phone, Hughes quickly impressed Musial with his self-assurance in bargaining as he asked Stan to pay him a $1,000 bonus for each victory he gained for St. Louis. "I told him bonuses based on performance weren't permitted," Musial remembered, "but I liked his confidence." Hughes, looking like a dominant physical force at a strong 6'3" and 205 pounds, was confident that he could finally make the Cardinals' roster out of spring training in 1967, having spent the nine previous seasons in the minors in 18 different cities. "A lot of times, I figured it was do-or-die, and a lot of times I halfway died," Hughes said in reflecting upon all the crossroads he faced coming up through the minors. "One of the biggest reasons I hung on was that I never had any serious arm troubles." He was 9–4 with a 2.21 ERA at Toledo in 1966, striking out 132 batters in 110 innings with four shutouts. After a three-inning stint with the Cardinals in September, he then followed up with 11 wins in thirteen starts in the winter leagues in Puerto Rico, in addition to two wins for his championship Santurce team in the playoffs. Hughes was bespectacled, an assistance for his near-sightedness that had him 20/350 in one eye and 20/375 in the other. He admittedly was lucky to see *anything* without help, for that matter. "Without my glasses, I couldn't recognize my own mother," he noted. This prospect was especially frightening in consideration of the nickname his Cardinals teammates bestowed upon him, the "Sniper," as he once fixed the scope of his beloved rifle (unloaded) by zeroing in on pedestrians from his hotel room in Atlanta. In fact, as soon as he claimed his personal bags at the airport when the Cardinals traveled, Hughes would nonchalantly sling the rifle over his shoulder in walking out of the terminal and catching a cab — signifying, like Gibson's regular brushback pitches, a different era altogether. Hughes would be battling young Nelson Briles for the fifth starter's spot, as Briles was looking to bounce back from a 4–15 campaign in 1966. Both men had developed a no-windup style of pitching in the minor leagues under the direction of coach Billy Muffett, soon to be copied by modern pitchers everywhere. Until that time, most pitchers waved their arms in a downward motion before beginning their delivery; under Muffett and some other coaches of the late 1960s, some viewed this action as wasted motion and wasted energy.

For the Cardinals' bullpen in 1967, Schoendienst planned to rely primarily upon Briles and rookie Ron Willis from the right side, along with veteran lefthanders Hal Woodeshick and Joe Hoerner. Hoerner, in coming over from the Houston organization, was sparkling in his first season with the Cardinals in '66, posting impressive numbers of a 5–1 record and 13 saves, the latter figure good for seventh-best in the National League. Hoerner had originally been in danger of being out of a job that spring, as Schoendienst was ready to cut him after a poor performance in Florida. After injuries to Woodeshick and reliever Don Dennis, however, he took advantage of the opportunity and made the regular-season staff. Hoerner had been a star outfielder in his high school career, but had sustained broken ribs and a separated shoulder in a serious car accident before graduation. Nonetheless, he recuperated well enough to start pitching with a semi-pro team in Dyersville, Iowa — the town which, over a quarter of a century later, would be the filming site for the famed baseball movie *Field of Dreams*. It was while pitching for Dyersville that he impressed the coaches of the Waterloo team from the Midwest League, and was soon signed to a professional contract by the Chicago White Sox organization. A year later in 1958, he suddenly collapsed on the mound while pitching, and it was discovered that Hoerner had a muscle irregularity near his heart that needed to be monitored. In 1961, he was selected by the Houston Colt .45s in the expansion draft, and made his big league debut two seasons later. Possessing above-average movement on all of his pitches, Hoerner relied on a hard slider that he developed during his minor league odyssey as well as a strong fastball. Coming to the Cardinals, Hoerner would quickly become known as the team's official prankster. His favorite pastimes included taking a fungo bat, standing at home plate in the new Busch Stadium, and hitting golf balls out of the park — over the light embankments and everything, where no batted baseball would dare to go.

Willis had appeared in four games as a 22-year-old in 1966 after dominating hitters in the minors at Indianapolis for most of the season. He was a native of Tennessee, and had met his wife, Becky, at a minor league hockey game in Memphis the previous winter where Willis made ends meet in the off-season by working as an engineer at the rink. It was clear that Willis had many people from the family turf ready to support his bid to make the major leagues. His uncle Barnard ran a farm in Tennessee, and was so excited about the prospect of his nephew making the Cardinals that he planned to go out and purchase an expensive radio to hook up to his tractor so that he could follow the games; Ron, however, warned him against doing so before the final cut-downs of the roster were made that spring. And Ron's father, Tolbert, a truck driver, had lost sixty pounds in the past year in worrying about his son's baseball career, a stretch in which he lowered his weight from 300 to 240 pounds. And yet another uncle, Marvin, wanted Ron to list Willisville as his official hometown in the Cardinals records, claiming that he family had founded the town from whence he came ("It's actually just on the side of the road," Ron said of the hamlet. "There's nothing there."). The family, in fact, made a move to St. Louis a few years earlier, as Willis had helped lead Kirkwood High School to the Missouri state baseball championship in 1961 as a center fielder (Ron's family moved him from Tennessee to St. Louis when he was twelve, figuring that he would have a better chance to develop as an athlete in the city). Consequently, the $10,000 he received from the Cardinals on the night of his high school graduation allowed Willis to help his family purchase the note to the farm back in northwest Tennessee. Starting his career as an outfielder in the organization, Willis was made into a pitcher in his stop at Brunswick, Georgia, where he was hitting .255 before being informed about his position switch from manager Owen Friend, a former second baseman for the old St. Louis Browns. Even though the news came on a night in which Willis went 4-for-4 with a home run against Thomasville, he remembered still being agreeable to the move. "I didn't have too much confidence as a hitter," he recalled. "If a pitcher got two strikes on me, that was pretty much it."

Woodeshick, after suffering through a few rough years as a starter, had found his niche in the bullpen. In 1963, he posted a 1.97 ERA as a reliever; a season later, he led the National League in saves with 23, developing one of the best sinkers in the game. Like Hoerner, Woodeshick had arrived from the Houston club as left-handed help for his new team.

If anyone was anxious for a winner in St. Louis, it must have been Gibson. For in 1965 and '66, he became the first pitcher in more than forty years to have back-to-back seasons of twenty wins for a second-division team. He knew, however, that there was quality behind him. "There were stars on the 1967 Cardinals, but no star mentalities," Gibson would later reflect. "If a player was caught looking at the stat sheet, for instance, we fined him on the spot." Gibson, of course, was referring to the kangaroo court that most teams held, as a way of passing the time before or after a game if for nothing else. A "judge" would sit in consideration of the evidence — say, a batter failing to get a run in from third base with less than two outs — and then decide if a fine was in order — say, five or ten dollars. At the end of the season, this money was used for a party for the team. But soon it would be time for serious business, as the Cardinals executives spent the fall and winter of 1966 looking for one more way in which they could strengthen the '67 outfit into a contender.

3. Building a Champ;
The Champ Goes Down

Show me a guy who's afraid to look bad, and I'll show you a guy you can beat every time.

— Lou Brock

The Cardinals were satisfied with nearly all the position pieces they had in place to begin the 1967 campaign, as the St. Louis club was looking for just one more stabilizing, veteran presence on the field. A new top-notch infielder would have been ideal; they came up with another plan which they believed would be even better. They found a man who had long been looking for a change of scenery, and welcomed him into the fold.

In a move that surprised the baseball world, New York Yankees outfielder Roger Maris came to the Cardinals in a trade on December 8, 1966, which was actually an indirect culmination of a year-long search for a third baseman for the Cardinals. The Redbirds had traded the seven-time all-star Boyer — just a year after his MVP season — to the Mets in October 1965 for Al Jackson and infielder Charley Smith, just a week before White and Groat were sent packing with Uecker to Philadelphia (Boyer's brother, Clete — whom Ken had faced in the 1964 World Series — was beginning 1967 with a new team himself, as he was traded to Atlanta. There were seven brothers (and 13 total children) in the Boyer family, with five of the boys playing professional baseball). "Boyer was booed more than any outstanding player the Cardinals ever had," Broeg lamented after the deal was made. "But criticism never bothered him — at least, he didn't let it show." Broeg was not impressed with the move, saying Smith played third base "like a plumber" — which was at least literally true, as Smith applied that very trade in the off-season months.

54

On the flip side, many felt that Caray was overly harsh on Boyer when he made poor plays in the field, and not complimentary enough when he succeeded, thus painting much of the St. Louis public opinion of the third baseman in disfavor.

Smith, who would hit .266 with ten home runs at third base for St. Louis in 1966, was then dealt for Maris just fourteen months after his arrival in St. Louis. Instead of Maris, the original trade rumor had Eddie Mathews coming from the Braves to fill the hole at third base. Maris, gaining fame from his stressful-yet-successful pursuit of Babe Ruth's single-season home run record in 1961, had been trying to recover from a recurring hand injury during his final years in New York. Maris made the "mistake" of chasing the home run record just as widely-distributed electronic media — otherwise known as television — were entering the cultural mainstream, coupled with a barrage of newspaper men who seemed to prefer that his teammate Mickey Mantle break Ruth's record instead. He never felt that he gained respect with the people of New York, despite winning a Gold Glove and an MVP award an entire year before the home run saga took place. With the pressure mounting during the stretch run of the 1961 season, Maris began pulling out chunks of hair as a result of the tension, while his smoking became incessant. Because of the hand injury suffered in 1963, he had not played a full season since 1962. He would re-injure the hand with bone chipping in June 1965, and along with the fading Mantle and Whitey Ford, it was yet another glaring sign of the crumbling Bronx Empire that had ruled for over forty years. There were rumors everywhere that 1967 would be Mantle's last season, possibly also involving a move to first base to save his ailing knees. Maris, however, disagreed with the underlying philosophy to the idea. "Certainly Mickey can play first base," he said. "but I don't think he will, at least not for long, because the wear and tear on his legs will be greater there than in the outfield. And even if the throws aren't as long, they can be more demanding at first base."

Growing up in the Great Plains region of Fargo, North Dakota, Maris had originally signed with the Cleveland Indians for $5,000 in 1953 instead of going to play for the University of Oklahoma. Thinking of himself as simply a contact hitter in his younger days, it wasn't until Maris met up with manager Jo Jo White at one of his minor league stops at Keokuk, Iowa, that he truly learned to pull the ball and develop his impressive power. In his major league debut in 1957, he hit a game-winning, grand-slam home run in the 11th inning, a promising sign of things to come. He was traded from the Indians to the Kansas City A's on June 15, 1958; on December 11, 1959, Maris would be sent to the Yankees for Don Larsen, Hank Bauer, Marv Throneberry, and Norm Siebern.

When Maris was traded to the Cardinals, he was planned to be the only new position player from the Cardinals' sixth-place team in 1966. "I was sick and tired with the situation in New York," he said as he arrived for his first spring training with St. Louis. "Here, I've been quite pleased with everything. Maybe it's because there are baseball men running things here in Red and Stan, but I've definitely found a relaxed atmosphere." How much longer would he play? he was asked by reporters. "To play on, and draw an attractive salary might sound economically smart, but that's not the way I'm built," he informed. "I want to have a good year, but I'd expect to produce or call it a career." To make matters even more comfortable, Maris and his wife had purchased a home in Independence, Missouri, just outside of Kansas City and within easy reach of St. Louis. He would agree to a contract for $75,000 for the 1967 season with the Cardinals, and upon arriving in Florida, he had also resumed interviews with reporters—a courtesy that he had all but shut down in the last few years with the Yankees. "I would have liked to have been liked than disliked," he concluded about his experience with the newsmen in New York. "Just wearing a different uniform this spring seems to have made some difference."

Although he did not need his new slugger to hit home runs all the time, Schoendienst was concerned about the condition of Maris' legs, and was not about to let him get out of shape. "He's up to about 20 laps in the outfield," Red said of his outfielder's workout regimen shortly after he reported for duty. By the third week of March, Maris had his weight down from 210 pounds to 203. One of the more excited people to see him with the Cardinals was the other relative newcomer, Cepeda, who was very impressed with the right fielder as a human being. "He's good people," the first baseman said about Maris, who had remembered meeting Cepeda way back in spring training of 1958 while Maris was still with the Indians. "He's a man, and he's for real. Everybody on this club loves him and if you ask me personally, I don't think they come much better." There had been a reported underlying jealously between Cepeda and superstar Willie Mays in San Francisco, but Cepeda now saw the value of fortifying a well-rounded team that could produce a pennant-winner. "I understand what it means for a fellow like Roger to come here," he added. "What happened to me with the Giants is exactly what happened to Roger with the Yankees. I know what it means for him to come to a club like this where everybody looks to help each other."

Cepeda, like Maris in preseason camp with the Cardinals for the first time, also was enjoying his new spring environment in St. Petersburg. "I like this very much," Cepeda said in his broken English as he bounced around in the Florida sun, comparing this location with his previous spring training sites with the Giants. "I sweat more, but I breathe more easily than in the higher altitude of Arizona." And most concern about Cepeda's knee being healthy seemed to have been put to rest, even though he required a half-hour of treatment on it from trainer Bob Bauman every day before taking the field. "Playing 35 games of winter ball helped," the first baseman said of his activities over the previous few months. "It made up for missing all of 1965 and part of 1966." It was certainly time for the players to roll into shape, or at least maintain their progress. Brock, as one example, had upped his weight ten pounds from a rigorous off-season weight training program, reverting to his playing weight from college. In acquiring the extra muscle, he felt confident in swinging a heavier bat, moving all the way up to a 35-ounce stick as opposed to the 32-and-a-half he had been using. Brock knew that speed was still his game, however, as he did not want to regress from his Cardinals record of 74 steals that he had established the previous summer. He was also reminded by the coaching staff that he had set another team record in 1966 — 134 strikeouts, a stat that told him to concentrate on line drives and not the long ball.

The Cardinals took roost in the spring at St. Petersburg's Al Lang Field, their waterfront home for preseason ball since 1938. When they arrived, they found inspectors that had been sent by the office of Major League Baseball commissioner William Eckert. The workers were making a tour of all the spring training parks, making sure that the lights were in proper working order. Complaints had earlier circulated in both Florida and Arizona about the dangerous level of dimness that the poor quality of lights offered in most of the exhibition stadiums.

While Cardinals fans were happy to hear of the impending arrival of Maris, the question was asked — what was to be done about the gaping hole at third base, most recently plugged by the departed journeyman Charley Smith? The plan was immediately revealed, although it may have been obvious given the recent acquisition of Maris as part of Smith's exiting. The former right fielder Mike Shannon was to move to third base, an experiment that the Cardinals were confident would succeed. "There are several good reasons to move him there," Schoendienst said of Shannon's proposed new home. "In the first place, we have a surplus of outfielders. We have Lou Brock, Curt Flood, Roger Maris, Alex Johnson, Ted Savage, and Bob Tolan. But we need a third baseman, and I prefer Shannon because he has the best bat of anybody we might consider for third base." It was reasoning that was supported by Broeg. "The men in the middle of the infield won't hit much," the writer pointed out, in reference to Javier and Maxvill. "So that's all the more reason why a third baseman able to bat with more authority than Charley Smith a year ago is necessary in a lineup expected to score more." And as for Shannon himself, he was confident in making the switch, as he had made position changes previously in his career.

The Cardinals, in fact, were looking for *all* the bats they could muster — for as to the poor offensive season in 1966 to which Broeg was alluding, they had scored only 571 runs, their lowest total in nearly fifty years (tracing back to 1919, when the club played only 137 games). The simple equation was that Shannon was expected to hit a great deal more than Smith, and the Redbirds felt they had made a steal. "Shannon didn't become a really good hitter until last year," Schoendienst added. "Before then, he'd see someone hit a home run, and then immediately he'd try to hit the ball farther. He kept trying for home runs, and that's what the pitchers want you to do.

"Another reason is that Mike will take on anything, and give it a real try. He's that kind of guy. I really believe Mike will become a great major leaguer."

Almost as soon as the trade for Maris was announced, Shannon began working outside in the cold St. Louis December at learning the new position when it became apparent his move was going to take place. "The football Cardinals still were in St. Louis, and we would work out alongside them at the ballpark," Schoendienst remembered, "hitting him [Shannon] ground balls by the dozen. It was cold out there, and we even took him to Forest Park and worked out there." When Forest Park got too crowded with pedestrians and the new stadium was not available, the coaches would take Shannon to old Fairgrounds Park for more groundballs (old Busch Stadium was not a possibility as a workout facility, as it was already in the process of being converted into a Herbert Hoover Boys' Club). With his toughness and athleticism, Shannon reminded many of the old-timers of former Cardinals great Martin, a star of the Gas House Gang in the 1930s who also made the conversion from outfielder to third baseman. Like Martin, if there was a ball that Shannon couldn't stop with his glove, he would simply knock it down with his broad chest and pick it up.

All of the Cardinal players were under contract by the second day of spring training on March 2. In addition, all of the players were in camp with the exception of the late-arriving Javier, who traditionally needed extra time to return from the Dominican Republic. (Also needing extra time this year was Brock, who was pinched in Perry, Florida, for driving too fast. When he had only $30 on him in answering a $35 charge of driving 80 miles per hour in a 65 mph zone, Cardinals traveling secretary Leo Ward had to post bond for him.) Schoendienst had allowed the players a generous amount of extra time in the batting cage on the first day of camp, with Maris still looking happy to be out of New York and apparently healed from his hand injury. Musial was bemoaning the lack of depth in the infield, and was determined along with Schoendienst to spend the next few weeks seeking quality extra players for those positions. "Any time anybody talks trade, they want an infielder," Stan said. "And that's one of the reasons we're hanging on to all those we have." Musial was scouring the rosters of the other major league teams, also looking for one man to be a pinch hitter off the Cardinals' bench. Perhaps Musial should have activated himself, as his mother had earlier suggested; his vision was still the best on the club at 20–15 after physicals of all the players had been performed on the first day by team doctor I. C. Middleman. To gather as many ideas as he could for his new job, Musial was meeting daily with two of his most trusted confidants, in addition to Schoendienst — Ward, who had been the Cardinals' traveling secretary for the past thirty years, and Jim Toomey, who had been the club's public relations director for the past twenty. During spring training, he also tried to visit daily with Bauman to keep abreast of the health of the players. Musial was being careful to look for familiar faces that he could trust; for a week before spring training began, the manager of the Cardinals' farm club at Tulsa, Charlie Metro, resigned, saying that he wanted to take a job in Denver as a banker. Before the end of the month, however, he surfaced with the Cincinnati Reds organization. "He could have leveled with us," a disappointed Musial said.

As big-league training camps were starting to rattle with activity in March 1967, the United States was still coming to grips with the horror of its first space program disaster. The Apollo 1 capsule, a craft designed to push the then-known limits of the outer skies, burned during a training exercise on January 27 and killed all three astronauts aboard: Roger Chaffee, Ed White, and Virgil Grissom. Undaunted, the administration of United States president Lyndon B. Johnson announced that the American space program would nonetheless press forward with more research, testing, and experimentation. Just two weeks later, the Lunar Orbiter 3 would be placed into service, providing fantastic images of the moon's surface in advance of an expected manned exploration of its surface in the future. Along with the continued war in Vietnam, tensions were rising at home as well as abroad. Troops from the Soviet Union and China were involved in a stare-down on the Tibetan border that separated the two countries, a show of force from both sides after Chinese protesters had harassed the Soviet embassy in Peking on February 4. Later that month, certain facets of the Johnson administration would come under scrutiny from New Orleans district attorney Jim Garrison, who was determined to re-open the examination of the assassination of Kennedy from four years earlier, just as Kennedy's body was about to be moved to its permanent burial plot in Arlington National Cemetery.

In the midst of the spring training exercises commencing and the anticipated launching of the regular season, the war in southeast Asia was requiring that more young men from America be called to fight. Among those chosen by the Selective Service was a boxer from Louisville, Kentucky, named Cassius Clay, who on March 22 would defend his world heavyweight championship with seventh-round knockout of Zora Folley at Madison Square Garden in New York. But Clay's world — and the world all around him — was changing drastically. He was ordered to later report to Houston on April 28 for his induction into the United States Army after being drafted, but was seeking an injunction to preclude the event in trying to challenge the constitutionality of the Selective Service Act in federal court. A judge denied the injunction, however, stating that the 25-year-old Clay "could not challenge the act's constitutionality until he either permitted himself to be drafted or failed to comply with the induction order." Clay, who had recently changed his name to Muhammad Ali, had his attorney, Hayden Covington, file a 67-page statement that protested his entry into the army on the grounds he should be granted an exemption for his current status as a Muslim minister, a plea that had already been denied by multiple federal judges. "If Clay is inducted," Covington warned, "we are fighting a war and sacrificing justice to win it." Clay, changing his stance, was now protesting the injunction on the grounds that no black members were on the draft board where he was selected in his hometown of Louisville. Attorneys for the government, meanwhile, contended that Clay was seeking "not equal treatment, but preferential treatment." Even with his imminent induction, it was discussed that Clay might possibly schedule one more bout before he entered the army, a proposed match against former champion Floyd Patterson in Nevada, or perhaps even Tokyo, Japan. Clay was looking for at least $250,000 in guarantees from boxing promoters before he would agree to the bout. When Nevada denied him a license to fight, Clay shifted his attention to Pittsburgh. Pennsylvania governor Raymond Shafer subsequently ordered the Pennsylvania State Athletic Commission to forbid the fight from occurring in his state, even after the commission had already approved the bout. All interested eyes next fixed on the end of April, when Clay would either accept or refuse his induction into the army, with the latter choice carrying extreme consequences.

Back in the baseball world, the Cardinals were taking nothing for granted in spring camp, as this time they wanted to carry over their momentum when heading north. In 1966, as they finished the regular season in sixth place, the Cardinals had previously completed the spring schedule with an impressive 18–9 record, the best in the National League. The other spot at which Musial and Schoendienst were concerned about depth was at the catcher's position, as McCarver had endured a grueling 148 games behind the plate in 1966. Two possibilities for relief existed in veterans Dave Ricketts and Johnny Romano, the latter with extensive experience in the big leagues. Romano was a 32-year-old backstop from the shores of eastern New Jersey, and it would be his first venture into the National League. He had spent nine seasons with the Chicago White Sox and Cleveland Indians after initially signing with Chicago for $4,000 in 1954 and turning down scholarship offers to play basketball in college. After hitting 38 home runs for Waterloo in 1955 — a single-season record for the old Three-I League — Romano was an All-Star with the Indians in 1961 and 1962, when he hit a combined 46 home runs and 161 runs batted in. Romano, however, had always battled a weight problem in his career, and the White Sox gave up on him in 1966 as they shipped him to the Cardinals that December for Don Dennis and outfield prospect Walt Williams. Up to 235 pounds at one point, he had reduced himself to a more-trim 210 as camp began in St. Petersburg. He was foreseen as the most efficient backup choice to McCarver. "I just hope I get the chance," he told Broeg. "I like this club. I think it can win, and I know I can help." Ricketts, a star in both baseball and basketball himself at Duquesne University, had been with the Cardinals organization for over ten years. But the club was getting slightly impatient with his development, as Ricketts had played in a total of just 14 major league games (which accounted for a mere 37 at-bats) heading into the 1967 season. Ricketts had almost quit baseball altogether to further pursue his career in teaching when the Cardinals signed Romano. "I was about to give it all up," he remembered, "but my wife told me, 'You've already made your arrangements to stop teaching in late February. Go down [to spring training] and give it one more try.'" And even though Ricketts had hit over .300 four times in the minor leagues, a starting job in the majors never appeared. "I think clubs never trusted me to be a number-two catcher, and didn't feel that they could afford to keep a third catcher on the roster," he reasoned. "They'd get a good-fielding, weak-hitting catcher for the number-three spot, and they'd use up another roster space with someone to hit for him." His brother, Dick, played basketball with him at Duquesne and was the first draft choice of the NBA's St. Louis Hawks in 1956.

To polish his transition to third base, Shannon was some days taking 200 ground balls and 200 bunts in the Florida sun. He would appear at the practice yard behind the wall at Al Lang Field with Schoendienst at 9:30 each morning, earlier than the rest of the team was required to show up. Soon after spring training started, however, Red was mandating that all of the pitchers and the entire coaching staff join him and Shannon at 9:30 as well, so they could go over bunt coverages and pick-off plays as a unit. Schoendienst himself laid down the bunts, as Shannon and the pitcher learned to communicate on fielding the ball. Shannon barely had a chance to catch his breath as Schoendienst grabbed a fungo bat and began the ground ball barrage at him.

"I feel sorry for Mike," a half-chuckling Maxvill said to a reporter as they peered at the scene from across a distance, while a zooming two-hopper off the manager's bat painfully caromed off Shannon's shoulder. "He's giving it the old try. Red has been hitting balls like that at him every day. Mike really wants to make it. Why, he even asked me to write down all the play situations I could think of for a third baseman so he could study them."

On March 8—the day after Jimmy Hoffa began serving an eight-year prison sentence for his attempt to bribe a jury — Shannon made his first "pub-lic" appearance at third base, participating in an intra-squad game. The club-house boys at Al Lang Field were getting used to the routine that Shannon held, a routine which was very familiar to their counterparts at Busch Sta-dium. Shannon liked to change his baseball cleats regularly, and normally at least three times a game (once before batting practice, once before infield practice, and a final time before the start of the game). Schoendienst had wanted to throw Gibson for at least a couple of innings that day, but decided that Bob would be happy with a longer start and postponed his debut until the first traditional exhibition game against the New York Mets. This went against Gibson's typical request of his manager, as he normally never wanted to tip his hand to any teams he would be facing during the regular season. "I asked Schoendienst to pitch me only against American League teams in spring training whenever possible because I didn't want to show myself to National Leaguers," Gibson once wrote. Bob was eager to get going, though, and the skipper handed him the ball. The big right-hander was also looking forward to a full season in the cavernous new stadium in downtown St. Louis—for in not even a complete season in the new ballpark in '66, Gibson had lowered his home runs allowed total from 34 to 20, and the entire pitching staff improved from 166 down to 130. In addition to playing part of the season in the larger ballpark, he attributed his success to a better mixing of his pitches. "Usually I will not throw a curveball after the sixth inning," Gibson revealed. "When you're tired, that's when a curveball is dangerous. You're not pulling down on it as hard as you should, and it hangs ... admittedly, I go into most games planning to rely on the fastball and the slider." Shannon got only one chance in the intrasquad game, a ground ball after which he threw wide to Javier covering at second on an attempted force play. At his alma mater the two days later, the University of Missouri named 32-year-old Norm Stewart as the head coach of their struggling basketball program. Like Shannon, Stew-art was a two-sport athlete at Mizzou, playing both basketball and baseball before graduating in 1956. When the Detroit Tigers paid a visit to St. Peters-burg a few days later, manager Mayo Smith called Shannon "one of the most improved players in the National League last year."

Shannon handled two easy chances without an error in the first spring game of the year, as Gibson and the rest of the Cardinals lost to the Mets 5–3 on March 11, with the 76-year-old Casey Stengel throwing out the first pitch to Musial. Stengel, the winner of seven World Series titles with the Yankees, was the Mets' first skipper when the club was formed in 1962 and was relieved 96 games into the 1965 season. "A half-dozen games should be enough to tell about Shannon," Schoendienst affirmed about the infield experiment, "but I'm sure now he'll make it at third base." Broeg wrote that "[Schoendienst] is banking heavily on Mike Shannon to prove in the 28-game exhibition schedule that a Germantown Dutchman knows a third baseman when he sees one in a St. Louis Irishman who never played the position before."

The Mets—along with other clubs—were just as interested as the Cardinals in seeing how Shannon would do at third base, as all teams were thirsting for heavy-hitting infielders. Devine, now with the Mets, tried to use his familiarity with the St. Louis organization as an advantage. "We know that if Shannon makes the switch for the Cardinals," he told the press, "they'll have an extra infielder — probably Jerry Buchek or Phil Gagliano. I'd be interested in Buchek or Gagliano. I feel like I know them.

"This is only the talking stage. It is nothing hot. The Cardinals want to see Shannon in some spring training games before they make up their minds. And if they decide they want to trade, then we'll have to see if we have anyone who can help them." Especially by today's standards, Devine's comments were quite generous towards the Cardinals, as teams are often hesitant to work a trade to the betterment of another rival club. But Devine — even with all of his clashes with Branch Rickey — was still a product of the Rickey School, whose textbook stipulated that you never cheat the other guy in a deal, because you may want to go back and trade with him again at another time. In addition, the Mets were seen as no serious threat to others in the National League anyway, consistently in the basement of the standings. Indeed, Buchek would be gone in less than a week, traded to the Mets in a five-player deal that primarily drew another utility infielder to the Cardinals in Eddie Bressoud. Buchek, a native St. Louisan and graduate of McKinley High School, had been trying to stick with the Cardinals for the past six years, first arriving for a taste of the big leagues in 1961 at the age of 19. He had received a $65,000 bonus to sign with the Redbirds two years earlier.

The addition of the eleven-year veteran Bressoud — who in his off-time from baseball had become a high school teacher and counselor —fortified the Cardinals bench, which also consisted of Gagliano, Ed Spiezio, and Jimy Williams in the infield and Tolan, Johnson, Savage, and Tito Francona in the outfield. Gagliano, like McCarver, grew up in the middle of Cardinals country in Memphis, and was in his eighth year with the organization and was a two-time all-star in the minor leagues as a second baseman. The coaches liked how he could play multiple positions as well as being a strong bat off the bench. "Phil almost always gets a piece of the ball, and he has the ability to hit to all fields," Cardinals batting coach Dick Sisler said in his support. "He has learned to go with the pitch, especially in our park and other large parks." About his ability to handle the bat, Schoendienst added, "Gag has a good eye, as he doesn't swing at many bad pitches. A big thing is that you can play ball with him; you can hit and run, and count on him to hit behind the runner." Spiezio, meanwhile, had grown up not too far north of St. Louis on Interstate 55 in Joliet, Illinois, and had crafted his game at Lewis

University and the University of Illinois before joining the Cardinals in 1964. He had batted .311 for Tulsa in 1965 after nailing the ball for a .515 average in spring training with the Cardinals that year. Then, that autumn, he came up to the Cardinals and won three games with home runs, one of which had beaten the Pirates in a crucial game for Pittsburgh in the midst of the pennant race. While injuries had sent him back to the minors for most of the year, Spiezio was satisfied with the progress he had made in recent weeks. "I feel that I improved a lot at third base by playing winter ball," he said about his recent experience in Venezuela. Working on his hitting, however, was another matter. "You couldn't get any batting practice," he complained. "They didn't turn on the lights until fifteen minutes before game time in order to save electricity. We had to play catch in the dark. But I hit about .500 in the last ten days in Caracas, and after that I batted about .340 in the Dominican Republic." Williams, a skilled fielder and having arrived from the West Coast and Fresno State, had received 11 at-bats in his first taste of major league action in 1966, and many in St. Louis held out great promise for his future in the Cardinals infield.

The Cardinals were excited about Johnson being the most help in the outfield, even though he was in camp without a contract being signed. "Moody, unpredictable Alex Johnson," as Broeg had described him in an article, "a right-handed hitter with bulging biceps and feet that twinkle when he wants them to, offers batting potential. That is, if he's not dealt." He had hit .355 at Tulsa the previous season as Spiezio's teammate. If he was able to stick with the big league club, Schoendienst's plan was for Johnson to platoon with left-handed hitting Maris in right field. "If Roger isn't hitting well, there's no sense in getting him tired," the manager said. Johnson's running speed was also top-notch when he put forth the effort, as verified by Philadelphia manager Gene Mauch. "He's faster than anyone in the National League, including Adolfo Phillips of the Cubs, at going from the plate to first base. Johnson can do anything—if someone can get it out of him." Mauch's colleague—Phillies' assistant coach George Myatt—concurred, and even went further in his assessment. "Including Lou Brock, Willie Davis, and Maury Wills," he insisted. "No question, Johnson's the fastest, when he wants to put out."

Tolan, batting from the left side like Maris, was a frontrunner for one of the top utility jobs as he displayed fleet running ability in the outfield as well as adept footwork around first base. "A lot of people, including myself, had doubts that Tolan could hit big-league pitching consistently," Sisler revealed. "But he's made us all sit up and take notice. So far this spring, he's hitting the ball harder than anyone on our club." What partially hindered the baseball progress of both Johnson and Tolan, however, was their intermittent service in the army reserve. The 31-year-old Savage, meanwhile, had recently turned down an offer to be a high school basketball coach in order to take one more chance at continuing his major league career, as he had not been a starter since his rookie year in 1962 with the Phillies.

The Cincinnati Reds trained up the road from the Cardinals in Tampa, and on March 10, a shocking story hit the headlines from their camp. Pitcher Ted Davidson, who had won five games and saved four more for the Reds in 1966, was shot in an alley the previous night as he departed a local restaurant. When assistance arrived for him, Davidson informed the police that it was his ex-wife, Mary Ruth Davidson, who had shot him — once in the abdomen and once in the shoulder. The authorities caught up with Mary Ruth in an isolated bar that was less than a mile from the Reds' spring training complex, and she had a .22-caliber revolver in her possession. Over in the Dodgers' camp at Vero Beach, the Los Angeles team was losing one of its main offensive forces of the decade in shortstop Maury Wills. Nonetheless, the Dodgers were attempting to regain their focus, as their successful run through the 1966 regular season in the National League was stymied by a four-game sweep at the hands of the Baltimore Orioles in the World Series, which included being shut out in the last three games (in addition to the last six innings of Game One, for a World Series record of 33 straight scoreless frames). Wills had been traded in December to the Pirates for Bob Bailey and Gene Michael, as he had seen his numbers drop off in 1966. He had hit .273 and stole 38 bases in the past season, his lowest marks since his rookie year of 1959 (with the exception of 1961, when he pilfered 35 bags). He had led the league in stolen bases in each of his full seasons in the major leagues— including a single-season record (at the time) of 104 in 1962 — but in '66 fell to third behind Brock and Sonny Jackson of Houston, due in part to a leg injury that he had sustained. It was also charged by some on the team that Wills had become too assertive in executing his duties as the Dodgers' captain. "Losing Maury is no big loss," star outfielder Willie Davis had mentioned. "It might even help us. He wasn't a bad guy, but a lot of guys didn't like him, and I was one of them. I think Maury got a little too big for his pants. He was always trying to exert more power than he should have had as captain." Part of the problem, Davis revealed, stemmed from Wills accusing Tommy Davis of not returning early enough from an injury that caused him to miss significant time in 1965 and 1966.

But without a doubt, the biggest loss for the Dodgers was the sudden and inexplicable retirement of Koufax, their indomitable run-stopper who donned his Dodgers uniform for the last time in their disappointment at the World Series. He was beaten by the Orioles' impressive 20-year-old pitcher, Jim Palmer, in Game Two, a contest in which Koufax's normally sure-handed center fielder Davis committed three errors in a row. In blanking the Dodgers 6–0, Palmer became the youngest pitcher in history to author a shutout in

World Series play. Ironically, Koufax was calling it quits after his most dominant regular season and as he was reaching his prime, as he posted a record of 27–9 at the age of 30 during the 1966 campaign. It was rumored that Koufax had been frightened by the arthritis that had formed in his pitching elbow from two years earlier, and that he did not wish to strain the arm any further. Led by Koufax, Don Drysdale, Claude Osteen, and 21-year-old rookie Don Sutton, the Dodgers had inched ahead of the Giants and the Pirates at the end of the regular season in '66. With their outstanding pitching staff, a prolonged losing streak was hardly possible (in 1966, the Dodgers never lost more than four in a row). Some had felt that Koufax and Drysdale had planted a poison in the organization before the season began, as they announced they were holding out together. They decided that, for contract negotiations with the club, they possessed more power if joined as one. They demanded a three-year contract for both of them at a cost of over a million dollars. After a 32-day siege the club held firm, however, as Koufax finally inked on the last day of March for $130,000 while Drysdale would take home $105,000 for the year. Drysdale finished the season with a record of 13–16, and went on to lose the first and fourth games in the World Series. Even without his southpaw sidekick in Koufax, Drysdale was determined to return to the top of the statistical charts in the 1967. "I had too much weight across the chest last year," Drysdale attributed his problems, as he displayed a new figure in which he weighed 15 pounds less— at 210 — as spring training for the new season began. "I'm young enough to pitch another five years, if I can do so effectively. We're going to have our best hitting club in five years, too— especially at our home park. I think we're going to fool a lot of people who've been writing us off." Drysdale was filling his free time with other pursuits, which included a venture into acting and his nurturing of young thoroughbred race horses.

In addition to the absence of Koufax, another lefthander was on the mind of the Dodgers. Schoendienst announced that he planned to start Jaster — the man who had shut out the Los Angeles men five times in 1966 — in the Cardinals' second game against them during the first week of the regular season at Busch Stadium (Washburn, conversely, had a career record of 2–8 against Los Angeles, as Schoendienst was reserving judgment on where to use him in the opening games — even though seven of Washburn's Dodgers losses had come against either Koufax or Drysdale). In addition to Jaster and Hughes, also getting a long look in camp for the Cardinals' starting rotation was a 24-year-old named Jim Cosman, a native of New York state who had stunned the Cubs by hurling a two-hit, complete-game shutout at them in his big league debut on the last day of the season in 1966 at Busch Stadium. It had been his first start of any kind on the season, as he had appeared solely in relief 54 times in the minor leagues to that point in the year. He had been up with the St. Louis club for nearly three weeks, having been recalled from the farm team at Tulsa, but had yet to take the field in the majors. In addition, he did not learn that he was starting the final contest of the '66 schedule until twenty minutes before game time. Three years earlier in the minor leagues, while sporting a 1–9 record at Brunswick, Georgia, it looked as if Cosman would struggle to ever be promoted as his $700-a-month salary was cut nearly in half by the organization. Cardinals coach George Kissell, however, saw the raw ability in the 6'5", 210-pound right-hander and gave him some simple advice. "Keep your eyes and ears open, your mouth shut, and hum the ball," Kissell said.

"For every half-dozen grapefruits he threw," the coach revealed to the press about the pitcher's potential, "he'd throw a ball as small as an aspirin. I not only liked him and his solid family background, but I liked his eagerness and his competitive spirit." Cosman took it to heart, and reversed himself with a 12–1 record in 1964 at Rock Hill, North Carolina. A relief role with the Cardinals was another possibility for Cosman, as the bullpen was an increasing concern for Schoendienst and his pitching coach, Muffett. Willis had been shaky since arriving at camp, prompting Red to consider using Briles once again in the fifth spot in the starting rotation and moving Hughes to Willis's place in the bullpen. Unfortunately, the young Briles had seen his development slowed as well, as he had been unable to pitch in nursing a pulled muscle in his side. Briles needed all the work he could get, trying to re-establish himself after losing his last eight decisions for the Cardinals in 1966 en route to his 4–15 overall mark. A young scholar, guitar player, and attendee at Santa Clara and Chico State universities in California, Briles was still a question mark on the staff even though he had recently posted a 12–3 record while pitching in the winter leagues in Puerto Rico. His first stint in professional ball occurred a bit further to the north — in Alberta, with stops in towns such as Medicine Hat. "They enjoy their baseball, but their ballpark was on a river, and they had the biggest and most bugs anywhere," Briles recalled. "Some games had to be interrupted because of the bugs. So many of them would swarm onto a light bulb that the bulb would pop. One time, nearly all the lights in the place went out, so they had to turn them off to get rid of the bugs." As a youngster, Briles helped with the family income by loading the boxcars of trains. As an adult, he was fluent in Spanish, Russian, and French, and actively sought to learn other languages as well.

Near the end of spring training, the San Francisco Giants were concerned about the absence of their star pitcher, Juan Marichal. By March 27, Marichal had been holding out for 29 days — one of the longest holdouts to date in major league history — when he was granted a $100,000 contract with the team. Marichal, however, spoke as if he didn't need spring training. "I'm in good shape," he proclaimed. "I think I can pitch the opening game of the season if they want me to." Especially targeting Marichal and the Giants was

Gibson, looking to make amends for his three losses in three tries to the San Francisco club in 1966 as St. Louis would face them for four games in the season's first week. Gibson became the first Cardinals pitcher in the spring to go seven innings in a game on March 29, as he used 114 pitches in beating the Dodgers even though he struggled in retiring only one of the first six batters he faced. Cepeda was nearing a .400 batting mark for the spring, giving signs to the Cardinals and the rest of the league that he was in store for a big year in '67, his first full season in St. Louis (Brock and Shannon were the other hot hitters for the exhibition schedule, batting .373 and .364 respectively by the end of March). Indeed, the Cardinals were happy to have him on their side — especially the relief pitcher Woodeshick, who never liked to face Cepeda in a crucial spot during a game. "Orlando was always one of the hardest guys to walk," Woodeshick said. "He's ready to swing at anything that's anywhere close to the plate. He doesn't like to walk, especially with men on base." The other newcomer in Maris, however, was continuing to struggle physically. In addition to his hand ailment which had resurfaced, Maris in late March had developed bursitis in his ankle and was playing less and less with each passing day of the spring schedule. On Easter Sunday — March 26 — Maris had finally recorded his first home run in a Cardinals uniform in following up his four hits from the day before. It also marked the first day in nearly two weeks that Javier had been in the lineup, as a bruised hip had kept him out of action. "Hoolie" celebrated his own return with a home run of his own off Tigers lefthander Mickey Lolich, in addition to a double. Furthermore, the starting rotation looked to be juggled for at least the first part of the season, as Carlton had sustained a hurt knee after a line drive had struck him on the 27th. Al Jackson went into his place for the time being; but when Jackson was pounded for twenty hits over nine innings in an exhibition game on April 3 (and worse, against the Cardinals' farm team from Tulsa) he was just as quickly pulled out of the rotation as Hughes was suddenly given the number four spot. "Jackson didn't have a thing out there," a disgusted Schoendienst said afterwards. "In fact, he's looked good only once all spring." And Hoerner was temporarily disabled as well, having been struck by a pitched ball in the knee while batting in a Grapefruit League game, and then re-injuring the joint when he twisted it in covering first base on a ground ball. Nonetheless, the lefthander wasn't discouraged. "This is the best spring I've ever had," Hoerner said in recalling that he had nearly been cut from the squad the previous March. "Slow starts had been the story of my life."

With the injuries and inconsistencies on the pitching staff, people were wondering when Musial would pull his first trade as the general manager. While it did not involve a pitcher, the Buchek deal had made that a reality two days earlier on April 1. Devine (in making his fourth trade since being named general manager of the Mets) had hinted repeatedly that Buchek would be a candidate to start at second base for the Mets, an impossibility in St. Louis with the presence of Javier (this, despite the fact that Schoendienst was a bit nervous in starting the season with an already banged-up Javier in the lineup every day). Bressoud, in turn, had been coveted by Schoendienst and Musial as a solid back-up at shortstop for Maxvill, giving the young Jimy Williams an opportunity to play every day in the minor leagues and gain experience. In addition, Bressoud was envisioned as a late-inning defensive replacement for Shannon at third base.

In advance of the opening of the regular season, the executive council of Major League Baseball met the same day as the Buchek trade to discuss issues such as expansion and player salaries. Commissioner Eckert, a former lieutenant general in the United States Air Force, announced that "the council's sentiment was that expansion was inevitable, but not at the present time." It had been recommended by the players association that the council support its bid to raise the minimum player salary from $7,000 to $12,000, while Eckert hinted that the council would support a raise that brought the figure to $9,000. Also on the table was the topic of possible inter-league play, a concept that was unanimously favored by the American League but dismissed by the Nationals.

The Cardinals had thirty players on their roster during the first week of April as spring drills drew to a close. They needed to be down to 28 by Opening Day, and then down to 25 players by May 11. It was presumed that Pat Corrales and Williams would comprise the remaining cuts, with the club wishing for both men to accumulate at-bats in the minor leagues in lieu of sitting on the bench in St. Louis. Corrales was assigned to catch for Tulsa, while Williams would be honing his skills at the farm team at Little Rock. Schoendienst was particularly excited about the future prospects for the young shortstop. "He'll be back up, maybe in 1967," Red predicted about Williams. "He's a big-league shortstop already. He has learned fast, has a good batting eye, and is going to be a tough out." Williams finished the spring batting .333 and did not strike out a single time in exhibition play.

The Cardinals bats were hot as they prepared to head north, as the team batting average for the spring did not dip below .300 until April 1, which was also the first day in which they were shut out. Maris, in terms of his physical state, was looking better and better each day; the promising rookie Tolan was batting near the .400 mark, tops for the club; McCarver, like Williams, hadn't struck out all spring after being the fifth-toughest player in the National League to strike out in 1966; and even the typically light-hitting Maxvill was smacking the ball around the park, as he was at the .300 level himself. Suddenly, there was nowhere for Sisler to place what he called the vaunted "Green Dagger"—a rubber knife that clandestinely went into the locker of a player who was mired in a slump. The private consultations that Sisler was conducting with Maxvill, however, were obviously paying off. "We'd work hard and long, even after a regular workout or game," Sisler said of the grueling drills to which he subjected Maxvill, who was now the recipient of extra work as opposed to Shannon. It was becoming a common sight to see Sisler and Maxvill headed to the batting cage after practice, each lugging as many balls in a bucket as they could carry for Sisler to fire at the shortstop. "I tried to get Maxie to stand closer to the plate so that he could handle the outside pitch. I urged him to hit the ball up the middle and to right field with some snap. He learned to wait longer for the ball instead of pulling the first pitch to third base for an easy out ... if he can hit .260 or .265, he can be a valuable man."

Maxvill nodded in agreement. "After I'd ground out, Dick would say, 'Keep pulling, Dumbo, and you'll hit .100.'" The shortstop had improved his average slightly from .222 to .244 between 1965 and 1966, although he was as high as .280 in early September of '66. McCarver was also seeking an improvement in his batting average, which had dipped slightly to .274 in the past season. "I don't know if I can make up 26 points in one year," he surmised about the possibility of reaching the .300 level in the regular season, "but I think I might have a good chance if I avoid another bad start like the one I had last season. I haven't hit .300 since 1960 at Memphis." McCarver had admittedly put a lot of pressure on himself in 1966, as Schoendienst had originally placed him in the cleanup spot in the batting order. After being moved to the fifth spot and later to sixth, McCarver relaxed and drove the ball with more regularity in the second half of the season.

Schoendienst, along with coaches Muffett and Sisler, had spent the down time at spring training by angling for kingfish in the outer reaches of Tampa Bay. Musial, meanwhile, had been invited to go on a cruise on the 119-foot yacht that Busch had in the harbor. As the crew of coaches drifted out on their fishing boat on Good Friday, appearing alongside them in another craft was the Cincinnati Reds' catcher Johnny Edwards and pitcher Jim Maloney. "John and I caught ten kingfish," Maloney would say upon coming back ashore. "But Red and his gang were pulling them out right and left. They caught 78 — and they kept rubbing it in by keeping us posted of their catch total on radio. Then they yelled, 'This is how the season is going to go for you, too!'" Among the best boatmen in the group was Muffett, born in Hammond, Indiana, outside of Chicago but growing up a Cardinals fan in Fort Worth, Texas. He would work his way through the minor leagues to spend six seasons in the majors with the Cardinals, Giants, and Boston Red Sox in the late '50s and early '60s. By the spring of 1967, Muffett had just recently replaced St. Louis native Joe Becker as the Cardinals' pitching coach, as Becker felt he was being forced out of his position by Howsam as a scapegoat for the staff's fall from success after two mediocre seasons. With Howsam giving Schoendienst a few recommendations for Becker's replacement, Red decided to go with his own choice in Muffett, who had previously been the Cardinals' minor league pitching instructor. "He understands pitchers and their problems because he pitched," Gibson pointed out simply about Muffett. Becker, on the other hand, had been a catcher with the Cleveland Indians in 1936 and 1937. "I never could understand why catchers were supposed to know so much more about pitching than the men who actually do it," Gibson continued. Added Hughes, "He's not aloof, but more like one of the guys. He kids around, and corrects a pitcher in a manner no one can resent." The batting coach, Sisler, another St. Louis-area product like Schoendienst and Muffett's predecessor, Becker, had a big league career as well. He was a rookie first baseman in the Cardinals' world championship season of 1946, and four years later became an All-Star with the Philadelphia Phillies. Before joining the Cardinals, Sisler had managed the Cincinnati Reds to 89 wins and a fourth-place finish in 1965. He had also been a sociology major while attending Colgate University, and used a cerebral approach when trying assist a ballplayer with his hitting technique.

For boating and fishing enthusiasts around the St. Louis area, meanwhile, the big optimism for the warming months of 1967 was the much-anticipated opening of Carlyle Lake in Illinois, located approximately 50 miles east of St. Louis off of U.S. Route 50 and about five miles from Schoendienst's home in Germantown — much to Red's delight. The man-made lake, which by the time of its final filling in 1969 was planned to stretch across 26,000 acres, was thought to be the new paradise for the St. Louis-area outdoorsman. "Its low, unbroken shoreline and breadth will make it ideal for sailboaters, who are being provided a special sailboat harbor," forecasted Tim Renken of the *Post-Dispatch* in the summer of '67. Builders had stocked the lake with one and a half million bass the year before, most of which had grown to nine inches in length.

While Schoendienst, Muffett, and Sisler were enjoying their fishing poles on the Florida Gulf Coast, other coaches on the staff preferred quieter times back at camp. They included Joe Schultz and Bob Milliken, also former major league players who rounded out the brain trust. They would all soon meet and determine who would be wearing the "Birds on the Bat" in St. Louis for the beginning of the season. After further discussion, the final decision on the position players would Cepeda, Maris, Brock, Maxvill, McCarver, Javier, Shannon, Flood, Romano, Gagliano, Tolan, Savage, and Johnson. The pitching staff would consist of Gibson, Hoerner, Washburn, Jackson, Woodeshick, Briles, Jaster, Carlton, Willis, Hughes, and Cosman.

The Cardinals finished their exhibition schedule with a trip to Washington, D.C., on April 8 and 9 to play the Senators of the American League. Schoendienst was not at all pleased with the sloppy 7–4 and 8–5 losses that occurred on the stop. "The way we played the last two days, it looked like the first day of spring training," he muttered. Fortunately for the Redbirds, just over 8,000 total people had shown up to watch over the course of the two days. Shannon had been given both days off, hoping to heal a pulled muscle in his leg in time for the opener at Busch Stadium against the Giants on the 11th, as the club was scheduled to get to St. Louis in time for a light workout on the 10th. Cepeda hit the last of his team-leading five spring home runs in the finale, while Shannon paced the club in exhibition RBIs with 20 and Tolan was the batting champ for the preseason at .394. Of slight concern was the fact that Maris had hit only .225 in spring play, but this figure was largely dismissed with the nagging injuries he endured while getting into shape. Off the mound, Washburn led the pitchers in Florida with a 1.73 ERA.

The sportswriters had collectively picked the Cardinals to finish fifth in the National League in 1967, with six of the 88 writers polled selecting the Cardinals as the pennant winners. The final tallies looked like this:

1.	Pittsburgh (35 first-place votes)	1,289 total points
2.	San Francisco (26)	1,178
3.	Atlanta (10)	860
4.	Philadelphia (4)	816
5.	St. Louis (6)	813
6.	Los Angeles (3)	803
7.	Cincinnati (3)	775
8.	Houston (1)	457
9.	New York	273
10.	Chicago	250

The Cardinals were not the only team in the National League experimenting with a new third baseman. The Pirates had risen as the top choice of the writers, in part, because of their acquisition of the speedy Wills from the Dodgers. Wills' acquisition was seen as a fortifying addition to their established lineup of tough hitters, which included Roberto Clemente, Matty Alou, and Willie Stargell (even though the hefty Stargell was currently in danger of a hefty fine from the club, as his contract stipulated that he needed to be down to 215 pounds by the start of the season; he had reported to spring drills at 230, and was not able to lose much weight in the preceding weeks). Clemente was becoming increasingly despondent in Pittsburgh, even going so far as to assail the club for a lack of effort. "Some are laying [*sic*] down and not giving one hundred percent," he told the media one evening after a Pirates' loss in the spring. The unsung hero in the group was Alou, who was the reigning 1966 National League batting champ with a .342 average, and whom Broeg likened to a "soda bottle" in trying to view Alou's diminutive five-foot-nine stature playing so deep in the vast outfield of Pittsburgh's Forbes Field. As Willie Davis had mentioned, Wills was mostly a welcome absence from the Dodgers' camp. But the Pirates embraced their new infielder, looking to place him at third with the established Gene Alley already manning the shortstop position, which was Wills' typical post. Many writers felt it would be a loss for the Dodgers that would come back to haunt them, as the defending champions had seen themselves go into free-fall to sixth in the minds of the predictors for 1967. "The feeling here," Broeg opined from his office in St. Louis, "is that Wills will retaliate with a tremendous season to lead the Pirates to the pennant ... with Koufax, the Dodgers could win without scoring. With Wills, they could score without hitting. But those men are gone." Broeg's league forecast had the Cardinals placing fourth, just ahead of the Philadelphia Phillies. "Fourth or better," he qualified his statement. "That how the Cardinals look to these bifocals." And in Cincinnati, the Reds' fortunes rested on the shifting of Pete Rose — owner of over 200 hits in each of the past two seasons—from second base to the outfield, and the development of a 19-year-old catcher named Johnny Bench. The position switch of Rose was in part an attempt to get the talented Tony Perez into the lineup every day (and move current third baseman Tommy Helms to second), but it was also a shell game, trying to cover up the biggest void to which Cincinnati fans were still trying to acclimate themselves. It was the loss of former Most Valuable Player Frank Robinson in the outfield, who completed his first year in Baltimore in 1966 as the American League MVP.

The Giants, with their combination of Mays and Marichal, were regarded as their usual formidable threat. The newcomer to the pennant chase was the Atlanta Braves, starting their second season in Dixie. Starting the inaugural '66 campaign in the South in poor fashion, the club rushed to fifth place in the last third of the season under new manager Billy Hitchcock, as the new skipper logged a 33–18 record in relief of Bobby Bragan. In November, they had picked up Clete Boyer from the Yankees to fill the void at third base, adding another home run-hitting bat to a lineup that already included Hank Aaron (coming off his third home run title in 1966 as he clubbed 44) and Rico Carty, a promising pick-up from the American League. Boyer would be taking the place of Eddie Mathews at third, as the long-time Brave (and owner of 493 homers himself) was traded to Houston on New Year's Eve of 1966. Meanwhile, the city of Milwaukee — whom the Braves had jilted — yearned for another major league team to take its place. In fact, in a survey conducted in early 1967 by the *Milwaukee Journal* newspaper, only repairing the local freeways ranked ahead of securing another big league baseball team as the biggest local priority, listed ahead of the other issues presented on the survey such as the improvement of schools and the lowering of taxes.

In Chicago, Durocher was confident in the strength of his Cubs team despite its last-place finish and 103 losses in 1966, his first year back as a manager after sitting out '65 in contemplating his next move after the Busch-Keane-Devine fiasco at the end of the previous season. Leo was sticking to his plan of playing his talented youngsters, including catcher Randy Hundley and infielders Glenn Beckert and Don Kessinger — all under the age of 25 who all saw the field regularly in 1966. "We've got several kids just an inch away from greatness," Durocher told the media in spring training from Arizona, "and they could come to the fore right now." Hundley was definitely one cut out of the old-school mold, which Leo appreciated. "You can't get him out of there," Durocher said of Hundley's endurance. "I gave him a rest one day, and he was like a caged lion. He wouldn't shut up. You have to cut the uniform off him." Kessinger was the same, another hard worker who in taking up switch-hitting in the middle of the season saw his batting average rise 73 points from 1965. The two veterans in the infield were the legendary shortstop-turned-first baseman Ernie Banks and third baseman Ron Santo, who were both optimistic about the Cubs' fortunes as always. "I've just turned 27 years old," Santo announced, the captain of the club. "And it looks like we might make it to the top before I'm through." Banks, in limited duty in the spring, had been batting .419 on March 30, even though it had been yet another spring in which Durocher had been searching for someone to replace him at first base. The unknown variable in the Chicago lineup was a young, talented outfielder from Panama named Adolfo Phillips, whom Durocher always felt was not putting forth full effort. Nonetheless, the manager did not want to give up on the gifted youngster. "Branch Rickey once said that it's dangerous to get rid of a kid who can run and throw and has power — damn the attitude," Leo asserted. "He could become an $80,000-a-year superstar. He's got all the tools; he's got everything going for him. It's a question if he can play up to his potential, if he can adapt himself, and how much he wants to push himself." Phillips had arrived to the Cubs a few days into the 1966 season, knocking 16 home runs and stealing 32 bases, but also striking out 135 times in only 416 at-bats with the Cubs. On the mound, Durocher was particularly excited about a 24-year-old youngster named Ferguson Jenkins, who was converted into a starter in the latter half of his rookie season in 1966 after displaying a resilient arm from the bullpen in the first half of the year.

Despite the disagreements that Durocher had with Rickey during Leo's days as a player for the Cardinals in the 1930s, Rickey knew full well the leadership qualities that Durocher, the captain of Frankie Frisch's Gas House Gang, possessed. "If I had a ball club that had an outside chance at the pennant," Rickey would always say in introducing him, "I know no other man I would prefer to have as manager."

Before the start of the 1967 season, Schoendienst took a piece of paper and an envelope out of his desk. Sitting very thoughtfully, he made a few notes on the paper, placed it in carefully in the envelope, sealed it, and put it in his jacket pocket. The piece of paper listed how he predicted the 1967 National League pennant race would finish. He was most optimistic about what he had seen in St. Petersburg. "We've had the greatest weather in years, our boys have stayed healthy, and judging from our hitting, we ought to be able to score a few more runs than we did last year." Lou Brock included his own optimism about 1967. "The pitching staff is better because of more experience. Now, we've got two of the best power hitters in baseball [in Maris and Cepeda]; a year ago at this time, we had none. Overall, we've got much better depth." Added Maxvill, "We're as well-balanced as any well-balanced team in the league."

The American side of the standings was seen as a three-team struggle among Robinson's Orioles, Minnesota, and Detroit, with Baltimore envisioned as edging the pack. More than 25 million fans had attended major league games in 1966, and with the exciting pennant races that were anticipated, league presidents Cronin (American) and Warren Giles (National) expected the 1967 figures to top that total.

As the 1967 season opener approached, Rodgers and the rest of the grounds crew at the new Busch Stadium were still struggling to familiarize themselves with the automatic field tarpaulin that was one of the many mechanical wonders of the new ballpark. As they practiced putting the tarp onto the field, it took over an hour for the gadgets to remove it, far longer than satisfactory standards. Rodgers had transferred most of his on-field duties to Ed Fuchs, a representative of the Civic Center Redevelopment Corporation that oversaw the operation of the new stadium and its surroundings. "When the cover is operating as it should, we can get it up and out in two minutes or less," Fuchs assured the public (and Cardinals executives). "Then it takes about a minute or so to remove it, and 15 or 16 seconds to lower it into the pit." The idea behind the innovative new system was to avoid the hassles of a stumbling crew laying the tarp in the midst of a heavy rain — which had been taking the stadium grounds crew as much as fifteen minutes — thereby saving precious moments as the playability of the field is preserved. "We just need practice with it," Fuchs summarily said. "We'll roll it out and work with it when the Cardinals go on the road."

Maris noticed one flaw about the arrangement of the park — a glare that hit the fielders in the eyes when the sun shone on the box seats around home plate. "When the sun is shining on those field seats," Maris said, "you just can't see the ball when it's hit. You just have to guess out there. There's a lot of concrete in this park, and the ball blends into it. Most parks have a blind spot somewhere, but I never had one playing right field in Yankee Stadium." The Giants came to the downtown stadium to open the season on April 11, with their ace Marichal slated to go against Gibson. The openers around major league baseball were being played in the midst of turmoil in yet another part of the world, for four days earlier the Arab-Israeli War had erupted. Israel ultimately triumphed over Egypt, Syria, and Jordan, and in doing so gained control of the Gaza Strip and other key posts in the Middle East.

Both Gibson and Marichal had increased their workloads in the previous two weeks, with Marichal using an exhibition start against Santa Clara University as a final tune-up for the major league season. Heading into the game, the Cardinals were the only team against which Marichal did not have a winning career record, as his all-time mark versus the St. Louis men stood at an even 12–12 (while his winning percentage against all other teams was over .700). It would be the third Opening Day start for Gibson, which included 1966 against Jim Bunning and the Phillies which was rained out after one inning of play. Gibson's batterymate, McCarver, took a moment on the way north to St. Louis from spring training to celebrate the opening of his new restaurant in Memphis. Meanwhile, members of both the Giants and the Cardinals would meet for a dinner in their honor in St. Louis the night before the first pitch, given by the St. Louis Knights of the Cauliflower Ear and taking place in the magnificent Khorassan Room of the Chase Park Plaza. With Jack Buck as the emcee, light-hearted jokes were exchanged between Schoendienst and the San Francisco manager, Franks, the last chance for civility before going to battle for the rest of the summer. The Knights' main honoree was Musial, who was presented with a gold clock from the hosts. "It's a pleasure to be among you," the great one responded simply. The gift was presented by Robert Hyland, who not only served as the president of the lodge but was more widely known as the innovative and loyal general manager of KMOX radio, the home for Cardinals baseball since the 1950s.

In the locker room before the first game, Brock sauntered over to the hi-fi record player that Cepeda had lugged into the room. Lou slapped on a record that cranked out the tune "A Fistful of Dollars," and announced to one and all that, at the end of the season, the Cardinals would have a fistful of dollars themselves from all the championship money they were going to win.

Temperatures were in the mid–50s as the Cardinals made their way onto the field, making a appreciative lap around the field in open automobiles as they were escorted by a Marine Corps color guard. A crowd of just over 38,000 saluted them, anxious for the season to get underway. They would soon witness one of the most auspicious beginnings by a Cardinals pitcher in team history. After Schoendienst's wife, Mary, calmly walked to a microphone on the field and sang the national anthem, Gibson and his comrades took their positions as he was determined to become a one-man wrecking crew.

He blew through the young outfielder Ken Henderson to lead off the game, fanning the 21-year-old on four pitches. Next was Jesus Alou, brother of Matty and Felipe, the latter of whom had taken the first official swings in the ballpark eleven months earlier. Alou was no match for Hoot as well, flailing at three pitches that never neared the bat. Boiling over with confidence, the great Willie Mays provided no resistance either, as Gibson struck out the side as the crowd flung itself from the seats in an explosion of cheer (the next time up, Mays would be robbed in right-center field on a spectacular diving catch by Flood in the fourth inning). Gibson strutted off the mound towards the dugout in his usual stoic gait.

In the bottom half of the first, Brock showed off the skills that Cardinals fans had remembered from summers past. He singled off Marichal, promptly stole second, and went to third on Flood's bunt. But even though the Cardinals would put two more base runners aboard in that inning, they would not score. Gibson returned to his business and fanned the imposing McCovey, whose long, vicious swings seem to send the whole stadium into a vacuum when he missed. Next was Jim Ray Hart, who went down swinging as the fifth straight Gibson victim to open the game. It tied a National League record for the most strikeouts to open a game, a mark shared by Bob Bolin of the Giants from the previous year and Dazzy Vance of the Dodgers from 1926. Some were beginning to wonder if Big Bob was going to allow a ground ball all summer, let alone a base hit. "He was busting the bats right out of their hands," Maxvill would say later about those first two innings of the 1967 season. Javier and Maxvill started the Cardinals' second with singles, as Marichal knew that he was running into immediate trouble as the Cardinals drew first blood in the scoring column. Also helping in the offensive effort was the newcomer, Maris. "It was nice to hear a reaction like that for a change," the Cardinals' right fielder said of the enormous ovation he received the first time his name was announced. "It's been a long time. I almost thought those days were gone." Maris went 2 for 5 on the evening, even in the midst of a pronounced shift that Franks had ordered when Maris came to bat. Shortstop Hal Lanier (whose father, Max, won 101 games for the Redbirds from the late 1930s to the early 1950s) was sent into shallow right field, while third baseman Jim Davenport moved behind the second base bag. Henderson, playing right, moved over onto the foul line; and Mays, the centerfielder, shifted into the right-center field gap. "I've never had much luck going to left field," Maris himself admitted. Nonetheless, just after Brock's home run in the second, he was able to punch a ball to the left side — guarded loosely only by the third baseman, Hart — which he was able to leg out to second base for a double. "The big thing was that Roger didn't challenge the shift," added Dick Sisler. "In a park with a short porch [the inviting stands of right field in Yankee Stadium], you'd have to challenge. But in a park like this, you're better off going to all fields." Schoendienst, confident in the ability of Maris to han-

Lou Brock steals second base after getting a single in the Cardinals' first at-bat of the 1967 season on April 11 at Busch Stadium, diving in safely just ahead of the tag by the Giants' Hal Lanier. Calling the play is umpire Augie Donatelli. (*St. Louis Globe-Democrat* / Archives of the St. Louis Mercantile Library)

dle the bat, even suggested that the slugger consider bunting for base hits if teams continued to shift on him.

When Maxvill singled in the seventh inning, it was the fourteenth hit off Marichal, the most he had ever allowed in a major league game. Next up was Gibson, and after he tapped a dribbler down the first base line, he collided with Marichal and knocked the mitt off the San Francisco pitcher's left hand, causing a bruise. It looked for a moment that tempers would flare between the two, as the charge by Gibson was thought by some to be retaliation for an inside pitch from Marichal earlier in the game, but nothing more came of it. After Shannon re-injured a lingering pulled muscle in his left side, Gagliano took his place at third base and promptly knocked a home run at the plate, more than enough offense for Gibson to cruise to a 6–0 five-hitter to start the year. Alou and McCovey would each be his strikeout victim three times on the night, part of the total of 13 that Gibby posted in hurling the shutout, one strikeout short of his career high that he had accomplished against the Giants in 1966.

"It's about time I beat them," Gibson told the writers after the game. "I had pitched so many good games against this club, but I always seemed to get beaten. My slider was my best pitch tonight, but I had a good fastball, too." He was still one win shy of the .500 mark for his career against the Giants, as his personal totals stood just below Marichal's mark against the Cardinals at 11–12.

In other National League openers, Wills proved to be an immediate asset to the Pirates, as he got two hits and a stolen base in Pittsburgh's 6–3 win over the Mets. In Houston, Eddie Mathews got quick revenge on his old team of fifteen years, the Braves, as his seventh-inning triple tied the game and paved the way to a 6–1 win for the Astros. Jenkins blew past the Phillies by a score of 4–2 at Wrigley Field in Chicago, a promising start for the usual back-hanger Cubbies. And also on the 11th, a highly-touted 21-year-old named Rod Carew made his big-league debut in the American League for the Minnesota Twins, going 2 for 4 as the Twins lost to the defending world champion Orioles in Baltimore 6–3.

After the unusual one-game meeting with the Cardinals, the Giants made their way to Atlanta to play the Braves. Back in the Giants' hometown of San Francisco, however, 10,000 people would take to the streets on the 14th to protest the Vietnam War, while a similar large demonstration would take place in New York City the next day. The Cardinals, meanwhile, welcomed the Dodgers to St. Louis. And as expected, the Dodgers-master Jaster got the ball from Schoendienst. He pulled off an 8–4 win against Osteen in the first contest of the series, pitching scoreless baseball into the seventh inning on 145 pitches to run his blanking of the Dodgers to 52 straight frames (a Drysdale-versus-Washburn match up had been washed out the night before after two scoreless innings—the first rain-out in the new Busch Stadium — and was re-scheduled for a makeup on June 11 as part of a double header), while Hughes was able to finish off the final two innings for the win. Sitting clandestinely in the outfield bleachers at the game was the National League president, Giles, wearing a long overcoat and dark glasses to conceal his identity. "I like to go around the park and hear what people have to talk about," he said. "Sometimes you pick up a lot of ideas from the fans. I talked to quite a few of them. I don't think they knew who I was."

Jackson beat Sutton the following day behind two homers by Brock, 13–4, as temperatures soared into the 80s for the afternoon game that was shown on national television, featured as NBC's Game of the Week through the call of Curt Gowdy and Pee Wee Reese. The broadcast also marked the debut of Koufax as a third member in the announcer's booth, the first of 28 games he was scheduled to work and the origin of an ill-fated second career choice that the great lefthander would later regret. He had practiced for a few innings in the first Dodgers-Cardinals game over the local Los Angeles television station, but still could not get comfortable. "It's frightening," Koufax said of his first moments in front of the camera. Seeing his former Dodgers teammates for the first time in months, some of them even had trouble recognizing him. "I quit smoking and put on about 15 pounds in three weeks," Koufax noted, "so I went back to smoking." It was also the same day that the 18-year-old phenom named Gary Nolan gained a victory for the Reds via eight innings of work in his first major league appearance, besting the Astros 7–3.

The hot bats continued for the Cardinals through the first week of the season, as Brock homered five times in the first four games and the Redbirds streaked out to a 6–0 start. The streak was one win shy of the club record for season-opening victories, beating Houston at home behind Gibson and winning the first two games of a West Coast road trip at San Francisco ("Lou can do it all!" Flood shouted in the locker room after a two-homer performance against Houston on April 16. "He can hit, he can run, he can field, and he can throw. What else is there?" Brock yelled over to him, "I can bunt, too— but they don't know that yet!"). Three of the homers came on the first pitch he saw in the at-bats. And while Schoendienst was pleased with the outcome, he still wished to see his leadoff hitter be more patient. As a tribute to the leftfielder, Gibson sneaked over to the record player in the locker and played "Fistful of Dollars" once again after his latest powerful performance. Brock then stood on a stool and announced to everyone that the song would be heard every day for the rest of the season.

On the trip to the bay area the Cardinals would miss Mays, as the outfielder had pulled a muscle in his leg in diving for a gapper that was hit by his fellow home-run slugging contemporary, Aaron, as the Giants had been visiting Atlanta (while it would be several seasons before Aaron would challenge Babe Ruth's all-time home run record, in 1967 he was erstwhile leading all active players with a .317 career batting average). In the first game with San Francisco, Washburn and the Redbirds disposed of their other star pitcher, Gaylord Perry, by a 2–1 score. Normally dominating St. Louis, Perry had been 4–0 with a 1.06 ERA against the Cardinals in 1966. Jackson suffered the first St. Louis defeat of the season in the finale at Candlestick Park, as Bolin and the Giants downed the lefty 7–5. It wasn't the loss that bothered Schoendienst so much as a crucial play that helped form the outcome. With the bases loaded for the Giants in the second inning, Jackson failed to throw home for a sure double play after getting a ground ball back to the mound. He instead hesitated, and threw a wild toss to Maxvill at second. The runner charging the bag was safe, and it led to five runs for San Francisco. "You have to have your mind in the game at all times," the angry manager growled afterwards. Experiencing the team's first loss after six straight wins to open the season, Schoendienst was not about to settle for complacency. "Everybody in the National League is too evenly matched to afford mistakes like that. Just one mistake like that and they'll beat you. There's no such thing as little mistakes— there are only big mistakes."

The victories were also somewhat soured with the news that Hoerner and Woodeshick, the two primary lefthanders that Schoendienst possessed out of the bullpen, were each dealing with a lower-body ailment. Hoerner aggravated a chipped bone in his foot, an injury that was first sustained in the middle of March during spring training even though he had shut opponents out in his last 17 innings of Florida work. Woodeshick, meanwhile, was being slow to recover from a sprain to his left instep when he stepped on a baseball during batting practice before the opener with the Giants.

Weather had once again prevented the Cardinals from facing Drysdale, as rains hit Los Angeles on April 21. Drysdale was part of the cast that officially went down in the first rainout at new Busch Stadium the previous week, and now had been the scheduled starter in what became the first rainout for the Dodgers since they had moved to southern California from Brooklyn in 1958, breaking a string of 737 uninterrupted games that had been played at the Los Angeles Coliseum and Dodger Stadium.

The Cards would split the six games they played at Los Angeles and Houston on the remainder of the trip. Gibson extended his record to 3–0 by beating Drysdale 3–1 in the first game in L.A., a game broken open by a bases-loaded single by Flood off Drysdale in the eighth inning, as the outfielder had hit safely in all nine games the Cardinals had played so far on the season. Like with the Giants, Gibson had struggled recently against the Dodgers, as it was his first victory in seven tries against manager Walter Alston's men. The following night, Washburn did not last four innings, as he gave up six hits and six runs in a 9–3 loss. Shannon returned in the final game of the series, as he had not seen action since being removed in the fifth inning of the season opener with his pulled muscle. Unfortunately he suffered another setback, as a first inning fastball from Sutton pinned Shannon's thumb between the ball and his helmet as the Cardinals third baseman threw up his arms to guard himself against the tight pitch. X-rays were negative, but once again Shannon had to leave the game. The game turned out to be rarity — a loss by Jaster to the Dodgers, as he allowed two home runs in the third inning to Jim Lefebvre and Lou Johnson. The offensive star for the Cardinals in the defeat was Brock, who with three hits lifted his average to .451 in addition to stealing three bases in the game.

In going to Houston, the Cards were making their first visit of the year to the Harris County Domed Stadium — or as it had commonly become known, the Astrodome. The strange, space-age indoor arena had opened for business two years earlier, and Astros officials liked to claim that no batted ball would ever hit the roof, which stood 208 feet above the playing field. Hoerner, nonetheless, would defiantly and self-amusingly hit fungoes against the peak whenever he was in town, just as he liked to slug golf balls over the roof at Busch Stadium. While it was a unique playing environment, the

Astrodome was a venue to which no visiting team looked forward with its poor sight lines and unpredictable air flow. Gibson for one, though, enjoyed the comfortable surroundings, especially in his remembrances of the old outdoor Houston ballpark. "I remember one Sunday afternoon when I pitched in 115-degree heat and lost 12 pounds," he described about the old Colt Stadium, currently serving as a parking lot to the northwest of the Astrodome where the Houston franchise played as the Colt .45s for three seasons from 1962 to 1964. "Another time, it was so hot that we had to leave our pitcher for the night part of a day-night double header in the air-conditioned hotel. We also don't miss those king-sized mosquitoes at the old Houston park — some of them needed saddles." It was the third season in which the Astros were playing in the climate-controlled structure, dubbed by team owner Roy Hofheinz as "the eighth wonder of the world" after its $35 million construction was finished in 1965. With an air conditioning system which was sporadic in its expurgations, several visiting teams accused the Astros' grounds crew of turning the system off when the home team was batting to minimize air resistance to the flight of the ball. Originally, stadium officials had tried planting Bermuda grass on the playing field, which sat nearly thirty feet below street level. Before the start of the 1966 season, however, the decision was made to use artificial turf after trouble was found in keeping the natural surface viable (because of the difficulty of seeing fly balls in the building, the panels in the roof needed to be changed from the transparent variety that had been installed. When the change was made, the grass soon failed to grow). A separate carpet was set aside for use in gridiron games by the American Football League's Houston Oilers, while the dirt underlay which fed the original grass remained in place after the artificial surface was put down.

The Cardinals (as well as most teams around the league) had just switched to new, unbreakable helmets in 1967, which was somewhat of a disappointment to McCarver, who in the past had made a habit out of smashing the protective batting gear in moments of frustration. After striking out in a crucial situation in the second game of the series at Houston, McCarver returned to the dugout to commence his assault on his lid. He slammed the helmet down on the ground and began jumping on it — but surprisingly, to no avail. Glancing at it for a second with a confused face, he resumed his attack. The helmet refused to crack or even dent, when at that point someone on the bench told Tim that the club had gone to the new-and-improved model that would not disintegrate. "We'll see about that!" he shouted, as he relentlessly continued to stomp. The head armor wouldn't budge, however, and McCarver finally surrendered.

On April 28 — the day after the Cardinals left town in taking two of three from the Astros — Cassius Clay arrived at the Houston Selective Service Induction Center with 45 other army draftees, as the venue change was made at the request of Clay's draft board in Louisville as anti-war demonstrators continued to parade outside the building in that city. Just five days earlier, Clay had appealed for the second time in a week to the United States Supreme Court to avoid the induction, but for the second time was denied. Quiet and cooperative at the outset of the proceedings, Clay passed the pre-induction physical examination. An hour later, when his name was called to take the oath and be sworn into the army, he refused to answer and did not step forward in the affirmative, a tradition of the induction ceremony. Twice more his name was called, and again he failed to respond, even after a quiet whisper of encouragement into his ear by a nearby officer. In not answering the summons, Clay immediately became culpable for a federal charge potentially resulting in five years imprisonment or a $10,000 fine or both. While his lawyers vowed to continue a legal fight, no remaining federal court that could hear his case — from the district court in Louisville to the Sixth Circuit Court of Appeals in Cincinnati to the United States Supreme Court — agreed to do so.

That same afternoon, the World Boxing Council and the World Boxing Association stripped Clay of his heavyweight titles, and the New York State Boxing Commission revoked his license. Defiantly, Clay screamed that he would "take my title to prison with me." He also claimed that the title should be returned to him, as he asserted that other countries were supporting his cause. Clay mentioned that he was considering a fight with George Chuvalo in Montreal as part of the on-going World's Fair known as Expo '67 occurring in that Canadian city. An ambassador from the United Arab Emirates also invited Clay to fight there, saying that most countries in the Middle East would continue to recognize him as the champion. "That's great — I would love to fight in Cairo any time," Clay responded when he heard the statement from the diplomat, with the boxer a little mixed up with his geography. "I have been there four or five times; I like it. Soon, they [the boxing councils] will *have* to give me back my title, because with all the Asian countries behind me, I am a threat."

Clay did not meet with much sympathy, at least in the press. Broeg, with the tap of a typewriter, summarized the feelings of many in the nation that the fighter had insulted. "Clay has lost the respect of virtually all who accept the small obligations that go with the large benefits from citizenship in this freest of all societies," he wrote. Broeg suggested that Clay be allowed to keep his title, but leave the country. "No one here should ever want to pay to see him fight again ... this plea is as phony as a three-dollar bill. Rather than jail him, why not exile him and deny him forever the country he refuses to serve? For one, though admiring his boxing skills, I would no longer walk across the street to see him fight."

United States Attorney Morton Susman, who would be handling the prosecution against Clay, wanted to press forth with charges against the boxer immediately. He told the newspapers that it could be eight weeks before merely an indictment would be levied. "Even then, it may be two years before this can be fought out in the courts," Susman cautioned those who were expecting a quick decision on the matter. "Meanwhile Clay — or Muhammad Ali if you wish — will be free to keep on fighting and preaching." But just two months later, Clay was ultimately convicted of draft evasion, as a jury took just over twenty minutes to find him guilty. The maximum being imposed by the bench, Clay was sentenced to five years in prison. For the two years while his appeals were heard, he would not fight and announced his retirement in 1970. He returned in October of that year, however, to fight Jerry Quarry in Georgia, as the state had no boxing commission to confirm the licensure of prize fighters.

The Cardinals found themselves at home on the first of May, having just recently lost three in a row to the Pirates at Busch Stadium to drop in the National League standings after their strong start, with all the teams now chasing the high-flying Reds:

	W	L	Pct.	GB
Cincinnati	15	5	.750	—
Pittsburgh	8	5	.615	3.5
Chicago	8	6	.571	4
St. Louis	9	7	.562	4
Atlanta	9	7	.562	4
Philadelphia	8	8	.500	5
San Francisco	7	9	.437	6
Los Angeles	6	10	.375	7
New York	6	11	.362	7.5
Houston	5	13	.277	9

In addition to the power pitching of Jim Maloney, the Cincinnati ball club was receiving a surprising performance from the 18-year-old Nolan and converted outfielder Mel Queen off the mound. Nolan had just beaten Seaver and the Mets in the Reds' most recent game on April 30, and Queen had defeated Perry, another Giants hurler in Mike McCormick, and the Astros' Larry Dierker among his victories in the first three weeks of the season. The Reds—like the Cardinals, a second-division team in 1966—arrived in St. Louis on May 2 brimming with confidence, looking to take a permanent stranglehold on the league lead for the rest of the summer.

4. Young Arms on the Rise

When I knocked a guy down, there was no second part to the story.
— Bob Gibson

Spring's cool night air still had seven weeks left, but the vectors of heat and smoke coming from the downtown ballpark on May 2 suggested that the dog days of summer had already arrived. The heat source was the laser-beam firings of Gibson and Maloney, considered by some as the two supreme power pitchers of the league with Koufax having departed. "Nobody throws as hard as Maloney, in my opinion," Gibson had stated at the time. "He's the only guy who can simply overpower you. You know he's going to throw the fastball, but you still can't catch up with it." It was the first start in ten days for Maloney, as he had been suffering from a sore shoulder since taking the mound on the 22nd of April at Houston. Long well-known to the east in the Ohio River valley of the Cincinnati region, Maloney had been gaining national acclaim over the decade with his fastball being timed at 99.5 miles per hour back in 1965, the season in which he authored two no-hitters (each of which had lasted ten innings). In 1963, Maloney had surrendered the 3,630th and final hit in the career of Musial at Sportsman's Park; also in that season, he tied the Reds' single-game strikeout record with 16 against the Braves on May 21 (when Musial had bounced the sixth-inning single to right field on that last day of the 1963 season to score Flood from second, the ball had just barely skipped past a gritty young second baseman named Pete Rose, who was completing his rookie year on the final afternoon of the season). While never leading the league in strikeouts, Maloney had already used his overpowering fastball to fan over 200 batters in four straight seasons through 1966. The

Cardinals started slowly against him, but Shannon broke through with a three-run double in the fifth inning as the third baseman had switched from a 39-ounce stick to the 33-ounce variety in an effort to attain more bat speed against the hard thrower. McCarver, on the other hand, had changed to a bat that was two ounces heavier. "Willie McCovey and Willie Mays kidded me about the one I was using," the catcher said in reference to his former 32-ounce club. "They called my bat a 'baby bat' and McCovey would pick it up and act like he was using it as a toothpick. And you know what? Now McCovey's using the baby bat." Meanwhile, Shannon's infield mate, Javier, had credited *his* recent batting success to new eyeglasses, as the second baseman was nearing the .300 mark after two seasons in the .220s.

Maris ended an 0 for 21 slump by producing an RBI single in the sixth, more than enough for the dominant Gibson to gain his fourth victory in a 5–0 shutout and steal the marquee away from Maloney. It was truly a dominating performance for the man from Omaha, as he limited the Reds to two hits in striking out twelve (including six in a row) over the first seven innings, all while laboring through a case of the flu. Despite the whitewashing, a Cincinnati writer strangely suggested to Reds manager Dave Bristol afterwards that Gibson didn't appear to be throwing as hard as usual. The manager responded, "Well, he looked to *me* like he was throwing hard, and I didn't even have a bat in my hands."

New to the Cincinnati radio broadcast booth was former Reds pitcher Joe Nuxhall, who had announced his retirement before the season began. Nuxhall, 39, had amassed 135 victories in his career, but was most famous for being the youngest player to appear in a major league game in the modern era. Four days after the Allies landed on the beaches of France in June of 1944, Nuxhall appeared in two-thirds of an inning for the Reds, walking five and giving up two hits in the ninth inning as part of an 18–0 demolition that the Cardinals had deposited on Cincinnati. Nuxhall, from the suburban Cincinnati town of Hamilton, Ohio, was signed the previous February only after attaining the permission of his parents and high school principal. After seven years of seasoning in the minor leagues, he would rejoin the Reds' staff in 1952.

Washburn, who had struggled in his two previous outings, followed up Gibson with his own two-hit shutout of the Reds the next night, his 2–0 win in an hour and forty minutes made possible by two more RBIs off the bat of Shannon — and with his lighter-but-destructive bat remaining in the lineup, it supported the fact that his transition to third base was thus far a wise one. The stellar performance by Washburn had been only his fifth complete game since 1963, as he was seeking to regain strength in his injured right shoulder.

After the two blankings of the Reds, the Cardinals headed north on Interstate 55 to meet Durocher and his Cubs at Wrigley Field for a three-game series. Wet, cold grounds met the two teams in the opener, as the Cubs got to Hughes in the sixth to snap a scoreless string of 23 innings by Cardinals pitchers to beat the Redbirds 5–3. The winning pitcher for the Cubs was St. Louis native Ken Holtzman, a 21-year-old lefthander whose National Guard unit would be summoned to active duty the very next day (Holtzman had left the University of Illinois as a sophomore in 1965; ironically, the day after he learned of the activation of his guard unit, it was announced that the university was being placed on a two-year athletic probation for financial improprieties). Holtzman, who led Cubs pitchers with 171 strikeouts in 1966, needed to report for training on May 22, giving him two or three more starts before Durocher would lose him for most of the next six months. "I've got to be an idiot if I were to say I'm glad Ken is going," the manager responded when receiving the news about Holtzman's upcoming duty call. "But his country comes first, and baseball second." Then, in an obvious reference to Clay's demonstration, Durocher added, "Our guy took a step forward — not backward." Clay's final appeal to be reinstated as the champion would soon be denied by the World Boxing Association, who announced that a ten-man tournament would be set up to determine the new titleholder. Karl Mildenberger of Germany was listed as the number-one contender, to be joined in the tournament by Joe Frazier, Ernie Terrell, Thad Spencer, Floyd Patterson, Jerry Quarry, Jimmy Ellis, Leotis Martin, George Chuvalo, and Oscar Bonavena of Argentina.

Hoping to ease the departure of Holtzman on the starting staff was another pitcher by the name of Don Larsen, now 37 years old and pitching in his final major league season as part of the Cubs' roster on the season. He would appear in only three games for the Cubs on the year, however, pitching four innings while not gaining a decision. In so ending his career, Larsen would not only be remembered as the last man to pitch a perfect game in the World Series (for the Yankees in 1956), but also as the last remaining man to have been on an active roster of the St. Louis Browns before the franchise moved to Baltimore in 1954.

Jackson reversed the Cubs by the same score of 5–3 the next day, with Cepeda clubbing two home runs (giving him four on the season) while Flood tied the National League record for consecutive errorless games by an outfielder with 205. Flood felt as comfortable in Wrigley Field as any visiting outfielder ever had, as he routinely flew into the vine-covered bricks for many fly balls over the past nine seasons at the Chicago ballpark. Lou Boudreau, a former major league all-star and manager in the American League who was now broadcasting for the Cubs, was thoroughly impressed with the St. Louis center fielder. "I haven't seen a thing that Flood can't do," Boudreau told his listeners on WGN radio. "He gets as good a jump on a ball as Willie Mays does. He has absolutely no fear of walls. His first thought is to get the ball." Flood set the new record the next day, handling his 206th miscue-free game in succession that included 504 chances. Gibson (4–2) lost the complete-game duel with the Cubs' Rich Nye in a 5–4 score, however, a game in which Shannon (hitting .341 in the past two weeks) had actually tied the score with a home run in the ninth inning. Schoendienst, meanwhile, was becoming increasingly frustrated with outfielder Alex Johnson, as Johnson had been planned as an effective measure against any left-handed pitching (like Nye) that the Cards would face. Johnson, however, had seen his batting average dip to .103 on the young season, with the Redbirds sporting only a 3–7 mark against southpaws (while combined as the starting right fielders in the last 13 games, Maris and Johnson together had been hitting .089 with a 5 for 56 mark). The poor performance was prompting the manager to give Tolan and Spiezio a more lengthy audition in the outfield, or perhaps simply leaving Maris in the lineup even if a left-handed starter was scheduled by the opponent. For the most part, however, Roger knew that he was still in the midst of a platoon situation for the first time in his career — and he welcomed it. "Being in and out of the lineup hasn't bothered me," he said of half-time duty. "In fact, at times it has made me stronger."

In the wake of the incident involving Clay and the draft board, there was concern about security at the upcoming event in his hometown which drew a big crowd every year. On May 6 the Kentucky Derby was scheduled to be held in Louisville, where Martin Luther King, Jr. and a handful of supporters were planning a protest. Over two thousand National Guardsmen, state troopers, and city and county officers were assigned to patrol the premises. Fortunately, all on hand enjoyed the afternoon without incident, as Proud Clarion — a 30-to-1 longshot — found his way to the winner's circle at Churchill Downs, winning by a single length over Barb's Delight and taking home $119,700 of the $162,000 purse. Damascus, the heavy 8-to-5 favorite, sprinted to third place for show. Until recently, Proud Clarion was not envisioned as a challenger by anyone — including his trainer, Loyd Gentry, who only a couple of months earlier had recommended to its owner John Galbreath (a former owner of the Pittsburgh Pirates), that the horse be sold. Moreover, winning jockey Bobby Ussery was a last-minute selection in substitution for the regular rider. The crowd at the race was estimated to be approximately one-fourth less than the usual 100,000 expected figure, which was attributed to the imposing security presence at the track. The only disturbance came when a lone firecracker was shot over the guardsmen's heads, landing in the infield immediately after the race was finished. No one was hurt by the missile, and hardly anyone had even noticed.

The road trip for the Cardinals continued in Pittsburgh after leaving Chicago, as they took two out of three from the Pirates in the venerable Forbes Field. The old ballpark stood adjacent to Schenley Park and the University of

Pittsburgh campus, and a within a few years, its home plate would sit guarded for posterity under glass in the lobby of the campus's new Posvar Hall as the Pirates would play in the new downtown facility to be known as Three Rivers Stadium. After Washburn beat Juan Pizzaro in the opener, Carlton — who had solidified his spot in the rotation in the wake of Jaster's recent inability to throw strikes — was able to pick up his second win of the year with eight innings of strong work in the middle contest on May 9. As a rookie, Gibson was already calling Carlton's curveball "one of the best in the league." Cepeda started showing his hot hand as well in leading the offensive charge in the Steel City, going 4 for 4 and raising his batting average to a National League-best .384 — one day after his one-year anniversary of being traded to the Cardinals — and having gotten on base in 15 of the 22 times he had been to the plate on the current road trip. He even had a hand in the home run that Maris hit off lefthander Woodie Fryman, a 400-foot bomb to right-center field and his very first in a Cardinals uniform after 261 in the American League. "I called the shot from the bench," Cepeda proudly announced afterwards, thumping his chest. "I knew Roger was going to hit one out."

"I'm glad he knew it," Maris countered, "because I certainly didn't."

That same night in Philadelphia, Hank Aaron also thought he had not gotten enough of a ball for a home run. He chopped one off Jim Bunning which sailed over the head of Phillies centerfielder Don Lock, and Aaron was told by his base coaches to keep running. He charged across second, rounded third, and darted through home plate ahead of the throw in what would be the only inside-the-park home run of his career. A few days later, however, he would be embroiled in a verbal joust with Braves broadcaster Milo Hamilton. In making a speech to the Braves' booster club one afternoon with the Pirates in town, Hamilton — who had begun his major league announcing career with the St. Louis Browns in 1953 after starting in professional ball in Davenport, Iowa, four years earlier — said to the audience, "We all know how great Hank Aaron is and what he has done, but when it comes to making the All-Star selection, right there is the right fielder." Hamilton was pointing to the Pirates great Clemente in the audience — not Aaron — to which the Atlanta player took great offense. Hamilton's point may have been in reference to the fact that Clemente entered the series with the Braves leading the National League in hitting with a .402 mark, while Aaron hovered near .300. It was not the only bit of dissension to hit the Braves in the early part of the season; manager Bill Hitchcock had earlier fined 17 of the players $250 each for missing curfew while on the road in Cincinnati. Not backing down from any of the players, Hitchcock also announced that any further recidivism by the culprits would result in the fines being doubled. The manager was particularly angered in light of the team's poor play, as they simultaneously dropped all three contests in Cincinnati and had fallen to seventh place.

A week later in Philadelphia, voters in the city — perhaps tired of opponents turning such tricks as Aaron did in the spacious outfield of Shibe Park — approved a $13 million bond to build a new stadium in south Philly. For assisting Aaron in his round-trip was the great distance to center field in Shibe, a whopping 447 feet in 1967. The expanse was to be shortened to 410 feet for the 1969 season, one year before the ballpark's expiration.

As the Cardinals left Pittsburgh to return home to face the Mets, Savage and Cosman were cut from the team on May 10 and were optioned back to the farm team at Tulsa, in part a casualty of the team's decision to go with three catchers in McCarver, Romano, and Ricketts. Savage, however, preferred to try his luck with another major league club, feeling that his chances of ever returning to the Cardinals were nil. "If nobody wants you, what's the use in going back to Tulsa?" he said to the writers. He was particularly confused about his departure in light of the fact that the batting average of Johnson was now down to .083 (Broeg pointed out, in fact, that the Cardinals' bench had hit a combined .163 throughout the first month of the season, a decidedly-unacceptable figure if the pennant chase was to continue). Even more playing time had been required recently of Johnson, Savage, and Tolan, as Maris had injured himself in a freak domestic accident. While at home, Maris jumped out of bed when he thought he heard a noise on an intercom coming from one of his children's rooms. In the process, he cracked a bone in his big toe when it struck the door to the room.

A returning bout of wildness, meanwhile, had caused the demise of Cosman. The Cards still held out much future promise for the stocky right-hander, however, hoping that he could regain the form he showed in his dazzling, season-closing shutout of the Cubs in 1966.

Flood was maintaining a 13-game hitting streak on May 13 with the Mets in town, as he and Gibson were presented with their 1966 Gold Glove awards in a ceremony at home plate (Schoendienst actually went out to accept the award for Gibson, as Bob did not want to be disturbed during his pre-game warm-up routine). Jackson beat Seaver in the opener of the series, but Gibson — who heading into the evening owned a career record of 15–2 versus New York — was silenced by Buchek's homer and the effectiveness of opposing pitcher Jack Fisher in a 3–1 score, Fisher being a man who had lost a combined 38 games over the previous two seasons for the Mets including a whopping 24 in 1965. The split with New York was followed by a two-game sweep by Washburn and Carlton of Philadelphia at Busch Stadium, despite the fact that the Phillies tied a National League record in the first game with their eleventh-consecutive errorless game. The streak would end the next night, as Philadelphia third baseman Dick Allen booted a ball to leave the team one game shy of establishing a new standard. The real story of the evening, however, was McCarver, as the regular catcher switched roles and instead came off the bench to be the hero. Given a night of rest with Romano in the starting lineup, McCarver entered as a pinch hitter for his fellow backstop in leading off the top of the ninth with the score tied 2–2. On a 1–1 pitch from Dick Farrell, McCarver drove a ball which was described by Wilks to be "just short of Chouteau Avenue" (Wilks may have had his orientation wrong, as a ball heading towards Chouteau would have been out of play to the first base side). In any event, the ball did land fair in the seats for a home run, as a raucous group of Redbird players and coaches greeted a screaming McCarver at home plate to celebrate the win. Among the first to meet him was his friend Shannon, who himself was hitting .353 with 17 RBIs in only 69 at-bats, to go along with only three errors in appearing to already master his strange new position at third base.

In between the contests with the Mets and Phillies, the Cardinals had traveled to Tulsa to play their farm team on May 15. Shining in an opportunity to make his case to return to the starting rotation, Jaster permitted only two hits and no walks in six innings, but the Cardinals still lost to the Oilers 4–3, with the home club picking up their four runs off Hoerner in the eighth to the delight of the local crowd. The individual that stole the evening, however, was a 20-year-old pitcher from Topeka named Mike Torrez, who in only his second year of professional baseball was already beginning to impress the St. Louis brass. "He can really fire it in there," Schultz noted, "and he has a good curve, too." Standing an imposing six feet, five inches tall, Torrez pitched the final inning of the game, blowing Cepeda away with a strikeout. Despite his youth, he was immediately put on the short list of throwers to assist the big league club in the event of a roster emergency.

On that same night in Cincinnati, Clemente would enjoy his finest day as a Pirate, knocking a double, three homers, and driving in all of his team's runs, despite Pittsburgh losing to the Reds 8–7. And with the victories over the Phillies, the Cardinals had won five of their last seven by May 17 which had leap-frogged them over the Pirates into second place, trailing the front-running Reds by four games. That date also marked the start of their longest road trip of the season, which would take the club through New York, Atlanta, Philadelphia and Cincinnati, and through the end of May as well.

Maris, having recovered from his household accident of breaking his toe, was in the lineup in making his return to New York to help the Cards tackle the Mets. Even so, the suddenly injury-prone Maris was banged up in the first game of the road trip once again, as Javier's elbow caught him in the ribs as the two collided in pursuit of a pop fly (Cepeda was part of the entanglement as well, and suffered a couple of bruises as a result). Maris was booed loudly each time he stepped onto the New York dirt at Shea Stadium — although neutral parties in the stands could not decide if it was because he was an opponent or a former Yankee. Upon probing the area around first base, Maris drew some conclusions about his new league. "There are more hard infields in the National League," he noticed. Then he added, "There are more low-ball pitchers, too." Despite his general unwelcoming, Maris graciously signed autographs during batting practice as he leaned over the railing near the visitors' dugout. A few moments later, some New York photographers who were stationed nearby asked him to pose for a few shots with his former Yankees teammate and current Mets coach, Yogi Berra, who was watching his three sons, Larry, Tim and Dale, shag flies in the outfield. "C'mon, Yogi," Maris hollered across the field when the photographer came calling. "They want a couple of rejects!"

Gibson, missing a scheduled start because of a rain-eliminated contest against the Mets the previous week in St. Louis, assumed control with eight strikeouts in the first four innings of the first game and cruised to a 6–3 win. Jackson followed the next night with a close win, 11–9, as did Washburn, 3–2, who was helped by the eighth home run of the season by Brock (in addition to stealing his fourteenth base) and the second by Maris. Washburn's effort was the first complete game victory by a St. Louis starter in nearly two weeks, giving the bullpen a much-needed rest. And Jaster's revitalized work as part of that bullpen (in logging two saves since being dropped from the starting rotation) had now allowed him to rejoin the starters along with Gibson, Carlton, Washburn, and Hughes, as he would take the spot of the struggling Al Jackson (and his 4.86 ERA). Briles had been recently ineffective as well, as Musial was considering packaging him and Woodeshick to another club in a deal for a different pitcher. Muffett had been working with Briles to help him adopt a no-windup style, as they called it, in an effort to keep Briles' pitches from sailing on him, a technique that Hughes had recently begun using with success as well. Meanwhile, Musial and Muffett were certainly refusing to give up on Jaster. "Every team in the National League could use help in pitching," Musial pointed out, "but it seems like there isn't much available. That's why I've said that this could be a hitters year in our league." When asked about the possibility of now bringing Torrez to the big league club, Musial — while impressed with the youngster — said simply, "he's not ready." It was becoming readily apparent that the bullpen would be a source of concern all summer long, as the team would have to rely upon the deep starting staff to go far into most games.

Hughes would salvage the only win for the Cardinals in the series at Atlanta, as the bespectacled right-hander threw a 5–0 shutout on May 25 against Dick Kelley. Gibson had been beaten 2–0 the night before on a one-hitter orchestrated by the Braves' Denny Lemaster, as Alou popped a two-run homer in the fifth inning for the game's only scoring. Pat Jarvis had disposed of Briles in the first game, as the native of Carlyle, Illinois, entered in relief of Wade Blasingame in the third inning after which the Braves scored the decisive runs. The residents of Carlyle — approximately 50 miles to the east of St. Louis— were so proud of Jarvis that they had built a special radio tower in town that was able to pick up the Braves' broadcasts from Atlanta, a project that was devised and overseen by none other than the Carlyle chief of police. Back in 1960, Jarvis had been signed by Detroit Tigers scout Joe Mathes— by accident. Mathes, who had been driving through southern Illinois in search of prospects, had originally stopped in Carlyle only to eat lunch. He decided to stay, however, in hearing that the All-Star Game of the Clinton County League was to be played that night. The league included a collection of eight teams from various small towns around the county (including Germantown, the home of Schoendienst), and the fierce competition among them remains in place today. Ex-pros, ex-college players, ex–high school players, and full-time wannabes still suit up and fight for the likes of Germantown, Aviston, Beckemeyer, Trenton, Carlyle, Centralia, Breese, and Bartelso. "He picked up our weekly paper — it comes out on Thursdays— and read that the Clinton County All-Star Game was that night," Jarvis remembered of Mathes' visit to Carlyle that would change his life. "So he stayed in town." Jarvis, however, never knew that he was being watched during the game. "I went to St. Louis the next day to see the Cardinals play, and when I got home, my mother told me Mathes had been to our house. She kidded me about it — she told me that he wasn't coming back. But Mathes showed up the next Tuesday and signed me. I left for a Tiger farm team at Decatur the next day." Jarvis later married a Carlyle girl, Dena Zimmerman, and the couple had two young sons by the time he reached the major leagues. His grandfather, Ben Galyean, had also been a well-known player in the area, and still carried the nickname of "Sock" around Clinton County. "Everybody calls him 'Sock,'" Jarvis said. "You can just draw a sock on an envelope and mail it to Carlyle, and he'll get it."

Not making the trip to Atlanta was Shannon, who was put on a flight back to St. Louis as he claimed to be feeling "progressively worse" from a viral infection he sustained three weeks earlier. Fluid was found in his lungs by physicians, and he was told to stay home and await the team's arrival back home. "The bad weather we've been having on the road hasn't helped," the third baseman said about his condition, also revealing that he previously had battled pneumonia twice back in 1957 and 1959. "It's been a struggle to move around, and a struggle just to get dressed." In the interim, Gagliano and Spiezio manned the hot corner for the Redbirds.

Brock had been a steadying influence on the offense, hitting safely in eleven straight games as the team took two out of three from Philadelphia on the next stop on the road. The left fielder, who had entered the month of May batting an even .400, had hit only .237 thereafter; Tolan, in fact, had recently told him, "Don't worry, Lou ... only 13 more days, and May will be behind you." May, in fact, had never been kind to Brock. In May 1962 with the Cubs, he was benched after poor showings; twelve months later, a pinched nerve put him out of the lineup; twelve months later, a May '64 slump prompted the Cubs to ship him to St. Louis; in May of '65, his shoulder was fractured after being hit with a Sandy Koufax pitch; and, of course, he was benched for the grand opening of Busch Stadium in May 1966 in the midst of his record pace for strikeouts. Brock didn't like to use a particular word, but he confronted it. "I was conscious of the jinx at the start of the month," he said, "and I was determined to not let it happen again. But it was turning out the same old way." Before the end of May 1967, however, he had suddenly regained his stroke due to a dietary change (he claimed) in logging three hits in support of Carlton's 8–3 win over the Phillies on May 28 (after Jaster (3–11) gained a victory the night before with four innings of flawless relief help from Briles, the other formerly-struggling pitcher). "I really like that Carlton," noted former major league player and manager Charlie Grimm, now a scout for the Cubs. "He reminds me of the good young lefthander we got from the St. Louis area, Ken Holtzman. They're both relatively inexperienced, but both throw really hard and show great promise." Big-band leader and renowned trumpet player Harry James, a long-time Cardinals fan, said hello to the team while in Philly. "I've already made arrangements to take off anytime in October for the World Series if the Cardinals make it," James revealed. "I'll have my band out in center field for the first game in St. Louis."

Not forgetting the speed portion of his offensive game, Brock had also stolen 21 bases in 25 tries to date. His overall average was back up to .345, having batted just over .300 for the usually-cruel month and over .400 during the course of the recent, tiring road trip. Brock had credited his recent success at the plate to the milkshakes that Woodeshick had been providing him before the games. In fact, their pre-game routine would become the same every day. The pair would find an eating joint near the ballpark in any given city, and Woodeshick on cue would say to the waitress, "A milkshake for this man," in patting Brock on the shoulder. Sometimes strawberry, sometimes chocolate, sometimes vanilla — but always, seemingly, full of hits. Even with baseball players being superstitious as a rule, Brock was well off the charts in comparison with his mates. Before going with the milkshakes, he had tried ordering rare-cooked steaks in restaurants to break a bad spell at the plate, despite the fact that he had always ordered them well-done in the past. At other times, if he had enjoyed a stretch of games in which he got several hits or stolen bases, he would insist on wearing the same uniform pants every day, regardless of whether or not they were stained or even torn. Each day, club house supervisor Butch Yatkeman — who had started working for the Cardinals as a batboy in 1924 — would collect the dirty laundry for cleaning. When on one of his hot streaks, Brock would hide the pants from Yatkeman in any way he could. He first tried stuffing them in the small open slit under the locker, but Yatkeman "would go right in after them, like a terrier digging out a bone," according to Jerry Gibson. Next, Brock tried placing them on top of the locker and up against the wall, where presumably the five-foot-tall Yatkeman couldn't get to them. But Butch, with great instincts for clubhouse orderliness, simply grabbed a stepladder and found the stash. Out of ideas, Brock even wore the lucky pants *home to his house* on occasion, hiding them under his slacks as he left the ballpark.

Brock's success continued on the road as he lengthened the hitting streak to fourteen games at Cincinnati. After Gibson was triumphant over Mel Queen in the opener, the Redbirds dropped the final two contests of the three-game set, however, one-run losses that could have catapulted St. Louis into first place. The final battle was particularly stinging, as Hughes had thrown a perfect game for seven innings, after which he was touched for two runs. Tolan, inserted in center field for the injured Flood who had pulled a hamstring, homered in the third to stake Hughes to a 1–0 lead. Undaunted in surrendering that lead in the eighth, the Cardinals loaded the bases in the ninth with nobody out; unfortunately, a routine double-play ball to Reds shortstop Leo Cardenas ended the game. Inexplicably, Cepeda had failed to head home as the ground ball was hit off the bat of Gagliano, despite the fact that Cardenas was playing deeply to concede the run. Cardenas flipped the ball to second baseman Tommy Helms, who in turn fired it to Deron Johnson to complete the expected twin-killing. Johnson then turned his attention towards home, and saw an extra opportunity. He whistled a fast one to catcher Johnny Edwards, who tagged the lagging Cepeda to give the Reds the victory.

Although the final game in Cincinnati was a disappointment after the momentum gained in the set at Philadelphia, the Cardinals had held their own on the 12-game road trip, posting a 7–5 mark which placed them second to the Reds in the standings on May 31, just as A.J. Foyt was rifling off his third victory in the Indianapolis 500 in navigating through a five-car crash on the race's final lap. The end of May 1967 also marked the Cardinals' best record at the Memorial Day milepost in nearly twenty years:

	W	L	Pct.	GB
Cincinnati	30	17	.638	—
St. Louis	24	16	.600	2.5
Pittsburgh	23	17	.574	3.5
San Francisco	23	19	.547	4.5
Chicago	21	19	.524	5.5
Atlanta	22	21	.511	6
Los Angeles	19	23	.452	8.5
Philadelphia	17	23	.425	9.5

	W	L	Pct.	GB
New York	14	25	.358	12
Houston	15	28	.348	13

After their slow start to the season, the Giants posted the best record for the month of May, going 17–10 (a .630 winning percentage) while the Cardinals played the second-best ball over the same stretch at a .600 clip (15–10). The defending champion Dodgers, however, seemed to be fading already — as everyone knew that they were missing their star pitcher. "You know Koufax would have won seven games by now — seven, at least," Schoendienst claimed in looking at the standings.

Back home in St. Louis, Ritenour High School honored its baseball team for its recent claim of the Missouri state championship. Leading the charge was senior left-handed pitcher Jerry Reuss, who finished the season by throwing five shutouts in the state tournament. However, a junior pitcher named Bill Todd (who owned a 10–0 record himself) won the final game against Columbia Hickman. Altogether, Reuss and Todd held their tournament opponents to an .098 batting average. Reuss, at 6'6" and 200 pounds, was an outstanding basketball player as well, but baseball would be his sport of choice for the future. A week later, he would be the second-round choice of the Cardinals in the amateur draft, and would ultimately make his big-league debut with St. Louis in 1969 at the age of 20, throwing seven shutout innings in a game at Montreal in September of that year and gaining his first major league win. His biggest success would come later with other clubs, however, including All-Star Game appearances with Pittsburgh and Los Angeles in 1975 and 1980, as well as contributing a victory to the Dodgers' 1981 World Series win over the Yankees. He retired from the Pirates in 1990, ending a major league career that spanned three decades.

On May 30, the legendary Yankee lefthander Whitey Ford had announced his retirement from the game, having pitched in only seven games in 1967. The final appearance for the "Chairman of the Board," as Yankees catcher Elston Howard had nicknamed him, had come earlier on May 21. He lasted only one inning in a start against Detroit at Tiger Stadium, a game in which an equally-ailing Mantle made an error at first base as he painfully creaked towards a ground ball that he could not handle (Mantle would homer in the game as well, however, and it was his fifth in the last six days). Ford, not able to recuperate from a painful bone spur in his elbow and from a second surgery on his shoulder that had been performed the previous August to alleviate circulation problems, had earlier posted what would be his final win on April 25 in Yankee Stadium against the White Sox at the age of 41. It was the end of a career that began in 1950 when, as a rookie, Ford was elevated from the farm system to work in Yankee Stadium and subsequently reeled off nine straight victories in leading New York to the championship. The year before, Yankees manager Casey Stengel had received an anonymous phone call, urging him to bring Ford up to the big leagues that season; to his dying day, Stengel was convinced that it was Ford himself who had called. In addition to retiring with a .690 winning percentage — best in the twentieth century among winners of 200 games or more — Ford was also leaving the game with ten World Series victories, which remains the record and also constituted the standard for all post-season victories before the advent of multi-round playoffs (on the negative slate, Ford also holds the record for the most World Series losses with eight). Just one week earlier — on May 14 — Mantle had hit the 500th home run of his career off Stu Miller of the Orioles, as a young fan jumped out of the stands and patted him on the back as Mantle made his historic way between third and home. Eyes now turned to Eddie Mathews, who stood next behind Mantle among active players at 495 (with Mays possessing 546). Mantle had promised his wife the night before, on Saturday, that he would hit one for her on Sunday — Mothers' Day. "She's like Whitey Ford's wife — she doesn't know anything about baseball," Mickey said of her. "Once, shortly after we were married, she brought her family to a game. When everyone got up to stretch in the seventh inning, she and her family went home — they thought the game was over." The ball struck for his 500th home run was returned to Mantle by 16-year-old Louis DeFillippo of Mount Vernon, New York. Mantle rewarded the youngster with some other memorabilia, as the ball was sent to Mickey's home in Dallas for careful keeping. The bat used, however, belonged to his teammate, Joe Pepitone. "He'll have to fight me for it," Pepitone announced to everyone about the keepsake. The events surrounding the waning professional moments of Maris and Ford were the final artifacts of an era, hallmarks of a general Yankees dominance in the American League that had its origins the mid-1930s when Babe Ruth had left the game, Lou Gehrig was on the verge of retirement, and a young centerfielder named Joe DiMaggio was appointed to carry the "mantle" of responsibility until passed to Mickey. Mantle and Ford would together be elected to the Hall of Fame in 1974, with Mantle being only the seventh player in history to enter on his first ballot. Just as Ford had saved his greatest moments for the big stage, Mantle's 18 home runs in World Series play remain a record today.

With Mantle's inevitable fade, some were sure that that epoch of the dominant home-run hitter was nearing its end. "There's no 700 homer hitter in sight," Broeg stated, "but [Henry] Aaron, just 33, is a prime candidate for 500 or more ... the Bambino's 714 seems certain to stand the test of time."

The Cards were looking forward to the long homestand after the lengthy road trip but a torrential rain greeted them, the fifth washout of the young season to date for St. Louis. As a result, the visiting Braves played only one game at Busch, a 5–4 victory by Washburn on the first of June as a two-out triple in the tenth inning by the up-and-coming youngster Tolan plated Gagliano to win the game. Tolan, now batting .343 in part-time duty (12-for-35), was making a claim to be a regular somewhere in the field.

June 2 marked the first visit from the neighbors to the north, a date on the calendar to which all baseball fans in the Midwest annually awaited with interest. The Cubs, themselves surprisingly above .500 for the month of May (14–13), had gotten extensive mileage out of their young position players and pitchers that Durocher had thrust into the lineup. For one, the old Cardinal Durocher was impressed with the crowds that had shown up to watch baseball in the new park in St. Louis. "If only Sam Breadon could see this!" he exclaimed, referring to the former Cardinals owner's vain attempts to make money during the cash-strapped days of the Great Depression (a time in which Breadon had asked Durocher to take a pay cut on his annual salary from $8,500 to $5,000 between the 1933 and 1934 seasons, a nearly 40 percent decrease that Durocher at the time called "a request that is most unfair"). The Cardinals—currently averaging about 23,000 fans per home date in 1967 — had set a franchise-record with an attendance of 1,712,980 in 1966 with part of the season having been played in the new ballpark. That figure was only fourth-best among the National League, but still topped every club in the American League. It was starting to be rumored around baseball circles that St. Louis in 1967 could finally top the National League in customers—something it had not done since 1901. It also made Broeg wonder in a column, "Will St. Louis, the same French fur-trading post once joshed for non-support of great ball clubs, turn the two-million trick?"

The lone mistake made by Carlton in the opener was a home run pitch offered up to none other than Ted Savage, who was picked up by Chicago after being cast aside by the Cardinals only weeks before. The young Carlton, however, continued to solidify his regular spot on the mound in beating veteran Curt Simmons 2–1, who was 38 years old and in his last season in the major leagues, long removed from his success as one of the "Whiz Kids" on the 1950 Philadelphia Phillies' National League championship team. Carlton had a no-hitter maintained until the sixth, when Kessinger smashed a single through the infield to break the ice. Simmons was impressed with his precocious opponent, who admitted he used to imitate the elder when they were teammates briefly when Carlton first arrived to St. Louis in 1964. "Carlton pitched a great game," Simmons said afterwards. "Give me my fastball and that kid's curve, and I could be around a while longer." Once again it was Brock leading the offensive charge, who in hitting his team-topping eleventh home run also drove his club-leading RBI total to 34, while lengthening his hitting streak to 16 games. In a preview of what would become one of the great pitching matchups in the league for years to come, Gibson dueled with Jenkins in their first meeting ever in the middle contest, as the Cubs beat the Cardinals right-hander 7–5. In the game, Gibson batted left-handed for the first time since he was in the minor leagues; he had actually abandoned switch-hitting upon entering the majors, but figured he would give it a try in light of his .138 average to date in the 1967 season. Perhaps also distracting to Gibby was the fact that his regular catcher was out of town. The Cardinals had been rotating Ricketts and Romano into the lineup during the Cubs series, as McCarver was away on his duty with the Army Reserves. More help was apparently on the way at the position — albeit a few years off. For in the amateur draft later that week, the Cardinals (before taking Reuss) would select high school catcher Ted Simmons from Southfield, Michigan. At six-foot-one and 185 pounds, Simmons was described in the St. Louis papers as "a good athlete, with good batting power who can play the outfield as well." Another St. Louis team filling its roster with new players that week was the Blues, the city's brand-new entry in the National Hockey League. Their first choice in the expansion draft was the all-star goaltender from the Chicago Blackhawks, Glenn Hall. Later, their twenty-first and (second-to-last) pick was a defenseman named Bob Plager, who would ultimately join brothers Barclay and Billy on the St. Louis Arena ice as well.

The final game of the Cubs series on June 4 saw Flood's string of errorless games come to an end, marking a total of 227 consecutive contests and 568 straight chances without a miscue when he dropped a fly ball. On the play, the Cubs' pitcher, Nye, lofted a high one between Flood and Brock in left-center, and the two collided as the ball fell free. Although baseball propriety anoints the center fielder with possession of any ball he can reach (a stance that Flood kept in his disagreement about being cited for the error), the scorer — sportswriter Neal Russo of the *Post-Dispatch* — decided that the flight of the ball made it Brock's to catch with Flood interfering. Russo felt obligated to make an explanation of his decision after the game. "It was most difficult to see the streak end short of an out-and-out error of physical commission," Russo announced in a dignified move, "but in my judgment, based on many similar plays that I have scored and seen scored, the error belonged to Flood for bumping left fielder Lou Brock as he was about to make the catch of a fly ball." The defensive lapse notwithstanding, the Cards won behind a three-hit complete game by Hughes and Brock's thirteenth homer, putting them ten games over the .500 mark with a record of 27–17 and three games behind the Reds.

Houston followed the Cubs into town, and surprised the Cardinals by taking three out of four games from June 5 through 8. The Astros had been mired in ninth place with a 17–31 record before coming to St. Louis, as Jaster, Washburn, and Carlton all suffered losses before Gibson (7–5) salvaged the final game. Carlton left his contest in the sixth inning before the lion's share of a humiliating 17–1 defeat was brought upon the club (Woodeshick and

Willis allowed 11 runs between them in the seventh and eighth), as Houston pounded out a team-record 23 hits off Cardinals hurlers. The Astros had entered the game with a .229 team batting average, and conversely wound up enjoying a .479 night. Towards the end of the evening, two fans jumped over the railing and positioned themselves on the rubber and behind the plate in the Cardinals bullpen, tossing an imaginary baseball to the delight of the other observers as if to offer their services to the hometown pitching staff. The evening was sour all around, as Brock saw the end of his twenty-game hitting streak as well. Listening to the ballgame on the radio, a butcher at a St. Louis supermarket had dozed off for a nap, and a short time later, awoke to Caray saying, "Seventeen to one." Later surprised to hear about the outcome of the game *and* the length of his nap, the butcher said, "I thought they were giving the time."

Maxvill was benched in the midst of the team's offensive struggles, as he was batting .228, the quotient of a recent 0-for-26 tilt. Schoendienst felt that he needed a rest, and opted for Bressoud at shortstop, who himself was hitless in 22 at-bats on the season. When Maxvill was given opportunities to play, his glove provided stability in the Cardinals infield. This was brought to the fore on June 13, when despite enduring another 0-for-3 night at the plate, he made five diving plays which Schoendienst estimated had saved the club four runs — part of a 7–4 victory for Hughes over the Pirates. A highlight of the evening was Captain Larry French of the United States Navy swearing in a hundred new recruits in a pre-game ceremony on the field before the opener. French had also distinguished himself in another career, winning 197 major league games as a pitcher for the Pirates, Cubs, and Dodgers from 1929 to 1942. While Maxvill's job was considered to be generally safe, Musial and the rest of the front office were now looking to deal a position player — possibly one of the extra outfielders — to another club for a pitcher before the trade deadline of June 15 appeared.

Gibson's effort in the finale was enough to propel a four-game sweep of the Dodgers, the next opponent in Busch Stadium, keeping the Cardinals within two and a half games of Cincinnati in closing the long homestand (the Reds, meanwhile, were providing drama for their fans each and every day, having just set a major league record with their eleventh consecutive one-run game, a stretch that ran from May 28 to June 7 — with five more one-run games in a row earlier from May 21 to 26. Cincinnati's record over this entire two-week unit of nail-biters was 9–8). In the first game against Los Angeles, Cepeda hit the 250th homer of his career as Hughes (4–2) drove in the winning run himself in the seventh inning for a 3–2 final. "I hit .364 at Tulsa in 1962," Hughes was quick to point out to the press, letting them know that he was no stranger to the offensive side of the game. "And I was used as a pinch runner 26 times in one season in the Pacific Coast League." As the writers quickly cross-referenced the veracity of his claim, the records did indeed show that Hughes was 12 for 33 with two home runs for the Oilers in '62. Cepeda, like Shannon, had recently decided to go to a lighter bat — although Orlando was more likely to change bats more whimsically. Cepeda had been using a 40-ounce club, but scaled back to a 35-ounce choice as he "had not felt too strong lately." The milestone homer wound up inside the park, as the ball hit the top of the wall and came down on centerfielder Willie Davis's head. Once back in the dugout, the proud Cepeda was then challenging speedsters Brock, Tolan, and Johnson to a footrace.

In traveling to Pittsburgh, the Cardinals fell in the opener 7–5 as Carlton (4–3) allowed Maury Wills' first homer ever in Forbes Field. But the Redbirds came back to take the series with a pair of 7–4 wins behind Hughes and Gibson, the former being the game in which Maxvill flashed his aforementioned quintuplet of defensive gems with Hughes throwing 135 pitches in the victory, according to the notes of Gibson — who was, in customary fashion, "doing the chart" for the current evening's hurler as he, Gibson, was scheduled to take the mound the next night. Hughes was so impressive on the evening that, after the game, Musial tore up his old contract and rewarded the pitcher with a $2,500 raise. Hughes did, however, need the help of Hoerner, who fired four more pitches in the ninth inning to strike out the powerful Willie Stargell of Pittsburgh on the final play. In adding to the accolades of Maxvill's play in the infield, former Red Sox shortstop and current Pirates coach Johnny Pesky said, "Maxvill did it on the roughest infield around," speaking of what he considered the poor dirt at Forbes Field in Pittsburgh. "We have the hardest infield, about as hard as the infield at the old St. Louis ballpark when both the Cardinals and the Browns were using it." Pesky was referring to the quality of the playing surface at Sportsman's Park, which was often bemoaned by both the home and visiting players. It was the only stadium in which both a National and American League team played, and the grounds crew had little chance to improve it over the course of the season. And McCarver, returning from military duty, struck a first-inning grand slam in support of Gibson's eighth win while raising his season batting average against Pittsburgh to a lofty .458.

The Cardinals had an off day as they traveled from Pittsburgh to San Francisco on June 15, just twenty-four hours after China had completed its first successful test of a hydrogen bomb halfway around the world, in an attempt to re-assert its authority in the Asian region. It was also the Cardinals' last open date before the All-Star Break would begin on July 10, and Musial spent most of the day on the telephone, still trying to work a last-minute deal for a right-handed relief pitcher before the trading deadline appeared. Included among his calls were the Braves, Astros, and even Bing Devine with the Mets. But like most general managers around baseball,

Musial did not have a surplus of talent to offer other clubs, so few deals by any of the teams seemed imminent. "We've talked to four or five clubs in the last twenty-four hours," he explained. "Another reason we're not likely to do much dealing is that the other clubs aren't too eager to do business with the first- and second-place clubs." The Cardinals were still not pleased with the progress from Willis and Woodeshick out of the bullpen. Woodeshick, in particular, had been belted hard with a 7.47 ERA. "I can still pitch in the major leagues," he insisted to reporters as the trade rumors flew about the pitcher who had been in professional baseball since signing with the Phillies in 1950. "My arm has never felt better. I'd prefer to stay with the Cardinals; they've treated me fine." So, Musial stayed by the phone in St. Louis as the Cardinals headed west to face the Giants. They were five games ahead of San Francisco in second place, while the Redbirds continued to trail Cincinnati by a mere game and a half. The Reds, who continued to win a seemingly-endless string of one-run ballgames, were nonetheless hurt by a pair of critical injuries in the same game on June 16, casualties that would impact the National League race for the rest of the summer. Shortstop Leo Cardenas, an All-Star for the past three seasons, fractured the middle finger on his left hand when he was hit by a pitch from Bill Singer of the Dodgers and was expected to miss up to two months. Meanwhile, left fielder and up-and-coming superstar Pete Rose, who notched 205 hits in 1966, badly bruised his shoulder while making a diving catch in the first inning.

Despite now wearing enemy colors, Cepeda was the special guest at a luncheon of the Giants Booster Club upon returning to San Francisco, as he announced that he was leaving 25 game tickets for friends that he retained in the area. Looking to sock some long ones while in town, Cepeda — though traveling — had his usual large assortment of bats with him. At home in Busch Stadium, he would keep as many twenty bats in the dugout. Those that would not fit into the bat rack, he would lay in the corner up against the wall. In addition — according to Jerry Gibson's estimates — Cepeda kept as many as 30 more bats in the clubhouse, all of various lengths, weights, and widths of handles, which were used depending on how felt on the given day and what type of pitcher he was facing.

Even though it was the middle of June, a cold wind blew off the bay and embittered the 50-degree temperatures. Maris complained that the San Francisco chill had caused his back to stiffen, saying that "if this is your home field, you'd have to lose interest in the game." The Latin-born Javier agreed. "If I had to play 81 games a year here, I'd hit .120." But Hoolie came up strong in the opener, lacing a two-run single in the first inning that was part of the difference in a Washburn (3–3) victory, 5–3. Worried about his stamina during spring training, Washburn had nonetheless managed to pitch into the seventh inning in eleven of his twelve starts on the year. Carlton (4–3) faltered in the middle contest due to wildness, but Cepeda brought home an important victory in the finale in a complete game by Hughes (6–2), in which Cha-Cha planted his eighth home run high into the seats off the notorious spitballer Gaylord Perry, raising his batting average to a lofty .347 (Cepeda and McCarver, with his .330 clip, were at number two and number three in the National League batting race behind Clemente). And Maris, overcoming his sore back, went 2 for 3 to improve his own mark all the way up to .313 from the depth of the lower .200s he had endured just weeks before. It was an unusually-productive performance for Roger on the road, for while he was hitting .393 at Busch Stadium, he had maintained a modest .243 mark away from home. He also indicated that his throwing arm was feeling better than it had in years, never having quite fully recovered from when he crashed into an outfield wall in the minors way back in 1954. Meanwhile, Hughes had suddenly become the hardest starting pitcher to hit in the major leagues, allowing a miniscule 5.2 hits per nine innings.

More importantly, the Cardinals had parlayed their success with the recent misfortunes of the Reds, jumping to first place ahead of the limping Cincinnati ball club as the standings showed at the close of play on June 18 (the Cardinals, despite being a half-game behind the Reds, led the league in winning percentage, to date having only played 58 games to Cincinnati's 65):

	W	L	Pct.	GB
St. Louis	36	22	.620	0.5
Cincinnati	40	25	.615	—
Chicago	32	27	.542	5
Pittsburgh	32	27	.542	5
San Francisco	33	28	.540	5
Atlanta	31	30	.508	7
Philadelphia	28	32	.466	9.5
Los Angeles	25	36	.409	13
Houston	26	38	.406	13.5
New York	20	38	.344	16.5

The Houston Astros had climbed out of the cellar due, in part, to an improved pitching staff. It was a corps led by 22-year-old rookie Don Wilson, who fired a no-hitter the same day that the Cardinals ascended into first place. The victims were the Atlanta Braves, as the six-foot-three Wilson dominated them with 15 strikeouts, fanning five of the last six Atlanta batters that he faced and ending the game by blowing the ball past Henry Aaron on a 3–2 count. "He's the kind of guy that makes me want to retire from the game," Aaron said afterwards. "That kid threw about as hard as anybody we faced all year."

Wilson and the Astros would next be challenged by the new league leaders. One player that almost never seemed to have trouble navigating the hazardous course of fly balls in the Astrodome was Flood, but even he was wary of tracking batted balls in the strange, climate-controlled world. With the Cardinals taking a 5–4 lead into the bottom of the eleventh inning of the first game, Flood resumed the defensive heroics that he had established in his monumental errorless streak recently ended. With the Astros holding the tying run on second base in the person of Jim Landis, Bob Lillis hit a sinking liner to center on which Flood got a late jump. Using his instincts, Flood lunged in an effort to make a shoestring catch — an effort which, if he failed, would likely have allowed the ball to skip past him on the artificial surface and allow Lillis to win the game on an inside-the-park home run. Flood, however, was able to snag the ball with the tip of his glove before it made contact with the ground, as Landis never stopped running in the belief that it was sure hit. When Flood looked up to see the Houston runner rounding third, he simply kept running with the momentum that he had developed, and ran all the way to touch second base for the first unassisted double play by a National League center fielder in 34 years. The dramatic save preserved the win for Briles, who along with Hoerner had entered in relief of Gibson to beat the Astros' top lefty, Mike Cuellar, as the Cards had won for the sixth time in seven tries for extra-inning ballgames on the year. The shortstop Maxvill, who was not even needed in the final scene, stood and watched in amazement. "That had to be the greatest play I've ever seen in a clutch situation," he claimed. Added Bressoud, who had played with Willie Mays, "I'd have to put Flood right there with Mays as the best I've seen at getting to a ball. And Curt is just as sure-handed as Willie. Willie's only edge is in his throwing arm." The next victim in the Cardinals rampage was Houston pitcher Bo Belinsky, who lost to Jaster the following night 6–2 via Cepeda's ninth homer and two hits and two RBIs from the resurgent Maxvill. "If the Cardinals aren't there battling for a pennant in September," Belinsky predicted, "I'll be the most surprised person in the world." Belinsky, while certainly a serviceable major league pitcher for several seasons, was better known for his Hollywood exploits as he dated multiple movie stars (including Ann-Margaret and Tina Louise) and appeared in a number of movie bits. The St. Louis steamrollers moved on to Belinsky's old haunts in Chavez Ravine, as a two-game sweep of the Dodgers' Drysdale and Osteen made it a fantastic 8–2 road trip since they arrived in Pittsburgh on June 12. Again it was Maxvill shooting a key hit, gaining more confidence every day as his average continued to climb. "That Maxvill [now 4 for 7 on the year against Drysdale] has to be one of the most improved players in the National League over the past few years," an impressed Drysdale said. "Sure, he may not hit all the time, but I admire a guy who can help as much as he can with his glove when he's not hitting well." McCarver, plating the second Cardinal run in the 2–0 win over Drysdale with his seventh homer, was the hottest hitter on the road, batting .441 over the last ten games and raising his overall average on the season from .306 to .331.

This first contest in Los Angeles was costly, however, as Washburn — in the midst of a spectacular performance, hitting his stride in a hot streak as the summer months were approaching — dislocated and broke the thumb on his pitching hand as he was struck by a line drive off the bat of Johnny Roseboro. The right-hander had dominated the Dodgers until the mishap, forcing 12 of 18 outs on ground balls into the seventh inning. He exited while having posted 14 outs in a row after a walk in the second, also aided by two diving catches by Brock in left field, who was also now leading the National League with 27 stolen bases. Washburn's chipped bone was removed by a California surgeon shortly thereafter, and Cardinals trainer Bob Bauman announced that the pitcher would have to sit out at least a month, even though Schoendienst privately hoped it would be two weeks or less. Suddenly, the youngster Briles was now thrust into a prominent role in the rotation. But like Belinsky, Drysdale didn't think that the Redbirds' youth would impede their pennant charge. "The only big question is whether in the heat of a pennant race if some of their younger pitchers, starters or relievers, will react all right under the pressure," the Dodgers ace added. "But having so many experienced players who have been through it, as they do, should help the younger guys." Needing a complete game from a depleted, eight-man pitching staff (with Woodeshick nursing a sore arm), Carlton (5–4) came through with a 7–2 win over Osteen to cap the trip. McCarver claimed that "Lefty" was throwing harder in the ninth than he was in the first; "Steve was smelling the bacon," Flood added. And Spiezio, making his first major league appearance in the outfield in giving Maris the night off, came up with two key hits the spark rallies. Not to be out-done by his teammates, Javier had been contributing as well with a twelve-game hitting streak. The Redbirds now headed home to open an eight-game homestand, enjoying a full two-game lead over Cincinnati. What concerned Schoendienst and Musial, however, was the fact that there was no standout pitcher in the minor leagues to take Washburn's or Woodeshick's spot on the major league roster. Once a team that relied on pitching and defense, it was the Cardinals' offense that was now carrying the load, as evidenced by the impressive batting statistics for most of the starters on June 23:

	Average	HR	RBI
Cepeda	.339	9	44
McCarver	.333	7	33
Brock	.321	13	42

	Average	HR	RBI
Flood	.317	3	25
Maris	.303	4	21
Javier	.302	6	16
Shannon	.279	2	32
Maxvill	.218	0	11

Much of the attention in the sports world had recently shifted to boxing — or at least, the off-canvas exploits of one ringsman — as Cassius Clay learned the ramifications of his acts on June 20. Judge Joe Ingraham sentenced him to five years in prison and a $10,000 fine for his conviction by jury of "repudiation of United States Selective Service laws," the maximum penalty for such an offense. When asked by the judge if he wanted to say anything in his defense before the sentence was pronounced, Clay answered with a defiant "no." His attorneys planned to take the case to the U.S. Fifth Circuit Court of Appeals in New Orleans and on to the U.S. Supreme Court if necessary. In the meantime, Clay remained free on bond until the highest court possible decided the case in finality. Meanwhile, making positive headlines in the world of sports that day was Jim Ryun, as the sophomore from the University of Kansas ran the mile in three minutes, fifty-one and one-tenth seconds, topping the world record which he already held. With this current performance in front of nearly 12,000 spectators at the Bakersfield Memorial Stadium in California, Ryun now held the three fastest mile times in recorded history. At the same meet, a 19-year-old Californian named Paul Wilson also set the world record in the pole vault by surmounting seventeen feet, eight inches.

It was Cosman who was Musial's choice to take Washburn's place and join the team in St. Louis, the best option in a pitching world that was thin throughout most every organization. Cosman had spent the first month of the season with the Cardinals, appearing in only four games and logging six innings of work before returning to the minor leagues. Musial envisioned the big right-hander as having the most versatility of the choices from the farm clubs, as Cosman could be used both as a long reliever and a spot starter. Cosman most likely had an easier trip to Busch Stadium from Tulsa than the rest of the club, as their flight from San Francisco did not arrive at the St. Louis airport until 4:30 in the morning. Like the others, Brock hurried home in an effort to get a few hours sleep before having to go to the ballpark. But he unfortunately awakened before his desired time, jarred to consciousness by the rude buzz of his neighbor's lawnmower.

Complete-game wins by Hughes and Gibson against Philadelphia ran the winning streak to seven (and 15 of their last 17), the longest roll of success the team enjoyed since starting the season 6–0. Up the road, the Cubs had also just won seven in a row (their longest winning streak in thirteen years), and had crept up behind the Reds in third place, just four games behind St. Louis. Durocher had indeed brought a new attitude to the north side of Chicago, appearing to reverse the fortunes of the downtrodden club just as he had promised in taking over the club in early 1966. What had caused the recent change, that showed the Cubs with a 39–28 record and on the cusp of the pennant chase? "One of the things they eliminated," Durocher said of his troops, "was a defeatist attitude; call it a 'second-division attitude,' if you want. It's a different team. It plays as if it expects to win ballgames. But it's not about me—you have to have the players. If you don't have the players, they can't execute the plays you teach them. You've got to have the talent."

The Cardinals' recent success led to the largest crowd ever for a double header in St. Louis (47,014) the next day—Sunday the 25th—but the faithful were disappointed to see the Phillies take both games. The ball club then turned to the rookie the following day, as a series commenced at Busch with the Giants in town. Cosman was given the ball against Perry, who the previous year had logged 21 wins, 201 strikeouts, and garnered his first All-Star nomination. Perry was angered by his poor performance in his 4–1 loss to Hughes the previous week in San Francisco versus the Cards, and looked to dominate the game against the youngster to make amends.

But Cosman refused to be intimidated. Thinking that the rookie would be nervous, pitching coach Muffett suggested that he use the no-windup technique to focus his energy on the plate, and it worked. Cosman himself drove in the second run off Perry with a single, and ultimately took a 3–1 lead into the ninth when he struck out Ollie Brown to start the inning and then issued a walk. When Schoendienst summoned Briles from the bullpen for relief, Cosman walked off the mound to a standing ovation from the large crowd. Before Briles had completed his warm-up tosses, the cheers continued to be so loud that they pushed Cosman from the dugout for more recognition. Two outs later, Cosman celebrated his first major league victory, an important win that pushed the Cards to three and a half games ahead of Cincinnati. In the locker room, the smile could not be removed from Cosman's face; it would be the last of the good times on the homestand, however, as the Giants dominated the Cards by scores of 6–0, 9–1, and 12–4 to take the series. Upon learning that the Redbird hitters carried an impressive 30–12 record against right-handed starters but only an even 13–13 against lefties going into the series, San Francisco manager Herman Franks quickly planned to insert all southpaws—former Cardinal Ray Sadecki, Mike McCormick, and Joe Gibbon—onto the hill after Perry lost the opener, and the strategy proved effective, saving Marichal and fellow right-handers Bobby Bolin and Ron Herbel for other work. "The way things are going, the Giants just might lure Carl

Hubbell back to the pitcher's mound, even if the great lefthander from Carthage, Missouri, is 64 years old," Russo wondered about the current Giants farm director changing jobs. "It's not often that a club with a right-hander such as Juan Marichal will set him back in the rotation and move in a left-hander with Joe Gibbon's modest credentials." Hubbell, of course, was the Giants ace of the 1930s who gained legendary status with his consecutive strikeouts of immortal sluggers Babe Ruth, Lou Gerhig, Jimmie Foxx, Al Simmons, and Joe Cronin. The final contest was especially ugly, as Gibson allowed the first eight Giants batters to reach base, part of an 11-run first inning for San Francisco. When he left after 38 pitches and not recording an out, he was booed voraciously by the Busch Stadium crowd. Upon receiving the unfriendly good-bye from the home folks, Gibson tauntingly flung his cap in the air, which only increased the volume of the derision.

Despite the three-game disaster against San Francisco, the Cards ended June, 1967 still holding on to first place by a game and a half after winning the first contest in a trip east against the New York Mets. Now the closest competitors were the Cubs, whose spirited leader, Durocher, had continued their hot streak by eleven of their last twelve by the end of the month. Schoendienst kept true to the faith in his club, however, strengthened by his own strong Catholic faith that he cultivated from Clinton County. He liked to keep up on Catholic news, as he happened to read in the paper about some other cardinals—Pope Paul VI had just ordinated 276 new ones in Rome on June 26, one of whom was a young Polish bishop named Karol Wojtyla.

	W	L	Pct.	GB
St. Louis	44	27	.619	—
Chicago	43	29	.597	1.5
Cincinnati	43	33	.565	3.5
San Francisco	40	35	.533	6
Pittsburgh	36	35	.507	8
Atlanta	37	36	.506	8
Philadelphia	35	37	.486	9.5
Los Angeles	33	40	.452	12
Houston	27	47	.364	18.5
New York	25	44	.362	18

Sadecki's 9–1 victory in the Giants-Cardinals series was propelled, in part, from two home runs off the bat of Willie Mays. Mays was perhaps taking out some frustration on the Cardinals, disappointed with the news he had just received about not being named the National League's starting center fielder in the upcoming All-Star Game for the first time in fourteen years (in 1967, players from around the league voted for the starters, although they were not permitted to vote for players from their own teams. As in contemporary times, the league managers for the All-Star Game—who in 1967 for the National League was Walter Alston of the Dodgers—would select the reserves and pitchers). Heading into '67, Mays was already the career leader in All-Star hits (22), runs scored (19), stolen bases (6), and the only player to steal two bases in one All-Star Game. From the St. Louis squad, Brock and Cepeda were chosen for the starting lineup, with Gibson, McCarver, and Javier being figured for appointments as well. McCarver was second to Joe Torre of Atlanta for votes among the catchers, while Javier trailed Bill Mazeroski of the Pirates at second base. In the end, however, Alston would pass on Javier, as his final roster that he submitted on July 5 would show Tommy Helms of the Cincinnati Reds as the other second baseman for the team. Many thought that Javier was as deserving as any Cardinal. "From I've seen this year," Dick Sisler said, "Javier is Mazeroski's equal on the double play, and has better range in the outfield because of his speed." Added the understudy Bressoud, "Javier has always covered nearly as much ground as Mazeroski; probably more now." Since entering the league as a nineteen-year-old rookie in 1956, Mazeroski had been an All-Star and Gold Glove winner seven times, including every Gold Glove won at the position in the National League since 1962.

Down the road in Kansas City on June 28, another group of voters was affirming a much more important decision—at least to the vicinity. Citizens of Jackson County, Missouri—an area that encompassed Kansas City as well as suburban Sugar Creek and Independence—solidly passed a $43 million bond proposal to build separate new stadiums for the Athletics of the American League and the Chiefs of the National Football League. A two-thirds majority was needed for approval of the stadium measure, which was surpassed by more than 5,000 votes. Rumors were surfacing, however, that tempestuous A's owner Charles O. Finley would threaten to move the team out of the area anyway. "Charley Finley has never made any secret of his desire to get out of Kansas City," wrote Red Smith after the ballot results were announced. "The principal reason he was turned down in earlier attempts to move was that American League owners hoped to starve him into selling the Athletics.

"Now it appears that Charley is laying new plans, more quietly than in the past. With the A's in last place, he has an attendance decline of about 90,000 to support the argument that Kansas City isn't a big league town. The Jackson County Sports Complex may be built as a multi-million dollar monument to blind selfishness." Meanwhile, the far-off citizens of St. Louis paid little mind, as their club continued to steer towards pennant contention.

5. A Bad Break

Trust me, you have to fight. When people are wrong, you've got to let them know it.

— Orlando Cepeda

The Cards returned from Shea Stadium in New York with a draw of two wins and two losses on the one-city trip, but their confidence was still soaring. They were riding the high spirits of their catcher and leader, McCarver, who had batted .367 in June (and was at .340 overall, 62 points above his career average to that time), but who had to miss the July 2 double header against the Mets because of military duty — as did Tolan and Johnson, leaving the Cardinals shorthanded by three position players. Into McCarver's place went Ricketts, and the back-up backstop simply went 4 for 8 in New York to raise his batting mark in part-time work to .382 in 34 at-bats. And Cepeda had risen to take the league batting lead among qualifiers at .350, just ahead of Clemente, who by 1967 had already won the crown three times. Cepeda was also exhibiting more patience at the plate, evidenced by his 33 walks — only five fewer than his entire total for 1966. On the flip side was Shannon, still convalescing from his recent bout with infections in struggling through a .231 batting mark for the previous month. He was still improving defensively at third base, however. "It's a lot easier for me to play right field," he admitted, always remembering where his natural instincts remained. "But I like playing third because I'm helping the club. What means the most to me — and what will help me get better at third — is that Red has confidence in me."

In splitting the four-game series in New York, the Cardinals suddenly found themselves in a tie for first place with the Cubs on July 2, as Chicago had gone a blistering 15–2 in the last three weeks. It was the first time in four years that the Cubs had found themselves in first place, reminiscent of a fleeting moment in the top spot when they won on June 7, 1963, against the Giants in ten innings when Mays was picked off second base. "I just turn 'em loose and let 'em go," Durocher said about his boys in the Wrigley Field home locker room after they delivered the knockout blow in the Reds series. As Ron Santo was batting in the bottom of the eighth in the last game, he had to step out of the batter's box in deference to the roar of the crowd—for the Cardinals' loss in New York had just been posted on the scoreboard. The two neighboring teams had indeed turned the standings on its head. "Anyone suggesting before the season that the Cardinals would come up to the Fourth of July tied for first place would have been considered optimistic," Broeg wrote. "The same guy suggesting the Chicago Cubs as the party of the second part in first would have been considered nuts."

An important series for the Cardinals waited against the Reds as July opened. The Redbirds knew that they could quickly turn things into a two-team race with a sweep of Cincinnati in the quartet of games to come, while the Reds—treading water with a 43–35 record, scrapping to stay in the hunt—came to the St. Louis riverfront looking for a fight. They had just been pummeled in three straight at Wrigley Field by the Cubs, the white-hot team that had recently supplanted them in the second chair. A *Farmers' Almanac*-type tradition in baseball always held that the team in first place on the Fourth would be the favored sons of the baseball powers, destined to go on through the dog days of summer and win the pennant at the outset of autumn. There was a standing-room-only crowd of nearly 48,000 on hand to watch the first game of the series, and they were privy to baseball and non-baseball fireworks a day early.

The Cards raced far out of reach early in the game, plating seven runs in the very first inning against Reds pitchers Milt Pappas and Don Nottebart. When Brock reached first base in the second inning, he unsuccessfully tried to steal — which the Reds felt was unnecessary with the Cardinals' big lead, despite it still being in the early stages of the game. Later, both he and Javier were knocked down on pitches from Nottebart. When the Reds came to bat in the fifth, Gibson — who had a perfect game going until the moment, and who was already angry in remembering his poor performance against the Giants a few days earlier — threw a pitch behind the ear of Tony Perez. "I wasn't trying to hit him," Gibson explained. "If a pitcher is trying to hit a batter, the last place he wants to throw the ball is at the head, because it's the easiest thing to move." (Most pitchers are taught that if a batter is to be struck, it is best to go for the middle of the back.) On the next offering, Perez flew out to Flood in center. Crossing back over the field in returning to the Cincinnati dugout, Perez said something to Gibson as he crossed the mound — something that Gibson would only describe as "uncharacteristically nasty."

Gibson took a few steps towards him as he responded, as Cepeda made his way towards the two men "as a peacemaker," he would later claim. Things just had appeared to be calming down when streaking in from the Reds' bullpen came big Bob Lee, the 6'3", 230 pound relief pitcher whose teammates had nicknamed "Moose" and "Man Mountain." The imposing Lee was viewed as the enforcer on the club, and he contended afterwards that he thought Cepeda was going to take a swing at Perez. When Lee got to the scene, he bumped Cepeda out of the way but denied hitting anyone. "I didn't swing at anyone and no one hit me," Lee recounted. "I couldn't get at him [Cepeda], or I would have put his lights out. They held both of us back." The benches emptied, and Cepeda had his right first cocked just as Nottebart grabbed him from behind. Cepeda's and Lee's accounts were just two of many conflicting reports on the fight that ensued, which involved the St. Louis Police Department and even a small number of fans who made their way onto the field.

In the middle of the melee, Rose was punched three times in the back of the head by Cepeda, as the Reds' outfielder next found himself wrestling with Gibson and Helms in the Reds' dugout. They were soon joined by Tolan who, looking as if he was readying himself for a dive into a swimming pool, peeked at the group for a moment from the top step of the dugout and then hurled himself onto the pile. From his perch above the field, Jack Buck described the professional wrestling-type scene with amazement, telling the audience that Gibson was, one-by-one, hurling bodies back onto the field from the dugout floor.

The injury list from the fight was long and diversified. Bristol, the Reds' manager, had a gash on his leg from being spiked, as did Woodeshick; Nottebart's face was cut; Muffett pulled a muscle in his neck; Javier escaped being hurt, but had his prescription eyeglasses broken and had to finish the game wearing his reading glasses; Robert Casey, one of twenty St. Louis police officers at the scene, received a dislocated jaw in his attempt to restore order; and Helms chipped a tooth in addition to having an 0-for-4 night at the plate. "Helms went hitless against Gibson," Russo wrote the next day, "but Hoot didn't go hitless against Helms." And then there was Tolan, who didn't even play in the game but still managed to bruise his hand with his half-gainer onto the Cincinnati bench (Bauman was so upset with him that he wouldn't even treat his wounds). Among the large crowd watching the fracas, unfortunately and ironically, were at least 13,242 impressionable youths, admitted free of charge to the game through the Cardinals' complimentary ticket program for straight-A students.

It took the St. Louis Police Department 12 minutes to clear the field. Interestingly, Lee was the only player ejected from the game, but even a few of the Cardinals pointed to Brock's desire for a stolen base in the second inning as the cause of the mayhem. And even though he was defending Brock by throwing at Perez, Gibson used the occasion to suggest that he did not hold the greatest amount of fondness for the leftfielder. There were several on the Cardinals team — and Gibson was among them — who felt that Brock stole bases when it was unnecessary in an effort to do little more than augment his personal statistics. "While I regarded Flood as a brother," Gibson once revealed, "I thought of Brock merely as my teammate. We seldom talked, less often at length."

Although Gibson suffered a jammed right thumb in the incident, he continued on through the game, being relieved by Briles with two outs in the eighth inning after he had recorded twelve strikeouts. "It hurt, and it kept me from gripping the ball right," he said. Briles proceeded to strike out three of the four men he faced, nailing down a 7–3 Cardinals victory and Gibson's tenth, ending the raucous day which Gibson claimed "lit a fire in our bellies" in pursuit of the pennant, and kept them on pace with the Cubs. Schoendienst agreed, seeing a difference in this year's Cardinals team from his first two seasons in charge — especially the way in which it was conducting itself in a business-like manner. "You can't let a player take advantage of you, embarrass himself or the club, but if you understand him and he understands you, you don't have to worry. I've had to fine players the last two years, but not this season." Still, the manager was not promising anything to the press about the outcome of the schedule. "The only thing I'm sure of is that quail season opens on November 10th," the avid hunter stated. Unfortunately for Schoendienst and the rest of the Cards, Gibson would have to battle a physical problem in the coming weeks much more serious than his jammed thumb.

Boxer Joe Frazier, while preparing himself for the tournament that was to find a successor to Cassius Clay for the world heavyweight boxing title, took note of the melee and jokingly offered to hold a fighting clinic for the baseball teams. But he wanted his primary pupils to be the New York Yankees and especially outfielder Joe Pepitone, whom Frazier felt was taking too much of a beating during the Yanks' seemingly-frequent brawls. "Look at him," the boxer said of Pepitone. "He banged up his hands without getting a punch across ... all they do is hurt themselves instead of the other guy. Baseball players should know about combinations as well as double plays." Pepitone, spending his first year as a full-time outfielder after four seasons at first base, was not letting the distance from the main action as an outfielder prevent him from taking part in fights. Frazier, meanwhile, was successful in the first round of the tournament, brutally mauling George Chuvalo in a fight that ended 16 seconds into the fourth round. Chuvalo, a Canadian and veteran of 11 years in the professional ring and 62 fights, had his right eye entirely closed from Frazier's attacks; "His tough face was beaten into a bloody soufflé," according to Red Smith. It was reported to be the worst beating Chuvalo had ever taken in his career, and jumped Frazier to the top of the contender list by *Ring* magazine, passing Terrell and Mildenberger. Fifteen months earlier, Chuvalo had gone the distance with Clay, losing a decision on March 29, 1966, for the heavyweight title. After the fight, Frazier was immediately offered a $70,000 contract to fight Jerry Quarry in Madison Square Garden in the fall of 1967. Clay meanwhile, in the wake of the Frazier-Chuvalo bout, had absorbed another blow in his legal fight, with his request to fight in Japan denied as his passport was ordered surrendered by the courts. It was presumed that Clay, if allowed to fight abroad, would speak and act unpatriotically, and perhaps even constitute a flight risk. "The defendant does appear ready to take part in anti-government, anti-war activities," Judge Ingraham said in his ruling.

On the Fourth of July holiday against the Reds, the Cardinals were stopped in their tracks by the 19-year-old pitching prodigy Gary Nolan, who logged the first shutout on the year by a right-hander against St. Louis in winning 1–0, spoiling an equally-impressive performance by Jaster as Rose was driven home in the ninth on a double by Deron Johnson. Nolan threw harder than the Cards were expecting, using a four-seam fastball that got on top of their bats and induced many harmless fly balls. Nolan was well-rested for the game, having relaxed in his hotel room in downtown St. Louis while the brawl was taking place on the field the previous night. The first-round pick of the Reds in the 1966 draft, the young Nolan displayed no fear in challenging big league hitters through his rookie season. And Cosman, though allowing only one run in eight innings in an encore of his last start, nonetheless gave way to Briles in the tenth in losing to Maloney the following night 2–1, as the struggling Cardinals offense received a tongue-lashing from Schoendienst. The manager announced he was benching Brock for the final game of the Cincinnati series, as the leftfielder had been batting .186 since reaching a season-high of .354 on June 5. Brock's 0-for-5 performance against Maloney left him at .138 for the last 15 games with just one stolen base. The club responded with a thrilling 6–5 win in the final contest, with the villain Bob Lee surrendering the deciding run in the ninth. His nemesis from three nights prior, Cepeda, touched him for a single to center field that carried Tolan home with the game-winner. With three hits on the evening, Orlando's average sailed to .359, still at the top of the National League charts. And McCarver was as hot as his batting average, shouting profanities at umpires in every park until arbiter Harry Wendelstedt told him to cool it. "If a man in the tenth inning of a heated and important game can't say what I said," the befuddled McCarver explained, "then I don't know what this game is coming to."

Brock was right back off the bench after a one-game siesta, however, as Flood did not make the trip for a three-game series in Philadelphia, the final battles before the All-Star break. Flood suffered a contusion and pulled muscle in his shoulder after crashing into the center field wall in pursuit of a fly ball against the Reds, as Tolan took his place in center. Flood believed, however, that the shoulder had first been injured in trying to make a long throw to home plate back in early May in the cold, damp weather at Chicago's Wrigley Field. Still, his mere ability to grab almost every fly towards center continued to amaze all, even his teammates. "Watching Flood's catches," as Gibson described it in his autobiography, "is like looking at a pretty girl — each one is always the prettiest, until the next one comes along." The Cards took two of the three games in Philly, but Brock continued to struggle in posting a 2-for-12 personal performance on the trip. Nonetheless, he refused to go off his milkshake diet.

As with each team every year, the Cardinals took inventory of their 1967 campaign at the All-Star break, which began on July 10 and which found them exactly halfway through their schedule with a 49–32 record, three and a half games ahead of the Cubs. Chicago had cooled off considerably after their torrid rampage through June, having lost seven in a row heading into the break since tying the Cardinals for first place for a mere 48 hours on July 2 and 3, a drought that culminated with a four-game sweep at the hands of Houston in the Astrodome. "I'm just playing it day by day," the non-committal Durocher said when asked to forecast a second-half outlook for his club. "I won't predict where we'll finish." The Giants, meanwhile, had caught the Reds in a tie for third, with both teams five games back. According to Broeg's memory, it was the first time in ten years that St. Louis was in first place at the time of the "Mid-Summer's Classic." The appearance of the break also marked the Cardinals' first day off since June 15, and the extra rest was especially beneficial to the recovering Washburn. The pitcher planned to test his fractured thumb by pitching batting practice before the Cardinals' game with the Pirates on July 12, a make-up contest which cut the two clubs' All-Star break down by one day. The Cardinals needed Washburn to regain his form, as they figured that it would take at least 95 wins to claim the pennant, which left them 46 wins away — or three wins fewer than their first-half pace. Jimmy "The Greek" Snyder, a noted Las Vegas oddsmaker, still had the Cardinals as favorites in the National League at a 7–5 choice. Snyder's pick in the American League at the midway point was the Chicago White Sox at an 11–5 gamble, who with a 47–33 mark owned a two-game advantage over the Detroit Tigers and a half-game further over the Minnesota Twins.

*　*　*　*

The 1967 All-Stars met in sunny southern California at the new $24 million stadium in Anaheim. The stadium was a year old in 1967, and was considered among the classier new parks in the game. The press described it as "the heart of fast-growing Orange County, a hop, skip, and a jump away from

Disneyland." The 91-degree temperatures were actually a welcome change from the previous July, when the stars battled it out under triple-digit heat on the floor of two-month-old Busch Stadium. A crowd of over 46,000 settled in to imbibe the special baseball treat, only the second time that the classic was held in the region (the 1959 contest took place in the Memorial Coliseum in Los Angeles). The American League was led by Baltimore Orioles manager Hank Bauer, who had piloted his club to the world championship in 1966. Red Ruffing, a former Yankees pitcher, threw out the game's first ball to Lloyd Waner, a former Pirates outfielder, as both were entering the National Baseball Hall of Fame in a couple of weeks.

The two rosters not only comprised some of the best players in the game, but also a range of individual salaries that averaged a beefy $40,000 per year in dwarfing the pittance of the $22,000 that the average player in the major leagues was making in 1967. The *starters* in the All-Star Game, in fact, were making an "outlandish" $50,000 per man, and they were as follows:

National League	*American League*
Brock, lf (STL)	B. Robinson, 3b (BAL)
Clemente, rf (PIT)	Carew, 2b (MIN)
Aaron, cf (ATL)	Oliva, cf (MIN)
Cepeda, 1b (STL)	Killebrew, 1b (MIN)
Allen, 3b (PHI)	Conigliaro, rf (BOS)
Torre, c (ATL)	Yastrzemski, lf (BOS)
Mazeroski, 2b (PIT)	Freehan, c (DET)
Alley, ss (PIT)	Petrocelli, ss (BOS)
Marichal, P (SF)	Chance, p (MIN)

Despite the formidable list of participants, Broeg would be unimpressed at the end. "The contest was, among other things, the longest and perhaps dullest in a series that began as a sideshow to the Chicago World's Fair in 1933," he wrote. Nonetheless, the game drew an estimated 52 million television viewers—more than four times the number that watched the 1966 game from St. Louis, attributed to the later starting time that allowed more people to tune in. The 1967 affair stretched for three hours and 41 minutes, not being decided until the fifteenth inning when Tony Perez of the Reds socked a solo homer to give the Nationals a 2–1 victory and a 20–17 lead all-time. All of the runs in the '67 contest, in fact, came via the home run—and all by third basemen—for before Perez's game-ending drive, Brooks Robinson of the Orioles and Dick Allen of the Phillies had connected on solo shots. The loudest cheer erupted when Mantle, playing in his fifteenth All-Star Game, entered to pinch-hit in the fifth inning, only to be called out on strikes from the pitching of the Cubs' Ferguson Jenkins. "I threw two fastballs right down the pipe, and he swung through them both," a startled Jenkins told the reporters later. "It really surprised me to see him miss. The third strike just caught the corner." The pitchers truly dominated, as they punched out thirty batters with strikeouts including six by Jenkins, which matched an All-Star Game record. The game's two walks went to just one batter, Carl Yastrzemski of the Boston Red Sox. The man they called "Yaz," in fact, reached base five of his six times at the plate in lacing two singles and a double. Drysdale got the win, while a 22-year-old rookie named Tom Seaver from the New York Mets recorded the save, striking out Ken Berry of the White Sox to end the long affair. Berry had taken the place of Frank Robinson on the American League roster, who was suffering from blurry vision as a result of a collision with an Orioles teammate two weeks earlier.

Even the special All-Star circumstances could not provide a cure for Brock's bat, as he went 0 for 2 before Mays entered as a pinch hitter for him in the sixth inning. Cepeda also struggled, going hitless in six times to the plate on the evening, which now made him a paltry 1 for 27 in All-Star competition over his career. He did manage, however, to play in all fifteen innings at first base, while Bill Freehan of Detroit caught all fifteen frames for the American League (interestingly, the only non-pitchers that Bauer did not use were two other catchers—Paul Casanova of Washington, and even Bauer's own Andy Etchebarren of the Orioles). As for the other Cardinals in attendance, Gibson pitched a scoreless seventh and eighth while McCarver entered the game in the tenth and got hits in each of his two at-bats. It was part of the National League total of nine safeties, which included a double McCarver hit off Jim "Catfish" Hunter of the A's, who at age 21 had already been in the big leagues for three seasons with 25 major league victories. The marathon contest had pre-empted an hour-long special on Khrushchev that NBC had been planning to air for months, and originally scheduled to be aired after the game, but no one seemed to mind about the change in programming—especially the network. "A Russian spy in the standing-room crowd at Anaheim Stadium would have seen filthy capitalism at its most profitable best, or worst, depending on which side of the cash register you're standing," Broeg added.

Most noticeable was the fact that Gibson was his usual private self in the midst of his temporary teammates. As he normally did in such circumstances, he dressed into and out of his uniform quickly, said little to the other National League All-Stars, and kept to himself while on the bench. He never wanted to be known as a fraternizer with the "enemy" to any degree — even in the unique circumstance of an All-Star game. "I dressed and left quickly at All-Star games so that I wouldn't accidentally make a friend," he once had said plainly. He was true to form at this gathering, not wishing to be buddies with anyone to whom he may have to give a brush-back pitch later in the season during the heat of the pennant race. Joe Torre had noticed this previously, back when he had caught Gibson in the 1965 classic. "He wouldn't talk to me," Torre said, pointing out that, at the very least, he and Gibson needed to communicate on the signs for the pitches that he was going to throw. When Torre went out to the mound, he noticed he was talking only to himself. "Tony Oliva was at bat, and I said to make sure the ball was up-and-in, not down-and-in. He acted like I wasn't even there."

After the All-Star break, Schoendienst was planning was for Gibson to begin pitching on three days' rest instead of four.

*   *   *   *

Hughes, Jaster, and Carlton would precede Gibson in the series against the Pirates at Busch that opened the second half of the season, with the Cardinals winning two out of the three (while Eddie Mathews was belting his 500th home run in Houston). Cepeda remained very consistent, providing key hits in the two victories and having lengthened his current hitting streak to fifteen games, during which he was batting .414 (24 for 58). On the 15th of July in the final game of the set, Gibson took the hill against Pirate journeyman Dennis Ribant, anxious to shake off any rust lingering from the All-Star break in pointing the Cards toward the flag in October.

Carrying a 1–0 Cardinal lead into the fourth inning after Brock bunted for a single and Maris tripled him home, Gibson was very strong, not allowing a Pirates hit despite permitting four walks. Clemente led off the inning, catching hold of a pitch out over the plate and driving a screamer right back at the pitcher. It struck Gibson squarely on the right leg that he had just planted on the mound. The ball caromed around the infield for the first Pittsburgh hit of the day, as Bauman sprinted out from the dugout to check on him. "The leg was surprisingly numb at that point," Gibson noted. "I really couldn't feel anything." When Gibson told Bauman that he could continue, the trainer sprayed his shin with a freezing compound to dull any subsequent pain, and then trotted off the field. Gibson had figured that he had only suffered "a hell of a contusion," as he put it, but beyond that he expected to continue to play through the pain — just as brother Josh had taught him when he was growing up in Omaha. Next up was Willie Stargell, whom Gibson walked. After Mazeroski popped out, Gibson ran the count full on first baseman Donn Clendenon. Going for the strikeout on the 3–2 pitch, Gibson tried to put a little extra behind his ball. When his right leg hit the ground, his whole body collapsed in a quivering mass of agony. He went crashing to the ground in a crumpled heap, bringing down what many feared to be the Cardinals' pennant hopes with him. Gibson had snapped the small fibula bone about four inches above the ankle, which was discovered minutes later as he was rushed off to Jewish Hospital in St. Louis for x-rays. Just two innings after the cataclysmic event, Cepeda's homer that gave the Cardinals a 3–2 lead in the sixth was tempered with the bad news that reached the ballpark from the hospital's examination room. "The monkey's on somebody's back now," a forlorn Shannon muttered, who was nonetheless doing his best to try and celebrate his twenty-eighth birthday that night. "Somebody has to pick us up." Once again Schoendienst would turn to Briles, the swing-man on the pitching staff, to bolster the starting group in the absence of the ace. And now, the immediate, necessary return of Washburn to the rotation became all the more important. Briles would eventually squander Cepeda's homer and take the loss on the evening, part of a Cardinals relief corps that allowed four runs over the last four innings to drop the contest 6–4. Interestingly, Pittsburgh manager Harry Walker — one of the Cardinals heroes from their 1946 World Series victory over the Red Sox — would last only two more games (both of which were losses to the Braves) as he was fired with a 42–42 record for the season. Walker, however, would then be hired as the batting coach of the Houston Astros less than two weeks later.

Initial reports suggested that Gibson would be out anywhere from six weeks to two months; but in reality no one knew, not even the doctors. It could be sooner, or it could be much, much later. There was a feeling of "morbidity" in the St. Louis locker room, as Wilks described it, as the players gazed over towards the locker of Gibson, where he sat with a dejected head between his knees after returning from the hospital, a mound of plaster wrapped around his right leg and crutches at his side as reporters — who normally hounded the pitcher for a storyline — kept a respectful distance from him this night. Years later, Maxvill would tell *The New Yorker* magazine, "That was the most extraordinary thing I ever saw in baseball — Gibby pitching to those batters [Stargell, Mazeroski, and Clendenon] with a broken leg. Everyone who was there that day remembered it afterward, for always, and every young pitcher who came onto our club while Gibson was still with us was told about it. We didn't have too many pitchers turning up with upset stomachs or hangnails on our team after that."

An injury that did not make as many headlines as Gibson's — but nearly as important — was Javier re-aggravating a lingering hip pointer the night before, a stinger that had troubled him since spring training. It affected all aspects of his game, including the double-play pivot that had become routine with the smooth combination he had developed with Maxvill. Furthermore, the club was still without the services of Flood, who went on the disabled list July 6 with his shoulder injury.

The standings after the games on July 15 still showed the Cardinals in first place; but now, an ominous feeling of trouble appeared to loom on the horizon. Their main piece of artillery had been disabled, and his return was indefinite.

	W	L	Pct.	GB
St. Louis	51	34	.600	—
Chicago	47	38	.552	4
Cincinnati	49	40	.550	4
San Francisco	47	39	.546	4.5
Atlanta	44	39	.530	6
Pittsburgh	42	40	.512	7.5
Philadelphia	40	42	.487	9.5
Los Angeles	36	48	.428	14.5
Houston	34	52	.395	17.5
New York	32	50	.390	17.5

Gibson put Clemente in his own personal class with Ernie Banks of the Cubs—he did not want much to do with either one of them, and had no problem firing a close one at both. This feeling had existed before the Pirates outfielder struck Gibson in the leg with the line drive. "Clemente was similar to Banks to the degree that he would never shut up," Gibson claimed. "but I threw at him for a more substantial reason. As he and Bill White and others found out, I simply couldn't allow batters to lean across the plate." Gibson did not feel the broken leg was as serious as the fractured ankle he had suffered back in 1962. So despite the doctors' reports, he felt confident that he could return to the mound sooner than later. But a presumed quick return did not change the fact that he was still among the most competitive of all people walking the earth at the time, and was not one to be happy about being incapacitated in a leg cast during the middle of a baseball season—for any length of time. "The ache was not in my leg," he recounted, "but in my whole being. It's good form, I know, and standard practice for a ballplayer to say that he can't stand being out of commission, but believe me, I *couldn't* stand it. There was a pennant to be won, and I was hobbling around with crutches and a _____ cast." Doc Middleman fit him with a walking cast, so that he could continue to throw on the side. And to fend off the nagging questions about the progress of his broken leg, he soon would hang a sign around his neck with prepared answers to the usual questions. The sign read a simple list of answers, in which Gibson used a varying number of exclamation points to address the most frequently-asked questions on the list:

—Yes, it's off!!! [the permanent cast]
—No, it doesn't hurt!
—I'm not supposed to walk on it for one week!!
—I don't know how much longer!
—Ask Doc Bauman!
—Ask Doc Middleton!

Beyond the pain in his limb and the "ache in his whole being," as he put it, it was part of a subtle resentment that Gibson was developing about being in the center of attention. He simply wanted a measure of privacy, and he often expressed it in no uncertain terms. "One of the worst things about being in the limelight is trying to go somewhere and enjoy yourself without being bothered," he complained. "Your steak gets cold and you can't even go to the restroom without someone asking for an autograph. Ninety-nine out of a hundred want to talk about only one thing, baseball, and not many of them know much about it. It doesn't make for very interesting conversation." Some of his teammates viewed him as very inward and guarded, and via the media, much of the general public was getting that impression as well. Thus, despite the injury keeping him from helping the Cardinals to the pennant for the time being, his temporary retreat from the bright lights of the center stage may have helped Gibson in the long run of the 1967 season, as he would return hungrier than ever.

Gibson's dilemma was simply part of the diversion that baseball created for the public eye in the summer of 1967. For on the same night that he was injured, a riot had broken out in the racially-divided city of Detroit, only a prelude to more intense violence that the city would endure just days later. Similar riots had been occurring in cities across the country during the early summer of '67, including Tampa on June 11, Buffalo on June 27, and Newark on July 13.

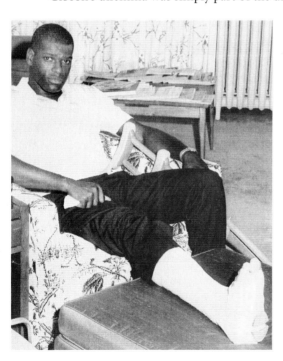

Bob Gibson attempts to relax at home with the broken leg he suffered when a line drive off the bat of the Pirates' Roberto Clemente hit him on July 15, 1967. (*St. Louis Globe-Democrat* / Archives of the St. Louis Mercantile Library)

When the Tigers and Yankees played in Detroit a week later on Sunday, July 23, the baseball world had been mourning the death of Jimmie Foxx the previous evening, the great slugger of the Philadelphia A's from the 1930s who in 1967 ranked only behind Ruth, Aaron, and Mays on the all-time home run list. Not far from the ballpark, Detroit police were called to break up an illegal tavern and gambling ring that had been functioning on Twelfth Street. All 82 people inside the small building were declared to be under arrest. When the perpetrators at the blind pig (as such establishments were called) were hauled out of the building by the officers, local blacks tried to block their path. The police were able to escort the perpetrators out of the area, but as soon the squad cars had left the scene, a window was smashed at a nearby clothing store as rampant rioting and looting commenced. Soon, some fans sitting in the upper deck at Tiger Stadium (at the time called Briggs Stadium) could see smoke billowing off in the distance, the source of which was unknown to them at the time. Later, Tigers pitcher Mickey Lolich — who had worked the first game of the double header against the Yankees that day — had already driven to his home in the northern Detroit suburbs when he received word that his 191st Michigan National Guard unit was being activated that same night, assigned to guard a public works supply building near the origin of the trouble on Twelfth Street. Lolich was one of 8,000 Guardsmen who would be activated to pacify Detroit over the next 48 hours. His teammate, Willie Horton, arrived in the middle of the chaos to plead with the crowd for calm; the violence, unfortunately, would only spread further. Even when word of the destruction reached the city's television stations, reporters were directed to downplay the event or not mention it at all, in an attempt to keep other parts of the city from being infected. The rampage continued throughout the early morning hours of Monday the 24th, and would surface to varying degrees throughout the following week. It was first announced that the Tigers' game with Baltimore on Tuesday would be postponed, but then the rest of the series was soon moved to Baltimore — a decision that made most of the Detroit players angry. "Moving the games to Baltimore and forcing a lot of our players to leave their families in that mess back home was one of the worst decisions I've ever heard of," Tigers pitcher Denny McLain told the press. McLain would proceed to shut out the Orioles 4–0 in one of the transplanted contests on July 27. "A man's family comes before anything, even baseball." McLain told his wife (who was the daughter of former Indians shortstop Lou Boudreau) to go stay at her parents' house in Chicago. Being from Chicago himself, McLain made plans to meet her there the following week, when the Tigers would arrive to play the White Sox.

The city of Detroit had been figuratively and literally encircled and quarantined from the rest of the world. "We're stuck down here," one downtown office worker said in a phone interview in the early morning hours on Tuesday. He was not planning to go back to his home in the suburbs any time soon. "There's no way to get out. Downtown is surrounded. I'm not going to try to get through any of that out there." Scattered individuals from the unruly mob had broken into weapon shops, and were posting themselves as snipers atop buildings with .22 caliber rifles, recklessly aiming down below at any uniform that resembled that of a police officer.

Smaller but similarly-dangerous scenes had broken out in other Michigan cities during the week as well, including Grand Rapids, Flint, Saginaw, and Pontiac, and also outside the state with incidents of violence in Toledo, South Bend, and Chicago. Before long, police in Detroit were able to round up the snipers with little difficulty. Late on the 26th, as army helicopters hovered over the city during a rainstorm to protect officers and soldiers on the ground, Michigan governor George Romney lifted the curfew that he had imposed on Detroit three days earlier. Romney also authorized the resumption of gasoline sales that had been halted in an effort to prevent further acts of arson. The pumping of gas into portable containers was still forbidden, however, as was the sale of liquor. In surveying the scene, Romney stated that "as far as I can determine, rebuilding this city physically is going to be a lot easier than rebuilding it socially."

It has been claimed by some that Romney initially hesitated to call for federal help in the situation, as he had been a political foe of President Johnson. Ultimately, Johnson would deploy the Third Brigade of the 82nd Airborne unit from nearby Selfridge Air Force Base, twenty miles from Detroit, to assist. When the smoke cleared on the 27th, 43 people had been killed and another 1,200 injured in the preceding days. The wave of insanity hastened the downfall of Detroit mayor Joseph Cavanagh, who was accused by some of sitting by idly and not preventing the situation in the first place. The riot in Detroit, mirrored with another similar outburst in Washington, D.C., just a week later, was a microcosm of the social unrest that continued to grip the world in the 1960s. On August 5, more violence erupted in the smaller cities of Wichita, Kansas, and Elgin, Illinois, in which a total of fifteen people were injured, five of them police officers. In Elgin, three people were arrested in the firebombing destruction of a downtown Sears and Roebuck store, a lumberyard, bakery, and a furniture business. The perpetrators were arrested by three o'clock in the morning, as new mayor E.C. Alft issued an emergency curfew. The domestic strife was still being compounded by the on-going war in Vietnam, a conflict which saw the Chinese presence step up dramatically in the summer months of 1967 as Johnson committed more American troops to the region.

Tension never seemed to grip the Cardinals, however, immune to the troubles of society in their playful world as the diverse lot of players always found a way to entertain themselves. On a trip to Atlanta at the end of July, the players were waiting on the team bus outside of Fulton County Stadium for a ride back to the hotel. When minutes had passed with no driver showing, which then turned into a half-hour, the general annoyance and grumbling on the bus continued to grow. Hoerner suddenly charged to the front, as the other players looked at his determined face, knowing that he had something drastic in mind. The pitcher planted himself in the driver's seat to the great delight of the most of the team, while a few had a fearful look. After a couple of minutes of struggling, Hoerner managed to put the vehicle into drive, and inched the bus forward as it shook—first from the rough shift of gears, and then loud cheers were heard from the back. Afraid that something awful was about to happen, Flood, Washburn, and Hughes scrambled out of their seats and out the bus door, and went to look for a taxicab. Schoendienst, Brock, and a couple of others were not aboard either, as they had exited moments earlier to search for the regular driver. Hoerner took off, and was able to make a couple of laps around the ballpark, following the circular driveway that orbited the stadium. He finally made his way out onto the freeway as the bus continued to rock with laughter and cheers. The cheers grew louder with each passing mile — especially from Cepeda, who was hollering, "GO! GO! GO!" The hollering quieted down when the bus passed a couple of police cars, but once a safe distance beyond the troopers had been achieved, the cheering began once again. At one other frightening point, Hoerner—of course not having calculated the height of the bus before leaving the ballpark—sped towards a low-hanging overpass, as all the passengers aboard were terrified and assumed crash positions. "From the stadium to the hotel, there's this one sign that says, 'Clearance, Ten Feet, Ten Inches,'" Tolan remembered. "I don't think bus drivers took that lane, but we did. Joe just zipped us right through there." Having safely squeaked the bus under the overpass, Hoerner then "skillfully" (as he would later put it) maneuvered the vehicle for the remainder of the ten-minute trip, avoiding any mishaps until the final hundred yards when he knocked over a sign after exiting the interstate. The bus screeched to a halt in front of the hotel lobby as the players piled out. Hoerner grabbed his key quickly and headed for his room, expecting some sort of reprimand from the club, the hotel, or the bus company. "The bus company picked up the bus in the morning," traveling secretary Leo Ward said simply, "and the fellow I talked to apologized for not having a driver at the park to bring us home."

Flood, who had just come off the disabled list after recovering from his shoulder injury, was angry at Hoerner for pulling the stunt, saying that he put the entire team's lives—or at least, their professional livelihoods—at risk. "We had money riding on that bus," Flood said. "Money, that is, in the form of a pennant—something that we were all working for, and something bad could have happened." Instead of a lecture, however, Hoerner and the Cardinals received an apology from the bus company for the tardy driver, while Schoendienst was just grateful that the team arrived unscathed. It wound up innocently being one of those amusing stories that teams share, one of the million moments that occur on a bus, a plane, or a dugout bench that builds camaraderie among men spending a summer together in the highs and lows of a baseball season.

That togetherness kept the Cardinals in first place through July, through Gibson's injury, and through the unstable situation occurring in American cities over the course of the month. The night before and into the day of the Detroit riots, the resurgent Cubs had once again climbed to the top and tied the Cardinals for first, but St. Louis was able to pull away once again as the Redbirds won eight out of nine games at the end of the month (including the taking of two of three from Chicago at Busch Stadium, a sweep of the Braves during Hoerner's adventurous bus navigation, and the opener of another series against the Cubs at Wrigley Field on July 31). McCarver remained as sultry as the weather, temporarily seizing the league lead in batting from Cepeda with a .355 average on July 18 before relinquishing it back. The two had been running away in a two-horse race before the recent onslaught of Rusty Staub of Houston, who was also closing in on the top spot. "I'd much rather hit .240 and win the pennant than bat .370 and finish seventh," said McCarver, who had recorded a .274 mark in 1966. Then, with a smile, he added, "Of course, you don't strive to hit .240." Shannon had also improved at the plate, logging 50 RBIs by July 25 which, despite having missed 20 games, placed him second ahead of Brock (47) and behind Cepeda (70) for the club lead. Brock was still in the midst of his struggles, however, enduring another famine with a 1-for-24 spell despite notching 35 stolen bases. And Gibson's absence from the pitching staff became quite obvious, as the Cardinals did not receive a complete-game performance from one of their starters from July 7 to July 28, at which point Hughes ended the string with a full effort in a 9–1 win over the Braves. Yet, even though the club had suffered substantial personnel setbacks, a collection of substitutes was picking up the slack. The injuries to Gibson, Flood, and Javier had been filled more than adequately by Briles, Tolan, Gagliano, and others (Cosman, however, had been loaned on July 16 to the Mets organization as part of the trade for Jack Lamabe, which in turn made room on the roster for Flood when he came off the disabled list on July 27). In addition, improvement from the bullpen contributed greatly to the Cards' hot streak at the end of July, at which point the standings showed them stretching their lead over the Cubs to four and a half games, and further distancing themselves from the rest of the National League:

	W	L	Pct.	GB
St. Louis	62	40	.607	—
Chicago	58	45	.563	4.5
Atlanta	52	47	.525	8.5
Cincinnati	55	50	.523	8.5

	W	L	Pct.	GB
San Francisco	54	50	.519	9
Pittsburgh	49	51	.490	12
Philadelphia	48	51	.484	12.5
Los Angeles	46	55	.455	15.5
Houston	46	59	.438	17.5
New York	39	61	.390	22

Even so, Schoendienst was far from being satisfied. "We've got to go .500 on the road from now on, and play .600 baseball at home the rest of the year," Red proclaimed. Keeping the laughter and looseness going, it would soon become commonplace for Cepeda, in the locker room after a Cardinals game — win or lose — to stand on top of what was called the "money trunk" (where players stored their valuables during the game) and lead the team in a series of shouts and cheers. Cepeda claimed to have over 2,500 record albums at his home (and 5,000 more at his home in Puerto Rico, he insisted), and sometimes he would play one in the clubhouse at random as an impromptu victory march. He had been nicknamed "Cha-Cha," a moniker given to him by former Giants pitcher Johnny Antonelli, who once had caught him doing some Latin dancing by himself. And when the Cardinals had completed their sweep of the Braves in Atlanta on July 30 with Willis' 7–5 win in relief of Jaster, powered by Maris' three RBIs, Cepeda — even though having endured an 0-for-5 night himself — had everyone laughing in the locker room as he rose on top of the money trunk once again and began speaking in his broken English (and broken Spanish).

"A week ago, the Braves beat us two and talk about pennant," he yelled. "But we showed them they are not playing the Mets or Houston.

"We are the Birds—*El Birdos!*"

"El Birdos! El Birdos!" his mates all yelled in reply, which became the official battle cry that continued through their shower, onto the bus (this time with the Atlanta bus company providing a professional driver), and back to the hotel as they crept along in stalled traffic. The three-game, series-record crowd for Fulton County Stadium had totaled nearly 125,000 and left the Braves' supporters confronting the fact their team now stood eight-and-a-half games behind St. Louis. The Cardinals themselves were suddenly caught up in this new-found enthusiasm and fellowship — seemingly a modern Latin Jazz version of the old Gas House Gang spirit. "I almost hate to mention it because it sounds high-schoolish," Gibson would recall years later. "I know we are professionals and that rah-rah stuff is not supposed to apply to us. And I know one more thing — I know that every player who came over from another team — all of them said the same thing. They have never been with a team that had as much spirit as our team." And, in the Gas House Gang spirit of Pepper Martin's Musical Mudcat band, El Birdos of 1967 had their own amateur collection of clubhouse musicians as well. Briles and Hughes would often pick away at the guitar (while Hughes added in some Arkansas yodeling as well), Spiezio massaged the accordion (his self-proclaimed stage name was the "Joliet Jolter" when he toured local clubs with Briles), and Gibson and Flood strummed away at the ukulele in fashioning an extemporaneous orchestra that always kept the others laughing and cheering. Briles was so fond of music, in fact, that he dragged his heavy 1960s tape recorder on the road to play his jazz favorites—long before the parade of MP3 players that is seen from sports teams traveling today—and entertainment that Briles preferred to the hotel room television. Soon, "El Birdos" was crafted into verses, and turned into an officially-recorded song. Sales of audiotapes of the song were brisk in the St. Louis area; Ray Cooley of Ackerman Buick-Opel, in fact, offered prospective customers a free El Birdos record just for coming into the dealership.

But while harmless locker room antics had been as old as the game itself, players in the 1960s—in reflecting the demonstrative feelings of the era—had become what some considered to be more inappropriately animated in their on- and off-field actions. The small, isolated scenes of expression in 1967 were further evidence to some citizens of baseball players reflecting the persona of the times, asserting their extended independence and revealing their rambunctious behaviors, just as their fellow young people had been simultaneously doing in anti-war demonstrations and other activities. During the Great Depression in the 1930s, the Gas House Gang Cardinals—along with the rest of the players on major league rosters who were fortunate enough to have jobs—had to suffer through massive salary cuts in conjunction with the difficult financial times (such as Durocher in his dealings with Breadon), just as their brethren in the business world or any other profession had to endure. Now, the cultural shift of the 1960s had placed an emphasis on more personal expression and a call for equality for the working class—and in baseball terms, the working class referred to the players, long seen as subjugated under the reserve clause which the owners held dear. The clause, which in essence kept the major league player as property of his club indefinitely through his career, came under official attack by the Major League Baseball Players' Association on August 1. In addition to calling for a minimum salary of $12,000 (to be raised from the current rate of $7,000), the Players Association also forwarded the following list of demands to the major league offices:

- That no player's salary could be cut more than 10 percent from the previous year (current stipulations allowed for a maximum 25 percent reduction)

- A possible reduction in the 162-game schedule
- Representation in national television financial negotiations, including the "Game of the Week" telecasts
- Increases in meal money, spring training allowances, and moving expenses
- Binding rules on the scheduling of day double headers, day-night double headers and "getaway" day games
- Impartial arbitration in player-management disputes

The issues were presented by the players in a stance of proposition to the owners. "No threats are being leveled," assured Marvin Miller. "This policy statement is a guide to negotiations with major league club owners, but we do feel that many matters, including minimum salaries, have gone far too long without action ... in addition to placing the player in the untenable position of being required to accept the club's proposed salary or leaving organized baseball, the reserve clause is of doubtful legality." When some argued that giving the players such power would ruin the game, Miller disagreed. He guaranteed the public that the MLBPA was not trying to turn everything in the game on its head. "We find no validity in the predictions that chaos will result from any change whatsoever. The solution of this problem lies neither in a sudden elimination of the reserve clause nor in the preservation of the status quo." The main target in the players' crosshairs was the immense amount of television revenue that was entering the game. For three days later, John Fetzer, president of the Television Committee for Major League Baseball, would announce a new $50 million, three-year contract with the National Broadcasting Company (NBC). This contract gave exclusive rights to NBC for transmittal of the World Series, the All-Star Game, and continued coverage of the Game of the Week from the 1969 through 1971 seasons. As the owners met separately in Chicago on August 3, however, most of the discussion turned into angry debate, fueled by the American League's unanimous desire to go to a two-division format for 1968. The National League owners would hear none of it. "We feel the pennant should be decided in the traditional manner," Giles, the National League president, said in support of his cadre. "We would object if the American League went ahead alone on this. Our main objection is we didn't have notice of this, and it needs study." Originally, the meeting of the owners was foreseen as a formality, a quick session twenty-minute meeting to ratify certain proposals put forth earlier by Commissioner William Eckert, such as the awarding of the 1968 All-Star Game to the Astrodome in Houston. When the divisional split was proposed, however, the minor squabble turned into a four-hour affair.

Ferguson Jenkins beat Briles in the second game at Wrigley Field to open the month of August and dismantle the Cards' six-game winning streak, with the Cubs winning their 59th game almost two months earlier than they had reached that mark in 1966. Outside the ballpark on the corner of Addison and Clark, optimistic vendors were selling buttons that read, "Chicago Cubs, World Champions, 1967." But the Redbirds got promptly back on track the following day as Carlton (10–6) and Hughes (10–3) swept a double header from the North Siders 4–2 and 7–1 before the biggest paid crowd at Wrigley in four years (37,164). Hughes, while pitching his second straight complete game (which constituted the Cardinals' only two in the past month before Carlton performed the feat in the second game), also posted seven strikeouts that matched him with Gibson for the club lead with 119. At the plate, Flood was batting an even .500 (14 for 28) since coming off the disabled list, raising his overall season average to .322. Also contributing was a rejuvenated Brock, who had hit safely in his last eleven games, including six hits in the double header. He credited his turn-around to disposing of his efforts to try for the long ball. "I'm just not a home run hitter," Brock said plainly, thinking that attempts to be one had affected his performance at the plate in the middle portion of the '67 season. "It's still a thrill — and a surprise — when I hit one. My job is to get on base." It was Cepeda who really impressed Durocher, however, a player whom the Cubs' manager had an opportunity to claim in a trade from the Giants before he finally landed in St. Louis in May of 1966. "If Cepeda had come with us, he would have hit a zillion home runs," Leo mourned, even though Cubs owner Phil Wrigley had just provided the manager with a new two-year contract extension. "With the closer fences here, he'd have maybe 60 home runs, maybe enough for a new record."

The disheartened, second-place Cubbies were now five and a half games back, prompting Wilks to write in his *Post-Dispatch* column, "Chicago hasn't had so many ashes to clean up since Old Lady O'Leary finally decided to buy milk out of bottles." The Redbirds had batted nearly .300 — and Brock, nearly .400 — on this most recent road trip, in which they had gone 6–1.

The double header sweep on August 2 was the start of another winning streak, this one running to five contests (and making it 13 of their last 15) that included a three-game sweep of the Reds back at St. Louis that lengthened their lead to eight and a half games beyond the next closest contender, the San Francisco Giants. The Reds' opener on August 4 showcased a much-needed 5–0 win for Jaster (7–5), his first victory since July 14 and only his second complete game on the year. It was also Jaster's first shutout of the season, and also his first blanking of an opponent since he turned the trick five times against Los Angeles in 1966. The following evening, a night-game record crowd of 48,019 (just 75 spectators shy of the overall stadium record) at Busch watched Brock extend his new hitting streak to twelve (which would continue to thirteen the next night), en route to a 4–3 triumph for Willis out of the bullpen in relief of Washburn. When asked by reporters how he had shaken his slump (in addition to avoiding swings for the fences), Brock pointed across the locker room from his stool. "That man over there," he said in waving a finger at little-used catcher John Romano. Romano had noticed that Brock was gripping the bat too tightly, causing a myriad of problems when he approached the ball. "Louie couldn't figure out why he kept fouling off pitches to the opposite field," Romano explained. "It's a matter of relaxing. Ernie Banks does it by tapping his fingers on the bat just before swinging. Orlando Cepeda relaxes by rocking at the plate." Romano suggested Brock take a looser grip on the bat, and since he tried it, Brock had gone 22 for 47 (.468) and had raised his season average from .270 to .293. "When a man gets desperate, he'll even discuss hitting with a .130 hitter," Romano joked about himself. Briles (6–5) and Willis combined to cap off the domination of Cincinnati, 3–2, in the final game of the series behind Cepeda's twentieth homer, a long one into the upper deck of the left field stands at Busch. It was also Orlando's 85th RBI, which continued to lead the major leagues.

The losses pushed the once league-leading Reds to fifth place and eleven games back. Sensing that the Cardinals were running away with the pennant, the Cincinnati club now started planning for the future. In doing so, they finally unveiled a hot new catching prospect named John Bench from their minor league system. Nonetheless, their situation was not as dire nor as perplexing as the defending champion Dodgers. The men from Hollywood were the next guests in Busch Stadium, who somehow managed to take two of three from the Cards without Drysdale, but still found themselves eighteen games behind the pace when the series ended on August 9. Drysdale, winner of only eight games on the year, had suffered a re-aggravation of a back injury as well as a fractured finger on his glove hand, ailments that most figured would have the star right-hander incapacitated for the remainder of the season. He had first hurt his back on July 27 in pitching against the Mets, when during the game he worsened the injury by sliding into third base. Despite the fact that Drysdale would be able to return to the mound on August 9 against the Cardinals, it all but spelled the end of a most disappointing season for the Dodgers, their pennant-winning club of 1966 led by Drysdale and the departed Koufax and Wills a distant memory.

The Cardinals, meanwhile, only wanted no disturbances in their progress on the field. "The boys have to remain themselves and keep loose," warned hitting coach Sisler about maintaining the large lead in the perilous final weeks of the season. "They don't have to look ahead to a certain series. Of course, they're thinking about a pennant. It's all over town. The coaches' job is to keep the boys calm and keep them from pressing." Sisler then reminded everyone of early August from ten years ago, when the Cards held first place but quickly went on a nine-game losing skid, surrendering the top spot to the Milwaukee Braves who ultimately took the flag. But Sisler also pointed out that it would take more than a nine-game skid to overtake this Cardinals club, as the '57 version held only a half-game lead on Milwaukee. Such ominous tidings had presented themselves in the first two contests against the Dodgers, as Los Angeles defeated Carlton and Hughes to snap the St. Louis hot streak. To make matters worse, Cepeda was ejected from the second contest for uttering profanities at plate umpire Stan Landes, an action that would cost him an additional two-game suspension and a $100 fine. Cepeda had allegedly used a particular phrase — a specific arrangement of words that a poster placed inside the locker room warned players not to use — that carried an automatic suspension. Cepeda denied saying it, but other umpires Al Barlick and Augie Donatelli confirmed that he did. In essence, Cepeda would miss three full games, as his ejection took place in the first inning. It took the Dodger-killer Jaster to correct things in the finale against none other than Drysdale, a 3–2 win that was credited to Willis for his one inning of work in the top of the eleventh. Two of the Cardinals runs came via solo home runs by Brock (his fifteenth) and the first of the season for Bressoud, who was starting the game at short for the injured Maxvill and who had entered the game just 6 for 49 at the plate for the season. Shannon ended things in the bottom of the eleventh, when he doubled off Dodgers reliever Phil Regan and moved to third on walks to Maris and Gagliano. Then Bressoud, displaying a great penchant for drama in one lone evening, looped a foul pop up down the right field line. It was chased down by Los Angeles first baseman Wes Parker who, although the fly not being very long, feared that Shannon might try to tag and score. Parker hurried a throw towards home plate that one-hopped catcher Jim Campanis and skipped all the way to the backstop, actually allowing Shannon to strut home easily with the game-winning tally. "Drysdale showed a lot of guts," Schoedienst commented afterwards, as everyone knew that the Dodgers' starting pitcher could hardly stand up straight with his injured back.

The Dodgers' triumphs set the stage for two of the most important series of the year to date for St. Louis, a four-game test against the Giants followed by three with the Cubs, a week which held the National League sway in the balance. San Francisco had relinquished second place back to the Cubs, standing at nine games behind St. Louis with Chicago a half-game ahead of the Giants as the current leading contender. The stadium had been vacated for the weekend by the other St. Louis Cardinals— those of the National Football League, who were on their way to Shreveport, Louisiana, to play an exhibition game against the brand-new expansion franchise, the New Orleans Saints. The Saints, losers in their first game with a 16–7 preseason loss to the Los Angeles Rams the previous week, would be facing the Cardinals' second-year, 23-year-old quarterback, Jim Hart, who provided the Big Red with promise for the future. NFL commissioner Pete Rozelle, meanwhile, was in the process

Orlando Cepeda (30) is ejected in the first inning of a game against the Dodgers on August 8, 1967, at Busch Stadium for arguing balls and strikes with home plate umpire Stan Landes (not shown). Attempting to restrain Cepeda from further contact with Landes are (left to right) umpire Mel Steiner, Cardinals manager Red Schoendienst, umpire Augie Donatelli, Tim McCarver, Dick Sisler, and Joe Schultz. (*St. Louis Globe-Democrat* / Archives of the St. Louis Mercantile Library)

of considering changing the name of the championship game between the professional leagues to something other than the "Super Bowl," as it was coming to be called. Other titles being considered were the "Merger Bowl," the "Summit Bowl," and simply "The Game" (it was currently called officially the "AFL-NFL World Championship Game" — however, as one writer put it, "By the time anyone could get all that out, television would have missed the first commercial. So, the label 'Super Bowl' became popular").

With thoughts still on baseball for the citizens of St. Louis, however, the South Side Kiwanis thought that they had provided good karma for the Giants series, as they presented Cepeda with an award as "The Most Valuable Cardinal of 1967," even though it was a bit early in the calendar for such a designation. And although he would have to sit out the first game of the series with his suspension, a banner hung from the upper deck of Busch Stadium greeting him upon his return: it read "Vamos El Birdos!" Loosely translated, the message trumpeted, "Let's Go Cardinals!" In the locker room, Cepeda's teammates jokingly went up to him and re-introduced themselves.

Cepeda's counterpart, the powerful Willie McCovey, provided the difference in the first game. The strong first baseman launched a long three-run homer to the seats in right field in providing Mike McCormick a 5–2 decision. McCormick, who had shut out the Cardinals six weeks earlier at Busch, won in spite of the various heroics of Brock. The outfielder pushed his hitting streak to seventeen games with an infield hit in the first inning, then promptly stole his thirty-seventh base of the season, and later robbed Willie Mays in the fifth with a diving catch of a line drive in the left-center field gap, a play in which Brock was "parallel to the ground" and "slid about 20 feet" after catching the ball from the wet turf that had endured a pre-game drizzle, according to reports.

In between his at-bats, Cepeda was like a caged tiger in the dugout, pacing back and forth while staring angrily out onto the field. Like Gibson, he could not stand being out of the lineup, and champed for his opportunity to strike a blow, particularly against his old team. He appeared at the plate in the sixth inning against Gaylord Perry with the game tied and two outs. Maris was on first, the product of his own hustle as well as that of Flood. Maris had tapped a grounder to second baseman Hal Lanier, who in turn flipped to the shortstop and former Cardinal Dick Groat at the bag in pursuit of a double play. The combination of Flood going in hard at second and Maris going through hard at first allowed Roger to reach, however, and kept the inning alive. The crowd then revved with excitement, as the big man approached the box with an opportunity. Cepeda soon found a mistake from Perry, and deposited one far into the left field stands, staking Briles and the Cards to a 2–0 lead as the premises were whipped into a frenzy. Briles, with perfect help from Hoerner, was sparkling in getting his seventh win, 2–1, pitching into the eighth inning while allowing one unearned run in what Muffett called "his best performance of the season." Russo noted that it was only the fifth start for Briles after 35 straight trips out of the bullpen, as the young pitcher continued to fill the Gibson void strongly. While it was Briles' first major league win over the Giants, it was not the first time he had faced the San Francisco outfit. As a sophomore at Santa Clara University in 1961, Briles had pitched five shutout innings against the Giants, a performance in which he allowed one bunt hit, and had struck out Mays and McCovey. "That was my biggest game ever," Briles would later say of his feat. Additionally, his father had passed away two weeks before the game. "That game was for my dad." When Briles' school days were over, it was the Giants who offered him his first pro bonus of $10,000. Briles turned it down and after playing one year of semi-pro ball, signed with the Cardinals for five times that amount.

After the Redbirds had beaten the frustrated Perry for the fourth straight time on the year, the rejuvenated hero Cepeda was of course leading the cheers on top of the money trunk once again, hollering in between bites of a large watermelon he was holding in both hands. "Da me cinco," Cepeda said to Javier's six-year-old son Julian, Jr., in the locker room. Other players soon followed suit in the English version, telling the future second baseman to "Gimmee five."

The night of August 12 saw the largest crowd in the history of the young ballpark, as a total of 50,797 jammed into their seats at Busch to watch Lamabe arrive in relief and beat the Giants 3–2. The overflow gathering barely surpassed the previous mark of 50,763 that had been recorded at a Big Red Cardinals' football game the previous year. Leading the offensive charge this time was Flood, who in recent days had gone from .304 to .330 since coming off the disabled list — thanks to a .450 (27-for-60) clip after getting fully healthy on July 28. Lamabe had been working with a distracted mind, as he and his wife, Janet, had been expecting their first child, and both were hoping that the magical moment would occur with the Cardinals still in St. Louis on the long current homestand. But a new child and new-found major league success weren't the only changes occurring in the Lamabes' lives. Before a game a short time later, the players crowded around the television in the locker room as they watched Janet appear on the game show *Eye Guess*. Navigating successfully through the contest, she walked away with a new car, oven, stereo, luggage, and an expensive collection of wines.

"Hey Jack!" one of the players yelled, "you're going to have to use your World Series check to pay the taxes on all that stuff!"

And over the past few weeks, Lamabe had been spreading more than just pitching, game-show, and father-to-be tips around the clubhouse. He and Hughes had also had recently taught Gagliano and Jaster the "art" of chewing tobacco, a habit which was, in reality, practiced by relatively few major leaguers at the time. "When things get a little tense on the bench," Hughes said, "Gag and Jaster will now come up and ask for a chew. For me, I started on the stuff when I was twelve years old. I remember my first time — I was on the golf course, and I got sick as a dog. There was a bamboo thicket on one hole, and I went into the middle of it and lost my lunch. I didn't want anybody to see me.

"It was a few years before I came back to it, which I did to keep my mouth and throat from getting dry. Atlanta is the only town in the league where you can get a good plug. Nice and soft — not hard. Some plugs are so hard they can make your jaws sore." Jaster, like Gagliano, denied that it was a habit. "It's just something to do," he said nonchalantly.

The beatings sent the Giants into fourth place, twelve games back of St. Louis, and the San Francisco media now began looking for scapegoats. Not even the usual sacred cows appeared to be now safe. For the first time in his career, Willie Mays was taking criticism about his declining skills in the field. He was eight for his last 57 after the series with Cardinals, and had batted only .211 with two home runs since the All-Star break as some were suggesting that he should consider stepping aside and let younger outfielders get some at-bats. "I'm not able to do everything as well and as often as I once did," he conceded, "but I still think I can do a pretty good job. I like to think that I can play three or four more years, but I wouldn't want to stay on if people were just feeling sorry for me and thought that I couldn't help the club." He was hitting .280 overall with 15 home runs, numbers that Mays felt would be judged better if posted by a lesser-caliber player. "A day game after a night game gets tougher all the time, and I just can't play double headers anymore," he continued. "I'll be all right if I can get a day or two off every now and then." By mid–August, he stood 360 hits shy of 3,000 for his career, and was now second to Ruth all-time in home runs with 557.

Groat, the former Cardinal and current Giant, was now convinced that the St. Louis club could not be caught in the standings. "The only way any team can catch them now is to do what we [the Cardinals] did in 1963, win 19 out of 20. The Cardinals aren't going to collapse — they have too many professionals who have been down this road before." This was Groat's assessment as he watched the Cards down the Giants again on August 13 by a score of 2–1, resulting in the eleventh victory in fifteen decisions for the stunning Hughes, even though the former Cardinal Sadecki held his old friends to only five hits. Keeping track from a distance in Chicago, Durocher added his worry about the Redbirds. "They're a balanced ball club," he pointed out about Schoendienst's unit. "They've proved that they can win without Gibson, and they're getting the breaks and making them, too." The Cubs were next as an offering, with the Redbirds beating them in three straight at Busch in two one-run games and one two-run contest. In the opener (a victory for Al Jackson), Flood skidded across the plate with the winning run in the ninth as the team rushed to greet him. Cepeda picked up the outfielder and hoisted him triumphantly into the air, nearly breaking Flood's back in the process.

Included in the victory party at home plate was Gibson, who now was able to throw lightly on the side but was still more in anguish from his inability to help the team than from the pain in his leg. That didn't stop the ribbing he continued to take from the other players, who showed no mercy in giving the competitor some flak. "Get out of the clubhouse!" Maxvill would holler at him. "Put on a uniform or get out! You're eating up too much of our food spread after the game, and you're taking up valuable space on the training table!" Since Gibson went down with his broken leg, St. Louis had gone 23–11, and was an even more amazing 19–3 against winning ball clubs since July 23, which included San Francisco (3–1), Atlanta (5–0), Cincinnati (3–0), and Chicago (8–2). The six wins in the last seven games over the Giants and Cubs left the Cardinals thirty games above .500 for the first time on the year — and with their largest lead of the season — as the standings in the morning papers of August 17 showed:

	W	L	Pct.	GB
St. Louis	74	44	.627	—
Atlanta	62	53	.539	10.5
Cincinnati	64	55	.538	10.5
San Francisco	62	56	.525	12
Chicago	64	59	.520	12.5
Philadelphia	60	56	.517	13
Pittsburgh	56	63	.471	18.5
Los Angeles	51	65	.440	22
New York	49	69	.415	25
Houston	49	71	.408	26

The hot streak at home was all the more important in light of the fact the Cardinals were leaving on an 11-game road trip to the West. Keeping in step with hallowed traditions, Brock was still playing the song "Fistful of Dollars" on the stereo in the locker room after each win. The concept of money continued to swirl around the club, as newspaper men were always quick to point out their robust salaries. Butch Yatkeman, in fact, had written the following on the chalkboard of the locker room:

EL BIRDOS NEVER LOSE ON PAYDAY

And nobody dared to erase it.

Superstition, always prevalent among baseball players, was beginning to run rampant on the Cardinals — whether in dealing with on-field play, clubhouse music, money matters, milkshakes or any other number of things. When the milkshakes were working and Brock would have several good days in a row at the plate, he would try to parlay his luck by continuing to use the same bat — even after it had broken. Some painters were finishing some final touches on the one-year-old ballpark in St. Louis, and Brock borrowed some of their special tape to keep his magical stick in one piece; after a few more uses, it soon shattered into many. Other dietary customs beyond milkshakes took hold of the team as well after the Cards had strung together the streak. Trainer Bob Bauman was asked to continue making his tomato rice soup every day — the same broth he had made before the game when the streak had begun. Finally, when the players had become tired of the soup but were still winning, they decided instead to paint half of a baseball red, call it the "tomato rice soup ball," and use it for infield practice every day until the streak was over, only to be caught by Sisler when Cepeda threw it in the dugout at the start of an inning. When Cepeda mistakenly threw the tomato rice soup ball into the stands one day, he had to hustle after it and offer the fan two brand new baseballs in its place. "We're not superstitious," Bauman added. "We just like to change the pattern now and then when things go wrong."

While the Redbirds were threatening to run off and hide with the National League pennant, the Chicago White Sox had seen a large lead give way to a two-game deficit to the Minnesota Twins over in the American League, as the Sox lost pitchers Tommy John and Jim O'Toole to injuries. Also coming on strong were the Boston Red Sox, three games in back of the Twins on the dazzling pitching of Jim Lonborg. Unfortunately, the Boston pennant drive appeared to take a horrifying derailment two days later. Outfielder Tony Conigliaro was struck in left cheekbone on a pitch from the Angels' Jack Hamilton, nailing him just below the eye socket. While Conigliaro was recovering in Santa Maria Hospital in Cambridge, Massachusetts, for the rest of the season, the Red Sox were suddenly scrambling to find a replacement for their All-Star player. Meanwhile, a separate (but soon related) story was occurring with another American League franchise.

By mid–August Charles O. Finley, the wealthy, 50-year-old insurance man from Chicago, had convinced most people in the game — and most residents of Kansas City — that he was now ready to move the A's out of town, the team that he had owned for the past six years. "The 'O' is for owner," Finley would often say proudly and unabashedly. He made public his plans of having an outside consulting firm study which of the three cities of Oakland, Seattle, or Milwaukee would best suit his franchise for the future. This, of course, did not sit well with western Missouri taxpayers — particularly those of Jackson County, who had recently approved the $43 million bond for the construction of a new ballpark. Jackson County residents, in fact, were planning a night at Municipal Stadium to show their support for the players in the midst of their disdain for the owner. The A's were stuck in last place, seventeen games below .500 (52–69), as Finley attempted to shake things up — and a recent incident had given Finley cause, or so he thought. On a team flight, there had been reports of lewd behavior by pitcher Lew Krausse and first baseman-outfielder Ken "Hawk" Harrelson, neither of whom Finley had ever liked very much. On August 18 (the same day that Conigliaro was beaned), Krausse was fined $500 and suspended immediately for four days by Finley for "rowdyism and conduct unbecoming a major league player," while manager Alvin Dark was fired and Harrelson was given his outright release two days later — making him, in one sense, baseball's first free agent in the modern era. The remaining A's players had decided unanimously to write Commissioner Eckert to list their disputes with the owner. Meanwhile, many in the media wondered why Finley had waited over two weeks to impose punishment in the matter. The negative publicity about Finley was growing so strongly, in fact, that many potential markets for his major league franchise — including the city of Milwaukee — were not interested in his operation taking hold on their premises. Finley, meanwhile, staunchly announced that he would not make any decisions on moving the franchise until October 1. While Harrelson was out on his own, Krausse would receive a full hearing on the matter from Eckert the following month. The case caught the attention not only of the players union, but also of the National Labor Relations Board, which on September 7 would file an unfair practices charge against Finley, claiming that the owner "has threatened individual employees in an attempt to coerce them into withdrawing their impending grievances." This issue came to light when Krausse insisted that Finley had pressured him into signing a document, one which had Krausse agreeing that the fine and suspension were justified. Krausse then passed along the contents of the statement to the wire services, as well as the hometown newspaper, the *Kansas City Star* — an act that Krausse later regretted. "Before I signed that document, Finley looked at me and said, 'Lew, you want to play baseball, don't you?' Doesn't that sound like a threat?" While he could not correct that mistake, Krausse was most certain of his next move. "He's through scaring me," the pitcher said of Finley as the case went before baseball's highest office. "I love baseball and I owe a lot to it, but if that man doesn't trade me I'll hang up my glove. I don't want to play for Finley again. As soon as you think you can confide in him and trust him, he burns you." Krausse, however, would remain with the A's for two more seasons before finishing his career in 1974 after playing for other teams, including the Cardinals for one game the year before.

Sid Bordman, who covered the A's for the *Star*, was also on the plane when the alleged "rowdyism" took place, and would later claim that he witnessed no improper behavior by any of the A's personnel. The chartering of flights was a process that major league teams were only beginning to utilize by the mid–1960s, and the Trans World Airlines flight on which the supposed problems occurred was a commercial trip with non-A's passengers aboard. Bordman and witnesses went on to suggest that any recognizable trouble on the plane began when other passengers — not ballplayers — were unable to obtain liquor during the trip. Earlier, Finley had fined pitcher Jack Aker (who also happened to be the A's player representative to the MLBPA) for a curfew violation. The betrayed feelings of most A's fans in Kansas City were summed up by a local fan named Paul Grimsley, who sent this letter to the Kansas City newspapers:

This area has supported the Athletics very well, considering the frustrations brought upon us by Mr. Finley's threats of moving, complaints of stadium facilities, and so forth. Many of us believe that a great deal of the blame for the team's low percentage of wins compared to losses also can be laid at the door of Mr. Finley. A team's quality of performance is greatly affected by morale. Insecurity, upset [players], change of leadership, to name just a few, affect morale. Now it is being revealed that they are subjected to Gestapo tactics.

Grimsley was referring to Finley's handling of the incident on the plane, after which a team meeting was held and a virtual no-confidence vote was given about the owner. Or, as another fan in downtown Kansas City summarized the situation, "When you want to insult somebody around here, you just call him 'Mr. Finley.'" Harrelson, meanwhile, was released by Finley on August 20, and was not the least bit concerned about any commotion that he had caused. "When I sign with another team," Harrelson said with a laugh, "I'm going to send Charley Finley a dozen red American roses and a thank-you note. He's a menace to baseball." The unfolding scenario was becoming obvious; the Red Sox, with their sudden gap in the outfield, signed Harrelson immediately for a $75,000 bonus. In facing New York at Yankee Stadium the next day, Harrelson would homer in his first at-bat for Boston. While never becoming a superstar, Harrelson's personality made him popular with fans and the media alike. "He's skillful with golf sticks, a pool cue, a bowling ball, gin rummy, and other gimmicks and gadgets with which he's hustled a buck since he was a 17-year-old bridegroom," Broeg noticed. "He's the best golfing ballplayer, though he'd really like to be the best ball-playing golfer." One legendary story around the A's clubhouse had Harrelson losing $400 in a bowling match to a local competitor, then angrily throwing his bowling ball and shoes into a pond in disgust at the defeat. An hour later, Harrelson retrieved the ball and shoes, went back to the bowling alley, and promptly won back his $400 from another challengee. "I go into sports on a dare or as a lark," Harrelson described himself simply, "and I'm naturally good. A 'hot dog,' they call me, but I don't mind. They'll remember me." Back in 1959, Finley had spent $30,000 to sign the 18-year-old Harrelson.

As China was announcing that it had shot down two American planes that had violated its airspace, the Cardinals' hot streak was finally stopped on August 20 at Houston in a 2–1 loss for Jaster. It was followed by an 11–4 beating that Washburn took with Spiezio, Romano, and Bressoud in the lineup as several of the regulars took advantage of a rest. In scoring the most runs against the Cardinals by any club since June 29, the second Houston victory was powered by six doubles and was particularly savored by their manager, Grady Hatton. "Your club was due for a bad one like this," he told a friend of his who hailed from St. Louis. "You have only one of these a week. We have six of them."

The Cardinals would miss Marichal in the series in San Francisco on their next stop near the end of August, as the Giants' ace was struggling to recover from a pulled leg muscle that had kept him out of action since the first of the month. After the early–August series in St. Louis against the Giants, Javier had been batting .385 against San Francisco for the season, while Cepeda had been swatting the ball at a .417 clip against his former club (25 for 60). On August 26, Marichal told the media that he might miss the rest of the season, as the leg did not seem to be healing as quickly as he had hoped. "I think that will be all this year," he said after losing to the Braves that night, allowing eleven hits in less than five innings of work. "Right now, I think it's impossible for me to pitch."

McCormick became the National League's first 17-game winner in 1967 when he stopped the Cardinals' winning streak on August 23 with a 6–0 shutout, with McCarver, Shannon, and Maris on the bench for the third game in a row with a variety of minor injuries. The Cards would have been happy to know it would be the last time they would face the lefthander on the year, as McCormick held a perfect 3–0 record for the season against the Redbirds. In fact, McCormick, Bob Veale of the Pirates, and Jim Maloney of the Reds were the only pitchers to beat St. Louis three times on the season to date. Despite their general success, the Cardinals were barely over .500 for the year in day games with a record of 22–20, while holding a sparkling 55–27 mark at night. However, the amazing Hughes ran his record to 13–4 the next day with a shutout of his own, a 2–0 masterpiece in what was the fifteenth loss of the season for the bewildered Perry. The game was a scoreless deadlock until the ninth when Tolan — who had been stuck in a 3-for-33 funk — delivered with a pinch-hit single to score McCarver and give the Redbirds the lead. In the bottom of the eighth, Brock had kept things scoreless by making two back-to-back leaping catches in left field to retire Tito Fuentes and Lanier. The Cardinals would thus finish their season series with the Giants with an 11–7 record, while Cepeda did more than his part against his erstwhile companions with a final .419 average for the year against San Francisco. "Nice going, Sniper!" Cepeda yelled to Hughes from across the locker room.

It was time to head south to Los Angeles, where the Cardinals would miss yet another team's ace, as misfortune had befallen Drysdale and the Dodgers once again. The pitcher had re-injured his back yet another time, slipping as he stepped off an elevator in a hotel on the Dodgers' last road trip. Nonetheless, Singer provided some stability for Walter Alston's men as he beat the Cards in the first game of a double header on the 25th, 2–1, in front of the largest crowd of the season at Dodger Stadium (40,740). Singer was one of the few hurlers that had mastered the squad from St. Louis, as it was his seventh straight victory against the Redbirds. But Briles, designated as the man as having taken Gibson's spot in the rotation, ran his record to 5–2 since

Gibby's injury after beating the Dodgers on August 27. Flood was asked if the Cardinals were really missing Gibson after all. "Are we? If we had him, we might be 22 games in front," he responded. The bullpen had been particularly effective in recent weeks, as Hoerner (logging his fourteenth save in Briles' win) had allowed just three earned runs in his last 29 innings of work, and Willis just two in his last 27. Lamabe, meanwhile — perhaps the most unknown variable on the relief corps entering the season — had not been scored upon in sixteen innings, a stretch covering his last eight appearances.

For the leader of the offensive side, it was just another day of celebration for the colorful Cepeda, as he announced he was hosting a party afterwards with his achievement of "Cien Carreras Enpujadas" — or "one hundred runs batted in" — for the fourth time in his career, his personal equivalent of a Cinco de Mayo fiesta in August. The first baseman appeared to be getting hotter as the summer wore on, ending the day by having posted 28 RBIs in the month of August alone — with four days still remaining. Clemente remained a bit hotter, however, as he maintained his slight lead in the batting race with a 3-for-5, two-homer performance against the Braves in Atlanta on August 29. "I really don't think about the batting title, or Cepeda," Clemente said after the game as his victim back in July — Gibson — had pitched batting practice for the Cardinals that same evening, his first work since being injured on July 15. "If you start thinking too much, you don't do well. I just go out and get my hits." If Clemente was nonchalant about his individual competition, it was the St. Louis *team*, however, that was drawing the true respect from around the league. While the Cardinals were in Los Angeles, the admiring Dodgers manager, Alston, made yet another comment about the seemingly-indomitable nature of the St. Louis men. "They can kill you with speed. They also have an important ingredient: most of their frontliners are having good or excellent years at the same time. Their defense is good enough. Their pitching is deep and excellent. And their shortstop is very underrated." The shortstop of whom Alston spoke was, of course, Maxvill, who was hitting only .220 with one home run in nearly four hundred at-bats. His daily presence in manning left side of the dirt was so strong, however, that all of his offensive liabilities were more than tolerable, just another aspect of the diversity of the Cardinals' weapons that Schoendienst had at his disposal. The "spare parts" came through again on the 30th, as Jaster and Willis combined to shut out the Mets in Busch Stadium. Brock was doing his best to test New York catcher Jerry Grote on the basepaths, whom Brock deemed as currently the best-throwing backstop in the National League. "For quickness and getting rid of the ball, I have to pick Grote," Brock said after being blanked for steals in the series. "John Bateman of Houston has a stronger arm, but not the accuracy that Grote has. By 'accuracy,' I mean getting the throw at the knees or lower." Jaster, still trying to earn respect as a bona fide starter, had been allowing an average of a scant two runs per nine innings in the previous two months.

This collection of multiple talents was bonded stronger every day through confidence and togetherness, a team that still boasted a ten-game lead at the end of August as the rest of the league began to merge towards the middle:

	W	L	Pct.	GB
St. Louis	83	51	.619	—
Cincinnati	73	61	.545	10
Chicago	72	62	.537	11
Philadelphia	68	62	.523	13
San Francisco	70	64	.522	13
Atlanta	67	64	.511	14.5
Pittsburgh	64	69	.481	18.5
Los Angeles	60	71	.458	21.5
Houston	55	80	.407	28.5
New York	51	79	.392	30

Unlike in the National League — where the Cardinals were simply seeking to avoid collapse and gradually extend the distance between themselves and the rest of the field — the American League continued to deal with the clutter of Boston, Minnesota, Detroit, and Chicago at the top of the standings. The Red Sox took over sole possession of first place from the White Sox on August 26, as they beat Chicago at Comiskey Park 6–2. In taking a half-game lead with a 72–56 record, it was the latest in the season that Boston had been in the top spot since October 1, 1949. The Twins, however, remained right on their heels as their ace pitcher, Dean Chance, amazingly threw his second no-hitter of the month on the same day. Minnesota would take the lead by a percentage point the following afternoon. Chicago was hanging tough despite their poor hitting, which was remedied by the great pitching of their 1967 All-Stars Gary Peters and Joe Horlen (the latter of whom would soon throw a no-hitter against the Tigers on September 11). Also helping off the mound was Tommy John, and a young rookie recently recalled from their Indianapolis farm club named Carlos Cisco, a California kid and attendee of the University of Northern Colorado who had pitched twelve innings of scoreless ball in his first two major league appearances. Although he was not permitted by White Sox manager Eddie Stanky to finish either contest, Cisco had proven his mettle. "This is the second time in a row that this fellow has pitched his heart out," Stanky said after Cisco's encore, a game in which he had been no-hitting the Red Sox in Fenway Park into the seventh inning when he was relieved by Hoyt Wilhelm. He allowed a walk to Yastrzemski and a single to

George Scott before exiting the game, at which point even the partisan Red Sox crowd gave him a loud ovation. "It's pretty difficult to take a guy out with a 1–0 lead. I'd hate to do that to my own son. But we're fighting for $10,000 a man [World Series money]." Stanky, in fact, was even fighting his own players in pursuit of a pennant. In the second game of a double header at New York the following week, White Sox third baseman Pete Ward was ejected for arguing balls-and-strikes with umpire Emmett Ashford. Stanky then rushed out from the dugout to prevent Ward from any further penalty, at which point the player shoved Stanky aside. The 165-pound Stanky then jumped the 205-pound Ward from behind and wrestled him to the ground, the two men clawing at each other as if mortal enemies. The manager, the whole time, was simply trying to protect his player. "I get a broken back, I can manage from a hospital bed," Stanky reasoned. "But I need Pete tomorrow. And when he pushed me, that convinced me that he was out of his mind.... I was fearful of a brush-up with the umpire that would have cost him one or two more days."

And even though things were rolling for the Redbirds, Gibson was at the end of his purgatorial rope and ached to return to work — regardless if it temporarily disrupted the machine, for all knew that the machine would be stronger in the long run with him a part of it. He had been on the shelf long enough, and few people were still willing to get in his way. Some reminded him of the fall of Dizzy Dean, the great Cardinals pitcher who tried to return too early from a broken toe suffered in the 1937 All-Star Game, a decision that ultimately caused him to alter his delivery, develop a sore arm, and cut short his career. "Anytime they want me to pitch, I'm ready," Gibson fired off as politely as he could. "It's up to them now. I can pitch."

The "they" to whom Gibson was referring was Dr. Middleman and the other team physicians, now holding out as the lone middlemen between the anxious athlete and the pitching mound.

6. Recovery

I don't think any ballplayer could ask for a better place to play than in St. Louis.

— Roger Maris

Complacency had yet to strike the Cardinals as they stormed into September with a four-game sweep of the lowly Astros at home, highlighted by Briles' (10–5) shutout in the third game and Hughes' one unearned run and fourth-straight four-hitter in the finale, raising his record to 14–5 for the best winning percentage (.737) in the National League. The Cardinals' magic number had dwindled to 16 (the combination of their wins and the second-place team's losses needed to clinch the pennant), and their league lead had extended to a season-high twelve games over the second-place Reds and Cubs. Briles' 5–0 domination was another chapter in the amazing turnaround of the 23-year-old pitcher, filling in for Gibson impeccably as he was just twelve months removed from his awful stretch run in 1966 when he had lost his last eight decisions. While the Cardinals were appreciative of his ability to step in for Gibson, they also felt that Briles could be effective once again out of the bullpen in the future. In any event, Briles was happy to simply be succeeding at the major league level. "Relief may not be as glamorous as starting," he pointed out, "but relievers are making a lot more money than they used to. And if you can make a lot of money, you can throw the glamour out the window." Schoendienst and then-pitching coach Joe Becker had a hand in the turnaround, as they identified an egotistical flaw in Briles that is common in many young pitchers—equating strikeouts with success. Over the off-season before the 1967 season, Schoendienst asked Briles, "How many hitters do you expect to strike out in a game?" And without hesitating, Briles responded "ten," thinking that was what his manager wanted to hear. Becker, who was sitting in the room, was dumbfounded. "Ten! You'll be lucky if you strike out five!" Becker's point was taken by Briles, and already understood by Schoendienst—that to be an effective pitcher in the major leagues, Briles needed to learn how to record outs in any fashion necessary and not rely upon his own skills, which were only slightly above average.

Houston, while maintaining a winning record (37–33) inside the still air of their Astrodome home, was now a dismal 18–50 on the road after their collapse at Busch, their seventeenth loss in their last nineteen tries away from home. A bright spot for the Texas club had been the play of young second baseman Joe Morgan, who although being only 23 years old had already been an All-Star in 1966 and the Astros' regular keystoner for all three seasons that the franchise had been in existence. The diminutive (5'7") Morgan had been churning up the base paths in the summer of '67, having been successful in his last 19 stolen base attempts with a total of 25 thefts on the year.

Cepeda was named the National League Player of the Month for August by gathering three-fifths of the fifty votes from the sportswriters (the surprising Lamabe—never before experiencing extended success in the major leagues—finished second with his 24 innings of scoreless relief. Briles garnered two votes for fifth place behind Bunning and Maloney). Cepeda had batted .352 in collecting 38 hits over the month. The arrival of September also permitted the expansion of the rosters, as the Cards recalled Cosman (who had been on loan to the Mets' Jacksonville farm club), Mike Torrez, and Wayne Granger from the minors pitching help, as well as infielders Jimy Williams and Steve Huntz. Neither Huntz nor Williams had been a large threat at the plate, with .260 and .237 batting averages respectively. Nonetheless, the pair would provide Schoendienst with more options in the later innings for defense and speed, particularly in working with Shannon at third base. In addition, both looked to soon see time at second base as Javier was expected to miss nearly a week with a pulled muscle in his lower back.

When the Cards returned home to play a Labor Day double header with the 66–70 Pirates on September 4, it was rumored that Gibson might be available for a few innings of work in relief. Ironically, it was the first time that the Pittsburgh club had set foot in Busch Stadium since Gibson was injured back on July 15. Said Dr. Middleman, "I'm turning Gibby over to manager Red Schoendienst, and he can pitch whenever Red wants him to." Even though he threw batting practice at full speed for 20 minutes, it was nonetheless decided that his rest should continue. The Pirates would ruin the holiday for the hometown crowd—which was the largest in baseball on the day at 43,960—with a sweep, 10–8 and 9–3, on the strength of 32 hits. The one-day stop by the surprising Pittsburgh club raised its record for the season against the Cardinals in Busch Stadium to 7–2, by far best mark in the league. "It's hard to believe they're where they are in the standings with that kind of hitting," Schoendienst mentioned after the licking that his boys endured (the Cardinals had more than reciprocated the treatment to the Pirates, however, as they had won 26 of the last 32 games at Pittsburgh). Jaster never recorded an out in the opener before exiting in the first inning, allowing Wills, Alley, Clemente, and Stargell to reach base. Washburn didn't fare much better in the nightcap, being belted for nine hits and five runs before three innings were in the books. The good news was that Brock had found his batting stroke; he nailed three home runs on the otherwise-dismal day, running his season total to 19 and surpassing his previous personal mark of 16. Ricketts, in filling in for McCarver, hit his first homer of the season as well. "That's the first time I've ever hit a ball out of our stadium — even counting batting practice," he said proudly.

With McCarver away on another requisite stretch with the Army Reserves, Schoendienst decided to sit Gibson until his "personal catcher" had returned. And despite another interruption in his work, McCarver still had plenty of time left in the season to set the team record for home runs in a season by a catcher. He knocked his thirteenth of the year in helping Carlton win the final game of the series, and now stood one behind Gene Oliver's mark of 14 set in 1962. And as the Cards hit the road, success had followed them — not only in Pittsburgh, but in nearly every city at which they stopped. The Cards were maintaining a winning record at every other team's home park, figuring out to a 41–24 record overall as the visitor in 1967.

Gibson returned to the mound on September 7 in New York as the Cardinals faced the Mets for the final time on the year, an evening after Briles had opened the brief series with yet another victory in what was, in essence, his second consecutive shutout as he permitted one unearned run in winning 3–1. Mets manager Wes Westrum would last only two more weeks with the club, deciding to resign on September 19 with a record of 57–94. The move was framed in the papers as having caught Devine and others in the Mets' front office off guard. "Since his decision took me by surprise, I was unable to immediately offer him another position," Devine said in reference to the possibility of Westrum remaining with the club in another capacity. "My own preference would be for him to stay on as a personal assistant to me." After being an assistant coach with the club for one year, Westrum had first been named the interim skipper when Casey Stengel broke his hip on July 25, 1965, ending a major league playing, coaching, and managing career for Stengel that had stretched back to 1912. Westrum was given the permanent job in 1966, and under his leadership, the Mets had escaped last place for the first time in team history as they finished seven and a half games ahead of the cellar-dwelling Cubs. In 1967 the outfit had returned to its previous misfortunes, however, and Westrum was not satisfied with his own performance. Assistant coach Salty Parker was given charge of the club for the remainder of the 1967 season, but the Mets' ownership was clandestinely making plans to pursue former Dodgers great Gil Hodges as the permanent replacement, who was currently under contract as the manager of the Washington Senators.

As Gibson took the hill for the first time in nearly six weeks, he wore a plastic protective wrap on his healing lower right leg that resembled a small hockey shin guard. Over the time of his absence, his teammates had sprinted out from a four-game lead in the National League to an 11½ game advantage, with a 36–20 record during that stretch. After being staked to an early benefit on a homer by Maris—his ninth on the year, and his first since the 29th of July—Gibson went five innings as he struck out four while allowing eight hits and one walk in posting an easy win, 9–2. Afterwards, Hoerner came up and gave him a hard time. "Big deal," Hoerner grumbled. "You rest for two months and pitch five innings." Then, Hoerner glanced at the sportswriters that had crowded around Gibson's locker, and shook his head again in disbelief. "All that ink for only five innings." Next, Carlton could not resist chiming in. "Hey Hoot—those were my nine runs that you stole today!"

To which Gibson responded, "Yes, but I've been keeping track of all those runs I should have been getting instead of Nellie [Briles]."

That same day, it was announced back in St. Louis that the Cardinals' front office had been given permission by Major League Baseball to print World Series tickets, with home games being scheduled in the National League park for October 7, 8, and 9. While the Cardinals were the only team in the National League allowed to produce the tickets at this juncture, the four American League teams in the pennant hunt — Minnesota, Chicago, Detroit, and Boston — all were permitted to do the same, as the four stood in a virtual tie for first place (Minnesota and Chicago, with 78–61 records, had a winning percentage of .561; Boston and Detroit stood right behind at 79–62, good for a .560 mark). Both leagues were directed to set World Series ticket prices as follows: $12 for box seats, $8 and $4 for reserved seats, and $2 for a spot in the bleachers.

On September 8, word was released that Hughes and the Mets' Seaver were named the co-winners of the National League Rookie of the Year Award as presented by United Press International (the award was announced early in this era). Hughes started the Cardinals' game in Pittsburgh that day, but could not hold on as the Pirates logged a 4–3 win in ten innings in spite of the 1,000th hit in Brock's career, a first-inning single. Back behind the plate was McCarver, but his understudy, Ricketts, was planning to leave the team to travel five hours to the east to Pottstown, Pennsylvania, after getting word of the death of his father. The Bucs' victory was credited to Bruce Dal Canton, the first major league decision for the local 25-year-old who was only a part-time pitcher for the Pirates—his main occupation was as a high school science teacher in the Pittsburgh suburb of Burgettstown. "I got a standing ovation at a pep rally for the football team this morning," Dal Canton said with a grin. He had recently been recalled from the club's Macon, Georgia, farm team, and would continue to offer his teaching services to Burgettstown High while the Pirates were at home. Carlton returned in dominating fashion the following evening with a 6–0 shutout; now with a record of 13–8, he was well beyond his spring training goal of ten wins (Carlton, in fact, now had ten wins on the road alone, to go along with a 3–4 record in Busch Stadium). Ricketts—back in the town where he starred in baseball and basketball at Duquesne University—delivered an important RBI single. It was Saturday the 9th, and Ricketts had received word from his brother in Pottstown that their father's funeral would not be held until Tuesday—the family had given Dave their blessing for him to stay with the Cardinals for the time being. "Dad brought us up to be ballplayers, and he made a switch-hitter out of me," Ricketts said of his father, who had been a notable professional and semi-professional player in eastern Pennsylvania in days gone by. "The saddest part of it all is that we're so close to the World Series, and it would have been nice if he could have been around for it." Ricketts drew some respectful cheers from some former college classmates and other Pittsburgh fans in the eighth, a small collection that had lessened from the meager 6,500 present at the start of the game, as he threw out Maury Wills trying to steal with St. Louis ahead 3–0. The day's rest for McCarver was important, as the regular Cardinals catcher was nursing a bone bruise on the middle finger of his glove hand. It had been ailing him so much that he was trying to catch every pitch in the webbing of the glove, away from the palm.

The Pirates won the finale of the series the following day 8–7 on the strength of a four-run eighth inning off Jackson and Hoerner, as the Redbirds were nonetheless able to show off their latest pitching phenom. Mike Torrez made his major league debut to put out the fire in the inning, striking out the only batter he faced (Donn Clendenon) after turning 21 just two weeks earlier. "There's nothing different about pitching here from pitching in Tulsa," the youngster said in thinking about his minor league experience. "There are just more people in the stands here." Torrez gave the Cardinals' coaching staff yet another option from their deep stable of pitchers, and Schoendienst was looking for a way to get him a start before the season was over. But the manager did not want to alter the work schedule of his regular five-man rotation, in an effort to keep them sharp for an expected appearance in the World Series. For some of the most loyal Cardinals followers, the National League title was not only expected, but actually a forgone conclusion. For after the game, an angry Cardinals rooter hollered at Pittsburgh coach Hal Smith from over the Pirates' dugout as Smith was walking towards the home team clubhouse.

"Hey — quit stalling our pennant drive — we've got World Series plans to make!" the bitter St. Louis fan yelled.

"Well, you people did quite a job of stalling our pennant drive last year," Smith responded, in reference to the Pirates' ultimate third-place finish, three games behind the Dodgers for the flag. "You helped stall us all the way out of it." Smith was referring specifically to the pair of one-run losses that the Cardinals pinned on the Pirates, nearly a year ago to the day — two losses that struck a severe blow to the Pittsburgh club in advance of the season's remaining three weeks in 1966.

Making baseball news on the West Coast were the exploits of the San Francisco ace Perry, who was pursuing former Giants' lefthander Carl Hubbell's National League record of 47 straight scoreless innings pitched. In 1966, Perry had tied Gibson for third place in the National League with 21 wins and made his first All-Star appearance. Hubbell was currently the Giants' farm system director, and Perry would fall just six innings short of his mark. He allowed the Cubs to scratch in the seventh inning of a game on September 10, although Perry would hold on to win 2–1. His previous three outings had included shutout victories over Houston and Los Angeles, sandwiched around an even more amazing feat — his firing of 16 scoreless innings against the Reds in Cincinnati on September 1, only to get a no-decision in a 21-inning win picked up by the Giants' Frank Linzy. Due to poor run support on the part of the San Francisco offense, the 28-year-old Perry's overall record for the season still stood two games below .500 at 13–15; nonetheless, it was because of the Giants' pitching staff that the club had jumped to second place ahead of the Reds and Cubs, but still a distant eleven games from the Cardinals with 18 left to play. In the following summer, Hubbell's record would see a more vicious assault from all angles.

Even with the return of one of the most dominant pitchers of the decade to the rotation, Schoendienst was still not about to let the established momentum be altered. Briles remained a part of the starting staff, and was given the ball on September 11 against Philadelphia. The Phillies were a quality team at six games above .500, but were driven into submission by the hottest pitcher the National League had witnessed in the past six weeks. Briles once again went the distance, scattering eight hits on 139 pitches in a 5–1 win, his seventh in a row and the first time the Cards had beaten the Phillies' ace lefty Chris Short in over two years. It was the 90th win for St. Louis, and dropped their magic number to eight. The win also mathematically eliminated the Pirates — the preseason favorite by 35 of 88 national sportswriters to take the flag — with nearly three weeks yet remaining in the schedule. McCarver provided the offense, going 4 for 5 to push his average back over .300 after recovering from his bruised finger. Since Gibson was damaged on July 15, Briles had posted a 1.70 ERA in 85 innings. And also during that stretch — just as his former pitching coach, Becker, had predicted — Briles was averaging almost exactly five strikeouts per nine innings.

As the regular season was drawing to a close, Finley was reinvigorating his bid to move the A's out of Kansas City. It would take the unanimous approval of his fellow American League owners, scheduled to meet on the matter on October 1, who had previously denied his request twice in 1963 and 1964. Much fallout continued to plague Finley in the aftermath of the confrontation with Harrelson, Krausse, and Aker, but he knew that it was time to make his move. Unfortunately for him, Finley had established a track record of being less than publicly truthful about his intentions during such negotiations. In 1964, he categorically denied any intention of moving the club until the date of the owners' meeting; now, he was taking the same basic stance in 1967. But with his current chance drawing ever closer, his plans were revealed. Seattle would be his first choice, contingent upon the city getting a bond vote passed to build a new baseball stadium. In the event that Seattle could not get a stadium deal done, Finley's plan would then turn his attention to Oakland. Some of his colleagues hoped that another denial would force Finley to give up on baseball altogether. But despite their general annoyance with Finley, the other American League owners were intrigued with the idea of another one of their teams on the West Coast, challenging the dominance of the National League in the new territory (at the time, only the California Angels in Anaheim were the only American League team west of Kansas City). On September 16, Cronin told the press — much to the chagrin of the people of Kansas City, who were particularly anxious about the fate of the team — that an announcement on the movement of the club would have to wait until the World Series was completed.

Gibson made his return to the Busch Stadium mound the next night (September 12), emerging from the dugout to a strong reception from the 20,000 present. The home team disposed of the Phillies in just over two hours, as Gibson fired 90 pitches in combining with Jaster for a 6–0 shutout while slapping two base hits himself. Gibson was his old stingy self, permitting the Philadelphia men only five singles and a walk. "How do you like that," muttered Oliver, a former Cardinals catcher who appeared in the game as pinch hitter for the Phillies, and who held the single-season home run record for Cardinals catchers, which McCarver was chasing. He popped out weakly to Javier in the seventh against Jaster, just after the starter had exited. Oliver was the first of eight straight batters that Jaster retired in order to end the game for his third save. "Gibson is out for six weeks, and he gets more hits in one night than I do in a month!" Oliver wailed. "But he's just that type of athlete — he can be out for two months and still be okay. He's always in shape." The game-winning hit was delivered by Maris, who though in dropping to .270 on the year had knocked in the go-ahead run for the sixteenth time on the season. Also adding two RBIs was Maxvill, giving him fifteen in the same number of games. Most on the team figured that Maxvill's recent success was due to the new t-shirt that his roommate, McCarver, had given him. The shortstop, in the name of continued good luck for the ball club, had been sporting an old shirt beneath his uniform jersey that was perforated with holes and reeking from perpetual wear. McCarver's gift, however, had rescued Dal from the pinched noses of his teammates.

Rick Wise, the opposing pitcher who was beaten on the evening, added his own amazement about the resiliency of the Cardinals' starting hurler. "Gibson didn't pitch like someone who just had a broken leg. He pitched like someone who was getting ready for the World

Dal Maxvill, the Cardinals' sure-handed shortstop and native of Granite City, Illinois, just across the river from St. Louis. (*St. Louis Globe-Democrat* / Archives of the St. Louis Mercantile Library)

Series." The ERA of the St. Louis pitching staff before the All-Star break had been 3.57; since, it had dropped more than a run per game to 2.53, and they were now looking for more victims with their main man back in the fold. Cepeda, while going 0 for 3, was nonetheless the ending point of 13 ground ball outs from the effectiveness of Gibson and Jaster. And once again, he was leading the post-game cheers on top of the money trunk in the locker room. "FIVE MORE TO GO! FIVE MORE TO GO!" he had the players yelling, as their preseason goal of 96 victories was that close.

After losing the finale to the Phillies, the Cards went to Cincinnati and ripped off three straight at Crosley Field, holding the Reds to a total of three runs in sweeping the set and lowering their magic number to one. They faced, in essence, a high school battery in the first game. Carlton pitched a 4–0 shutout (the second in a row, running his scoreless inning string to 26), coupled with a three-run homer off the bat of Shannon, his twelfth, a golf shot on a low-and-away pitch that cleared the distant wall in right field. Sent to the mound by the Reds was their 19-year-old phenom, Nolan, who was being caught by the organization's other 19-year-old prospect in Bench. Despite struggling at the plate, Bench — who entered his first major league game two weeks earlier on August 28 — still showed signs of physical greatness, and promise for the future, both at and behind the plate. "He has good moves and doesn't drop many balls," Cardinals coach Joe Schultz commented about Bench during the series. "But you can't judge a kid from one game. Bench does seem to have an adequate arm, though."

Despite the promising youngsters taking the field for the Reds, the local sports attention that week in Cincinnati had shifted to professional football. Paul Brown, the winner of three NFL championships as coach with the Cleveland Browns, was thought to have had successfully landed an expansion franchise in the rival American Football League for the Queen City. However, disagreements between Brown and AFL president Milt Woodard about financial entrance requirements for the franchise held up the final authorization, and Brown was given one week to amend his proposal (he was seeking the same monetary terms as had been recently given to the aspiring New Orleans Saints of the NFL). Back in 1946, Brown had been part of another new challenger to the NFL's dominance, as he was given charge of the Cleveland franchise of the All America Football Conference, with the team donning his surname in his honor. While fans in the city of Cincinnati pondered what the future on the gridiron, the Cards spent time watching an NFL game on television in the locker room after the final contest of the Reds' series on Sunday, celebrating Cepeda's 30th birthday while also keeping an ear to the score of the San Francisco Giants' game being played in Pittsburgh. The cheers rang loudly when news was learned of Clemente's homer in the ninth that downed the second-place Giants 5–4 and put St. Louis within one win — or one San Francisco loss — from their eleventh pennant since 1926 as the club headed to Philadelphia. And after losing to St. Louis for the thirteenth time in eighteen games on the year, Pete Rose just shook his head. "There's no way, no way at all, that the Cardinals can lose the World Series," the Cincinnati native of the Western Hills neighborhood said. "I don't care what team they play. They have such momentum going, it's unbelievable. It was that way the whole weekend."

Just when one thought that caution off the field would be the order of the day for the Cardinals, Hoerner suddenly struck again with his driving antics. As the team was passing the time in Philadelphia airport, waiting for a ride to the hotel, Hoerner once again took transportation matters into his own hands. He found an airport vehicle on the tarmac that had a luggage trailer attached to the back. Hoerner playfully jumped behind the wheel, while as many as 15 Cardinals teammates even more playfully jumped onto the trailer as a leisurely spin was taken around the runway. The vehicle was pulled over by security personnel, with no more than a laugh exchanged by Hoerner and the officer as the abductors relinquished the ride. Hoerner was evidently looking to operate some type of vehicle, for before the team's plane took off from Cincinnati, Hoerner had donned a captain's hat and made his way for the cockpit. "Oh, no you don't!" hollered his teammates as Maris and Javier grabbed him before he could make further progress up the aisle.

They were as confident as a team could be, off to one more destination before claiming their manifest destiny. As the Cardinals took the field at Connie Mack Stadium in Philadelphia on September 18, a win would secure another National League championship for the proud franchise, something very few considered possible for St. Louis after their mediocre season the previous year and being given 12–1 Vegas odds to take the title at the beginning of the '67 sea-

Dal Maxvill's partner on the doubleplay was the slick-fielding second baseman Julian Javier, one of the greatest pursuers of pop flies at the position. (*St. Louis Globe-Democrat* / Archives of the St. Louis Mercantile Library)

son. The ball was entrusted to Gibson, the man who clinched the flag with his win against the Mets on the last day of the '64 season, and he traded shutout innings with Phillies starter Dick Ellsworth before the Redbird bats came to life in the sixth. Maxvill started things with a single to right, and was sacrificed to second by Gibson. Brock followed with his 32nd double on the first pitch he saw to score his shortstop, while Javier followed suit in jumping on the first offering with a single to plate Brock. Javier, who had seen his batting average drop every season from its peak of .263 in 1963, was now up to .290 with 62 RBIs. After Cepeda walked, Shannon laced a two-out double for two more runs and a 4–0 lead. Gibson had tired early in his two previous starts since returning from his broken leg, but was determined to go the distance for his team in this important contest. He had allowed only one hit into the seventh inning when Tony Gonzalez and Bill White led off with a single and double. Gibby recovered, however, to record the next eight outs with ease. When the former Cardinal White re-appeared at the plate with two out and nobody on in the ninth, only he stood between St. Louis and the 1967 pennant. Gibson, looking to go 15–4 for his career against Philadelphia, reached back for one last fastball and induced White to fly weakly to Tolan in right field; Tolan had taken over defensively for Alex Johnson two innings prior. Tolan squeezed the ball as all the gray-uniformed Redbirds sprinted to a celebratory rendezvous point near the pitcher's mound.

The cramped, aged visitors' locker room in Connie Mack Stadium "had shrunk all the more because of cameras and other equipment," as described by Russo. The writer also remembered that the Dodgers had clinched the pennant in the same room one year ago. Cosman was dancing on top of the trainer's table, while Cepeda was leaping around the room in a frenzy, bumping into someone or another with every other step. "How many more we gotta win?" He asked his teammates. They hollered back, "NONE! NONE!" Schoendienst was kidnapped in uniform by his troops, and dragged into the shower where he was doused with a mixture of beer, champagne, and water. Bob Bauman and Butch Yatkeman were next, and when Musial showed up on the scene to offer his congratulations, he was next to receive an impromptu bath. Colonel Busch was first on the scene with the early exit from his box seat, but had almost missed the event entirely due to business elsewhere. "We've been so busy with two new breweries going up," he explained, "I had to pull away from a lot of things to get to today's game. But I couldn't be happier; this has just been marvelous." The beer mogul joined in the fun, pouring a Budweiser over the head of Schoendienst as well. Busch had such confidence in his boys—especially Gibson—that he left his box seat in the eighth inning to head down to the locker room in advance of the celebration. The party would continue later that evening, as Busch hosted the team at a dinner at the Old Bookbinders restaurant in Philadelphia. Included in the room were the wives of Gibson and Al Jackson, which constituted the first time (except for spring training) that Mrs. Gibson had accompanied her husband on the road during the baseball season. The remainder of the wives were simultaneously enjoying a party hosted by Mary Schoendienst back at their new house in Creve Coeur, Missouri, a suburb of St. Louis, into which the Schoendienst family had moved back on June 8. Red had been so consumed with the pennant race that he had no time for interior decorating. "Pick what you want," he told Mary when asked about the trimming for the inside of their new home. Back in Philly, the party increased in its raucousness when Hughes tried to calm everyone down. "Remember boys, I've still got to pitch tomorrow." Several of the players were asked to come to podium and say a few words. One of them was Maris, who frightened everyone with hints of retirement.

"This is a great way to go out," he said to the audience. "Everybody has to be turned out to pasture at some time."

Amidst the stunned silence of the crowd, Maris then turned to Busch and said, "I'll take a 50 percent pay cut if I can have a beer distributorship," to which everyone burst out in relieved laughter.

And to which Busch replied, "How about a distributorship for 35 home runs or 90 runs batted in?"

In the last two months—even with Gibson out for almost all of that time—they had compiled a 26–7 record against the "first division" clubs of San Francisco, Cincinnati, Atlanta, and Chicago. And aside from being tied with the Cubs on top of the standings on a couple of dates, the Cardinals had not relinquished the National League lead since claiming it on June 18. With the Cardinals officially clinching the flag three months after that date on the 18th of September, the standings looked this way at the end of the day's play:

	W	L	Pct.	GB
St. Louis	95	56	.629	—
San Francisco	81	68	.544	13
Chicago	82	70	.539	13.5
Cincinnati	81	70	.536	14
Philadelphia	77	72	.517	17
Pittsburgh	75	76	.497	20
Atlanta	74	76	.493	20.5
Los Angeles	68	82	.453	26.5
Houston	62	88	.413	32.5
New York	56	93	.376	38

Lost in the Cards' overwhelming advance over the course of the summer was the tremendous effort displayed by Durocher's Cubs, an overachieving team which most felt was destined for another second-division finish. As the Cardinals were clinching in Philadelphia, an individual achievement was hailed by the Chicago men in Atlanta. Jenkins, the 24-year-old pitcher acquired by the Cubs from the Phillies only the year before, set the club season strikeout record with 206, besting the mark set by Orval Overall in 1909. Along with Durocher, General Manager John Holland—who had been trying to mold a winner with the North Siders since 1957—were certain that the pieces were in place for a serious championship run in 1968.

With any remaining dramatics finished in the National League, none of the Big Four in the American League would yield, continuing what was one of the more amazing pennant races in recent memory as one game still separated Minnesota, Chicago, Boston, and Detroit. The White Sox remained in the American League hunt thanks in part to the on-going success of the amazing rookie Cisco, who complemented the other talented young pitchers on the Chicago staff. On the 15th, Cisco authored his first complete game in the big leagues, facing only 33 batters in a ten-inning shutout of the Indians at Comiskey Park played before a mere 4,300 spectators (the night before, an array of Chicago pitchers had held Cleveland scoreless for seventeen innings in winning 1–0, with the first eleven frames crafted by Peters). Once again, it looked as if Cisco would be a hard-luck victim, as it was not until the tenth inning when the Sox would score their only runs to secure the victory, powered by a walk-off grand slam by Don Buford. "Our last two extra-inning victories definitely puts the pressure on the Twins," the confident Stanky asserted to the media. "They know that our players can bounce back." Minnesota was being led by the indomitable power hitting of Harmon Killebrew and the leadership of Chance off the mound, while Detroit was getting balanced offensive production from Bill Freehan, Norm Cash, Al Kaline, and Dick McAuliffe. In Boston, meanwhile, almost equal attention to the championship chase was being paid to the personal exploits of Yastrzemski, who was threatening to follow Frank Robinson of the Orioles from 1966 in pursuit of another Triple Crown. On the 21st, he kept the Red Sox in the four-way tie for first with a dramatic ninth-inning hit that led to Boston's 5–4 win over Cleveland. It was over Robinson whom Yastrzemski was maintaining a slight lead in the American League batting race with a .316 mark, while his 41 home runs and 108 runs batted in continued to slightly outpace Killebrew. Scoring in both leagues was down overall, however, and the statistics were piling up as proof. On September 27, Lolich would throw a 1–0 blanking for Tigers at the Yankees, the 146th shutout on the year in the American League which tied a record set in 1909 (furthermore, it was also the 33rd 1–0 game in the American League on the season). The major league season record of 164 shutouts, set by the National League in 1908, appeared safe. But many around the game were beginning to question the origins of the sudden dearth of scoring.

After Hughes silenced the Philly bats with yet another shutout the following day (supplied with a lineup full of substitutes, as Bressoud, Spiezio, Ricketts, Tolan, Gagliano, Huntz, and Alex Johnson all got starting assignments in a 1–0 win), Carlton finished up the series in looking to extend his scoreless-inning string. It was broken at 29 as the Phillies tallied in the third stanza, but Carlton continued to dominate by striking out 16 batters over eight innings — including the first four hitters he faced, and later, seven in a row — in celebration of his pitching coach Muffett's 37th birthday. Nonetheless Carlton lost 3–1 as Short once again found his personal dominance of the St. Louis club and prevented the Redbirds from having a perfect six-game road trip. Spiezio took advantage of another start in left field in giving Brock an extended rest, nailing his third homer for the Cardinals' only run. The strikeouts by Carlton were two short of the major league mark for a nine-inning contest at the time (shared by Koufax and Bob Feller), and one shy of the Cardinals' record set by Dizzy Dean in 1933. In addition, the combination of 25 strikeouts between Short and Carlton was one shy of the big league record by two pitchers as well. Carlton struck out each batter in the Philadelphia starting lineup at least once, including Ricardo Joseph and Billy Cowan three times each. He had no idea how many whiffs he was piling up until the end of the seventh inning, when after fanning his 15th Phillies batter, a fan hollered out the total to Carlton from over the Cardinals dugout as the team came off the field. "Hearing about the possible record at that point broke my concentration, but I still kept trying to get the strikeouts," Carlton admitted afterwards. "But I made a bunch of other mistakes tonight, and that's why I lost." Even though the Cards were losing in the eighth inning when Carlton came to bat, he was allowed by Schoendienst to hit so that he could remain in the game and pursue the record, since the pennant was already in hand. The Phillies, of course, were more than impressed with the young lefthander. "You say he's only 22 years old?" asked leftfielder Don Lock. "I'd like to trade places with him." Again taking the dietary credit for his teammate's success was Woodeshick, who while earlier had provided milkshakes as a batting remedy for Brock now had introduced Carlton to the power of cherrystone clams for the first time before the game.

The Cardinals' plane flew into Lambert Airport in St. Louis at about 1:30 A.M. local time on the 21st, but the early hour didn't keep a large flock of bird followers from greeting their heroes at the terminal. As they departed the plane, fans threw fake money into the air at Cepeda, who returned the gesture with a hearty laugh.

Reserves in the starting lineup continued to be the order of the day with the flag in hand, as the Braves took on the Cards back at Busch Stadium. Hoerner, due in part to inactivity in the past week, allowed three walks in the ninth inning to charge a 4–2 loss to Willis, who had preceded him. Willis had pitched a perfect eighth, and then allowed Felix Millan to reach on a bunt single to lead off the ninth when Hoerner appeared, who allowed Aaron to plate Millan with a sacrifice fly for the go-ahead tally. Because of the success and stamina of the Cardinals' starting pitchers, it had seemed like weeks since Hoerner had pitched in a ballgame, working only two innings over the past twelve days. The fans—as well as Schoendienst—had held their collective breath when Cepeda was hit in the wrist by a pitch from Ron Reed in the first inning. Tolan immediately took over for him in moving from center field to first base, as the slugger was removed from the game for precautionary reasons as x-rays taken later proved to be negative. The pain would linger, as Cepeda endured an 0-for-4 performance the following night, making him 1-for-27 over the past two weeks. Flood, meanwhile, had streaked past him for the club lead with a .332 average, good for fifth in the National League as Cepeda sat sixth. Cepeda, who at the end of August was batting .349 but was at a .230 clip since, was struggling in the RBI department as well, failing to drive in a run in the past week. Nonetheless, he continued to lead the National League overall RBI chase by two in having posted 108 by September 23, two better than Henry Aaron and Jimmy Wynn of Houston (Aaron, by this point, had already led the National League in RBIs in four different seasons; if he did so for a fifth time in 1967, he would break the record that he currently shared with Rogers Hornsby). Al Jackson was given a rare start in the second game of the series, having been used by Schoendienst as a left-handed specialist out of the bullpen for most of the season with the establishment of the other starters. Jackson finished with over three innings of sparkling relief after a tremendous beginning by the youngster Torrez, leading the Redbirds to a 5–4 victory in twelve innings. Jackson held the Braves at bay until the bottom half of the third extra stanza, at which point the rookie Huntz pinch-hit for him and delivered a single with two outs, which was similarly followed by Tolan and ultimately Shannon for the game-winner. The heroics made happy spectators of the 32,000 in attendance, pushing the Cardinals' home attendance for the season over the 2,000,000 mark for the first time in club history — just as had been predicted in spring training, as the team had been looking forward to their first full season in their spacious, beautiful new home. It signaled a shift in the paradigms of power in baseball; for with all their success over the decades, the Cardinals had always had to play financial second-fiddle to their associates in New York and other East Coast locations. Despite the charm, history, and feelings towards Sportsman's Park that the city always held, the club now finally had a modern ballpark with which to compete.

September 23 would mark McCarver's turn to make a trip to the infirmary, for as with Cepeda 48 hours earlier, he was also the recipient of a negative x-ray after a pitched ball hit him on the foot. All St. Louis hitters would be quieted on the evening, as the Cards' last regular-season loss at home was pinned on them by the local boy, Jarvis, with the right-hander from Carlyle going toe-to-toe with Gibson for a complete-game win, 2–1, in front of many of his personal fans from Clinton County. Gibson held a 1–0 lead entering the seventh, having retired 17 Atlanta batters in a row, but a throwing error by Shannon — his second of the game, giving him 29 at third base for the year and the total with which he would end the season — led to the two Atlanta runs. The home schedule ended the following afternoon with a 5–4 triumph for Jaster over the Braves, as Schoendienst refused to reveal to the media his pitching plans for the World Series, with the exception of letting it be known that Gibson would take the mound in the opener. That afternoon in Pittsburgh, kicker Jim Bakken of the football Cardinals was simultaneously nailing an NFL-record seven field goals that pushed the Big Red past the Steelers 28–14. All of Bakken's kicks were 33 yards or fewer, as he also missed attempts from 45 and 50 yards away. The feat — also performed amidst a swirling wind, and with Bakken working with a new snapper and holder — left Bakken one shy of the league record for consecutive games with a successful field goal of 14, set by Lou Groza in 1951.

The last regular-season game in St. Louis was celebrated afterwards with a party for the players and their families at Stan and Biggie's, Musial's restaurant in the central part of the city that he operated with local businessman Julius "Biggie" Garagnani. They had opened the establishment in 1949, and in 1961 moved to a larger location near the St. Louis Arena on Oakland Avenue, just west of Kingshighway. When Biggie died in 1967, his son Jack took over and provided patrons with the top-flight level of service they had come to expect. The business soon grew to include resort communities in Clearwater Beach and Miami Beach in Florida. Despite the obvious success that the place was enjoying, Stan was always worried about it going under. "The quickest way to a million bucks," Musial would joke, "is to start with two million and open a restaurant." Particular favorites on the menu included veal scaloppini marsala, fettucini a la Romana, and the specialty of the house, the breast of chicken cacciatore.

As Harry Caray started his role as the emcee of the event, he invited several of the Cardinals up to the front of the room. Cepeda decided to talk, but not into the microphone — imagining that he was in front of his locker on the money trunk at Busch Stadium after a game with his dirty uniform on, instead of at a fancy dinner. "I'm very happy to be in St. Louis!" he yelled. "My English is not good looking, but everything else is beautiful." Cepeda perhaps was referring to the beautiful music to which everyone had just been privileged. The owner of the establishment — also the owner of 3,630 National League hits — had brought his famous harmonica for the enjoyment of all.

When the party had died down, the Cards made a final visit to Wrigley Field on September 27 for a contest against the Cubs. The Redbirds, having most of the starters back on the field to prevent rust, fell short in an 8–7 loss as Hoerner was causing concern with another poor performance out of the bullpen. The lefthander recently revealed that he had been nursing an injured right foot as well, having been spiked by the Phillies' Johnny Callison while covering first base in a game back on September 13. The ultimate victims were Jackson and Torrez, as the former permitted a game-tying homer to Santo in the ninth and the latter the game-winning single to Cubs' catcher Randy Hundley. But Brock, in going 4 for 5 on the day with two home runs in the seventh and ninth innings (giving him 21 on the year, as well as 200 hits), broke Flood's three-year-old club record for at-bats in a season with 680. Earlier in the game, Brock had slightly injured his hand while sliding into a base. Though the outfielder displayed no ill effects with his power demonstration later in the contest, Schoendienst afterwards chose to sit him out for most of the remainder of the regular season. The decision, while prudent, would prevent Brock from making a run at the then-major league record of 696 at-bats for a season, set by Woody Jensen of Pittsburgh in 1936. Was it Woodeshick's milkshakes that were striking again in the left fielder's favor?

Not this time, for his current juice was supplied by a couple of lemon cream pies that Mrs. Katie Brock had packed for Lou and his teammates for the road trip. Mr. Brock hungrily gobbled up most of one of the pies on the plane, and did the same to the other at the team hotel in Chicago, much to the disappointment of his teammates who were hoping for a bite (the feast that Mrs. Cepeda had provided for Orlando was downed quickly as well, a serving of Puerto Rican stuffed chicken with rice that, like with Brock's pies, the rest of the team observed longingly). Buck, while on the air with KMOX radio, wanted to know if the food truly helped. "Oh absolutely, Jack," Lou responded. "It's what keeps me going." Brock was now batting close to .400 with 15 home runs for his career against his former team, including a .434 mark and six round-trippers in 1967. And while the Cardinals continued to be generally well-balanced in their performance, some American League scouts were telling the contenders in their league that the Redbirds might be susceptible to left-handed pitching in World Series play. On the year, the Cards held a 68–36 record against right-handed starters, with only a 30–24 mark versus lefty starters. The reason for the mediocrity against southpaws could be seen in the batting averages of the left-handed Cardinal regulars against left-handed pitching — such as Maris (.221), McCarver (.256), Tolan (.200), and even Brock (.245). Furthermore, no one off the bench had been able to help, as none of the right-handed substitutes had a higher average than Alex Johnson's .240 mark against lefties.

The Cardinals left the Windy City in quicker fashion than expected, as the final game of the Cubs series was rained out (since the game would have no bearing on the final standings, it would not be re-scheduled, leaving the Cubs and Cardinals with only 161 games played at season's end, with all other league teams having played the standard 162). Gibson spent the free days watching the Chicago White Sox and other American League teams on television, hoping to get a preview of the Redbirds' remaining potential opponents in the final round. A lone game still separated Minnesota, Detroit, Boston, and Chicago, with each club having four or fewer contests remaining. "It really won't matter which team we play in the World Series," Gibson murmured while slouching in a chair in his hotel room, glancing at the screen. "I feel that our pitching is as good as that of any of the American League teams, even Chicago's." Gibson was the only regular starting pitcher whom Schoendienst wanted to throw for a long duration in the season's final week, as the manager felt that Gibson's arm needed to "toughen up" in gaining stamina after being idle with the injury for six weeks. Four floors up from Gibson's room, Schoendienst was watching the White Sox as well, and figured that the Chicago club would be the one his club would be facing for the world championship. Down the hall, trainer Bob Bauman was cleaning up his room instead of cleaning up wounds, as he was awakened to the rain leaking in through his window and spraying across the floor by the fan of the air conditioner.

Indeed, nothing had yet been decided in the American League — including the final destination of the A's franchise. On September 29, a member of the city council in Kansas City announced that they were going to fight any intentions of Finley to move the team out of the area. The council members defiantly announced that they would be present at the October 18 meeting of American League owners, at which Finley was expected to unveil his wishes. When Alvin Dark became the seventh field manager that Finley fired in the past seven years, 121 games into the 1967 schedule, Finley's detractors pointed to a continuing atmosphere of instability within the organization. And while most baseball observers around the nation wanted Finley to relinquish control of the club, he staunchly reiterated his desire not to sell. The members planned to accentuate — in addition to other evidence of Kansas City being a superlative baseball town — the approval of the bond vote for a new stadium by the city residents, a measure which passed by more than two-thirds of the ballots (Finley, however, had long stated that he was not impressed with the locals' fervor in getting a new ballpark). An imagined compromise by some would be Finley's exit and the simultaneous granting of a new expansion franchise to Kansas City for 1968 or 1969. Meanwhile, on the other side of the state, the St. Louis ball club would finish the regular schedule in chilly Atlanta against the Braves, as the "Capital of the South" was where the latest managerial casualty had recently taken place. Amidst temperatures that had dropped as low as the upper 30s, Billy Hitchcock had just been fired in his second season on the job, leading the club to a disappointing 77–82 mark after a promising 33–18 record under his guidance to finish the 1966 campaign. Ken Silvestri, who had been serving as the bullpen coach, was given the interim reins of a club loaded with talent. The Braves had won 85 games the year before, but had not gotten steady offensive production aside from established stars in Aaron and Joe Torre. Silvestri would direct the team in the final three contests of the season against the Cardinals, games that were meaningless on paper, but perhaps significant to Silvestri's future with the club.

The Braves fought hard for their new leader, but as with most of the regular season, the Cardinals disposed of them easily in three straight with outstanding pitching, defense, and just enough offense. Gibson, in his final regular season start, was precluded from achieving his fourteenth win, but received help after nine innings of work from Willis (6–5) in gaining a 3–1, 11-inning victory for the club. In the final turn at bat for the Cards, Shannon drove home Flood with his 77th RBI for the win, the fifteenth time on the year that a Shannon hit had decided a game in favor of St. Louis. As had been alluded to by Schoedienst, Gibson had been permitted to labor a bit longer than the other Cardinals starters in going a full nine innings. McCarver reported that his fastball was as rapid as ever, according to his statement to Russo after the game. "I had to wonder about his endurance, because he didn't have much of a chance to run when he was out with the broken leg," Muffett told an Atlanta newspaper man. "But he showed in his third and fourth starts after coming back that he could go all the way ... he's still the same fierce competitor that he always was." With his recovery complete, Gibson was set to start Game One in the World Series on October 4, regardless of the American League opponent. Muffett also had season-ending praise for the Cardinals bullpen, pointing especially to the work of lefties Jaster and Jackson in recent weeks. In addition, Jackson had paced the entire pitching staff in their friendly intra-position battle for top honors in batting average among the pitchers with a .258 figure. Hughes (16–6) would cap a magnificent rookie campaign with another 3–1 upside the following night, marking the first time since World War II (and only the fifth time ever) that the Redbirds had won 100 games in a season. Hughes' success was due in part to the socking Cepeda, who drove in the difference with two RBIs, advancing him that same number beyond Aaron for the league lead with 111. Not allowing any sort of momentum turn heading into the World Series, Briles finished the regular schedule with 5–2 win on the last day in just an hour and 53 minutes, going eight strong innings capped by the fifth save for Lamabe. It landed the Cards a final regular-season record of 101–60, the most wins by a St. Louis club in 23 years.

While the Redbirds had caused most of the month of September to be a yawner in the National League standings, little of the drama in the American League had still failed to cease, even into the schedule's final hours on October 1. As the Cardinals had finished their showers and were jumping back into their street clothes after the closer in Atlanta, they watched with great interest the game between Boston and Minnesota on the clubhouse television. The Chicago White Sox had been pared from the pennant race two days earlier, as they inexplicably lost a double header to the lowly A's on September 27. "I thought we were gone — dead," Yastrzemski said, speaking of the apparently-insurmountable task of climbing over the other teams to the pennant. "When I heard that Chicago had lost twice to Kansas City, I could hardly believe it." Soon after the collapse of the White Sox, the Detroit Tigers — having to play two double headers in two days due to earlier rainouts — were eliminated with their loss to the Angels in the second game on September 30, leaving the Twins and Red Sox with one winner-take-all battle at Fenway Park. Detroit's season had perhaps ended two weeks earlier on September 18 anyway, when their star pitcher, McLain, dislocated his toe in an accident at home and was lost for the remainder of the season. When Tigers' second baseman Dick McAuliffe grounded into a double play to lose in their final game, it was a tense, grueling end to a tense, grueling summer in the Motor City, as smoke was still seen smoldering from the riot-torn buildings off in the distance beyond Tiger Stadium.

It was now ace against ace, as Dean Chance of Minnesota would face off against Jim Lonborg of Boston for the decisive ballgame between the two squads. Interestingly, the week before, most of the Twins players had voted to not give a World Series share to their former manager, Sam Mele. Mele had been fired on June 9 after 50 games, in leading the Twins to only a .500 record as he was replaced by Cal Ermer. There were 11 players and assistant coach Billy Martin, however, who announced that they would — out of their own pockets — pay a full share for Mele anyway, provided that the club made it to the series. Mele had previously led Minnesota to the American League flag in 1965 with a franchise-record 102 victories that stands to this day. While the steady Lonborg was seeking his 22nd victory, it was Yastrzemski upon whom Boston rested its hopes — the ball club, the fans, and the entire city. In rising to the call, the man they called "Yaz" would attain an astonishing ten hits in his final 13 at-bats of the season — including a 4-for-4 performance on the season's final day — which not only gave him the American League Triple Crown, but the Red Sox the pennant as well (Yastrzemski had also hit .523 over Boston's final twelve games). Trailing 2–0, Boston powered to a five-run sixth inning that included hits by Lonborg and Yastrzemski that chased Chance, also a twenty-game winner, from the game. A key turning point had been the fumbling of a potential double-play ground ball by Zolio Versalles, the American League MVP from just two seasons earlier, which allowed Yastrzemski to come to the plate. And even though the 25-year-old Lonborg had never previously beaten Minnesota (and a third of his nine losses in 1967 came at the hands of the Twins), he dominated their hitters throughout the afternoon. As inspiration all day long, Lonborg had earlier written "$10,000" inside his glove — the figure he imagined to be the amount of a World Series check. And after Twins pinch hitter Rich Rollins grounded out to Rico Petrocelli at shortstop, Lonborg's Red Sox teammates stormed the field, and in celebration, ripped the jersey and sweatshirt right off his body in hoisting him on their shoulders. Writer Bud Collins was quoted as observing that "Lonborg was sucked into the crowd as though it were a whirlpool, grabbed, mauled, petted, patted, pounded, and kissed." As many fans joined the scene on the field, they seemed to have forgotten that at least two more (World Series) games would have to be played there this season — for chunks of sod, random items in the dugout, and even placards from the scoreboard were removed as souvenirs. Author Glen Stout noted the particular fanaticism of Red Sox follower Lawrence O'Brien of Somerville, Massachusetts. O'Brien was stationed with the U.S. Army in Vietnam, but when he heard of Boston's seizing of the pennant, he immediately requested an extension of his duty time in southeast Asia — for, in the short-term, it now meant an immediate 30-day furlough home. When he arrived back in Somerville, the *Boston Globe* newspaper had World Series tickets waiting for him.

Boston was celebrating its first pennant in 21 years, setting up a 1946 World Series rematch against the Cardinals that St. Louis had won in seven games.

In the time between the end of the regular season and the start of the World Series, much of the idle-time talk in St. Louis focused around the rise of the young pitcher Briles. He had won his last nine starts in the 1967 schedule, more than making up for the loss of the main right-hander in the rotation. "Things got dangerous when Gibson went down," Musial said, "But our young pitching saved us. We felt in the spring that this could be a first-division club." For some, however, the majority of the credit should have been given to Billy Muffett, the tutor of the pitching staff who had been directly responsible for the development of all the inexperienced hurlers on the staff. This was noted by reliever Hal Woodeshick, the former All-Star who unknowingly had already appeared in his final big-league game back on August 28. He would throw in only 42 innings on the year, gradually giving way to the powerful young arms on the Cardinals roster. "It was Muffett who changed Dick Hughes and Nellie Briles to the no-windup," Woodeshick was quick to point out. "Muffett brought along Steve Carlton, too, and he changed Ron Willis to sidearm. He had to have the young pitching come through when we left spring training, or we would've had nothing. They ought to triple Muffett's pay." Russo (who had been recently named one of the two official scorers for the 1967 World Series) pointed out that Carlton, Hughes, and Briles had a combined major league record of 9–19 in 1966; in 1967, the important trio had forged a mark of 41–19, an increase of 32 victories with no increased number of defeats. The club became so well-balanced and consistent, in fact, that it endured only one losing streak as long as four games, occurring far back in early May before the championship engine hit full throttle in the hot summer months. "Our present club has more speed than the '64 team," responded Gibson in comparing this outfit to the last Cardinals collection to win the pennant. Like the others, he agreed that the difference was seen on the mound. "Brock is twice the player that he was in 1964. The defense is about the same, but our pitching this year is stronger. Remember that in '64 we had to rely on three starters—Ray Sadecki, Curt Simmons, and myself. This year we have much more depth ... this is, without a doubt, the best Cardinal team with which I've played since joining the organization." And in perhaps the statistic that best illustrated their domination on the mound, the Cardinals pitching staff—since the last week of July—had orchestrated 38 games in which they permitted the opposition two runs or fewer.

A man who formerly held Musial's job revealed that he had seen no competition from the rest of the National League since the beginning of the season. "I saw the top contenders falling apart," Bing Devine reflected on his secretive preseason predictions from his Mets' office. Devine himself was responsible for bringing many of the current Cardinals to the club. "Cincinnati wasn't able to sustain injuries as well as the Cardinals did. Pittsburgh had a combination of obvious problems. Philadelphia suffered, among other things, from injuries and a lack of depth.

"San Francisco, surprisingly, had good pitching, but the Giants don't have much of a hitting ball club anymore. And Atlanta, in my judgment, was capable only of building up to a letdown. And with due respect to Leo Durocher, John Holland, and the Cubs, who have done exceedingly well — they did not have, however, enough experience in pennant pressure."

Personal plaudits were all around for the Cardinals hitters in view of the regular season final statistics. Brock led the National League in at-bats with 689, nearly doubled second-place finisher Joe Morgan (29) with 52 stolen bases for his second-straight theft title, and tied Henry Aaron for the most runs scored with 113. Brock also had 206 hits, good for second place behind Clemente (209), as were his twelve triples, one behind league-leader Vada Pinson of the Reds. Cepeda's RBI total of 111 edged out Clemente by one, as Orlando also was hit by twelve pitches, the most in the league. Clemente wound up with his fourth batting title, posting a .357 average which was the best by a National League leader since Musial's .376 mark in 1946. At this time, only Musial, Ty Cobb, Honus Wagner, Rogers Hornsby, and Ted Williams had won more batting championships than Clemente. Flood, with a hot September (and a .360 mark since coming off the disabled list in July), wound up fourth in the league batting race with a .335 average, best on the Cardinals (also, in the fielding department, Flood would join Gibson as Gold Glove winners from the Cardinals). In the past few seasons, Flood admitted that he had developed a habit of trying to pull the ball too much —certainly a mistake in the Cardinals' large new home park. "This year, he's gotten many hits up the middle and to right field," noticed Sisler by the end of the season. "He has also helped himself a lot by staying away from the low pitches he used to chase."

As a team, the Cardinals hit a modest .263, which nonetheless was good for second place in the league next to Pittsburgh (.277). An overall downward offensive trend in baseball had begun, as for 1967 National League batters had failed to achieve one hit in every four at-bats. On the pitching ledger, St. Louis had the top two hurlers in winning percentage in Briles (.737) and Hughes (.727), while Hughes allowed the fewest base runners per inning among starters in the league (.954). Aside from these, however, no individual pitching numbers stood out on the team; this was further testimony to the complete team job that was done on the mound, particularly by the youngsters, in the absence of Gibson. Additionally, with the novelty of the new Busch Stadium still drawing in the fans, the Cardinals far surpassed the two million mark in attendance, leading the National League with 2,090,145 patrons—the first time that the Cardinals had led the league in attendance in sixty-six years.

In actuality Yastrzemski did not, however, own a true Triple Crown, as he was only able to tie Killebrew with 44 home runs. The Red Sox left fielder cleanly swept the batting title (.326) and the RBI lead (121). Immediately after the game, reports swirled around Red Sox owner Tom Yawkey about his issuing manager Dick Williams an immediate two-year contract extension and a raise of $10,000; both men, however, said that they did not have the time for such discussions at this point. As the Red Sox celebrated their pennant in their tiny Fenway Park locker room, they hoisted Yastrzemski onto their shoulders, the man whom they knew would surely lead Boston to its first World Series title since 1918. They carried Yaz a few steps as if already parading down Beacon Street, but soon bumped into the wall in the small room and had to do an about-face. The Red Sox had not finished higher than fifth place in the past ten years, and they figured that destiny was now on their side. Perhaps the local praise of Yastrzemski, though, was getting a bit too high; for longtime Boston writer Joe Cashman—who had covered the Red Sox for decades—even claimed that "Old Number Nine [Ted Williams], sensational as he was, never was the complete ballplayer that Yaz has been this year." And fellow sports scribe Red Smith offered the following simple poem to the Red Sox heroes:

> This is the city of Boston
> The home of the bean and the cod
> Where Lonborg stands taller than Kennedy, Ted
> And Yastrzemski is some kind of god.

The Cardinals, meanwhile, scoffed at the Red Sox and the general quality of American League play, seeing the other side as having a lame-duck championship with the .568 winning percentage posted by the Red Sox (92–70) being the lowest in American League history for a pennant winner. Some of the more practical Redbirds were so indifferent to their potential opponent in the World Series, in fact, that they were rooting against the Red Sox for the American League flag—not because they feared Boston as a more qualified opponent, but rather because Fenway Park was smaller than the stadiums found in Minnesota or Detroit, and thus would provide a smaller World Series bonus check from gate receipts. As they watched the Red Sox's jubilant celebration in their locker room in Fenway Park, they saw the players tossing Lonborg and Yastrzemski around in congratulatory fashion. "Bruise their arms! Break their legs!" they hollered in innocent wishful thinking. There was one quiet voice in the cheerful crowd — that of John Romano, the backup catcher. He had batted only .121 in 58 at-bats during the season for the Cards, and he was named ineligible for the series by the team as they had to get down to the 25-player limit (the roster had enlarged when the Cardinals picked up pitcher Jack Lamabe from the Mets in July, a move originally made as insurance when Gibson was hurt). Nonetheless, Romano wished his mates well in the final round.

They were cocky and confident, but still with the knowledge of a job to do. And, despite possessing many young players, it was a St. Louis roster now filled with experience. In fact, many felt that McCarver — not Gibson — should have been the MVP of the 1964 World Series against the Yankees, as the catcher had batted a blistering .478 at the age of 23 as the Cards brought home the title. They saw this year's championship as another that was theirs for the taking, and Schoendienst was already organizing his pitching rotation to ensure that Gibson could start three games out of seven if necessary.

7. "Lonborg and Champagne"

Destiny is not something to be wished for — it is something to be attained.
— William Jennings Bryan

As the Cardinals embarked for Boston, it was the sixth World Series for which their traveling secretary, Leo Ward, had to make arrangements. According to Broeg, Ward had gone "a million miles with the team via train, plane, bus, and boat." It was Ward's 30th year in the position, as he was hired back in 1938 when the club's former secretary, Clarence Lloyd, had resigned and moved to Georgia to go into the wood finishing business. Lloyd had first employed Ward as a ticket-taker at Sportsman's Park in 1930, as Leo had been struggling to make a living as a plumber. He soon advanced to other jobs at the ballpark, including oversight of the press gate, organizing the Knothole Gang for boys and the Cardinals' Girls Club, and structuring the various try-out camps that the team held at Sportsman's Park (such as the one that had discovered Schoendienst as a ballplayer). A lifelong St. Louisan, Ward's father had been a bricklayer, having performed work on City Hall, Union Station, and other significant structures around town.

"I know you're going to have to spend my money, Leo," Breadon told the then-30-year-old Ward in 1938, handing him the official club checkbook as the Great Depression was drawing to a close — but with finances still tight. "Just don't throw it away."

The young man, who had been on the new job for five minutes, responded boldly, "I've never had an expenditure questioned in thirty years."

Soon after, Ward had learned very quickly that the job would involve needing to make quick decisions on his own. The World Series in Boston reminded him of one such particular incident in his first professional visit to the city, as Ward — extremely sentimental about his destinations — was always sad to leave a National League city for the last time in a season. "It was like saying goodbye to an old friend," he would say. But towards the end of his initial year as secretary in 1938, Ward and the Cardinals were more than happy to leave Beantown, having played a series in Boston against the Braves in late September just as a massive hurricane was striking the Atlantic coast. As the Cards and Braves were in the middle of their contest at 3:30 P.M. on the 21st, the hurricane made landfall at New Haven, Connecticut, 130 miles to the southwest. Boston somehow managed to avoid the storms long enough for the two teams to play a double header on the 22nd, as the worst storm in seventy years to hit the coast north of Virginia had killed over 600 as winds blew in excess of 120 miles per hour. It was a deadly torrent surpassed in that region in later years only by Hurricanes Hazel (1954) and Hugo (1989). With train service out of New England being rendered impossible, Ward spontaneously organized what was believed to be the first chartered flight of a professional sports team in history — a flight that, in all likelihood, would have been grounded under today's stricter regulations. The Cardinals boarded the plane and nervously flew together from Boston to Chicago for a series with the Cubs, eventually getting out of reach of the hurricane. A telegram caught up with Ward at the team's hotel in Chicago, a message that had been sent to Boston and subsequently missed him there. The note was from Breadon and read, "Do not think it advisable to fly — try some other means of transportation. Signed, S. Breadon."

Ward summarized the feelings of many about the Cardinals with Schoendienst and Musial in charge, men of impeccable character and baseball acumen. "Both Stan and Red were stars, top players who never displayed temperament and never would put up with a rotten apple if one was found in the barrel," he said, noting that over the years, the Cardinals seemed — at least to him — to have fewer disciplinary problems than other clubs. "As fine, decent men, as well as great players, they've got the complete respect of the men who work for and with them, on and off the field. This ball club is a joy to be around." Ward was not alone in his assessment of the job that the two men had done. For it had been announced on September 25 that Musial and Schoendienst were to receive the first (of what was expected to be many) awards from their work in 1967. The Elks Lodge Number Nine of St. Louis had bestowed upon the two men their Bruce Campbell Award for Meritorious Service, to be presented at a dinner in their honor on November 9. The award, though familiar only around St. Louis, was a great local dignity, as it was unanimously voted to Musial and Schoendienst by local sportswriters and broadcasters.

*   *   *   *   *

It had been an incredible reversal of fortunes for the Boston franchise, and the 1967 campaign was soon dubbed the "Year of the Impossible Dream." Before '67, the Red Sox had finished in the second division every year since 1958, and were only a half-game from the very bottom of the American League standings in 1966. The charge was led by the first-year manager Williams who, after starring at Beaumont High School in St. Louis, spent 13 seasons in the majors with a variety of clubs before retiring from the Red Sox as a player in 1964 (his family had actually moved to St. Louis from California when he was 13 years old). Back in 1953 as a member of the Brooklyn Dodgers, however, an accident at Sportsman's Park nearly ended his playing career. While covering the outfield, he charged in for a shallow fly ball off the bat of the Cardinals' Vern Benson. Williams dove for the ball and severely dislocated his shoulder in the process. Furthermore, doctors were later convinced that he did greater damage to the shoulder when he got up and threw the ball to third base, his right arm dangling precariously from the shoulder socket. In becoming a manager, he was the tenth skipper for the Red Sox in the past twenty years, having recently led the organization's farm team at Toronto to two straight International League championships. Williams immediately introduced a no-nonsense approach to leadership as the American League's youngest field general at age 38. "There will be no field captain," he told the press, in quickly stripping that honorary title from Yastrzemski. "No clubhouse meetings of the players with the manager excluded, no overweight players and no coddled athletes. The only meeting without the manager is when we'll meet to split up the prize money. The players have enough problems playing ball without running the ball club. We will have one boss—or rather, five bosses—me and the coaches. I will be the chairman of the board."

Williams continued to be without Conigliaro since August, when he had been hit in the face with a pitch. Instead, Conigliaro became part of the record-setting number of media correspondents taking their places in the press box for the World Series, as he wrote a daily column during the games for the Boston newspapers (Williams, Yastrzemski, and Lonborg were contributing pieces to the local pages as well). Meanwhile the man who was hired to replace Conigliaro— Ken "Hawk" Harrelson — had struggled mightily. After homering in his first at-bat for the Red Sox after signing with them in late August, Harrelson had hit just .200 for the remainder of the season after his debacle with the A's' owner Finley. In a further attempt to plug some late-season holes on the team, Elston Howard — the former great New York Yankees catcher — had been acquired by Boston on August 3 and had hit only .147 since. Nonetheless, Williams had given him the job behind the plate for the World Series in place of the Boston catcher for most of the regular season, Mike Ryan, who hit .199 himself during the year.

Schoendienst predicted that the Cardinals would win in six or seven;

Red Schoendienst and rookie Red Sox manager Dick Williams meet before Game Two of the 1967 World Series on October 5 in Boston. (*St. Louis Globe-Democrat* / Archives of the St. Louis Mercantile Library)

Yastrzemski, on the contrary, felt that it would take no more than six games for the Red Sox to take the title. Was he nervous before going into his first World Series, a reporter asked the Boston slugger? "Apparently, you didn't watch the last two months of the American League race," Yaz shot back. "After that, this will be like playing for fun — like playing stickball in the street." And the carefree Harrelson, despite his end-of-the-year slump, was most happy with his situation. "I'm the only man in baseball to have had a better year than Yastrzemski," Hawk told the writers in comparison to Yaz's Triple-Crown statistics. "I went from Charlie Finley to the World Series."

The Cardinals arrived with a police-escorted ride to their accommodations at the Sheraton Hotel in Quincy, Massachusetts, after taking a chartered United Airlines flight from St. Louis. When they arrived in Quincy, they were greeted by hostile Boston supporters who held out signs that read, "WE'RE #1— WELCOME #2." Some of them even reminded the Cardinals that the Red Sox had already beaten them once this year — in one game back in spring training in Florida, a 10–9 Boston win when Yastrzemski hit two home runs and had six RBIs on the day. In the unseasonably-warm eighty degrees in suburban Boston, the Cardinals arrived at their hotel rooms to find that the air conditioning system had already been turned off for the season — although some of them felt that it had been done to them on purpose.

Earlier that day, the Cardinals had held a light workout at Fenway Park to acclimate themselves to the grounds. The Cards were loose and laughing, especially when Gibson spotted a mounted Boston police officer during the ride to the park, and likened the cop to Paul Revere. "The Cardinals are Coming! The Cardinals are Coming!" Gibson yelled out the bus window to him, as everyone was having a good time. Gibson smiled again when, once inside the ballpark, he noticed seats in straightaway centerfield — which he knew would soon be filled with lots of white t-shirts, which are always tough on the batting eye. Even the normally-reserved Schoendienst was in a jocular mood, jumping in the batting cage for a round of practice swings during the workout. Red proved that he could still handle a bat, as he sent several balls crashing into— and a couple over — the outfield wall. The Cards were impressed with the traditional beauty of Fenway, the baseball basilica that had stolen the newspaper headlines with its grand opening on April 20, 1912 — even with those headlines having been printed just five days after the *Titanic* sank in the North Atlantic. The ballpark's name was derived from the Fens section of Boston in which it was built, a rather marshy area that was considered by many to be unsuitable for any other businesses. Red Sox owner Tom Yawkey had threatened to take the team out of Boston if a new ballpark wasn't constructed, but with the success of the 1967 club, it appeared imminent — at least to Broeg — that the city would nonetheless soon get a new state-of-the-art sports complex for all of its sports teams. "The way New England has reacted to this 100-to-1 long shot," he wrote, "you can be sure that Boston will get off its political treadmill to build that fantastic complex designed to house baseball's Red Sox, football's Patriots, hockey's Bruins, and basketball's Celtics."

The old oak seats creaked as the local fans nervously watched the series begin, hoping that this would finally be their chance to bring home their first world championship in fifty years.

The Cardinals' own Caray was at the NBC television microphone along with Curt Gowdy for the series, as Gowdy had left the Boston broadcast booth a year earlier for work on NBC's Game of the Week with Pee Wee Reese (Reese, meanwhile, was handling the World Series action on the radio side). Facing Gibson in Game One for the Red Sox was Jose Santiago, a 27-year-old right-hander who had grown up seven miles away from Cepeda in Puerto Rico and had fashioned a 12–4 record in the regular season for Boston (a mark which topped the American League for winning percentage). The Cards' first turn at the plate was a microcosm of the regular season, as Brock led off with a single and stole second. But after Flood struck out and Maris walked, Cepeda grounded into a double play to end the opening threat.

The 31-year-old Gibson then took the ball from home plate umpire Johnny Stevens of the American League, and nodded confidently to his shortstop, Maxvill, the man who had snagged so many grounders behind him during the summer. Maxvill had gotten insider tips on playing shortstop at Fenway from his understudy for the season — Bressoud — who had regularly played short for the Red Sox for four years from 1962 to 1965. Bressoud, in particular, had told Maxvill about the crazy bounces that the ball could take off the Green Monster — the infamous 37-foot-high wall in left field which, when a batted ball was sent against it, could shoot it back all the way to the nearby infield (the wall had actually only been green since the 1947 season, as it had been previously covered with billboards). To help him get ready for the task, Brock practiced by having fielded about 40 balls hit off the Monster by coach Joe Schultz's fungo bat during the previous day's workout session.

The big right-hander gave his searing look into McCarver's signs, and went to work with his normal rage towards the batter. While warming up in the bullpen, Gibson was being caught by Muffett, and the popping sound that Gibson's fastball made in Muffett's mitt made the nearby Red Sox fans "oooh" and "ahhh" with trepidation. Gibson readily admitted that he used his mysterious reputation among American Leaguers as a weapon — especially in All-Star and World Series play, as in the days before satellite television, the American League hitters had little chance to have previously seen him throw. In part because of Gibson's perceived angry demeanor, the Red Sox assumed that he threw mostly fastballs, when in fact Gibson revealed that he tallied many of his strikeouts on the slider.

He struck out second baseman Jerry Adair and third baseman Dalton Jones to start the Boston first inning. Next came Yastrzemski, and the one-on-one battle which all had anticipated was now on. Overpowered on a slider, Yaz popped out meekly in foul ground to Cepeda to end the first inning. Gibson was performing just as Woodeshick had predicted when the Cards arrived in town—for he forecasted that both Gibson and Hughes would have great success in Fenway Park (Hughes was scheduled to pitch the second game the next day) as both possessed not only above-average fastballs, but biting sliders that would keep Boston hitters away from the Green Monster — which despite its height, stood a mere 315 feet from home plate, inviting to right-handed hitters from all clubs. Woodeshick also pointed out that both pitchers had performed well in Cincinnati's Crosley Field during the 1967 season, a park which also had a left field wall that was relatively close to the plate.

The Cards loaded the bases in the second, but once again a double play foiled their chances to score as Gibson rolled a doomed ground ball to Jones. He grabbed his glove and returned to the mound to strike out Petrocelli and Reggie Smith in the bottom half, keeping the game scoreless.

In the preceding weeks, scouts around the American League had consistently reported that there was only one true measure that would shut down the Cardinals offense — keeping Brock and Flood off the base paths. But in the third, Brock reached again with his second single in three innings. Brock did not steal a single base in the 1964 World Series against the Yankees, and was getting anxious to show the American League his legendary jump. After two throws over to first, a distracted Santiago lightened up on his offering to Flood as he lined a double to the left field gap that landed Lou at third with nobody out. Then Maris — the man whose lone RBI in the 1964 series against the Cardinals (being a member of the Yankees) came on a home run in Game Six — drove home the first score of the 1967 World Series, a sharp ground ball to first that was scooped up by George Scott as Brock crossed the plate. Even with this breakthrough, however, though the next inning (the fourth), the Cardinals would have supplied themselves with nine base runners, but yet only had Brock's run to show for their efforts.

After Gibson struck out his namesake — Red Sox catcher Russ Gibson — to begin the bottom of the third, he quickly posted two strikes on Santiago. He got lazy with the third pitch, and left a curveball high up in the zone. Santiago — who had batted .190 on the year — jumped on the offering and drove the ball over the left-center field wall, tying the game at one as the fans cheered wildly. Gibson was so certain that the ball would not get out of the park that he did not even turn to look at Flood pursuing it to the wall. Gibson knew that Santiago was a serviceable hitter, as he had faced him previously in winter league play. But when he saw Santiago jogging around the bases, Gibson said to himself, "Where the hell is he going?" It would be, however, the only mistake that the Cards' ace would make on the day. He scattered three hits the rest of the way, displaying the prowess that the American League hitters had long feared. In the St. Louis seventh, the vaunted top of the order struck again as Brock singled, stole second, and was sent to third on a crafty ground ball off the bat of Flood. The center fielder deftly used an inside-out swing to dribble the ball to Scott at first, a selfless play to move the runner that always has the batter greeted with appreciative handshakes when he returns to the dugout. Next up was Maris, and he rang another seemingly-ordinary ground ball at the right side of the infield — but the ordinary grounder produced yet another run. Adair, who at the time held the major league record for second basemen for consecutive errorless games (89) and consecutive chances without an error (458), had been playing in close to stop the run from scoring, but was forced to make a diving play to his left which used up too much time. His only available play was to flip the ball to Scott at first, which allowed Brock to score the go-ahead tally in what would be the ultimate difference in the game for a 2–1 final score. In both instances, Santiago later admitted that he was trying to strike Maris out with pitches low and inside — pitches which precisely allowed Roger to pull the ball on the ground. In the ninth, Brock had a chance to break the World Series record for hits in a game with his fifth, but was instead walked by reliever John Wyatt. Nonetheless, with four hits, Brock now shared the record with five other Cardinals — Joe Medwick, Rip Collins, Whitey Kurowski, Joe Garagiola, and Enos Slaughter — among players from other teams. Days earlier, someone had cornered Philadelphia manager Gene Mauch on his prediction for the series. "Lou Brock will dominate," Mauch simply said.

Schoendienst had wanted a split leaving Boston at the very least, and now he had his wish. "Gibson made only two bad pitches the entire day," the manager pointed out, "the hanging curve that Santiago hit for a homer on a no-ball, two-strike count, and the leadoff hit by Siebern in the eighth." The Boston manager, Williams, recalled facing Gibson himself, as a batter, during a barnstorming tour by Williams' team after the 1960 major league season.

"How did you do against him?" a writer asked.

"Well, we survived the trip," Williams answered.

The box score from Game One:

St. Louis   0 0 1 0 0 0 1 0 0 — 2 10 0
Boston   0 0 1 0 0 0 0 0 0 — 1   6 0

Batting

St. Louis	**AB**	**R**	**H**	**RBI**
Brock lf	4	2	4	0
Flood cf	5	0	1	0
Maris rf	4	0	1	2
Cepeda 1b	4	0	0	0
McCarver c	3	0	0	0
Shannon 3b	4	0	2	0
Javier 2b	4	0	2	0
Maxvill ss	2	0	0	0
Gibson p	4	0	0	0
Totals	34	2	10	2

2B: Flood (1, off Santiago).
SB: Brock 2 (2, 2nd base off Santiago/Gibson 2).
Team LOB: 10.

Boston	AB	R	H	RBI
Adair 2b	4	0	0	0
Jones 3b	4	0	1	0
Yastrzemski lf	4	0	0	0
Harrelson rf	3	0	0	0
Wyatt p	0	0	0	0
Foy ph	1	0	0	0
Scott 1b	3	0	2	0
Petrocelli ss	3	0	0	0
Andrews ph	1	0	0	0
Smith cf	3	0	1	0
Gibson c	2	0	0	0
Siebern ph, rf	1	0	1	0
Tartabull pr, rf	0	0	0	0
Santiago p	2	1	1	1
Howard c	0	0	0	0
Totals	31	1	6	1

PB: Gibson (1).
2B: Scott (1, off Gibson).
HR: Santiago (1, 3rd inning off Gibson 0 on, 1 out).
SH: Howard (1, off Gibson).
CS: Smith (1,2nd base by Gibson/McCarver).
Team LOB: 5.

Pitching

St. Louis	IP	H	R	ER	BB	SO	HR
Gibson W(1–0)	9	6	1	1	1	10	1

Boston	IP	H	R	ER	BB	SO	HR
Santiago L (0–1)	7	10	2	2	3	5	0
Wyatt	2	0	0	0	2	1	0

BK: Wyatt (1).

There were no player casualties from the first game, but it was revealed afterwards that a St. Louis "injury" did occur with the sore arm of coach Dick Sisler, who threw batting practice to the Cardinals' hitters. Nonetheless, Sisler knew that his duty still had to be performed under any circumstances. "The show must go on," he announced in the usual superstitious Cardinals tone. "If I pitch batting practice one day and we win, then I have to pitch batting practice again before the next game. It's tough on the arm, but we can't change our good-luck pattern now."

Hughes took center stage in Game Two, the 29-year-old rookie who had performed so magnificently in the regular season with his 16 wins and the best base runners-to-innings-pitched ratio in the National League. Williams knew that he had to turn to his ace, Lonborg, as he did not want to leave town down two games to nothing. The six-foot-five Lonborg had been truly dominant in the American League during the course of the season, tying for the league lead in wins (22) while pacing the circuit in strikeouts (246). He had attended Stanford University on an academic scholarship as a biology major, and was a summer league teammate of Jim Palmer's in South Dakota before accepting a $25,000 bonus to sign with Boston in August of 1963. Despite not throwing as hard, Lonborg drew comparisons to Gibson and Drysdale in other ways by some sportswriters, as he was not afraid to pitch inside to a hitter, evidenced in that he also easily led the American League in hit batsmen with 19 (the next closest was Gary Peters of the Chicago White Sox with 11), twelve of which had occurred before the All-Star break. And although he had acquired a head cold in the previous twenty-four hours, Lonborg approached his task with serious determination.

As Hughes had done all season, however, he was not daunted by a supposedly-superior competitor, and matched scoreless innings with the Boston great for the first three rounds. At the start of the bottom of the fourth, he was immediately greeted with a homer off the bat of Yastrzemski, a symbol to the Boston fans that the tide was about to turn in their favor, a refreshing scene for the locals after Gibson had toyed with him in relative ease in four at-bats the previous day. They had been waiting for their main offensive threat to erupt, and a mist of confetti littered the stands as Yaz circled the bases. He had been embarrassed with his performance against Gibson, and joined Harrelson and Petrocelli at the park for extra batting practice long after everyone else had gone home from Game One.

The young Willis would replace Hughes in the sixth, as the starter received a lot of handshakes in the dugout for the lone earned run that he allowed. After Shannon muffed a double-play grounder, Willis permitted a sacrifice fly by Petrocelli to increase the Boston advantage to 2–0, and the game then crumbled upon the pitcher in the following inning. Lead-off batter Jose Tartabull walked, and was pushed to second on a single by Jones. Yastrzemski was due up, and Schoendiest decided to go with his proven southpaw, Hoerner, against Yaz's left-handed bat. It made little difference, as Yastrzemski swung mightily and launched a three-run homer into the stands as Hoerner's late-season struggles continued. Lamabe was able to finish the inning without further damage, but the 5–0 advantage was much more than Lonborg needed. When Brock had grounded out to start the St. Louis seventh moments before Yastrzemski's homer, he was the nineteenth Cardinal in a row to go down — leaving Lonborg only eight outs away from a perfect game in the World Series, something accomplished only once by Don Larsen of the Yankees eleven years earlier. Flood, hitting next, was able to coax a walk out of the right-hander, however, as the Boston faithful stood and cheered for over a minute in recognition of Lonborg's special day. One batter later, Petrocelli thwarted a Cardinals rally by snagging a hot shot off the bat of Cepeda that seemed destined for center field. Moving quickly to his left, Petrocelli flagged it down and tossed to Adair to force Flood. Curt would be the lone Redbird base runner on the entire day, save for a double that Javier sent to the gap in left-center in the eighth. The one-hit, one-walk masterpiece fashioned in 98 pitches by Lonborg was one of the greatest performances in World Series history, and put the Cardinals in a state of uneasiness for the foreseeable future. "It was pure agony when Javier got that hit," Lonborg admitted. "It was like somebody had just stabbed me with a knife." The pitch — as with Santiago's homer off Gibson the previous day — was a breaking ball that was up in the strike zone. "As soon as I released the ball, I knew that it was going to be a hit. I wish I could have taken it back."

It was only the fourth one-hitter in post-season play, and the first one in twenty years. Cepeda was shaking his head afterwards in bewilderment, as he was now hitting .075 for his career against American League pitching in All-Star and World Series games combined. An obviously-impressed Schoendienst compared Lonborg to Tom Seaver in the National League, the promising young right-hander of the Mets. But despite one of the greatest performances off the mound in big league history, it was still Yastrzemski who commanded the attention of the reporters in the dressing room. He stood triumphantly in his undershirt with each foot on a chair in front of his locker, a towel around his neck with one hand on his hips while sipping a bottle of Schlitz beer with the other. "We're pretty confident now that we can take this thing," he bellowed down to the writers. Lonborg, meanwhile, was removing his uniform pants — into the back pocket of which he had placed a paper horseshoe before the game. When one of the writers noticed the charm, Lonborg quickly denied that he believed in luck.

The box score from Game Two:

St. Louis   0 0 0 0 0 0 0 0 0—0 1 1
Boston   0 0 0 1 0 1 3 0 x—5 9 0

Batting

St. Louis	AB	R	H	RBI
Brock lf	4	0	0	0
Flood cf	5	0	0	0
Maris rf	4	0	0	0
Cepeda 1b	4	0	0	0
McCarver c	3	0	0	0
Shannon 3b	4	0	0	0

St. Louis	AB	R	H	RBI
Javier 2b	4	0	1	0
Maxvill ss	2	0	0	0
Tolan ph	1	0	0	0
Bressoud ss	0	0	0	0
Hughes p	2	0	0	0
Willis p	0	0	0	0
Hoerner p	0	0	0	0
Lamabe p	0	0	0	0
Ricketts ph	1	0	0	0
Totals	28	0	1	0

E: Shannon (1)
2B: Javier (1, off Lonborg).
Team LOB: 2.

Boston	AB	R	H	RBI
Tartabull rf	4	1	0	0
Jones 3b	5	1	2	0
Yastrzemski lf	4	2	3	4
Scott 1b	4	1	1	0
Smith cf	3	0	0	0
Adair 2b	4	0	2	0
Petrocelli ss	2	0	1	1
Howard c	3	0	0	0
Lonborg p	4	0	0	0
Totals	33	5	9	5

HR: Yastrzemski 2 (4th inning off Hughes, 0 on, 0 out; 7th inning off Hoerner, 2 on, 0 out).
SF: Petrocelli (1, off Willis).
IBB: Howard (1, by Willis).
SB: Adair (1, 2nd base off Willis/McCarver).
Team LOB: 11.

Pitching

St. Louis	IP	H	R	ER	BB	SO	HR
Hughes L (0–1)	5.1	4	2	1	3	5	1
Willis	0.2	1	2	2	2	1	0
Hoerner	0.2	2	1	1	1	0	1
Lamabe	1.1	2	0	0	0	2	0
Boston	IP	H	R	ER	BB	SO	HR
Lonborg W (1–0)	9	1	0	0	1	4	0

Before leaving town, several of the Cardinals players and their wives had visited the home of basketball great Bill Russell, the leader of many NBA championship teams for the Celtics. Briles, for one, was impressed with the spread of fare that was provided. "We had a lot of what you'd call 'soul food,'" said Briles, invited along as a guest of Gibson — the man whom Briles replaced in the rotation back in July — as Bob had hoped it would help Nellie relax before pitching the third game of the series in St. Louis. "We had some special ribs marinated in a marvelous sauce. We had rice, beans, cornbread, special greens, and candied yams. Russell's wife is a fantastic cook. She and K.C. Jones' [another Celtic] wife did all the cooking." Briles did not seem to be minding his important task ahead, as the music lover laughed and danced with his wife the entire evening at the Russell household. "Russell must have ten million tapes," he noticed. Briles had won nine in a row, and he would be facing Gary Bell, a ten-year major league veteran and former All-Star whom the Red Sox had picked up from Cleveland in midseason. Game Three would take place on Saturday, October 7, and network officials from NBC were hoping for a large television crowd (it would yet be several years before World Series games would be played at night).

The series shifted away from rickety Fenway to the newness of Busch Stadium, as the ballpark hosted its first postseason contest — of which St. Louis fans expected there to be many in the years to come. Despite spending a good portion of his childhood in St. Louis, Dick Williams understandably had no opportunity in the past seventeen months to visit the new ballpark in town. "I've seen pictures of Busch Stadium, and I watched the All-Star Game on television there last year," he said as he arrived. "But that's the closest I've been to it. I guess I'll be able to find it — I know the area." As the Red Sox held a practice session at Busch on Friday the 6th, Yastrzemski for one was not impressed with the conditions of the surroundings. "With this new sod in the outfield, the ball won't bounce true," he grumbled as he looked down near his feet. "And the infield looks lousy. It's spotty. I'm glad I'm playing in the outfield." Williams had another thought to offer about the stadium. "We won't change our strategy because we're playing in a new park," he added. "We will play our game." As he came off the field after the practice, Yaz was greeted with a handshake by Joe Medwick, the former Cardinals outfielder who was the last Triple Crown winner in the National League in 1937.

Being the first post-season game in the new ballpark, naturally a new single-game World Series attendance record for St. Louis was shattered as nearly 55,000 people passed through the gates. Rain had fallen the night before and then early into the day, preventing the teams from taking batting practice on the field, but the clouds had just given way to the sun when Briles took the mound at one o'clock central time. The youngster demonstrated early in the game that he was not intimidated. After retiring Tartabull and Jones to start the game, he took a page out of Lonborg's and Gibson's playbooks and hit Yastrzemski on the left leg with a fastball. Williams stormed out of the dugout, contending to home plate umpire Frank Umont that Yastrzemski was hit intentionally, but Umont made no further issue of the event. In the previous couple of days, a few of the Cardinals had voiced their displeasure at the numerous brushback pitches that Lonborg had fired at them in Game Two, and Williams felt that this was an obvious retaliation. Schoendienst was then summoned from the Cardinals' dugout to join Umont and Williams at home plate, at which time the umpire made it clear that — World Series game or not — no more tight pitches would occur without disciplinary action against the players. "I know that pitch was deliberate," Williams would say afterwards. "We can retaliate if we have to. Two can play the game." Williams pointed to the fact that the pitch was actually *behind* Yastrzemski, striking the left-handed hitter on the back side of his left leg as he stood in the batter's box, indeed an odd place for a brushback pitch (Williams soon argued another call with first base umpire Augie Donatelli in the second inning). A moment later, Yaz — who displayed no ill effects from the incident — tried to give the Red Sox an early advantage in attempting to steal second base after a pitch had bounced a few feet away from McCarver, but he was gunned down by the catcher. The Cardinals wasted no time in coming to Briles' support, as they scored three runs in the first two innings off Bell. Brock immediately commenced the attack after taking a curveball strike by stroking a triple to the gap in left-center, and was promptly plated on a single off the bat of the next hitter, Flood. After McCarver led off the second inning with a base hit, Shannon punched a homer into the stands for a 3–0 lead. A few observers felt that Williams' complaint in the first inning may have hurt his own pitcher; for in his effort to stay away from the Cardinals' hitters, most of Bell's pitches caught too much of the plate and were easily smacked around by the Cardinals' batsmen.

Briles kept Boston off the board until the sixth, when Mike Andrews scored from second on another base hit by Jones, who had matched Brock's total of six hits to date in the series. The Cards got the run back in the bottom half, however, as Brock's speed once again unnerved his unwitting American League counterparts. The Red Sox actually had Brock easily picked off first after he had reached on a bunt single, but a throwing error by pitcher Lee Strange allowed Brock to pick himself off the dirt and gallop all the way into third base with the ball caroming in the right field corner, with Brock's helmet flying off in a jet stream as he rounded second. Then Maris, the veteran of many an October game, shot a single to right field to put the game at 4–1. After another Boston tally in the seventh, Cepeda — who had been hitless in eleven trips to the plate in the series to that point — came through with an RBI double to score Maris, who had just garnered his second hit on the day, and make it 5–2.

In the ninth, a scuffle nearly ensued between McCarver and Boston center fielder Reggie Smith, as the catcher had shoved Smith out of the way in pursuit of Smith's pop-up in foul territory. In turn, Smith intentionally ran into McCarver while starting for first base, as Umont first called Smith out for interference and then had to separate the two men. It was the second out of the inning, and the fans then stood and praised the effort of Briles, who induced Adair to also pop out — this time to a waiting Shannon at third — to end the game.

It was another quick contest, completed in just over two hours in the inimitable Cardinals fashion of pitching, speed, and defense. "He deserved to win," Yastrzemski said of Briles, who along with the first-inning plunking had also caused Yaz to ground out to Javier at second base three straight times. "He kept the ball down. I had good swings, but I missed." Briles was in the middle of shaving in the locker room after the game when Koufax came in to interview him for television, as the former great lefthander offered his congratulations for his tenth straight win over the waning months of 1967. It was the seventeenth time the Cardinals had won a World Series game in St. Louis (which included two victories as the visiting team in Sportsman's Park in 1944 against the St. Louis Browns), but it was the first in their grand new home, a triumphant beginning for many imagined championships to come at the corner of Broadway and Walnut.

The box score from Game Three:

Boston   0 0 0 0 0 1 1 0 0 — 2   7 1
St. Louis   1 2 0 0 0 1 0 1 x — 5 10 0

Batting

Boston	**AB**	**R**	**H**	**RBI**
Tartabull rf	4	0	0	0
Jones 3b	4	0	3	1
Yastrzemski lf	3	0	0	0
Scott 1b	4	0	0	0
Smith cf	4	1	2	1
Adair 2b	4	0	0	0
Petrocelli ss	3	0	0	0
Howard c	3	0	1	0
Bell p	0	0	0	0
Thomas ph	1	0	0	0
Waslewski p	0	0	0	0
Andrews ph	1	1	1	0

Boston	AB	R	H	RBI
Strange p	0	0	0	0
Foy ph	1	0	0	0
Osinski p	0	0	0	0
Totals	32	2	7	2

DP: 1.
E: Stange (1).
HR: Smith (1, 7th inning off Briles 0 on, 0 out).
HBP: Yastrzemski (1, by Briles).
Team LOB: 4.

St. Louis	AB	R	H	RBI
Brock lf	4	2	2	0
Flood cf	4	0	1	1
Maris rf	4	1	2	1
Cepeda 1b	4	0	1	1
McCarver c	4	1	1	0
Shannon 3b	3	1	2	2
Javier 2b	3	0	1	0
Maxvill ss	3	0	0	0
Briles p	3	0	0	0
Totals	32	5	10	5

DP: 1.
2B: Cepeda (1, off Osinski).
3B: Brock (1, off Bell).
HR: Shannon (1, 2nd inning off Bell 1 on, 0 out).
Team LOB: 3.

Pitching

Boston	IP	H	R	ER	BB	SO	HR
Bell L (0–1)	2	5	3	3	1	1	1
Waslewski	3	0	0	0	0	3	0
Strange	2	3	1	0	0	0	0
Osinski	1	2	1	1	0	0	0
St. Louis	IP	H	R	ER	BB	SO	HR
Briles W(1–0)	9	7	2	2	0	4	1

Looking for extra karma in trying to take a 3–1 lead in the series, the Redbirds summoned a storied name from their past to throw out the first ball in Game Four. Frankie Frisch was a Hall of Fame second baseman for the Cardinals and Giants through the 1920s and '30s, after being an All-American football and baseball player at Fordham University. He was the manager of the famed world champion Gas House Gang Cardinals of 1934, Frisch's final year as a full-time player after being hired as the skipper by Breadon and Rickey halfway through the 1933 season. In that 1934 World's Series, Frisch had at his disposal the Dean brothers, Dizzy and Paul, who demanded to pitch as often as possible in order to carry the rest of the team on their shoulders. Before the seventh game of the '34 series, Frisch was pondering the possible use of veteran lefthander Bill Hallahan instead of Dizzy, as Hallahan had the fresher arm. "It will be Dizzy, you can bet all the tea in China," predicted John Carmichael of the *Chicago Tribune* before Frisch announced his choice for Game Seven. Paul had just mentioned to the press that Dizzy had lost twenty pounds from being overworked during the summer, but that he wanted the ball anyway.

Now, in October 1967, Gibson was well on his way to challenging Dean for the title of the greatest Cardinals pitcher of all time. In cool 55-degree weather in Game Four, he would be facing Santiago once again. In the process of adding to his statistical resume over the past several summers, Gibson was also establishing the same workhorse lore that made Dean as famous as his fastball, for Gibson was in the early stages of a remarkable string of games in which teams would fail to knock him out, a display that would stretch well into the 1969 season. Always expecting to complete games that they started, both Gibson and Dean were part of an era in the game long before terms such as "quality start," "middle relief," "set-up man," and "closer" entered the baseball lexicon. It was an era when a pitcher in the bullpen was not a very good pitcher, and no one wanted to be there.

Gibson smelled Boston blood from the outset, especially after learning that Smith and Petrocelli had been slightly injured during Boston's batting practice session (Smith had been hit in the ankle on a pitch from reserve outfielder George Thomas, while Petrocelli was struck on the knee by a hard grounder). With two outs in the top half of the first inning, Yastrzemski was able to cork a single off the right-hander, but Gibson came back with an overpowering slider to strike out Scott and end the threat. And not much after Santiago had finished his own warm-up tosses, Brock, Flood, and Maris had quickly parlayed hits to put St. Louis out in front 2–0. Brock had beaten out an infield hit to third, as Jones allowed the ball to take an extra hop towards the foul line, causing him to have to throw to first side-armed. "Anybody else but Brock, and I'd still have gotten him," Jones said later about the play. "But not that guy." Lou was moved to second on another single by Flood to left field, as part of the credit for Flood's hit could have been given to Brock with his feigned dashes towards second base that not only caused Santiago to pitch out twice to his catcher Howard, but also moved Petrocelli closer to the bag as Flood drove the ball in the hole. Maris then slammed a double between Yastrzemski and Smith that scored both runners. After Cepeda flew out to

right field, McCarver singled home Maris. Subsequently, Javier and Maxvill —
as usual, at the bottom of the batting order — also followed with hits that
scored McCarver as Yastrzemski "stood with his shoulders slumped, eyes
downcast" according to Wilks, already looking like a beaten man. Santiago
was then replaced with Bell (who had thrown only two innings in his start
the previous day), as Gibson then headed to the plate with a four-run advantage. He popped meekly to Yaz in left, but the Cardinals fans roared their
approval, anticipating that the four runs would be enough for the great hurler
to secure a win. Gibson would end the Cardinals' offensive assault in the third
inning as well, but not before Cepeda had started the inning with a double
off Jerry Stephenson and another onslaught from his mates that gave the Cards
two more runs. Stephenson's father, Joe, was a Red Sox scout, and had not
only signed his own son to a $65,000 professional contract, but also had inked
two other Boston pitchers that would appear in the game (Dave Morehead
and Ken Brett).

Gibson retired eight Boston batters in succession until Scott singled with
two out in the fourth, but Smith followed with an easy tapper to Cepeda at
first. The entire day for the Red Sox offense would follow in the same manner; Gibson would tease them by allowing a solitary hit or walk here and
there, but never anything that would amount to a sustained attack. He would
allow a total of only six base runners in going the distance, even though
Muffett did not think his thrower was working with his best stuff that day.
"Gibson didn't have that little extra zip this time," the pitching coach opined,
"but being the competitor that he is, he can get by with a lot less and still be
a helluva a pitcher. He's always relaxed, and doesn't care who's batting." Finishing up the pitching duties for Boston in the bottom half of the eighth
inning was the rookie Brett, who permitted a walk but allowed no further St.
Louis scoring in becoming the youngest pitcher ever to appear in a World
Series game at nineteen years, one month. (In 1924, Freddie Lindstrom of the
Giants took part in the World Series two months shy of his nineteenth, making him the youngest overall player in postseason history.) A couple of days
later, a random fan took out a paid advertisement in a Boston paper that lobbied Williams to give Brett more of a chance on the mound. "I ask all New
England fans to send telegrams to Mr. Williams at Fenway Park asking the
same," the ad concluded. The likable Brett, who had worked in just one game
in the regular season, was predicting that his 14-year-old brother, George,
would go on to an even greater baseball career than his own.

The score of 6–0 stood as the final, with people once again leaving the
ballpark just over a mere two hours after the contest had begun. And the
clutch-loving Maris, for the nineteenth time on the year and for the second
time in the 1967 World Series, had driven in the would-be winning run for
the Cardinals. "I know Roger is making $72,000," Maxvill admitted. "That's

a lot of scratch, but I don't care how much he's getting paid; he's earned it. He's earned it even if he got $270,000. I just want to see him back next year — I don't care if they have to pay him twice what he's getting now." Maxvill's comments, ironically, came on the eve of the Philadelphia 76ers announcing that they would make basketball star Wilt Chamberlain the highest-paid athlete in American history, providing him with a $250,000 salary for one year's play in the 1967–68 NBA season. Chamberlain had been holding out of the 76ers' pre-season practices, hoping for an increase from the $200,000 that he had made the previous year.

As expected, there were good feelings all around in the Cards' locker room. Schoendienst was asked by the reporters what he felt was the turning point in the game. "Gibson's shutout," he responded, followed by thunderous laughter.

The St. Louis pitching indeed appeared overwhelming to all observers, and the offense — led by their mercurial lead-off man — was providing more than enough punch for sustenance. "Bressoud was a good friend of mine when he was with Boston," Yastrzemski said after the game. "He told me that Brock has an uncanny knack of getting on base his first time up, and Ed was right." The Cards looked forward to wrapping things up in front of their home crowd the next day, the quintessential way to christen the year-and-a-half-old ballpark. With their backs against the wall and facing elimination, it was obvious that the Red Sox were going to run Lonborg out to the mound once again. Down the hall from Schoendienst's press forum, Cepeda — happy again now that he was hitting again — had returned to his perch as the lead Redbird in the locker room cheers.

"Do you want to go to Boston?" he asked his mates while atop the money trunk.

"No! No! No!" they yelled back.

The box score from Game Four:

```
Boston      0 0 0 0 0 0 0 0 0 — 0 5 0
St. Louis   4 0 2 0 0 0 0 0 x — 6 9 0
```

Batting

Boston	AB	R	H	RBI
Tartabull rf	4	0	2	0
Jones 3b	4	0	0	0
Yastrzemski lf	4	0	2	0
Scott 1b	4	0	1	0
Smith cf	3	0	0	0
Adair 2b	4	0	0	0
Petrocelli ss	3	0	0	0

Boston	AB	R	H	RBI
Howard c	2	0	0	0
Morehead p	0	0	0	0
Siebern ph	1	0	0	0
Brett p	0	0	0	0
Santiago p	0	0	0	0
Bell p	0	0	0	0
Foy ph	1	0	0	0
Stephenson p	0	0	0	0
Ryan c	2	0	0	0
Totals	32	0	5	0

2B: Yastrzemski (1, off Gibson).
Team LOB: 6.

St. Louis	AB	R	H	RBI
Brock lf	4	1	2	0
Flood cf	4	1	1	0
Maris rf	4	1	1	2
Cepeda 1b	4	1	1	0
McCarver c	3	1	1	2
Shannon 3b	3	1	0	0
Javier 2b	4	0	2	1
Maxvill ss	3	0	1	1
Gibson p	3	0	0	0
Totals	32	6	9	6

2B: Maris (1, off Santiago); Cepeda (2, off Stephenson); Javier (2, off Stephenson); Brock (1, off Stephenson).
SF: McCarver (1, off Stephenson).
SB: Brock (3, 2nd base off Morehead/Ryan).
Team LOB: 6.

Pitching

Boston	IP	H	R	ER	BB	SO	HR
Santiago L (0–2)	0.2	6	4	4	0	0	0
Bell	1.1	0	0	0	0	0	0
Stephenson	2	3	2	2	1	0	0
Morehead	3	0	0	0	1	2	0
Brett	1	0	0	0	1	1	0
St. Louis	IP	H	R	ER	BB	SO	HR
Gibson W (2–0)	9	5	0	0	1	6	0

WP: Stephenson (1).

Game Five saw the exact same official attendance figure — 54,575 — as the first two World Series contests in St. Louis, as the new Busch Memorial Stadium was stretched to capacity for the third day in a row. Finally it was Steve Carlton's turn, the young man who had seasoned himself in getting 28 big-league starts over the course of the year. He would give the Red Sox a look at a National League lefthander for the first time in '67, with the Cards a victory away from their second world championship in four years. But Lonborg, despite being only 25 years old himself, had an age and experience advantage over the St. Louis southpaw. Lonborg had already established himself as a big-game pitcher — at the very least, in the past week with the capture of the American League pennant and Game Two of the World Series — and he knew that the Beantown fortunes lay upon his shoulders.

Even though having not thrown in nearly two weeks, Carlton started sharply, with the only Boston base runners in the first two innings being a walk to Yastrzemski and a dropped third strike against Scott. The Cardinals defense had held up well to this point in the series, carrying over its spectacular play from the regular season. The wild card, of course, continued to be Shannon. For with all the progress he had made over 1967 in making the transition from right field to third base, all could have been lost if he suddenly fell apart in the Fall Classic. It appeared to be heading in that direction, as he muffed a bunt off the bat of Mike Andrews, a ball that squirted past Carlton near the mound and was intended by Andrews to be a sacrifice. In the end, Joe Foy — who was getting his first start in the series for the Red Sox at third base — was safe at second as was Andrews at first. "I broke for the ball, but then I saw that Steve had a shot at it," Shannon explained later. "But the ball got by him and bounced over my glove." Carlton was not unnerved by the play, as he got Yastrzemski next on called strikes, as Yaz protested to plate umpire Ed Runge by sarcastically dropping his helmet and bat at home plate — at which the St. Louis crowd booed him vehemently. But then Harrelson, making his first appearance in the series since his hitless performance in Game One, came through next with a single to left on a 2–1 count, and the Red Sox had scored the first run of the game in unearned fashion.

As steady as Carlton was, Lonborg appeared unshakable. With the paper horseshoe back in his pocket, he permitted a single to Maxvill in the bottom half of the third, then another to Maris in the fourth. Aside from these instances, the Cardinals' batters went back and forth from the plate to the dugout with regularity, with no St. Louis base runner reaching second until the eighth inning. Lonborg could not be touched, and his Red Sox headed into the ninth with the 1–0 lead still intact as a result of Shannon's boot, which appeared it would be the difference in the game. Washburn, seeing his first series action in relief of Carlton in the seventh after Tolan had pinch-hit, held the Boston attack in check for two innings before giving way to Willis. Willis allowed the first four batters to reach, which resulted in two more Boston runs after Lamabe gave up a single to Elston Howard. Lamabe actually made a very strong pitch to Howard on the inner half, but the Boston catcher was able to bloop the ball off his fists safely in front of Maris in right. "Howard jammed himself on the pitch," Lamabe said afterwards. "If he had hit the ball better, Roger would have made an easy catch." On the play, Reggie Smith—who had been on second base—ran through a stop sign from third base coach Ed Popowski, as Maris flung the ball towards home plate. The throw was high, but McCarver was able to flag it down and make a swipe tag at Smith. Reggie had already curled safely around the plate, however, and a three-run lead for Lonborg heading into the bottom of the ninth seemed insurmountable.

The top of the Cardinals order was up to face him, but it made little difference. Brock tapped meekly to Andrews at second, and Flood the same to Foy at third. Now, only Maris stood between Lonborg and his second straight shutout. The Boston hurler was keeping in form with recent times, for since the Cardinals beat the Yankees in a relatively high-scoring 1964 World Series, superior pitching had taken over the Fall Classic. In 1965, Koufax had fired consecutive shutouts at the Twins, the second one securing the championship in Game Seven; the tables were turned on his Dodgers in 1966, as the Baltimore Orioles had finished off the Los Angeles men in the World Series in four straight with shutouts by Jim Palmer, Wally Bunker, and Dave McNally in the final three contests. As Lonborg attempted to cement his name among the other pitching legends of the decade, he would have to get by Maris, the October superstar. With his own pride and that of his team on the line, Maris somehow was able to get ahold of a tough pitch and drive it over the right field wall, a home run which was Maris's sixth in World Series play and one which many people in the park missed as they had already begun heading towards the exits after the completion of the first two outs in the inning. Many of those same fans scurried back to their seats when Cepeda hit a line-drive, one-hopper toward the hole between short and third that was a sure hit, but the ball was flagged down by a diving Foy who righted himself and threw Orlando out to end the game. In finishing the contest, Lonborg became the first pitcher in baseball history to allow as few as four hits in two consecutive complete World Series games, evidence that his work was every bit as impressive as the moundsmen that had gone before him in years past. Williams, however, was still awed with the St. Louis lineup. "Brock is simply amazing," the Boston skipper said. "And the Cardinals have another flyer, but he doesn't play—that's Bob Tolan. But it's the old story—you can't steal first base."

Now the Red Sox—still facing elimination with another loss—would force the series to return to their rain-soaked home park, giving them a fighting chance to take the title. "Well, my wife wanted a little more of that great lobster at the Pier Four restaurant anyway," said Maxvill, resigned.

"We could have had lobster at *Musial's* restaurant," Schoendienst grumbled in response.

When the Red Sox arrived at Logan Airport back in Boston, nearly two thousand fans were there to welcome them as they chanted, "Sox in Seven!" A group of young fans—mostly obsessive, love-struck girls—had broken through a glass door in pursuit of a glimpse or a grab of the dashing young hero Lonborg.

The box score from Game Five:

```
Boston      0 0 1 0 0 0 0 0 2 — 3  6  1
St. Louis   0 0 0 0 0 0 0 0 1 — 1  3  2
```

Batting

Boston	AB	R	H	RBI
Foy 3b	5	1	1	0
Andrews 2b	3	0	1	0
Yastrzemski lf	3	0	1	0
Harrelson rf	3	0	1	1
Tartabull rf	0	0	0	0
Scott 1b	3	1	0	0
Smith cf	4	1	1	0
Petrocelli ss	3	0	0	0
Howard c	4	0	1	1
Lonborg p	4	0	0	0
Totals	32	3	6	2

E: Petrocelli (1).
2B: Yastrzemski (2, off Washburn); Smith (1, off Willis).
SH: Andrews (1, off Carlton).
IBB: Petrocelli (1, by Willis).
CS: Petrocelli (1, Home by Lamabe/McCarver).
Team LOB: 7.

St. Louis	AB	R	H	RBI
Brock lf	4	0	0	0
Flood cf	4	0	0	0
Maris rf	4	1	2	1
Cepeda 1b	4	0	0	0
McCarver c	3	0	0	0
Shannon 3b	3	0	0	0
Javier 2b	3	0	0	0

Maxvill ss	2	0	1	0
Ricketts ph	1	0	0	0
Willis p	0	0	0	0
Lamabe p	0	0	0	0
Carlton p	1	0	0	0
Tolan ph	1	0	0	0
Washburn p	0	0	0	0
Gagliano ph	0	0	0	0
Bressoud ss	0	0	0	0
Totals	31	1	3	1

DP: 2.
E: Maris (1), Shannon (2).
HR: Maris (1, 9th inning off Lonborg 0 on, 2 out).
Team LOB: 3.

Pitching

Boston	*IP*	*H*	*R*	*ER*	*BB*	*SO*	*HR*
Lonborg W (2–0)	9	3	1	1	0	4	1

St. Louis	*IP*	*H*	*R*	*ER*	*BB*	*SO*	*HR*
Carlton L (0–1)	6	3	1	0	2	5	0
Washburn	2	1	0	0	0	2	0
Willis	0	1	2	1	2	0	0
Lamabe	1	1	0	0	0	2	0

WP: Carlton (1).
IBB: Willis (2, Petrocelli).

In trying to develop as a pitching prospect in recent years in the Boston farm system, Gary Waslewski had been labeled as "lazy" early in his career by Williams, who had managed him not only with the Red Sox but in the minor leagues as well. "He was on me all the time," Waslewski remembered. "And as far as I'm concerned, it didn't do me a bit of good — he was hollering down a rain barrel. They [Williams and his coaching staff] were using all kinds of psychology on me, hollering and yelling all the time. All they're ever going to get from something like that is a sore throat." Nonetheless, Waslewski — a rookie of both Polish and Indian descent — wound up winning 18 games in helping Williams win the 1966 International League title at Toronto (ironically, Toronto would leave the International League in 1967 after a 78-year affiliation. The club's place in the league would be taken by Louisville the following season). In first signing with the Pittsburgh Pirates out of the University of Connecticut in 1960, Waslewski came to the Red Sox in 1965. At that point he was not even wanted by Williams in Toronto; the manager had his mind set on a couple of other pitching prospects, and Waslewski was thus offered back to the Pirates. When the Pittsburgh organization refused him, Waslewski was stuck in the Boston system, beginning his career at their Pittsfield farm club before rising back to Toronto. Enduring a variety of ailments including a collapsed lung, a bad back, and sore arm in spring training of 1967, Waslewski was originally sent back to Toronto for another season where he posted an uninspiring 5–6 record through midyear. An injury to Red Sox pitcher Darrell Brandon, however, opened a spot for him on the big league roster, and he contributed two victories to the club's pennant chase (including nine scoreless innings that he fired at the White Sox on June 15). Now far removed from their clashes in the minors, Waslewski and Williams put their differences aside and frankly discussed the importance of the upcoming sixth game, for which his manager was giving him the ball. "When Waslewski was with me at Toronto last year," Williams told the press, "I asked him to stop trying to be Thomas Edison. I told him to stop experimenting. Finally, he got rid of his slow curve and stuck to his fastball. I had to insult the devil out of him. I have every confidence in the world in him if he throws as well as he's capable of doing. He's the same type of pitcher as Jim Lonborg." Hughes, meanwhile, would give Fenway Park another try, scheduled to start for the Cardinals after losing to Lonborg in Boston in Game Two. "I hope it's cooler up here this time," Hughes told a reporter as the Cards' plane was about to land, noting that he had been bothered by the intense humidity that had gripped the New England area a week earlier when the Cardinals were greeted with non-functioning air conditioners in their hotel rooms.

Williams had raised the ire of the entire Cardinals team the day before, as he was quoted in a local newspaper as saying that Gibson "is the only St. Louis pitcher of any quality," despite the fact that Williams' hitters had produced a total of only eight earned runs in the first five games, as Dick Sisler pointed out. And the insult-trading did not stop at Fenway Park — it even continued over to the players' better halves. "The Cardinal ballplayers aren't the only ones who look down their noses at the Red Sox," claimed one Boston sportswriter. "Their wives look down their noses at the Red Sox wives. One day in St. Louis, they wouldn't even let the Red Sox wives sit down. A mink coat was stretched across three chairs in a room where wives congregated at Busch Stadium. Whoever owned the coat wouldn't lift a finger to move it." It was an accusation that the Cardinals women denied.

Just as Hughes had hoped, cooler temperatures — along with threatening skies — greeted the two teams as they arrived at Fenway on the morning of the 11th. Similar to the series games at Busch Stadium, each contest in Boston displayed the exact same sell-out attendance figure of 35,188 (except for the opener, which inexplicably had recorded 34,796 witnesses). Drawing first blood were the Red Sox in the second inning, as Petrocelli — who had been batting .071 in the series as he stepped to the plate — stunned everyone in the park with a blow over the fence in left. The Cards came immediately back in the third off Waslewski, who was making his first start in over five weeks. Brock came through with a clutch two-out hit to score Javier, who had led off with a double but could not be moved by Maxvill or Hughes. Brock then put his club ahead as the running game kicked into gear once again. He picked the perfect pitch and got the jump on Waslewski and Howard, sliding into second ahead of Petrocelli's tag for his fourth steal of the series. Flood — who, like Petrocelli, had been struggling with a .150 average himself in the five games played thus far — then stroked a single to left that fell in front of Yastrzemski, and St. Louis had a 2–1 lead in its quest to wrap things up that day.

However, a barrage of solo home runs greeted Hughes in the fourth, including a lead-off dinger by Yastrzemski and two-out shots by Smith and Petrocelli, the latter's second in as many trips to the plate (Petrocelli had actually been feeling ill before the game, and took a vitamin shot for an extra boost before taking the field). With the three balls leaving the yard, Hughes had set the record for most home runs allowed in a World Series inning. In addition, he had now tied the record for the most allowed in a total series with five. Furthermore, Yastrzemski also tied a World Series record with three home runs in a six-game series. The assault led Schoendienst to replace the starter with Willis, who precluded any further damage by getting Howard to roll out to Shannon and leave the Red Sox with a 4–2 lead.

Excellent relief work by Briles and Boston hurler Wyatt kept the score the same into the seventh, when the Cards mounted a charge. After Maxvill flied out to Smith in center to start the inning, Tolan batted for Briles and precisely did his job, reaching first base on four balls. Williams, as with his recent blurb in the newspapers, had warned his pitching staff that Tolan possessed the same dangerous speed of Brock, but the young outfielder had not been a factor as of yet in the series. Wyatt gave him several glances before offering up a very hittable pitch to Brock, and Lou drove the ball over the short outfield wall in right to instantly tie the game at four. Wyatt righted himself, as Flood and Maris finished the inning in the same manner that Maxvill had opened it. Running catches by Smith prevented St. Louis from taking the lead, and stemmed the momentum that Schoendienst's men had suddenly seized. But Lamabe — the hard-luck case in Game Five with the bleeder he allowed to Howard to permit the insurance runs for the Red Sox — became unnerved in the bottom half. This time he was able to retire Howard, the first batter of the inning, with an easy grounder to Shannon at third. The Red Sox then proceeded to shower him and his successor, Hoerner, with a bounty of hits that came from six out of the next seven Boston batters, resulting in four runs that galvanized the hometown crowd. Wyatt, now off the hook for allowing Brock to tie the game, was relieved by Bell. Cepeda, still struggling mightily at the plate, broke out in the eighth with a lead-off single, which Shannon followed one out later with a double as the Cardinals looked poised for yet another comeback. After Javier lined a screamer to Petrocelli at third for the second out, Maxvill worked a walk out of Bell to load the bases. Washburn — who had relieved Jaster in the top half (who in turn had relieved Hoerner), having gotten Howard to end the inning as he started it, with a groundout to Shannon — saw his turn come in the batting order, so Schoendienst told Ricketts to grab a bat, his last option among the remaining position players. Ricketts, who had been unsuccessful in his two previous pinch-hitting trips to the plate in the series, stood in against Bell with a chance to get the Cards back in the game once again. He caught a piece of a low pitch that he was able to drive fairly hard to left, but the smooth Yastrzemski was able to glide over and grab the ball with relative ease before it hit the turf.

A Maris single was all that could be had in the ninth, as Bell — the eleventh pitcher used in the game, a World Series record — closed things out as the Red Sox forced a winner-take-all on their home field for the following day. The momentum in the series was obviously now in their favor. Even though they already knew the answer, the Boston newsmen asked Williams who his starting pitcher would be in Game Seven. "Lonborg — and champagne," he responded to a roomful of laughter. To be sure, the setting was in place for the young right-hander to put a capstone on the most dominating pitching performance in World Series history, and more importantly to the people of New England, bring the long-sought title home to Massachusetts Bay.

The box score from Game Six:

```
St. Louis    0 0 2 0 0 0 2 0 0 — 4   8   0
Boston       0 1 0 3 0 0 4 0 x — 8  12   1
```

Batting

St. Louis	**AB**	**R**	**H**	**RBI**
Brock lf	5	2	2	3
Flood cf	5	0	1	1
Maris rf	4	0	2	0
Cepeda 1b	5	0	1	0
McCarver c	3	0	0	0
Shannon 3b	4	0	1	0
Javier 2b	4	1	1	0
Maxvill ss	3	0	0	0
Hughes p	1	0	0	0
Willis p	0	0	0	0
Spiezio ph	1	0	0	0
Briles p	0	0	0	0

St. Louis	AB	R	H	RBI
Tolan ph	0	1	0	0
Lamabe p	0	0	0	0
Hoerner p	0	0	0	0
Jaster p	0	0	0	0
Washburn p	0	0	0	0
Ricketts ph	1	0	0	0
Woodeshick p	0	0	0	0
Totals	36	4	8	4

2B: Javier (3, off Waslewski); Shannon (1, off Bell).
HR: Brock (1, 7th inning off Wyatt 1 on, 1 out).
SB: Brock (4, 2nd base off Waslewski/Howard).
Team LOB: 9.

Boston	AB	R	H	RBI
Foy 3b	4	1	1	1
Andrews 2b	5	1	2	1
Yastrzemski lf	4	2	3	1
Harrelson rf	3	0	0	0
Tartabull rf	0	0	0	0
Adair ph	0	0	0	1
Bell p	0	0	0	0
Scott 1b	4	0	1	0
Smith cf	4	1	2	2
Petrocelli ss	3	2	2	2
Howard c	4	0	0	0
Waslewski p	1	0	0	0
Wyatt p	0	0	0	0
Jones ph	1	1	1	0
Thomas rf	1	0	0	0
Totals	34	8	12	8

E: Petrocelli (2).
2B: Foy (1, off Lamabe).
HR: Petrocelli 2 (2, 2nd inning off Hughes 0 on, 2 out, 4th inning off Hughes 0 on, 2 out); Yastrzemski (3, 4th inning off Hughes 0 on, 0 out); Smith (2, 4th inning off Hughes 0 on, 2 out).
SH: Foy (1, off Briles).
SF: Adair (1, off Jaster).
HBP: Waslewski (1, by Briles).
IBB: Yastrzemski (1, by Briles); Petrocelli (2, by Washburn).
Team LOB: 7.

Pitching

St. Louis	IP	H	R	ER	BB	SO	HR
Hughes	3.2	5	4	4	0	2	4
Willis	0.1	0	0	0	0	0	0
Briles	2	0	0	0	1	0	0
Lamabe L (0–1)	0.1	2	2	2	0	0	0
Hoerner	0	2	2	2	0	0	0
Jaster	0.1	2	0	0	0	0	0
Washburn	0.1	0	0	0	1	0	0
Woodeshick	1	1	0	0	0	0	0

Boston	IP	H	R	ER	BB	SO	HR
Waslewski	5.1	4	2	2	2	4	0
Wyatt W (1–0)	1.2	1	2	2	1	0	1
Bell S (1)	2	3	0	0	1	0	0

HBP: Briles (2, Waslewski).
IBB: Briles (1, Yastrzemski); Washburn (1, Petrocelli).

Ironically, not all of the sports attention in St. Louis was focused on the Cardinals during the important week. For on the night of October 11, as the Cards and Red Sox were resting in anticipation of the winner-take-all finale the following afternoon, the St. Louis Blues of the National Hockey League were born. "Officials of the Blues are reluctant to predict a sellout," reported Wally Cross of the *Post-Dispatch*, "but a capacity crowd of 14,100 may be on hand for the opener. All of the $2.50 and $6.00 seats were sold out by yesterday, leaving only $3, $4, and $5 seats available." Back home along the Mississippi, the Blues skated in their initial regular-season game with the Minnesota North Stars to a 2–2 tie at the St. Louis Arena near Forest Park. The Blues, North Stars, Pittsburgh Penguins, Philadelphia Flyers, Los Angeles Kings, and the Oakland Seals had doubled the original number of NHL teams in 1967 to twelve, having received their official permission for entrance into the league back on June 5. The Blues would surpass everyone's expectations very quickly, beating the Flyers in seven games in the league quarterfinal playoffs the following spring, and also using seven games to dispose of the North Stars in the semifinals for an opportunity to face the mighty Montreal Canadiens for the Stanley Cup championship. With Montreal having several future Hall of Fame players on their roster, they swept the Blues in four straight games—despite enduring a fierce battle from the St. Louis men, with each game being decided by a single goal along with two being determined in overtime. It had been a foregone conclusion, however, that one of the expansion teams would make the finals, for they had been placed in a separate division since the start of the season with the "Original Six" in another, with each division staging its own playoffs to determine a league finalist. The warning of league president Clarence Campbell had, in essence, come true — the fear that under such a plan, an expansion team would be overmatched in the finals against an established club (but as displayed by the scores in the final round, it could be argued that the Blues were not overmatched, despite losing in four straight). Campbell had suggested that the entire league be thrown into the mix for a playoff format, but the league's board of governors instead decided to segregate the new and old franchises.

If all that occupied the mind in these days were opening-night hockey games and championship deciding baseball games, it would have been a simple world. But as St. Louis tried to focus its attention on sports, the domestic and international perils that the United States had endured over the 1960s dragged on. In Cincinnati that afternoon, six black students at Hughes High School attacked fourteen white students and were escorted off by police, chanting "black power" slogans as they were led into the squad cars; certain supermarket companies nationwide were being charged with collusion, allegedly conspiring to hike food prices in poor neighborhoods; and the conflict in Vietnam seemed endless, as the Department of Defense issued another draft call for December 1967 that solicited 18,200 more soldiers for the effort, up from the 12,100 that had been called twelve months earlier but down severely from the 40,200 that had received the obligation of induction in December 1965. The war was appearing to polarize the different segments of American society. "Let me say, as solemnly as I can, that those who would abdicate their responsibilities to this nation put it in jeopardy," Secretary of State Dean Rusk advised those who were considering evasion of any draft orders.

As the Blues were playing in St. Louis that night before Game Seven of the World Series, Gibson was instead looking for jazz. He wished for an opportunity to relax and get his mind off things, so he went to hear a personal friend of his, Les McCann, play the piano at a local jazz club. Gibson might just as well have stayed out of the hotel until the first pitch the next day, for a suspicious chain of events followed that would rattle his evening. Upon returning to the hotel around ten o'clock, he found that the air conditioning had once again been turned off in his room — not accidentally by Gibson himself before he left the room, but forcibly by the hotel management for "maintenance" reasons. Fighting a toothache as well, and with outside temperatures warming once again, he nonetheless laid on top of the bed and tried to sleep in the humid conditions.

The next morning, Gibson — short on sleep from the temperature in his room — came stumbling down to the hotel coffee shop to join McCarver, Maxvill, and their wives for breakfast before boarding the team bus to Fenway Park. Upon glancing at the *Boston Record-American* newspaper, they all noticed the headline, placed in large block print in a size that was usually reserved for declarations of war:

LONBORG AND CHAMPAGNE

They all looked at each other for a moment, and then laughed at the pronouncement while enjoying their coffee. While the five others—including Gibson's wife, Charline—had their food served promptly, the waitress informed the pitcher that his order had somehow "been lost." Nearly an hour later, the waitress brought Gibson some burned toast, which he tersely refused as the Cardinal bus continued to sit idling in the parking lot (Schoendienst and the coaches wanted to be sure that Gibson had some breakfast before they departed, so they decided to wait). Gibson stormed out of the coffee shop, as the evident tactics of the establishment had backfired—for despite the mistreatment, he was now all the more determined to single-handedly take down the Red Sox in the finale. He would not have to do it on an empty stomach, however. Broeg, who was also on the bus, suddenly asked the driver to allow him to depart when it paused at a stoplight. He jumped into a cab, and ordered the driver to take him to the nearest restaurant. He commanded two ham-and-egg sandwiches, placed them in a paper bag, and hurried back to the cab to intercept the grateful Cardinals pitcher in the visitors locker room at the stadium. Gibson gobbled down one of the sandwiches, left the other in its wrapper on top of his locker, and got down to business. "Anger was part of my preparation," Gibson would later say, defying the unscrupulous plans of the folks at the Sheraton Motor Inn in Quincy. "The people at the hotel, despite their best efforts to the contrary, were getting me extremely ready for the ballgame."

Once again, the aura of Gibson was striking fear in the hearts of the Boston men. He was going on three days' rest versus Lonborg's two, and the Red Sox knew they would have their hands full. "When I faced Gibson in Game Four of the 1967 World Series, it was the closest I ever came to being intimidated," the normally cocksure Reggie Smith stated. But Boston first baseman George Scott was more confident, and showed that many in the sports world had not forgotten the quips of the disposed Cassius Clay. "Gibson won't survive five," the Red Sox slugger said in mimicking the famous boxer.

The temperature in Boston read 63 degrees when it was time for the first pitch, as cloudy skies still dominated the backdrop. Cepeda had skipped batting practice, saying that he was tired of "using up all my hits" before the game started (his own explanation for his lack of batting prowess in the series). As Lonborg made his way in from the bullpen, the crowd rose in a gradual wave to give him a standing ovation. A moment earlier, when the Boston lineups were introduced, a "tenth man" was acknowledged — it was Conigliaro, making a momentary trip down from the press box to appear before the Boston fans for the first time since his beaning in the face back in August, as the fans gave him a rowdy salute as well. Meanwhile, back in St. Louis, fans nestled in before televisions and radios to monitor every pitch — including Mayor Cervantes, who had made sure that he had a prime place to watch the game. The mayor, his staff, and friends gathered in front of one of the eight TV sets that were in operation at Stan and Biggie's.

It took Lonborg only nine pitches to put the Cards down in the first, with the lone base runner being Maris, who logged an infield hit on a ball on which the pitcher could not cover first base in time. The bottom half offered a promising start for the Red Sox, as Foy coaxed a walk out of Gibson in the lead-off spot, causing an expectant cheer from the stands. Gibson proceeded to quell the uprising, ending the inning by catching Harrelson looking at strike three.

Williams was keeping a close eye on Lonborg, watching for signs of fatigue. The manager knew that even the best pitcher was worthless with no energy, but he relaxed a bit when Lonborg retired St. Louis with relative ease again in the second. Javier had knocked a two-out single to left, and subsequently tried to grab a run for the Redbirds by swiping second. But Howard, rekindling the defensive skills that once made him one of the great catchers of the past decade and the 1963 American League MVP with the Yankees, fired quickly to Andrews to catch Hoolie stealing. In the third, however, the first signs of Lonborg tiring became apparent very quickly. Maxvill — who had been thought of as a regular out by opponents all season long — came up with his biggest hit of the year, leading off the inning with a long triple over the head of Smith in center field. Lonborg recovered to get Gibson to line out to Foy at third, and Brock to pop up to Petrocelli at short, keeping Maxvill at third. A clutch hit was needed from Flood, and he promptly singled in putting the Cards in front. The team's speed came into play immediately once again, as after a Maris hit had sent Flood to third, Curt scored an important two-out run when a pitch got away from Lonborg and bounced to the screen behind Howard, plating the St. Louis center fielder for a 2–0 advantage.

With the Cardinals still holding the same lead in the fifth, Maxvill once again came to bat to lead off the inning. This time Lonborg, invigorated by a one-two-three inning he had logged in the fourth, jammed the shortstop and forced him to ground weakly to Foy at third. Next was Gibson, and although his reputation as a hitter and general athlete was well-circulated in the American League, he had been hitless in eight trips to the plate in the series after his lineout in the third. What followed from his bat, however, was one of the longest home runs seen at Fenway on the year — a soaring shot to the bleachers in dead center field, a tremendous display of power. When coupled with Santiago's homer in Game One, it was the first time in over forty years that two pitchers had hit the long ball in the same World Series. It was the solitary moment that shifted the tide completely in the Cardinals' favor. Now Lonborg, visibly rattled, permitted the St. Louis jackrabbits to get aboard as Brock singled and stole second. Before Flood would have a chance to take his base on balls, Brock took off for third and swiped it as well, the first time second and third had been stolen by a runner in one inning in World Series play since Babe Ruth accomplished the feat back in 1921. It was a vintage Cardinals inning, as Maris put another nail in the Boston coffin with a solid sacrifice fly to score Brock, giving the Cards yet another run as the Red Sox were facing a steeper and steeper slope on Gibson Hill that they would have to climb. The Red Sox were utterly baffled by Brock, as he was unlike any base runner they had seen over the course of the summer in the American League. "Lou has no specific weaknesses when he's on base," Dodgers pitcher Claude Osteen once stated. "He has so many different moves and so much speed, it's almost impossible to contain him."

Undaunted, the brash Scott tripled to lead off the bottom of fifth for Boston, and scored as Javier committed an error in handling the relay throw. The play had ended a string of twelve consecutive batters retired by Gibson since allowing the leadoff walk to Foy in the first inning. The stoic thrower went right back to work and retired Smith, Petrocelli, and Howard in succession to keep the score at 4–1.

The Cardinals had always made their living at manufacturing runs, so no one anticipated the turn that their offense would take in the sixth. They opened the frame with McCarver doubling to right field and Shannon reaching on an error by Foy. Next was Javier, and all expected a bunt from the meek little Hoolie in typical St. Louis fashion. Upon a visit by Williams to the mound, Lonborg convinced his manager to let him face the soft-hitting Javier. Expecting a bunt like everyone else, Lonborg pitched to him accordingly, offering a fastball high in the strike zone. Lonborg was surprised when Javier did not square to bunt, but instead chopped at the ball that carried far into the New England autumn sky. It landed well over the wall to the shock of all witnesses, and Javier carried himself around third with the Cardinals' seventh run in following McCarver and Shannon to the plate. Javier was coming off a career-high 14 homers in the 1967 regular season, but despite the World Series setting, much of this information was only slightly circulated to American Leaguers before the age of advance scouting and satellite television.

Gibson Hill had now become Mount Gibson, and the Red Sox were left without their rope and hooks.

And after the dramatics by Javier, few actually noticed a couple of batters later when Brock doubled to left. The feat gave him twelve hits for the series, which tied the all-time record.

The loudest shot heard in Boston since the incident at the bridge at Concord — Julian Javier's sixth-inning homer off Jim Lonborg in Game Seven, which gave the Cardinals an insurmountable 7–1 lead. Bob Gibson continued to silence the Red Sox' bats in taking the 1967 world championship. (*St. Louis Globe-Democrat* / Archives of the St. Louis Mercantile Library)

The man from Omaha sailed on into the ninth, with the only hit he permitted being a double to Petrocelli in the eighth which assisted in the scoring of a Boston run. As the Cardinals batted in the top half, Brock walked and stole second. When he got up from his slide, Smith — who had been running in from center field to back up the play — started hollering at him, saying it was unbecoming to be stealing second with the score being 7–2 in the ninth. But Brock shot right back at him, saying that Smith would have done the same thing if the situation had been reversed. Hearkening back to some ill feelings his own Cardinals teammates had for him during the summer in terms of his individual numbers, perhaps Lou did know that it was his seventh steal in the series, breaking another record set by Honus Wagner of the Pirates in 1909. Despite the controversy, the inning would end with no further Cardinals damage, as McCarver grounded out to Scott at first. The out was recorded by Brett, as the 19-year-old rookie got one more taste of World Series action.

Needing three more outs for the championship, Gibson sauntered to the hill in his unemotional way in the bottom of the ninth, as he had done before for thousands of innings in his life. First up was the proud Yastrzemski, Massachusetts' favorite son who offered the best chance to summon a comeback. Gibson made a rare mistake and Yaz jumped it, lining a sharp single to right as a hopeful murmur was born in the stands. Harrelson stood in the batter's box next, as Maxvill and Javier reminded the Cardinals outfielders to play deep and keep all balls in front of them, in order to prevent a big inning from evolving. It was at this point, the final inning of the year, when the Shannon Experiment at third base — which had begun with trepidation back in spring training — had finally come to full fruition for Schoendienst and the rest of the Cardinals coaching staff. Harrelson hit a hard ground ball to Shannon, who in turn snagged it quickly with his glove and threw to Javier and on to Cepeda, in executing what Gibson called "possibly the fastest double play I'd ever seen them pull off." On the eve of the regular season opener back on April 11, Broeg had almost prophetically written in his column that "if Mike Shannon can play a satisfactory third base defensively and if the young pitching comes up at least to last year's performance, the Redbirds—barring critical injury or misfortune — might go all the way."

Gagliano, Spiezio, Tolan, and the rest of the subs— who, while not playing a major role in the series, had certainly done their part to get the Cardinals *to* the postseason — were on the top step of the visitors dugout as Gibson kicked at the rubber one last time in 1967. He peered in toward the plate to find George Scott staring back at him, the man who twenty-four hours earlier had predicted that Gibson would not last through the fifth inning. Gibby reached back for one last fastball on a two-strike count, and umpire Johnny Stevens' right arm shot skyward. The Cardinals had won the World Series.

The unraveling of the Red Sox harkened back to another World Series demise for a Cardinals opponent — the Detroit Tigers in 1934. Heading into Game Seven at Detroit that year, the local faithful were confident in the home club, having won in St. Louis to send the series back to familiar turf. As in Boston, however, what the Detroit fans witnessed was the all-out implosion of their best pitcher (Schoolboy Rowe) and the entire team, erasing the chance to remedy years of disappointment in pursuit of a title. And, like Gibson, the Cardinals' great pitcher of the era — Dizzy Dean — took the team onto his own shoulders and down Rowe and the Tigers 11–0.

The box score from Game Seven:

St. Louis   0 0 2 0 2 3 0 0 0 — 7 10 1
Boston   0 0 0 0 1 0 0 1 0 — 2   3 1

Batting

St. Louis	AB	R	H	RBI
Brock lf	4	1	2	0
Flood cf	3	1	1	1
Maris rf	3	0	2	1
Cepeda 1b	5	0	0	0
McCarver c	5	1	1	0
Shannon 3b	4	1	0	0
Javier 2b	4	1	2	3
Maxvill ss	4	1	1	0
Gibson p	4	1	1	1
Totals	36	7	10	6

DP: 1.

E: Javier (1).

2B: McCarver (1, off Lonborg); Brock (2, off Lonborg).

3B: Maxvill (1, off Lonborg).

HR: Gibson (1, 5th inning off Lonborg 0 on, 1 out); Javier (1, 6th inning off Lonborg 2 on, 0 out).

SF: Maris (1, off Lonborg).

SB: Brock 3 (7, 2nd base off Lonborg/Howard, 3rd base off Lonborg/Howard, 2nd base off Morehead/Gibson).

CS: Javier (1, 2nd base by Lonborg/Howard).

Team LOB: 7.

Boston	AB	R	H	RBI
Foy 3b	3	0	0	0
Morehead p	0	0	0	0
Osinski p	0	0	0	0
Brett p	0	0	0	0
Andrews 2b	3	0	0	0
Yastrzemski lf	3	0	1	0
Harrelson rf	4	0	0	0
Scott 1b	4	1	1	0
Smith cf	3	0	0	0
Petrocelli ss	3	1	1	0
Howard c	2	0	0	0
Jones ph,3b	0	0	0	0
Lonborg p	1	0	0	0
Tartabull ph	1	0	0	0
Santiago p	0	0	0	0
Siebern ph	1	0	0	1

Boston	AB	R	H	RBI
Gibson c	0	0	0	0
Totals	28	2	3	1

E: Foy (1).
2B: Petrocelli (1, off Gibson).
3B: Scott (1, off Gibson).
SH: Andrews (2, off Gibson).
Team LOB: 3.

Pitching

St. Louis	IP	H	R	ER	BB	SO	HR
Gibson W (3–0)	9	3	2	2	3	10	0

Boston	IP	H	R	ER	BB	SO	HR
Lonborg L (2–1)	6	10	7	6	1	3	2
Santiago	2	0	0	0	0	1	0
Morehead	0.1	0	0	0	3	1	0
Osinski	0.1	0	0	0	0	0	0
Brett	0.1	0	0	0	0	0	0

WP: Gibson (1), Lonborg (1).

El Birdos were on top of the world. It was the sixth straight time that the Cardinals had won a seventh and deciding game in the World Series, and they had never lost in such a situation. Schoendienst had used the exact same starting lineup for all seven games, with surprisingly little help from the bench.

Of course, there was only one victory song to be sung in the locker room. The Cards grabbed each other by the hips and formed a conga line. Kicking outward as they danced in a circle around the room, they yelled, "*Lonborg and champagne — Hey! Lonborg and champagne — Hey!*" in a mock–Boston celebration. Meanwhile Gibson, who always acted dignified even after the greatest of triumphs, was simply munching away quietly on the other ham-and-egg sandwich that he left atop his locker. Ironically (in light of their dismantled air conditioning system back at the hotel), the team also found that there was no hot water in the visitors' showers at Fenway Park. They did not seem to mind, giving each other a celebratory dousing anyway with their uniforms still on their backs. Unfortunately, in the midst of the laughing and celebrating, there was a casualty. The top of a champagne bottle exploded in Hoerner's pitching hand, cutting tendons in his thumb and index finger. Even after treatment back in St. Louis, Hoerner would not regain complete movement in either digit until January, and his availability for the 1968 season would come into question.

Gibson, in pitching his third complete game in nine days, had tied the World Series record with five straight complete-game victories which dated back to his postseason inaugural in 1964. It was only the fifth time in history that a pitcher had won three contests in a seven-game championship set. He also tied the 62-year-old mark of Christy Mathewson for the fewest hits allowed in three World Series starts with fourteen, equaling the record that many thought — like many of the other laurels — would belong to Lonborg by the end of the day. In reflecting on the last few innings of Game Seven, Gibson said his right arm was so tired that he wished he could "take it off and hang it on a hook for the winter." In being named the series' outstanding player by a poll of sportswriters, he was awarded a 1968 Corvette by *Sport* magazine, the second time in four years he had won a free automobile for his performance in the World Series.

The personable Lonborg was quite cerebral about things in defeat, especially for a 25-year-old who had not been in the major leagues very long. He was lauded by writers everywhere for the tremendous season and overall World Series that he produced. "We've given a lot of people a lot of happiness, including ourselves," he said. "We're not going to be able to fathom the year until we sit beside a winter fireplace. We should have dinner together someplace and drink some fine wine, and maybe we will. Then we can sit across the table from each other and shake our heads." Some others in Boston were unyielding to the Redbirds, however, such as one local writer. "The Red Sox looked better in defeat than the Cardinals did in victory," the scribe believed. "Take Gibson out of the Cardinal lineup, and you've got a loser."

The Cardinals arrived back at Lambert Field at 7:20 P.M. St. Louis time with a gleeful crowd ready to greet them. As Maris got off the plane, he dismissed someone's suggestion of comparing the 1967 team to the Gas House Gang champions of 1934, saying that this Cardinals team wanted to carve out an identity of its *own* — inferring that another pennant should be in the cards for 1968. And as Bing Devine watched on television as the team he helped build made its way down the airport steps, he also saw the potential for the Cardinals of the late 1960s to be immortalized in history. "This club may not have the great stars — the Hornsbys, the Frischs, the Deans of the 1920s and '30s," Devine said, "nor certainly the same dynamics or color of the 1934 club. And, the potential of the 1942 Cardinals that left some of its talent in World War II.

"But, this club compares favorably with recent major league pennant winners — and just might show enough, long enough, to be regarded as among the great ones ever."

8. The Shaking
of a Nation

Our lives begin to end the day we become silent about things that matter.
— Martin Luther King, Jr.

Cepeda would soon be named the National League's Most Valuable Player for 1967, the Cardinals' first unanimous selection for the award. Nonetheless, he sought to improve upon his power numbers at Busch Stadium in 1968, for only eight of his 25 home runs came at home in 1967. Gibson, meanwhile, celebrated the series victory by going back to Omaha for "Bob Gibson Day," during which he was made honorary governor of Nebraska for an afternoon. He then returned to St. Louis to join the team for a three-day party at Musial's restaurant. His batterymate, McCarver, had finished a close second to Cepeda in the MVP voting. Earlier in the year, the catcher had been planning to spend the fall going back to Memphis State University to work on his undergraduate degree, but the World Series got in the way. "I only need 43 credits to graduate," he said proudly, alluding to the courses he had already taken at the University of Oklahoma as well as Christian Brothers College in Memphis. McCarver had turned 26 just after the conclusion of the 1967 World Series, and was already being regarded by many in baseball as the best all-around catcher in the game.

Almost two weeks after their triumph over Boston, the Cardinals took a goodwill trip to Japan. After a few days there, they got tired of eating their meals on the floor and searched for a more American-style restaurant. Perhaps basking too much in the enjoyment of tourism, they lost the first two games on the trip (resulting primarily from rustiness, not having played in ten days), but went on to win the remainder of the eight contests against a variety of Japanese clubs. During the trip to Japan, Musial — despite not having played in five years — remained the most popular Cardinal, abroad as well as at home. A few weeks after returning to the states, however, he would announce on December 5, 1967, that his tenure as general manager of the Cardinals was coming to an abrupt end, although he was staying on with the organization as a vice president. With the change, August Busch immediately knew he had to right an old wrong. He asked Bing Devine to return to his old job, as he was still working with the Mets in New York. Devine's heart belonged to the Cardinals, and had endured several run-ins with the Mets' chairman, M. Donald Grant, during his stay in Flushing Meadows. The most publicized of these included Devine's wish to trade relief pitcher Donnie Shaw, a pitcher whom the Mets had taken in the 35th round of the 1965 draft. Devine had a chance to ship Shaw to the White Sox for outfielder Tommie Agee, but the deal was nixed by Grant at the last minute. "How could you think about trading *my* Donnie Shaw?" Grant said to Devine, for some reason taking personal ownership in the player. This prompted Devine to resign, and when Colonel Busch came calling, he was ready.

Despite the team's overwhelming success in 1967, Schoendienst, Musial, and Devine knew that there were areas of individual improvement that were needed if a repeat championship was going to occur. One such area was the defensive play of Brock, who despite all of his offensive production had lead the National League in errors by an outfielder for the fourth year in a row (even though he had reduced the number from 19 to 13 over the past season). Another area of concern was the production of the bench, with more figured to be needed out of the utility players than what was provided in 1967, as the regulars were unusually fortunate in avoiding injuries. While Brock continued to struggle in the field, Clemente in 1967 had set a National League record for leading in outfield assists for the fifth consecutive season. And Clemente's teammate, the steady Bill Mazeroski, won the last of his National League-record eight Gold Gloves at second base, doing so even while having negotiated 158 more chances than any other player at the position over the course the season. But shortly after the Cardinals closed out their victory in the 1967 World Series and before their trip to Japan, numerous shake-ups began to hit the Pirates, as well as the rest of the big leagues. On Friday, October 13 — just 24 hours after Game Seven — Larry Shepard was installed as the new manager of the Pittsburgh Pirates. Danny Murtaugh, in his second (of what would be four) stints as the Pirates skipper, could fare no better than his predecessor, Harry Walker. Both men finished with .500 records (Walker at 42–42 and Murtaugh at 39–39), as the Pittsburgh front office looked for the team to rise above mediocrity. Interestingly, Walker was the man who effectively had beaten the Red Sox the last time the Cardinals played Boston in the World Series in 1946, as he sent home Enos Slaughter on Slaughter's

"Mad Dash," having scored all the way from first on a single for the deciding run with two outs in the eighth inning of Game Seven.

The following week, American League owners finally gave Charlie Finley his wish. Finley was granted permission on October 18 to move the A's franchise to Oakland, California, immediately. Local sentiment in Kansas City had boiled over so angrily against Finley, however, that Senator Stuart Symington took the matter before Congress, labeling Finley as "one of the most disreputable characters ever to enter the American sports scene." Before the end of the week, Finley — like Pittsburgh's ownership — would dispose of his interim manager, Luke Appling. Appling was able to post victories in only 25 percent of the A's' final 40 games, and would be replaced with Bob Kennedy, a man who previously had managed the Cubs from 1963 to 1965 and, in doing so, had broken up the infamous "College of Coaches," the ill-fated experiment by Chicago owner Phil Wrigley in the early 1960s to have several managers take turns guiding the club during the same season. Finley sensed a new-found opportunity, and spared no expense in intensifying the excitement for fans of American League baseball in the Bay Area. It was announced Sunday, October 22, that a local hero was coming home to help in the project. Joe DiMaggio, who more than thirty years earlier had launched the beginnings of his immortality in the game with his stardom in the Pacific Coast League, was returning home to serve as the club's executive vice president, a move by Finley that produced an immediate political benefit for him in his new area.

As a sort of consolation prize, the Kansas City area was assured by Major League Baseball that an expansion franchise would appear in the city by 1971. The action on the floor of the United States Senate by Symington had expedited the timetable, however, and with the assistance of Ewing Kauffman, it was decided that Kansas City would have a new team in the American League two years sooner. They would be joined in 1969 with Seattle as the other new franchise, as that city received permission to enter the league on December 1, 1967. Excited about the prospect of hosting a major league team, nearly two-thirds of the voters of King County, Washington, approved a ballot measure in February 1968 that authorized $40 million in bonds to build a new domed stadium in downtown Seattle, a facility that would hopefully attract an NFL franchise over time as well, to be similar in its layout to the Astrodome in Houston. In March, it was decided that the Kansas City entry would be named the Royals, while the Seattle club would known as the Pilots. There was also talk of expansion coming to the National League, and it was rumored that new franchises might be seen in the Senior Circuit as soon as 1969 as well. "Speaking only personally, I wouldn't be surprised if it happened," Devine said in early 1968. The owners of the existing National League clubs had voted 8–2 in favor of expanding, with August Busch and Philadelphia Phillies' chairman Bob Carpenter not present when the vote took place, and thus they had not cast ballots. Busch, however, demonstrated his support of the idea. "I can only speak for myself and the Cardinals," he announced, "but I feel the National League must go to twelve teams in 1969 when the American League does, if only to protect ourselves from losing too much talent to the other major league clubs in the draft of young players." In fact, Devine and other National League general managers were already circling their wagons, making initial lists of the 15 players on their rosters they would protect if an expansion draft hit the major league rosters once again. The front-runners on the list of possible new National League cities included Milwaukee and San Diego, while Dallas-Fort Worth, Buffalo, and Toronto were being considered as well. Busch also said that, despite the possibility of twelve-team leagues, he would not be in favor of divisional play. "I'm probably a minority of one," he added, "but I wouldn't like to see two six-team divisions because I'd hate to see a playoff system that would detract from the World Series, and along with that, I'd hate to see a loser get into the Series."

Oakland, however, would not be the only new city to see American League baseball in 1968. Chicago White Sox owner Arthur Allyn announced before the end of October 1967 that the Sox would play nine games in Milwaukee the following season, in an attempt (according to Allyn) to galvanize a fan base in a greater region around Chicago. The announcement sent shock waves throughout the corridors of power in baseball, as it was considered by certain observers to be an ominous prelude of a permanent move by the White Sox to the city 90 miles north. No team in the major leagues had played *any* regular-season home games outside of its home city in over sixty years, and many felt that Allyn's true motives were becoming all too obvious.

On the topic of expansion, Broeg chimed in by resurrecting Branch Rickey's idea of a third major league (which Rickey had wanted to call the Continental League), so as to not break up the current league (and soon to be divisional) rivalries that currently existed. The colorful Bill Veeck, who had sold his interests in the White Sox to Allyn back in 1961, suggested a four-division format in which the current teams would be thoroughly mixed with the expansion clubs. Veeck — never at a loss for creative ideas for changes to the game — in fact had been among the first to suggest the geographical alignment of the teams, a forerunner of the system that currently exists today. C.C. Johnson Spink of *The Sporting News* was predicting that owners of the new National League franchises would need to put up the whopping sum of $12.5 million to enter a team into play (the new American League franchises in Kansas City and Seattle cost approximately $5,250,000 each).

*   *   *   *   *

It had been 46 years since the New York Giants had been the last National League team to repeat as world champions. And as the Cardinals readied themselves for 1968, Musial cautioned them against complacency. "I told them not to forget what they had done last year," he said in a farewell tone in relinquishing his general manager's post, as workouts began at spring training. "And, that we all expected 'em to win a pennant and a World Series again," he added with a smile. Stan the Man was as relaxed as ever, enjoying the Florida sun with the weight of the general manager's responsibility off his shoulders. He now had time to roam, help with the Cardinals hitters, play golf, and even visit old Tinker Field in Orlando—the place where, in spring training of 1940, he had caught his spikes in tripping over a protruding piece of mud in the outfield. He fell and hurt his left shoulder, which at the time was his *pitching* shoulder. Unable to throw from the mound any longer, the organization gave him a try as a hitter, and he began rocketing baseballs with his bat all over the Sunshine State. Now, while having relinquished his previous office job, Musial had agreed to temporarily return to the field, aiding Schoendienst and Sisler in tutoring the St. Louis players. Many of the fans at spring training were excited to see his old number 6 roaming the pasture once again, flailing away with that famous old left-handed swing, a unique corkscrew design particular to Musial that was always described as "peeking around the corner." Now, instead of ripping into National League pitchers, that swing was shared in a more demonstrative mode, refining the minute points of the Cardinals hitters' techniques. There was some talk of rule changes coming to major league baseball in the next year or two, one of which would allow the addition of a tenth man to the batting order who would not play the field, but instead would act as a designated hitter in the lineup for the pitcher. While initially intrigued with the idea, the 47-year-old Musial shook his head and squelched any impending rumors about his return as a player after a five-year hiatus. "I don't know about Red," he said with another laugh, "but I quit in time. The ball was beginning to look about as small as a golf ball."

While the Cardinals were returning to baseball in relatively good physical shape, they appeared to be operating smoothly in the area of finances as well. Typically in coming off a World Series title, a team could expect a load of contract squabbles the following year — even in the days in which the reserve clause was still in full effect. Heading into the spring of 1968, however, the Cardinals management found themselves with relatively few problems, even though a couple of major headaches surfaced. On March 1, it was announced that Maxvill had signed a new contract, believed to be in the neighborhood of $37,500 for the 1968 season, which amounted to approximately a 33 percent increase from the previous year for the shortstop. It was the last day that players could report to camp without being deemed an official holdout, which now left two players in that category. This comprised both Javier and Spiezio, while Cepeda was under contract but had not yet reported to the club. Javier, while expected to arrive in camp a couple of days late, was nowhere near an agreement with the club. In fact, the words he used through his agent from the Dominican Republic were quite clear — "Pay me, or I quit." This prompted Devine to sic his assistant general manager, Jim Toomey, on the player to smooth things over. In his first attempt at contacting Javier, Toomey spent five hours on the phone — until 1:30 in the morning on March 1— unsuccessfully trying to reach him abroad. Toomey then called Musial at two in the morning for further advice, and Stan suggested that Toomey wait until the breakfast hours to contact August Busch at his winter home in Miami for further instructions. Ultimately, Toomey would find himself on a plane to the island to speak with Javier face to face. Javier had been offered even more money than Maxvill — $45,000 — but was seeking a deal more in the neighborhood of $50,000, nearly twice what he had made in the past season. After the meeting with Toomey, however, Hoolie would agree to the club's offer, and he signed the contract that Toomey had brought with him to the island in his briefcase. Spiezio, on the other hand, had not received permission to be tardy, and was not expected to be near a contract deal. Despite not being a starter, he was seeking to more than double the $10,000 he had received in 1967. Spiezio had asked Musial to intervene between him and Devine, but Bing was holding firm at Spiezio's 1967 rate, refusing to even accept a compromise offer of $18,000 by the reserve infielder (he would finally agree to a $16,000 salary on March 5). Even without Spiezio under wraps, the Cardinals payroll (counting coaches and other field staff) was now over $1 million, easily the highest in baseball history. Each of the members of the young pitching corps of Briles, Hughes, and Carlton had at least doubled their 1967 salaries, and according to the *Post-Disptach* the average salary of the positional starters had risen from $44,000 to $64,000 (Maris, with his pay staying at the 1967 rate of $75,000, was the only regular not to see a salary increase). Topping the list was Gibson, who would get $90,000 for 1968, a 12 percent increase from the previous year. As Toomey had done with Javier, Devine had made a special trip to Gibson's home in Omaha during the off-season to get his new amount settled in person.

Cepeda, meanwhile, had been jet-setting back and forth between St. Louis and his native Puerto Rico, attempting to sort out a legal misunderstanding that involved his name in the endorsement of a commercial product by the Swift Company during the off-season. Despite the paperwork, the 1967 National League MVP would arrive in camp in what he considered to be the best shape of his career, following a strict workout regimen over the colder months which he believed would correct a slump that followed him through the last few weeks of the '67 schedule. The slide led to his poor performance in the postseason, in which he batted a meek .103 with a lone run batted in against the Red Sox. "That's why I went to the gym when I wasn't

1967 ST. LOUIS CARDINALS
WORLD CHAMPIONS

FRONT ROW: Flood,Cepeda, Schultz, Muffett, Schoendienst, Sisler,
Milliken, Briles, Jackson, Maris.
SECOND ROW: Gibson, Hoerner, Willis, McCarver, Hughes, Carlton,
Cosman, Tolan, Javier, Shannon,Johnson,Bauman.
BACK ROW: Maxvill, Woodeshick, Jaster, Ricketts, Gagliano,
Romano, Bressoud, Spiezio,Brock, Washburn.

playing winter ball back home in Puerto Rico," he told the press. "I think I let down after we clinched the pennant, and I just didn't come back in the World Series the way that I wanted." His manager liked what he saw in the new version. "Cepeda played hard in Puerto Rico, even though I'm sure he would have like to have rested," Schoendienst noticed. "The way he reacted to the challenge won him a lot of respect from the people in St. Louis, many of whom didn't think that he could be a leader."

The new monetary deals among the players had prompted Broeg to do a comparison in salaries between the 1934 Gas House Gang Cardinals—one of his favorite teams—and the 1967 squad before the new contracts were signed:

1967 Cardinals		*1934 Cardinals*	
Maris	$75,000	Frisch	$18,500
Gibson	60,000	Martin	9,000
Cepeda	55,000	Collins	8,000
Flood	50,000	J. Dean	7,500
Brock	40,000	Orsatti	6,500
McCarver	37,500	Durocher	6,000
Javier	25,000	Medwick	5,000
Shannon	25,000	Rothrock	3,000
Maxvill	22,000	Delancey	3,000
Total	$389,500		$66,500

Jay Dean, better known as "Dizzy," would top out at $25,500 later in the 1930s. Medwick, meanwhile, was the only member of the Gas House Gang to play long enough to qualify for the Major League Baseball pension plan. Well after Medwick was through playing in 1948, the pension system was revised in the 1960s so that a player who had five years could draw $250 a month at age 50, or $643 a month if he waited until age 65. Ten-year men would get $500 at 50, or $1288 a month at age 65. For the Cardinals in 1967, the players also received the sum of $12 a day for meal money on the road in 1967, which would increase to $15 a day in 1968 (by 2005, however, major league players would be getting $90 a day). In addition, the players had received a nearly 75 percent increase in their daily allowance for spring training expenses. Times had certainly improved for the big-league ballplayer since the days of the Depression, but the Cardinals were still emerging as the lone big-money team outside of New York. The Players Association and the owners had just ratified their initial deal on February 21, an agreement that would last until midnight Eastern Time on New Year's Eve 1969. Within the reso-

Opposite: The world champion St. Louis Cardinals of 1967.

lution, the minimum major league salary had now increased to $10,000 — more than any member of the Gas House Gang had made, except for Frankie Frisch — who was pulling double-duty as the second baseman *and* the manager of the 1934 Cardinals. Baseball continued to top all professional sports in players' salaries, however, averaging $22,500 by 1968 according to Marvin Miller, with the NFL close behind at approximately $20,000. It was the Cardinals franchise, however, that was changing the game for the worse, according to *Sports Illustrated.* "Some highly-placed baseball people believe that, by paying so well, the Cardinals are undermining the very structure of baseball."

To help meet the new-age payroll of 1968, the Cardinals announced that they would continue the "new" process of accepting out-of-state ticket orders for games at Busch Stadium through Western Union wire services. Through the use of a telegram, residents in Illinois, Arkansas, Indiana, Iowa, Kentucky, Oklahoma, Tennessee, and out-state Missouri could place an electronic order — long before the arrival of Internet requests.

Other sports continued to fare prosperously in St. Louis as well. Fan attendance had swelled at the Arena for Blues hockey games, and a natural rivalry had developed with their neighbors to the north, much the same as a Cards-Cubs game in the middle of the summer. In early March of '68, the club published a letter in the *Post-Dispatch*, a portion of which revealed that business was even better than had been expected. "Due to the tremendous interest created by the rivalry with the Chicago Blackhawks ... the Arena has been completely sold out for Saturday night's [March 2] contest with standing room only available. This situation has caused many loyal Blues fans to be turned away. In order to not disappoint those who have supported the Blues in their opening season and who cannot be accommodated with seats for this contest, the St. Louis Blues, in cooperation with Falstaff Brewing Corporation, have made arrangements to telecast the final two periods beginning at 8:30 P.M. on KPLR-TV, Channel 11." It would be the first sellout in the franchise's history, and the first sellout for a hockey game at the Arena since an exhibition game had been played there nearly twenty years earlier. Indeed, a new sport had entered the St. Louis scene, as well as a new rivalry in the city's athletic competition with Chicago.

The major addition for the Cardinals in 1968 appeared to be at the catcher's position, where Schoendienst knew that a productive back-up behind McCarver was needed. On February 8 — the day that the St. Louis-based Boeing Company witnessed the first flight of its new 747 aircraft, and two weeks after the former Cardinals great Medwick was voted into the National Baseball Hall of Fame — the Cardinals sent Jimy Williams and Pat Corrales to the Reds for veteran catcher Johnny Edwards. Williams had batted only twice for the Cardinals in 1967, and eleven times in his initial season the year before. He displayed improvement in the minor leagues over the final months of the past year, but not enough to warrant the Cardinals' brass keeping him in their future plans. Corrales, meanwhile, was a catcher himself, and was behind the plate for 62 games with the Phillies in 1965 before appearing for 28 games with St. Louis in 1966. Edwards was much more of a known commodity, however, and it was an easy first deal for Devine in his second term with the club. Big and strong but slow, Edwards was nicknamed "Clyde" (as in "Clydesdale") for his clod-hopping base running, but had been a solid backstop for the past eight seasons, winning Gold Gloves and All-Star selections at the position in 1963 and 1964 while with the Reds, as well as another All-Star appearance in 1965 (in 1963, he had also set a major league record for putouts by a catcher in a season with 1,008). A degree-holder in ceramic engineering from Ohio State (he had done work for NASA and General Electric in the off season), Edwards was a high school teammate of golf legend Jack Nicklaus in Columbus before they both took their skills to the OSU campus. "Nicklaus was big and strong and the first-string catcher — not me," Edwards remembered about his prep days. He met his wife, Barbara, at Ohio State, and she traveled with him in his early days in the minor leagues. "In Nashville, most of the players lived in trailers," the catcher recalled about the couple's early life together. "Ours didn't have any air conditioning. And there were no shade trees. It was like living in a tin can."

Edwards also brought more post-season baseball experience to the Cardinals, having caught three games and batting .364 for Cincinnati as a rookie in their 1961 loss in the World Series to Maris and the Yankees. And despite another catcher stepping in front of him in the second-string slot for 1968, Dave Ricketts — who was now entering his twelfth year in the Cardinals organization — was understanding about the situation. "I felt sorry for [John] Romano last season, because he was a first-string catcher with no place to go," Ricketts said of the man who was released just before the World Series began. "He didn't know how to stay in shape while he was on the bench." Ricketts, while not lobbying for more playing time, nonetheless agreed with Schoendienst that McCarver would have batted well over .300 in 1967 if he had not been catching almost every day down the stretch run. "I had to stop them [other clubs] from running on me to become a good all-around catcher, and I did that last season," McCarver asserted confidently as he prepared for 1968. As practice began, a particularly cold late February and early March had struck Florida, but McCarver thought it was the perfect time to get in some preliminary practice time. Before many of the other players showed up at Al Lang Field in St. Petersburg, he had to drag Schoendienst out in the cold in order to get the manager to hit him some fungoes. "There's nothing like a blustery wind and a blue, cloudless sky to sharpen a catcher on pop-ups," he claimed. Another Cardinals deal in the off-season had also involved the Reds, as the two clubs exchanged reserve outfielders with Alex Johnson heading to Cincinnati for Dick Simpson back on January 11.

Al Jackson, meanwhile, had been sent to the New York Mets after the World Series victory to complete the deal that had brought Lamabe to the Cardinals over the summer. And rounding out the new (but older) faces in camp at St. Petersburg was shortstop Dick Schofield, a 15-year big league veteran who had first broken into the majors as highly-regarded, $40,000 "bonus baby" with the Cardinals in 1953, but had since made stops in Pittsburgh, San Francisco, New York, and Los Angeles. The switch-hitting Schofield — a native of Springfield, Illinois, just up Interstate 55 from St. Louis — had been a starter for only a couple of those years with the Pirates in the mid-1960s, but nonetheless afforded Schoendienst more veteran leadership on the field, and an able replacement at any of the infield positions. Schofield, however, initially did not sign the contract that the Cardinals had offered, and went to Florida without a completed deal.

The first 1968 Grapefruit League game for the Cardinals would be against the Mets on a cold, windy day on March 9 with Gibson starting on the hill, followed by Carlton and Briles, who each threw three innings. Gibson started the exhibition schedule by walking the Mets' leadoff hitter, shortstop Bud Harrelson, on four pitches. Next was Agee — just acquired by New York from the White Sox, and who Devine had wanted the year before — and Gibson's fifth pitched ball of the spring struck Agee on the left side of the head. The tourist-laden crowd gasped at the sight as the new Mets outfielder left the field on a stretcher, but he would not sustain any serious damage from the incident. The Cards' ace righted himself and threw three shutout innings, followed in suit by Carlton and Briles in their turns as well. Briles was extremely confident, coming off a 1967 season in which he won 11 of his last 13 starts. "I'd like to think with a few runs, no physical misfortune, and improvement, I can win twenty this year," he offered to the sportswriters. Simpson, the new St. Louis outfielder just acquired from Cincinnati, homered to provide the difference in a 4–0 win, helped by two hits each off the bats of Brock, Shannon, and the other newcomer in Schofield. Simpson was supposed to be the replacement in Cincinnati for Frank Robinson when the former National League MVP was traded to Baltimore, but such a scenario did not unfold. Simpson was a gifted athlete, a 6'4", 180-pound former track star in high school in California who was clocked having sprinted a hundred yards in 9.4 seconds, high-jumped six-feet seven inches, and long-jumped twenty-five feet three inches. "I had track and basketball scholarships offered by Arizona State and San Jose State," Simpson said, "but the $5,000 that the Los Angeles Angels offered to me in 1961 looked awfully big." Simply adding his physical prowess to the St. Louis outfield in any capacity excited Schoendienst. Additionally, Simpson thought that the locale would certainly suit him. "I like coming to a club that puts as much emphasis on speed and base running as St. Louis does," Simpson continued, foretelling what sounded like the utterings of manager Whitey Herzog's personnel on the Redbirds roster a couple of decades later. "It's a real good club with high morale. This is a tough lineup to crack, and I know there would have been an advantage to going to a team that was short on outfielders, but I just need the chance to play." The Cardinals envisioned Simpson not only pushing Tolan as the fourth outfielder, but also as a part-time starter for an aging Maris and Flood, the latter of whom dealt with a number of injuries in 1967. Since breaking into the majors with the Angels as a 19-year-old at the end of the 1962 season (the same year that he nailed a California League-record 42 home runs for San Jose), Simpson had never been able to secure a starting spot, appearing in a career-high 92 games as mostly a defensive replacement with the Reds in 1966.

The first game was the official start of an on-going spring of turbulence for Gibson. This was due in large part to the tremendous amount of racist hate mail he was receiving every day, most of it criticizing the success that the black man had accomplished in the 1967 season. Reading it casually and almost playfully in front of his locker, he was ultimately discovered doing so by a writer, who asked if he could print a few of the letters in his newspaper. When the hatred spewed forth in the public forum, Gibson received consoling letters from around the country a hundred times over. All the while, he was still directing his fury towards those National League players who stepped into the batter's box to face him. Watching him from behind the plate in a spring game during 1968, Baltimore Orioles scout Jim Russo was amazed with his velocity, and believed that Gibson was now throwing harder than anyone in baseball. "Two years ago, I'd have said Jim Maloney," Russo opined, in reference to the flamethrower from Cincinnati. "But now, I'd have to say Gibson."

Edwards, meanwhile, had looked comfortable right away in camp, homering in his first Cardinals at-bat—albeit unofficially. In the first intra-squad game a few days earlier on March 7, he took rookie pitcher Clay Kirby deep out of Al Lang Field, and everyone on the premises was impressed with his power. In the second official game on March 10, he caught all 14 innings of the contest, an affair that was mutually agreed as a tie at that point by Schoendienst and the Mets' new manager Gil Hodges after the St. Louis and New York clubs had scored one run each. In the first inning, Edwards threw out Art Shamsky, who was attempting to steal second, an eye-opener for Cardinals followers interested in the new backstop. Washburn, Jaster, Hughes, and Lamabe all looked sharp, as did Gibson—who returned to throw another inning in this game after being the starter in the pre-season opener the previous day. Edwards was awed with the new pitching staff that he was handling. "I was impressed very much not only with so few bases on balls [three over the course of the game]," he mentioned afterwards, "but also with the way that the pitchers moved the ball around the strike zone."

Stopping by practice the next day was another Cardinals catcher in Joe Garagiola, who was rounding up interviews with players for his new job as the co-host of the *Today* show on NBC television. Unable to resist the old tools of ignorance, the 42-year-old Garagiola — who had last played in the big leagues with the New York Giants in 1954 — strapped on the shin guards, chest protector, and face mask to catch batting practice. Garagiola would always be one of St. Louis's favorite sons, having grown up in the Italian neighborhood known as "The Hill" on the city's southwest side. Garagiola then (in his good-natured way) starting extolling the virtues of his "running" game, claiming that in 1952 he set a Pittsburgh Pirates record for playing in 118 games without grounding into a double play. "That," one bystander offered, "was because nobody was on base when you came to bat." Garagiola had spent the majority of his career with his beloved Cardinals, however, and was a year younger than another skilled catcher who also came from that neighborhood — Lawrence Peter Berra, better known as "Yogi." Berra had played in his final four games as a Met in 1965 at the age of 40, the capstone for the previous 18 years he had spent in the Bronx. It was during that time that he had led the Yankees to an amazing 15 pennants and ten world titles, while along the way achieving three Most Valuable Player awards for himself.

While professional baseball was readying itself for yet another season with the passage of winter, the war in southeast Asia raged on as an endless storm. On January 30, the North Vietnamese celebrated their Tet holiday with a major offensive against South Vietnamese and American troops; the following day, the U.S. embassy in Saigon would be assaulted by Viet Cong forces. The attack by the Communist troops would stall a few weeks later, as American and South Vietnamese forces would be able to recapture the fallen city of Hue. Bloody battles raged on through February and into March, when on the 16th, President Johnson displayed his optimism for the struggle in speaking to the National Alliance of Businessmen. "We are going to win the war, hopefully at the negotiating table, but on the battlefield if we must." That same day, Senator Robert F. Kennedy of New York — the brother of the president slain not five years earlier — announced that he too would seek the nation's highest office. To date, only Senator Eugene McCarthy of Minnesota had filed an intent to wrestle the Democratic nomination away from Johnson. "I will not run to oppose any man, but to propose new policies," Kennedy made clear to the press. "I do not lightly dismiss the dangers and difficulties of challenging an incumbent president, but these are not ordinary times, and this is not an ordinary election. I run because I believe this country is on a perilous course, and because I have such strong feelings on what must be done. I am obliged to do all that I can ... I seek to end the bloodshed, to close the gaps between the rich and poor, young and old, and to make America stand for hope."

Kennedy — in making the announcement in the caucus room of the Senate Office Building, where his brother had announced his own presidential candidacy in January of 1960 — said that he would enter the primaries "at least in California, Oregon, and Nebraska" in order to test the public's approval of his further pursuit of the presidency. Of course, he already had the approval of his powerful father. "Bobby is the most like me — hard as nails," Joe Kennedy, the patriarch of the family, said of his second-youngest son.

But just two weeks later — and three weeks after the first Battle of Saigon had begun — Johnson then stunned the nation with a broadcast he made on television, saying that he would not contest Kennedy, McCarthy, nor any other individual from the Democratic side. "I shall not seek, and I will not accept, the nomination of my party for another term as your president," he said plainly into the camera. It had been later revealed that Kennedy had already informed Johnson of his intent to run when Kennedy made his announcement on the 16th.

*   *   *   *   *

A point of emphasis among American League umpires for 1968 would be the enforcement of the "hands-to-mouth" rule, whereby a pitcher could not raise his pitching hand to his mouth while on the rubber. The National League had not adopted the new enforcement of the rule, however, and some were interested to see how it would be executed in the inter-league exhibition games. Nonetheless, some National League umpires had decided on their own to use the legislation by themselves. Leo Durocher, for one, thought the rule was misguided in the first place. The Cubs' manager showed that he was already in his own mid-season form, as he was ejected from a spring training game on March 13. His ace pitcher, Jenkins, had been roughed up by the Giants for six straight hits and five runs early in the game. Durocher then turned his attention to the new rule, which resulted in a shouting match with home plate umpire Mel Steiner after Jenkins had received a warning for going to his mouth. Steiner had previously ejected two Cubs from another spring game a couple of days earlier, and a couple of individuals in the Chicago dugout now showered the field with baseballs in protest after their manager was thrown out of the game. Two of the baseballs wound up whizzing by Steiner's head, while a third struck a photographer who was sitting nearby. Durocher would also draw the ire of an American League crew on March 23, when he instructed rookie pitcher Jim Ellis to deliberately touch his mouth with a three-and-one count on the batter. The result was ball four and a walk, but Durocher was chuckling loudly from his seat, as he was planning to intentionally walk the batter anyway. A few days earlier, Hoerner tried to make his own point about the seemingly arbitrariness of the new rule in a Cardinals spring game. While pitching against Boston, he motioned for rookie umpire Larry Barnett to come to the mound. When Barnett made it to the hill, Hoerner looked him in eye and spit into his own left palm, rubbing the saliva on the ball. "That," Hoerner said in self-satisfaction in attempting to teach a lesson, "is the same thing as putting your fingers to your mouth." The rule had previously stated that a pitcher, after being warned once for throwing a spitball, was to be ejected from the game on a second occasion. For 1968, a ball would be called on the first offense identified by the umpire, and a balk as well if runners were on base (unless the runner had reached base on the pitch via a hit, walk, or error, thus nullifying the call).

Another conversation around all the camps—and one that frightened many traditionalists within the game—was the possibility of artificial surfaces coming to every major league ballpark in the future. It had changed the way the game was played in Houston, and its long-term economy prompted most club officials to be interested in the idea. "I feel, as Stan Musial and Bing Devine do, that eventually all fields will have this artificial nylon ribbon to save wear and tear," Schoedienst admitted, as the team played a six-inning practice contest against their Tulsa farm club on the Astroturf on March 23 at the Redbirds' minor league complex. "But you couldn't use it on the baselines, or around the mound, or around the batter's box—I think the hitters have to be able to dig in more. Pitchers do, too." In general, the players appeared fond of it—as did the football Cardinals of the NFL and the St. Louis Stars of the newly-formed North American Soccer League, both of whom also shared the premises of Busch Stadium with the baseball Cardinals. In 1968 prices, it was estimated that it would cost over a half-million dollars to put the synthetic carpet in Busch Stadium. The surface, incidentally, had been partly developed across the river in East St. Louis, Illinois, by the Monsanto Chemical Company; the rug at the Cardinals' St. Petersburg complex had been a $30,000 gift to the city by Monsanto, as the company wished to show all visitors the usefulness of the new product. In addition, Monsanto was offering any interested teams a five-year guarantee on the surface, asserting that they had improved the product's quality since the original installation in the Astrodome in 1965. Nonetheless, no one from the Cardinals was jumping forward to pay the $550,000 price tag associated with its installation in St. Louis. Toward the end of the shortened game, Reuss—the former Ritenour High School star, and currently in the employ of the Tulsa team—threw two scoreless innings at an assortment of St. Louis regulars and reserves, giving credibility to his high selection in the previous year's draft. A lefthander, Reuss would enjoy the instruction of the most victorious southpaw of all time in the coming months, as Warren Spahn was the manager of the Tulsa team.

The Cards had gotten off to a good start on the spring schedule in 1968, winning ten of their first fifteen games while the University of California at Los Angeles was simultaneously racing to another national championship in college basketball under legendary coach John Wooden. While the mainstays of the Cards' starting rotation — Gibson, Carlton, Hughes, Briles, and Washburn — were pitching well in spring competition (Gibson, in fact, did not permit a run in spring training play until he met up with the Red Sox on March 16 at Al Lang Field, in front of an overflow crowd of past 7,000), the bullpen had been less than impressive, causing consternation for Devine as he pondered another move. One individual trying to crack the bullpen group was rookie Hal Gilson, a tall lefthander who was originally signed by the Cubs back in 1961 (and traded to the Cardinals system in 1965) but who had not yet made a major-league roster during his career. McCarver, meanwhile, was hitting the ball so well that some of his teammates jokingly suggested that he save some of those hits for the regular season. "My answer to that," McCarver responded, "is what Ray Floyd, the golfer, said when someone suggested he ought to save his practice-round birdies for the tournament: 'The way to get birdies when they count is to get into the habit of getting them when they don't count.'" Brock, meanwhile, was taking extra batting practice against left-handed pitchers to improve upon that aspect of his game. For with all his success versus right-handers in 1967 (he batted .330 against such hurlers), he had hit only .244 against southpaws. "I've cut down my strikeouts some, and I'm stroking the ball evenly," Brock assessed of himself in the middle spring workouts, trying to maintain a patient frame of mind at the plate in his duty as the Cardinals' leadoff hitter. "But I still can't get myself to do a lot of shopping around up there at pitches. I hit the first ball quite often." In off-season, Brock had made some extra money by spending a few weeks as a publicity carry-on with stops made by the Harlem Globetrotters basketball team.

By the third week in March, Javier was hitting .500 in exhibition play. But in actuality, the entire Cardinals team was terrorizing clubs around Florida at the plate, as if they wanted to prove that they were not a pitching-only outfit. Before the end of the month, several other teammates were joining Hoolie with impressive batting averages for the spring, including Cepeda (.400, with four home runs), Tolan (.395), Gagliano (.368), Brock (.364), Maris (.359), Edwards (.350), Flood (.340), and Shannon (.324). On top of them all, however, was a young outfielder named Floyd Wicker, a left-handed-hitting speedster out of East Carolina University. Wicker, leading the way at .625 (10 for 16), was making a serious case for a roster spot that was already crowded with position players in general, and outfielders in particular — for also making a good impression was the newly-arrived Simpson. Of greater concern to the team, however, were the nagging injuries that were becoming numerous. None appeared to be serious, but left all wondering which lingering ailments might cause a slow start for the team in the regular season. McCarver had an inflamed elbow which he had to dunk in an ice bucket every evening, originally resulting from being struck by a pitch from Cincinnati's Milt Pappas. Maris was gimping along with a pulled quadriceps muscle in his leg. And Hughes and Willis had strained their pitching shoulders, as Doc Middleman somewhat resembled a crazed attacker with a weapon, darting around the Cardinals' clubhouse to stab the infirmed with a syringe filled with cortisone. For McCarver, Middleman had used a cocktail of cortisone and novocaine, a combination that allowed the catcher to get through his duties each day at camp. X-rays of his elbow had been negative, but Pappas's pitch had struck him so hard that the imprint of the baseball's stitches were present on McCarver's arm for a week after the beaning. As for McCarver and the others, Middleman explained that "the shots relax the muscles and ease the spasms. I don't believe the pitchers are more than just tender, but we can't take a chance and push them or Maris." Schoendienst, however, was not concerned with the health of the pitching staff. He was satisfied in letting the regulars put in minimal work, giving him, Muffett, and the rest of the coaching staff an opportunity to watch the youngsters apply their trade. There was one spot open on the staff—the tenth—and Cosman, Torrez, Gilson, and Wayne Granger were battling it out for the honor. "Mike throws the hardest," Schoendienst said in assessing the group. "And when he's throwing strikes, he's definitely a major league pitcher. I believe he's got a bright future." The field had narrowed further on April 3 when Lamabe was cut, which then opened a spot for two of the new throwers. All four of the young pitchers were having ample opportunities to display their talents, as per Schoendienst's directives, no Cardinals starting pitcher had gone seven innings in a spring game until Briles did so on March 29. The man caught in the middle—literally—appeared to be Jaster, who with his string of shutouts against the Dodgers in 1966 had begun '67 as a main man in the rotation until the quick development of Carlton, Hughes, and Briles. Now, for 1968, it looked as if he was destined for long relief—or the title of "middle man" as it was now called. "Last year my goal was to start 30 games," Jaster recalled. "Now I'm in a different situation, fighting for the fifth starting spot. I hope I can get in the rotation to start 25 or 30 games, and maybe work in 40 or 45 total." Steve Huntz and two other players were assigned to minor league camp on the 29th, paring down the big-league roster to 29 men. The day after Lamabe was released, the four young hurlers all pitched in the same game. "We played 'em a dirty trick," Muffett said about the group, while laughing with and glancing at his accomplice, Schoendienst. "By pitching all four of 'em the same day, just after they'd learned about Lamabe leaving. And I know how it feels to realize there's a major league job waiting if you can cut the mustard."

Strong young arms certainly appeared to be a new trend elsewhere around the game, as there had been a buzz around the Mets' camp about the wave of fresh pitching talent which was giving hope to the New York club in its seventh year of existence. Seaver, the reigning co–rookie of the year along with Hughes, had jumped right into the rotation as a 22-year-old rookie in 1967, having pitched over 250 innings while logging 16 wins and 170 strikeouts. There were several others looking to join him, and on March 27, the Cardinals got a first-hand look at the pick of the litter. A twenty-one-year old named Lynn Nolan Ryan had actually appeared in two games for the Mets two years earlier, striking out six batters in three innings of work in 1966. He was reputed to have the most dominating fastball to enter the major leagues since that of Bob Feller, but rumors also persisted about the youngster's ability to find the plate. After Flood marveled to the writers about Ryan's stuff in collecting the lone hit against the phenom on this day, the newspapermen recalled a story that the old Cubs first baseman and manager Charlie Grimm had once shared about a pitcher whom one of his scouts had supposedly found out in the wilderness. The report came back to Grimm that no one could touch the hurler, save for one batter who hit a foul ball off him. "Forget about the pitcher," Grimm had wired back to the scout. "Sign the guy who hit the foul ball." And so it was on this day in St. Petersburg. For notwithstanding the hot Cardinals bats, five of the first six St. Louis hitters went down swinging against Ryan (Flood's triple was the exception). The prodigy left the game in the fourth inning to a chorus of cheers from the Cardinals-leaning crowd, as he even had outdone a sparkling performance by Carlton, who had struck out six and walked none through six innings of shutout ball himself. Ryan was replaced by other Mets pitchers (Billy Short and Danny Frisella) who were not as impressive but just as effective in a 1–0 New York win. Because of arm problems, Ryan had pitched in only 51 games in his three professional seasons to that point — but had also struck out 451 hitters in just 294 innings over that time. "If Nolan Ryan can survive his habit of hurting himself — the guy is either too fast for his own strength or as brittle as a nasty look — there is little chance that anyone who has seen him will soon forget him," one New York writer advised. The Mets planned to be extremely cautious with Ryan, as his namesake — Gary Nolan of the Reds, himself another precocious young pitcher — was about to be sent to the minor leagues within the week with his own arm trouble, a problem that would plague Nolan throughout his career. As a 19-year-old in 1967, Nolan had gone 14–8 for the Reds with 206 strikeouts, finishing third behind Seaver and Hughes for top rookie honors.

Undaunted by the imposing Ryan, the Cards righted their offensive powers and finished March with a 17-hit attack against the Braves on March 30, the third time in the spring they had reached that figure. Even the seldom-used Spiezio got into the assault, as he beat Atlanta with a two-run homer in the ninth. More importantly, the Cardinals had won 70 percent of their spring games (14–6, with one tie) to set the table for their pursuit of a championship repeat. Schofield was still holding out, but perhaps the dramatic homer by Spiezio inspired him, as the two men would be battling for a utility infielder's spot (with Huntz having been previously assigned to the minor league camp, and Bressoud — the other infielder who saw back-up duty with the Redbirds in 1967 — having retired). Schofield, not surprisingly, was then finally under contract within forty-eight hours.

Things were not so rosy in the camp of their pennant-winning counterparts, the Boston Red Sox, who were training in the city of Winter Haven, Florida, for the third year. The Bostonians had gone 8–16 in their exhibition contests, but were more concerned about the health of their star pitcher. Lonborg had suffered a broken ankle and an injured knee in a skiing accident on Christmas Eve 1967, and had yet to show any signs of being ready for the regular season. Another worry was the continuing struggle of their promising young outfielder Conigliaro, who was still convalescing from the eye injury he suffered the previous August 18 after being hit in the face with a pitch. Conigliaro had struck out in 22 of his 66 spring at-bats, hitting .143 while enduring lingering headaches from the incident. When his situation failed to improve, club officials had him sent back to Boston to visit with an eye specialist. While there on April 2, Conigliaro was unfortunately involved in a car accident which left his body even more bruised up, although not seriously injured. The Red Sox — more out of loyalty to the 23-year-old, but also out of hopes for his potential — stood by the infirm player and encouraged his comeback. However, when ultimately examined by three doctors in Boston three days later, he was offered a dim prognosis. The physicians described his future in baseball as "very doubtful," finding that he had virtually no depth perception remaining in the left eye, and that his vision in general was deteriorating. Conigliaro then visited his parents in the Boston suburbs, and attempted to remain upbeat. "This is one of the bad days, and I can't begin to explain how much it means to me to have the prayers and good wishes of so many good people," he announced. "But despite it all, I still feel that I am a lucky guy. I've realized my lifetime ambition to be a big league player ... and I want all these friends to know I'm not going to quit and that somehow, some way, there will be good days again." Conigliaro had started in right field for the American League in the 1967 All-Star Game just weeks before the incident, after having stormed on the scene in 1964 as a 19-year-old rookie with 24 home runs. There was a rumor of his returning to the Red Sox as a pitcher, a position where he sported a 14–2 record at Lynn

High School in Massachusetts. Ultimately, the gallant Conigliaro would work his way back and return to the big leagues in 1969.

Musial, now removed from the general manager's position and taking a panoramic view of the strength of the organization, spoke as confidently as any in the Cardinals family could remember him doing at the start of a season. "I don't think anyone is going to beat us, even if we don't win it as handily as we did last year," he said. "There's no question that club has improved. There's no question that Lou Brock and Curt Flood represent the best 1–2 combination at the top of the batting order in the more than 25 years that I've been with the Cardinal organization. As I said a year ago, this is a young but veteran club, and now it's a team with confidence, a good attitude, and a winning spirit. What we've got shows up over 162 games. No club — day in and day out, man for man, position for position — can do what our club can do."

The Cardinals were as relaxed as a major league team could be, passing the final days of spring training in an easy confidence while looking forward to returning home to St. Louis in defense of their championship. In the early evening hours of April 4, the team had just been enjoying its final few leisurely moments of the sinking Florida sun at their hotel. Suddenly, stunning news flashed before them on their television sets that would alter American life in a profound manner. It was announced that at 6:01 P.M. central time, 39-year-old civil rights leader Martin Luther King, Jr., had been shot as he stepped out on his second-floor balcony at the Lorraine Motel in Memphis. The downtown motel on Mulberry Street was a place where King and his associates had stayed previously on their visits to Memphis, but had never before encountered any hostilities at the site. King's chauffeur had just gone downstairs to warm up his automobile when he called out to the leader and suggested that he put on his topcoat, as the weather had turned cold. "Okay, I will," King responded as he stepped out onto the balcony to acknowledge the warning. Those would be his last words. The gunfire, coming from a squalid rooming house that perched over the motel from an incline across the street, had struck King in the upper neck and jaw with a single shot, and he was pronounced dead sixty-four minutes later after being taken to St. Joseph's Hospital in Memphis. King, the winner of the 1964 Nobel Peace Prize, had come to Memphis a week earlier on March 28 to assist 6,000 protesters in a demonstration of support of the striking city sanitation workers, a work stoppage that was already into its seventh week and causing unrest to escalate within the city. The night before the shooting on April 3, King had given what would be his last public speech to the Mason Temple in Memphis, entitled "I've Been to the Mountaintop." Among his final words, King said to the crowd gathered, "Let us rise up tonight with a greater readiness. Let us stand with a greater determination. And let us move on in these powerful days, these days of challenge to make America what it ought to be."

A .30–06 caliber rifle was found in a doorway of the rooming house, and was soon identified as the weapon used in the attack. The suspect, however, remained at large. After meeting the described assailant earlier in the afternoon, the landlady of the rooming house said that the man had made no immediate impression on her. "I don't believe I would recognize him if I saw him again," a woman who identified herself as "Mrs. Frank Brewer" had told authorities. Approximately three hours before the shooting, Brewer said that the suspect had knocked on her door and requested a room in the house. While she showed him a room that had a kitchenette, he then requested a sleeping room only, and one which faced the motel. Immediately, a massive manhunt ensued in the four-state area of Tennessee, Arkansas, Missouri, and Mississippi that surrounds Memphis.

Robert F. Kennedy was in Indianapolis at the time of the shooting, preparing to make a speech in his campaign for the presidency. Instead of clamoring for votes, he instead had to inform the gathering of the terrible news out of Memphis. "We can do well in this country," he spoke in a firm but emotion-laden voice, as many in the crowd were sobbing inconsolably. "We will have difficult times. We've had difficult times in the past. We will have difficult times in the future. It is not the end of violence; it is not the end of lawlessness; it is not the end of disorder. But the vast majority of white people and the vast majority of black people in this country want to live together, want to improve the quality of our life, and want justice for all human beings who abide in our land." While riots were breaking out in many cities across America, Indianapolis remained relatively quiet, and credit for the minimal violence was given to Kennedy's speech.

Opening Day in the major leagues had been scheduled for Monday, April 8, but was postponed until the tenth to observe King's funeral on the day in between, to take place at the Ebenezer Baptist Church in Atlanta. President Johnson, in a speech to the nation aired shortly after the incident, had already proclaimed Sunday the 7th as a national day of mourning and implored Americans to "deny violence its victory in this sorrowful time." Also appealing to the citizenry en masse was Jacqueline Kennedy, the wife of the slain former president. "I weep for Mrs. King and her children for this senseless, senseless act of hate," she announced, "which took away a man who preached love and hope. When will our country learn that to live by the sword is to perish by the sword? I pray that with the price he paid — his life — he will make room in people's hearts for love, not hate." Adding to the sentiment, former U.S. vice president and likely Republican nominee for 1968 Richard Nixon called on the country to "try a new spirit of reconciliation to redeem this terrible occurrence." And former Alabama governor George Wallace called the shooting "a senseless, regrettable, and tragic act." The killing gave new prominence to the Black Power movement, headed by Stokely Carmichael who asked blacks to quickly arm themselves and go outdoors. "We have to retaliate for the deaths of our leaders," Carmichael bellowed at a small news conference. "The executions of those debts will not be in the courtrooms. They will be in the streets of the United States of America." Carmichael added that "Bobby Kennedy pulled that trigger as much as anyone else," claiming that Kennedy was culpable for not seeking the prosecution of the murderers of civil rights workers from earlier in the decade while he was the attorney general. In only the next 26 hours that followed the King assassination, 19 people had been killed in urban rioting across America, with an additional 3,000 injured as violence took hold once again, just as the country had been quieted from the 1967 disturbances. Not wishing to see a repeat of the problems he personally witnessed from the previous summer, Michigan governor George Romney ordered 9,000 National Guard troops on alert in Detroit, where students at four high schools had walked out of their classes. Romney also sent 400 state troopers to assist the approximately 4,000 city police officers who were attempting to keep order (Romney, meanwhile, was scheduled to throw out the first pitch at the Tigers home opener on April 10 against the Red Sox). Across the state at Kalamazoo, black students had taken over the student union building at Western Michigan University, locking the doors and refusing to let any white students inside.

Some of the worst rioting occurred in Washington, D.C., where Baltimore Orioles pitcher Pete Richert was activated for duty with his National Guard unit. Richert, who had been traded in mid-1967 from the Washington Senators to the Orioles, was asked to stand guard with his unit at D.C. Stadium — the same place where he had been the starting pitcher in the season opener for the Senators in 1967. "It is very odd," Richert would say that Monday, overlooking an empty ballpark while dressed in his army fatigues with an M-16 slung over his shoulder. "There should have been 40,000 people and the president or the vice president here for a happy day. Instead, you have to be here under these circumstances. It's not fun." Standing alongside Richert was his former shortstop with the Senators, Eddie Brinkman, also on guard that day as it was announced that all Senators home games would be played in daylight hours until further notice. "There was always something going on," Brinkman recalled about those days to writer William Mead. "They would call me at home, and I'd have to go down [to National Guard duty] ... I just wanted the thing to be over with so I could settle back down to a normal life — play some ball." Brinkman and Richert were certainly not alone, as nearly a third of the major league players in the 1960s were serving in National Guard units.

Things were a bit more peaceful in St. Louis, where a commemorative march in King's honor was held on the 7th; it began at 1:30 P.M. under the Gateway Arch, and went westward along Franklin Avenue until ending at Forest Park. In later years, Franklin Avenue would be renamed Dr. Martin Luther King, Jr., Drive.

Magnifying such monumental events of the 1960s was the proliferation of the relatively-new media, television, which foreshadowed a larger culture of instant news that was becoming all-encompassing. This era was ushered in by news anchor Walter Cronkite, with his announcement of the shooting of President Kennedy on November 22, 1963, just over an hour after the event had occurred. CBS News had broken into its normal broadcasting of the soap opera *As the World Turns* when Cronkite first reported that shots had been fired at the president's motorcade in downtown Dallas. Moments later, Cronkite announced that the president was dead, and that the last rites had been administered. With the images presented on the television screen, it was a moment frozen in time in everyone's mind. "It is as though the entire nation had been in Ford's Theatre on April 14, 1865, and then at the barn-burning where John Wilkes Booth was killed two weeks later," the editorial in *Life* magazine offered the following week about the live, national consciousness of the event. "It is as though we had marched all the way with the Lincoln funeral train from Washington to Springfield, Illinois. Never has a whole nation lived a chapter of its history with such a searing immediacy."

Now, King's assassination — along with the daily reports of death from the war in Vietnam — served as another indication of the relentless onslaught of the modern media. It was four and a half years after Kennedy's shooting, and the coverage of King's assassination was even more acute.

Gibson had noted that, back in February, he had passed by King in the Atlanta airport. The two made eye contact and acknowledged one another, but nothing was said. "For the most part, ballplayers are able to divorce themselves from events of the real world," Gibson reflected. "Baseball is a self-absorbed sort of lifestyle that affords a certain detachment from many public concerns, but even for those of us in the game, there was no escaping the pervasive realities of 1968." Isolated riots had occurred near the ballpark in St. Petersburg, but did not affect any of the few remaining spring training games. Out of respect for King, however, the Cardinals and Tigers cancelled their final preseason affair that had been scheduled to take place on April 7, as they were the last teams remaining in Florida with all others having already headed north. The two clubs had played four games to end the exhibition ledger (with a fifth contest originally slated for the seventh), and split the contests to end the Cards' preseason record at 17–11–1 (one game better than their 1967 performance in the spring), while Detroit ended their preparations with a 14–15 mark from their off-season headquarters in Lakeland. Getting the start on the mound in the last contest for the Tigers was Denny McLain, a twenty-game winner in 1966 but who had stumbled to a mediocre 17–16 record in the past year. Instead of playing the fifth game against Detroit on

Sunday the 7th, the Cards gathered their gear and got on board a United Airlines charter jet that landed in St. Louis at 8:25 P.M. Just minutes before departing, Devine announced that the team had made the decision to postpone their opener with the Braves until Wednesday the 10th (which was originally scheduled as an open date), as the team would hold a light workout on Monday.

Overnight, life had been turned on its head. It was unmistakable that something was amiss in the order of things. For even while on the verge of a new baseball season — one of the perennial, eternal springs of optimism and hope in American culture — the shocking event in Memphis had served as a reminder to everyone that the United States, as well as the rest of the world, was still embroiled in an era of confusion and uncertainty, with seemingly no end in sight. Nevertheless, people still looked forward to a summer of 1968 that would hopefully be without the bloodshed of any more leaders.

Just two months later, however, another assassination would tear the country apart once again.

*   *   *   *

The Cardinals were the overwhelming choice to repeat as pennant winners in the National League, receiving over half the first-place votes of sportswriters as the season began. In the race for the remaining spots on the pitching staff, Gilson and Torrez found themselves on the plane ride to St. Louis, while Granger and Cosman were given their minor league assignments. Wicker (despite his tremendous spring) and first baseman Joe Hague joined Granger and Cosman in being the final roster cuts, enabling the club to get the list down the required twenty-five. (Devine, meanwhile, was unable to find a major league team willing to take Lamabe, so he was sent to work with Warren Spahn at the Triple-A team in Tulsa.) Granger was stunned by the news, for while not having appeared in a regular season big-league game as of yet in his career, he had held opposing batters scoreless in his last 13 innings of work in the spring. "Don't worry," Tolan told him in relaying the story of his own rookie year in 1965 at the age of 19, in trying to cheer up the 24-year-old. "I was back up before the season was over." Cosman was reported to be leaving the Al Lang Field locker room in tears, also having pitched magnificently in the spring. "This is the toughest part of a manager's job," Schoendienst uttered the words that so many professional skippers have used. "But at least, with expansion around the corner, I'm certain that these four promising prospects will be with us or another major league ball club no later than 1969." Gibson (1.64 ERA) and Jaster (1.89) were the stars off the mound as the spring statistics were totaled, while the performance of Briles (4.09), Washburn (4.85), and Hughes (5.68) caused consternation for the manager. Nonetheless, fans were expecting that the Redbirds would bring home their first consecutive pennant-winning seasons since 1943 and 1944. And there was no shortage of confidence among the players either, even from the normally-reserved Gibson. "Yeah, I think we'll repeat. I had a dream about it — we won with a long time to go, something like two months left in the season." Hoerner was even more specific, as he pointed to the upgrading of the bench. "We're improved. Simpson over Johnson is a big improvement, and Edwards over Romano, plus Tolan and Willis with a year's experience — Hughes too." Now Devine — in his second term as general manager — was making the stabilization of the bullpen his top priority. "Specifically, we hope to find on our own staff a good tenth pitcher," he said in obvious reference to either Cosman or Granger, "so that we can avoid going outside our organization to find another late-inning reliever. We know that there is good young talent on the staff, but the important thing is to have it ready to help now." Broeg was quick to point out that it was Devine who had previously secured most of the talent for the 1967 Cardinals, well before he was dismissed by Gussie Busch in 1964.

While the Cards were primed and ready, a repeat of 1967 was not expected on the American League side as the troubles that the Red Sox had been experiencing in the off-season had apparently taken their toll in the minds of the prognosticators. For overtaking them in the pre-season predictions for 1968 were McLain and the Tigers, jilted at the altar on the previous season's final day. Broeg, assured that at least the Cards would return to October play, was intrigued with the potential match-up. "A World Series between the Cardinals and the Tigers would be fun," he wrote simply on April 5. "Come to think of it, as the Redbirds proved in laughing all the way to the bank last fall, any series is a joy." Boston was placed a distant fifth by the writers, with none of them giving the Red Sox a single first-place vote — Detroit, Minnesota, Chicago, and Baltimore were imagined by the scribes to have better teams in '68. Trailing the Cardinals in second place on the National League side was predicted to be the Cincinnati Reds. "Cincy has a driving hustler in Pete Rose and tremendous talent in Tony Perez, Lee May, and of course, Vada Pinson," Broeg continued. "Questions might be how quickly John Bench responds to the pressure at number-one catcher, and how the Reds' pitching will fare without sore-armed Gary Nolan, who was sent to the minors." Even though Rose was fast becoming a superstar from the five major league seasons already behind him, like Johnny Edwards he had not forgotten the rough ways of the minor leagues that got him there. "We had to learn to sleep sitting up," he told a writer in early 1968, remembering how one of his minor league teams had to travel to their games in station wagons with eight men per vehicle. "Here in the majors, you fly everywhere and sleep in a real bed every night." He also was appreciative of the windfall of $15 a day the big-leaguers were receiving for meal money that year. "We got $3.50 in the minors," he added, "and I used to spend $2 for breakfast, so that left me a

$1.50 for the rest of the day. I always ended up spending some of my own money."

In addition to the Reds, also seen as contending were the improving Cubs under Durocher's leadership, and the Giants with their "Big Four" pitching staff of Marichal, Perry, McCormick, and Sadecki. (Durocher, incidentally, had been involved in a lawsuit against Aamco Transmissions Company during the spring of 1968. Seeking a million dollars in damages, Durocher sued the company for improperly using his name in advertising.) A dark horse was the Pirates club, whose pitching staff was greatly enhanced with the addition of Jim Bunning, as his 253 strikeouts with the Phillies in 1967 was tops in the National League. As for Detroit, Broeg joined his penning brethren in thinking that it was Motown's year in the Junior Circuit. "A healthy Denny McLain gives muscle to the pitching. The infield isn't the best defensively, but it's pretty good offensively. The outfield, like catcher Bill Freehan, is top-flight. It's headed by Al Kaline and Willie Horton ... this year, the Broeg Special is an inspiring season for Kaline, the classy Tiger who has waited 16 years to play in a World Series."

The Cardinals were generally healthy heading into the 1968 regular season, although Maris had spent yet another March trying to work through a pulled leg muscle. A badly-bruised finger which McCarver had sustained had healed, as he was ready to resume his arduous role as the everyday catcher, but with the capable Edwards in reserve. Willis and Hughes had been prevented from taking the mound as spring training drew to a close, as both were still fighting tenderness in their throwing arms. Each of the two, nonetheless, promised to be ready to go in St. Louis.

It would be the first time in the Twentieth Century that major league openers would be postponed by something other than inclement weather; not war, depression, nor any other cultural or political event had ever caused such a delay. As the major league ballparks of America opened for business, many of the cities had taken extra precautions in addition to the National Guard troops that would stand on watch to dispel potential rioting. Such was the case in Cincinnati, where the Cubs were getting ready to open the season against the Reds. The city government had issued a curfew from dusk to dawn, and had suspended the sale of liquor. Thus, the Cubs were stuck in their Netherland Hilton Hotel in downtown Cincinnati, unable to leave the premises as room service was the order of the evening. It was increasingly evident that the sports world was not immune to the rising social tensions, both domestically and abroad. It would be announced later in the week that the American Committee on Africa was calling on the United States to boycott the 1968 Summer Olympics in Mexico City. The committee, composed mostly of black professional athletes, signed a statement which protested the allowance by the International Olympic Committee of South Africa's participation in the games, a country that was viewed as rife with racial injustice and oppression.

At their practice session at Busch Stadium on Monday, April 8, the Cardinals pitchers took their turns at trying out the mound that had been assembled by the grounds crew. Muffett had wanted a slighter slope put in place, as he felt that a steep drop-off had a negative effect on his pitchers' follow-through during the 1967 season. Therefore, he had each of the pitchers throw ten minutes of batting practice to acclimate themselves to the new terrain. With Maris' leg problem, it was imagined that Tolan would get the Opening Day start in right field, particularly with his impressive .351 average that he had posted in the spring. But Roger said he was ready, and in fact Schoendienst would begin the same lineup that not only started the seventh game of the World Series against Boston, but that which started the 1967 regular season as well.

Naturally, all kinds of ceremonies were scheduled to be held in St. Louis to celebrate the world title from a season ago. Giles, the National League president, was on hand to present the pennant and world championship flags to Schoendienst, along with his co-captains McCarver and Flood. Customarily, the World Series flag would fly from a pole atop the stadium, while the flag for the National League title would go on display in the Cardinals' Hall of Fame underneath the building. In honor of his recent election to the Hall of Fame, Medwick threw out the first pitch from the pitcher's mound as McCarver squatted to receive it. Also making an appearance at Opening Day was the daughter of one of Medwick's teammates, 21-year-old Miss Beth Ann Walker from the Illinois side of the river. She had been chosen as Miss Redbird for 1968, a position that would employ her hospitality at organizational functions throughout the year. She was the daughter of Bill Walker, a former Cardinals pitcher and winner of twelve games for the 1934 Gas House Gang world champions. With Caray manning the microphone on the field as the emcee, the Cardinals paraded around the field in an open motorcade of cars, waving to their appreciative fans for a most-successful 1967 and a most-promising 1968. Busch Stadium was in beautiful form and ready to go in its second full season, receiving a $15,000 re-sodding job before the team had gotten into town (prior to the 1967 season it took $50,000 to repair the grass, as groundskeepers had been dealing with their first off-season of witnessing the progress of the turf after the stadium opened for play in May of 1966). But the big housekeeping rumor floating around town was, once again, the possibility of artificial turf being installed. "It's up to the Cardinals to decide if Astroturf would provide a suitable surface for baseball," said Glen Walsh of the Civic Center Redevelopment Corporation. "And nobody has decided who would pay for it. I know that Civic Center can't afford the $550,000 expenditure — not alone. There isn't enough cost-saving in maintenance and labor."

Because of some unsightly weather it was not a full house, as only 34,740 had come through the turnstiles for the opener. As the World Series hero Gibson took the hill, it was the fourth straight time he had done so for a Cardinals season inaugural. Despite his success in 1967 (albeit shortened by his leg injury), Gibson had nonetheless gone winless in two decisions against Atlanta in the past year, contributing to a surprising 10–17 mark that he held against the Braves over his career. Conspicuously absent from the Braves' lineup was one of their hard-hitting outfielders, Rico Carty. The talented Carty had first became famous in the winter of 1959 and 1960 for naively signing professional contracts with ten different organizations simultaneously from his home in the Dominican Republic. In the spring of 1968, Carty had been diagnosed with tuberculosis, and the disease would sideline him for the entire year. Of course, Schoendienst could empathize with the player, as Red had suffered the same malady in his young adult life. He sent Carty a letter of support. "You will especially miss baseball now that the season has started, but don't give up," Red wrote. "I'm told that you should be completely recovered for the 1969 season." Earlier in the day, Carty had sent an inspirational telegram to his Braves teammates, which read, "Best wishes for a win tonight, and for the National League pennant. With all my heart, I wish I was there to help." The sickness affected Carty's mind, and he would spend five months in a sanitarium before indeed making a remarkable comeback in 1969, playing in 104 games. In 1970, he would complete his recovery by leading the National League with a .366 batting average. For the interim, Mike Lum took his place in left field, with center fielder Felipe Alou and right fielder Henry Aaron in their customary spots.

Gibson forced three pop-ups from the Atlanta bats in the first inning, much to the delight of the home crowd. But matching him for the Braves through the early going was the Clinton County kid, Jarvis, who once again entertained the usual throng from nearby Carlyle. To make sure he was well-rested for the game, new Atlanta manager Lum Harris (who had won the permanent job over Silvestri) had sent two other pitchers, Phil Niekro and Tony Cloninger, to Carlyle with Jarvis for company. There were no sightings of the three at the "raucous" Carlyle Legion Hall the night before, so it was assumed that Jarvis had gotten the slumber he needed. The Clintonian permitted two-out walks to Maris and Cepeda in the bottom half, but then coerced McCarver into flying out meekly to Aaron to end the threat.

The Braves got on the board first in the second inning, thanks to an error by Brock that allowed Clete Boyer to score. Brock was handcuffed on a line drive off the bat of Felix Millan, and the misplay allowed Atlanta to draw first blood. Jarvis coolly kept them in control of the game; and when Maxvill popped out to Millan in foul territory to end the St. Louis fifth, it was showing on the scoreboard that the Cardinals had not managed a base hit to that point. Was Gibby going to be stymied by the Braves once again? As the former Clinton County All-Star made his way off the field, people in the stands—especially the Carlyle natives in attendance — began to murmur about the possibility of that unmentionable pitching feat looming on the horizon over the next hour.

His counterpart, Gibson, led off the bottom of the sixth, and Hoot decided that no one was going to show him up on the home field. He bounced a single between first and second into right field, as a double-dose cheer of relief from Cardinals fans and appreciation from Jarvis supporters filled the arena. Back to the top of the order, Brock made it appear that the Cards were seizing control as he shot another hit to center. But Jarvis composed himself again and retired Flood, Maris, and Cepeda to get out of a jam. The Cardinals would not score on Jarvis until Cepeda came to the plate again in the eighth and drove a ball into the right-center gap, scoring Flood (who had singled) to tie the game at one. Washburn, who had replaced Gibson after Tolan entered as a pinch hitter in the seventh, provided a second inning of effective relief in the ninth. It was only his second relief appearance since 1965, and it would be his last of 1968; nonetheless it serviced the task quite ably. In the bottom of the ninth, Maxvill — who was aching for a chance to contribute in a non-exhibition game since his .158 performance in the 1967 World Series—doubled with one out, as Dick Simpson made his Cardinals debut as Maxvill's pinch runner. Next, Ricketts was announced as the pinch hitter for Washburn, whereby Harris summoned Ken Johnson from the bullpen to replace Jarvis. Almost immediately the crowd rose to its feet, and Missourians and Illinoisans alike gave him a standing ovation. They had barely settled down when Ricketts jumped on the first pitch he saw from Johnson and stroked it into center field, chasing home Simpson and an opening-night win for the Cards 2–1, giving Washburn a quick victory. "Hey Washburn!" Hoerner yelled over from his locker. "Quit sucking up the relief pitchers' wins—you're supposed to be a starter!" Gibson, meanwhile, simply appeared grateful that the team was able to emerge on top. He was not able to strike out a single Atlanta batter on the evening. "Hoot is just snake-bitten by the Braves," Muffett shook his head afterwards. "That's three three-hitters he's pitched against them in the last four times he's faced them, and he didn't win any of them." In the locker room, Cepeda returned to his comfortable place from the previous summer — standing on top of the money trunk. "One hundred more to go! One hundred more to go!" he hollered to his teammates down below in getting the cheers for the new year started. To add to the celebration, it was time for Yatkeman to hand out vouchers to the players that they could redeem for free Anheuser-Busch products, which he would do on occasion. Often times, he would announce a rendezvous point for these distributions in advance, and he noticed that attendance for the meetings swelled when he posted the time and place in advance. Yatkeman also added proudly — just like on pay-day — that "El Birdos never lose on beer-slip day."

Elsewhere around the majors, attendance had dipped only slightly in inaugurals as compared to the first games of 1967, despite the postponements. In all, four out of the ten openers would involve shutouts, a harbinger of the demise of baseball bats that would arrive over the summer of '68. There was a glimmer of offense, however, as the grandest laurels of Opening Day belonged to Yastrzemski. Yaz belted two home runs — the latter being of the inside-the-park variety in the top of the ninth, the first such round-tripper of his career — as the Red Sox proved they were not going to simply hand the pennant to Detroit or any of the other contenders. Boston won in Tiger Stadium 7–3 as Petrocelli and Reggie Smith also added two hits. Getting the win was the newly-acquired Dick Ellsworth from Philadelphia, who looked to fill the huge void left by the off-season injury to Lonborg. At D.C. Stadium in Washington, the Twins won behind Dean Chance's four-hit shutout of the Senators. One of Minnesota's own was in attendance, in fact, as Hubert H. Humphrey was able to watch his beloved team as well as throw out the first pitch. Even as the vice president was loosening up his throwing arm, soldiers continued to patrol the grounds outside of the stadium, with Washington still being the epicenter of unrest following the King assassination. In New York, a mere 15,000 had shown up in the Bronx to watch the "lowly" Yankees, having finished 1967 in ninth place in the American League with a record of 72–90. This placement was actually an improvement over their final standing in 1966, which saw them in the cellar with a 70–89 mark, costing Keane his job and placing Ralph Houk on the hot seat. Before '66, never since 1925 had the Yankees finished lower than seventh (with that distinction occurring in that year only; in addition, their only sixth-place finish was Keane's first season in 1965). Furthermore, there had been worry of further delay in the openers for the Mets and the Yankees, as the grounds crew and custodians at both of the stadiums were threatening to strike. The Mets were not at home at Shea Stadium until April 17, but fortunately, a deal was struck for the employees at Yankee Stadium and the first game went on as planned. The club turned to Marian Moore for luck, as the poet performed the first-pitch duties at the New York ballpark. Mel Stottlemyre got the hometown team off to a good start, blanking the Angels 1–0 on four hits as the Yanks produced only three safeties themselves. Unfortunately, a twist of bad luck would strike the Bronx Bombers' promising launch, as star first baseman Joe Pepitone would fracture his elbow just four days later and miss nearly two months of the schedule. On the National side on Opening Day, the Giants scored three runs in the bottom of the ninth in rallying to beat the Mets 5–4, and the Phillies' Chris Short dominated the Dodgers and Claude Osteen in Chavez Ravine, posting his own shutout and striking out ten Los Angeles hitters.

Briles won his eleventh in a row the next evening to close out the Cards' quick meeting with the Braves, with Hoerner picking up the save in relief. Briles' streak now stretched back to his nine straight wins to finish the 1967 regular season, in addition to his victory in Game Three of the World Series. With a perfect 2–0 start at home, the Cards took off for Chicago. On the plane, Cepeda once again provided Gibson with a special Puerto Rican dish of shrimp and rice that Cepeda's wife had prepared, since the recipe had seemed to work wonders the last time that the team traveled. Some of the other passengers on the plane were tired, especially Schoendienst. "I planted 27 shrubs at home, and that's work," he grunted. Upon landing at O'Hare Airport, however, there were positive feelings throughout the Cardinals about arriving in the Windy City. The place held good memories for the club, as it was the spot where they had built a five-and-a-half game lead last August 2, and the lead would never get smaller than that for the remainder of the summer. Cepeda and Flood were particularly happy to disembark, as the two men had batted .371 and .393 against Chicago in the previous year. Even though the Cubs had faded from the 1967 pennant race, they were now counting on a core of young starting pitchers for their fortunes in 1968. Included among the group were Jenkins, aged 24; Nye, 23; Holtzman, 22; Joe Niekro, 23; and a veteran in the group, Bill Hands at 28. All of them, despite their youth, had already established themselves as quality major league pitchers in 1967. At the head of the class was Jenkins, who in '67 had tied for second place with Bunning in the National League Cy Young voting as he made his first appearance in the All-Star Game. Holtzman was just rounding into baseball shape, however, as he once again had been assigned to duty with his National Guard unit — this time, to quell the recent rioting in Chicago. "The young pitchers should be even better this year," Durocher predicted, "if they continue to learn the fine points of the game and follow the teaching of Joe Becker [the Cubs' pitching coach]." The entire Chicago roster tilted towards the youthful side, in fact, as over half of the 38 players that Durocher had in major league camp in spring training were under the age of 25. "Guys who want to stick with the big league club need to show something in a hurry," the manager warned. "There's no time for slow starters." Durocher knew that his club would not surprise anyone this year, for after being a last-place club in 1966, they were able to sneak up on the rest of the National League the following season. Now, they were expected to be in the upper division from the beginning of April onward.

The weather for the series began as unseasonably warm for Chicago in that part of the year, and the Cards' bats took advantage. In the first game, Carlton was the beneficiary of 17 hits— including five from Flood — in beating the Cubs 8–5. Hughes, however, next displayed the lingering effect of his sore arm, being touched for five hits and four runs in just over an inning of work in giving St. Louis their first defeat of the year 7–6 on Easter Sunday. The weather that day had suddenly turned cold, with winds pushing 30 miles per hour that played havoc with fly balls, particularly for Cardinals fielders, all day long. The Bleacher Bums in the left field stands resumed their heckling of Brock, once again chanting "Brock, as in rock!" in reference to his defensive liabilities. Nonetheless, Sandy Koufax — on hand to continue his short-lived and less-than-celebrated performance as a broadcaster for NBC's Game of the Week — felt that the St. Louis ball club would be just as strong as the version they put on the field in 1967. "The Cardinals look every bit as good as the club that won last year," the great lefthander noticed. "In fact, they look better, with additions like John Edwards and Dick Simpson ... the big thing is that the Cardinals have a guy like Bob Gibson who takes the pressure off of the young pitchers. The kids don't have to worry about many long losing streaks with Gibson around to help." The first road trip of the year concluded with another two-game sweep of the Braves in Atlanta (in the second game of which Cepeda continued a hot start by going 4 for 4 and upping his RBI total to nine in six games), before the Cardinals dropped a pair of heart-breaking 4–3 games in Cincinnati — both in twelve innings — and both won by the Reds' intimidating reliever, big Bob Lee, gaining a small measure of revenge for the pummeling he took in the Reds-Cards brawl in St. Louis the previous summer. Rose was the hero in the second game, tying things with an eighth-inning homer off Washburn and winning it in the twelfth with a double off Jaster. Meanwhile, the end was nearing for Crosley Field, as plans to replace the old ballpark at the corner of Western and Findlay in Cincinnati were underway with a new circular stadium planned for the Cincinnati riverfront — just as had happened in St. Louis.

A brand-new stadium in another city was already in operation. Big league baseball had hit Oakland, California, for the first time on April 17, as the A's took the field in the pristine Oakland Coliseum. Over 50,000 fans — many of them ringing cowbells — cheered their new team wildly and enjoyed an evening full of celebrations. Charles Finley, having gone through four general managers in the six years that he had owned the A's, was now making all player personnel decisions himself. Finley saw the event as a fresh start for his team, for the American League, and, not least, for himself, seeking redemption — at least publicly — from a good portion of the baseball world that had been soured by the manner in which he removed the franchise from Kansas City. Krausse also looked for redemption from his previous summer's run-in with the owner, getting the historic first starting assignment on the hill in the new structure. Unlike the opening of Busch Stadium two seasons before, the initial imperfections of the Coliseum appeared to be few and far between. The only missteps involved the umpires twice stopping play for approximately fifteen minutes, both times asking the grounds crew to tamp down some loose dirt that had appeared around home plate and the bases. The Baltimore Orioles spoiled the opener by winning 4–1 behind Dave McNally, but enthusiasm for the game in Oakland was soaring. "It may take a while," Orioles manager Hank Bauer mentioned, "but I think one day they may have a good ballpark here."

After the first week of the new season, people were noticing something strange that was occurring with the bats all over baseball — namely, their ineptitude, or at least that of the people swinging them. On April 15, a meeting between the Mets and the Astros in Houston would become symbolic of the remainder of the summer. The Astros scratched out a 1–0 win over New York — after 24 innings of play. The contest ended at 1:37 A.M. local time, marking it as the longest night game in major league history and two innings shy of the longest game ever played. It was the first time that any game had ever gone past twenty innings without a run being scored, as all the players, coaches, and fans involved were hanging on with their last ounces of energy. "That was a three-package-of-tobacco game," Houston coach Buddy Hancken sighed afterwards, "and I've just got one chew left." Approximately one-fifth of the 14,000 in attendance at the beginning of the game saw the finish, as Bob Aspromonte squibbed a hit towards Al Weis at second base. The Mets' infielder bobbled the ball as Norm Miller crossed the plate to end the affair. Two innings earlier, the flashy scoreboard had read, "THE JUDGE [Roy Hofheinz, the Astros' owner] SAYS HE'S READY TO GO TO BED ... LET'S SCORE A RUN." The number of innings grabbed the headlines the following day, but lost in the story was the 5–1 start to the year by the surprising Houston club which vaulted them over the Cardinals, and the overpowering performance by Seaver, the New York starter on the evening (and morning). In the process of cementing his place among the great hurlers in baseball for the coming decade, Seaver went the first ten frames for the Mets and allowed a mere two hits and no walks. The Astros, on the other hand, chose to utilize a greater combination of pitchers that, in sum, was just as effective. Those following the game in 1968 would soon see a complete season of dominance by the men on the mound, a wholesale shutdown of lumber usage that would precede major rule changes for Major League Baseball in 1969.

When the Cardinals returned for their second stint at home on April 19, Cepeda was given his 1967 National League Most Valuable Player award, while the team received their 1967 World Series rings from Commissioner Eckert before the final game of the series with the Cubs. The erstwhile released, retired, or traded Al Jackson, Alex Johnson, Woodeshick, Bressoud, and Romano were five of the 25 from 1967 that were not currently in uniform. Bressoud, after being released by the Cardinals, became the head coach at DeAnza Junior College in Cupertino, California. He was asked by one of his former teammates if he learned any lessons since he became a coach. "In our last game, we were ahead 14–0, so I took out most of my regulars and gave some of the scrubbinis a chance to play," he said. "We ended up losing 16–14."

Warren Giles wished to be there as well, but he was presiding over another matter of importance to the game. Giles was in Chicago with the owners of the National League clubs, announcing to the press that, after only a two-hour meeting, the owners had now formally voted — after months of vocal support — to approve the expansion of the league to twelve teams for the 1969 season. The two new cities had yet to be decided, and it was agreed among the executives that unanimity must prevail among them in the selection of the sites for the decision to be final. A narrowing to the five finalists had been made — including Dallas–Fort Worth, Milwaukee, San Diego, Buffalo, and Montreal — and a decision on the two winners was near. Originally, the league had planned on waiting until 1971 for expansion, but the strength of the proposals of the five sites allowed the process to move forward more quickly — in addition to the pressure placed upon them by the preemptive growth of the American League, as the Nationals sought to maintain a competitive balance between the two circuits. "We pretty much know who the owners would be in each city," Giles said, "and I think any of them could meet the conditions."

The night belonged to the youngsters in the Cubs-Cards opener. The 21-year-old Torrez got his second start in the major leagues (the first coming at the tail end of the 1967 season), and went nearly six innings before being relieved by his fellow rookie, Gilson, who made his major league debut. After a tough 1966 season in the minor leagues, Gilson had found reason for optimism the following year. "When I read the following winter that Warren Spahn was going to manage Tulsa in '67," he remembered, "I felt that if anyone could straighten me out, he could. I thought about quitting before that. I told Spahn that if I didn't show enough improvement in 1967, I definitely would quit. I was already 25." With two singles from Flood (who to date had hit in every game on the season), the result was a smashing 9–2 win. When Torrez tried out for the Cardinals at Sportsman's Park in 1964, he had thrown so hard to coach Vern Benson that Benson came into the clubhouse and asked that one of the regular catchers take over the rest of the duty, as his hand was sore from catching Torrez's blazing fastball. The Cardinals then gave him a contract that offered him a $20,000 bonus, which Torrez accepted — even though they later admitted — even to Torrez himself — that they originally thought it would have taken at least $40,000 to sign him. "But $20,000 was a lot of money anyway," Torrez reasoned. "My parents didn't know anything about contracts. With eight kids to support, there wasn't any money. I'm just thankful that God gave me a good arm." He was the son of Mexican immigrants who had settled in the Topeka, Kansas, area to work for the Santa Fe Railroad.

The post-game interviews, however, revealed a festering dispute on the Cubs between Durocher and his first baseman. Ernie Banks, who was starting his sixteenth year in the major leagues, failed to score from third on a high-bounding grounder that Shannon fielded well behind the bag. Durocher, who had been searching for Banks' replacement since he took the Cubs manager's job in 1966, felt that Banks should have crossed the plate easily — and it was the last straw for the frustrated Leo. "It's a disgrace not to score on that play," he muttered to the newsmen. "He's been in the league sixteen years, but he just won't get off the bag. I've told Joe Amalfitano [the Cubs' first base coach] that if Banks gets picked off first base, we'll give Ernie a hundred bucks. I'll betcha that in our eight games—what did we lose, six?—we've given Ernie the steal sign ten times. But he hasn't stolen a base. He steps one foot off the bag." Banks tried to respond in a positive but indirect manner. "I feel young. I am young. This is spring and you gotta be young in the spring. You gotta be a kid to play baseball. I'm a kid." In May 1968, Banks would pass Cap Anson for the top spot in all-time total bases for the Cubs with 4,150. Jenkins righted things for the Chicago ship the next evening, handing Gibson and the Cards their first home loss of the year 5–1 behind a first-inning homer by Billy Williams, as Jenkins had not walked a single batter in the 21 innings he had pitched thus far in 1968. The series was capped by another 9–2 St. Louis win on the 21st. Russo had pointed out that Briles, the victor, had gotten 25 runs of support in his three starts on the year — all wins— while Gibson had gotten only three runs in his three starts, totaling one loss for the Cards' ace. And as with the general downfall of baseball bats in 1968, the lack of run support on the evening would be a preview of much of the summer for Gibson, who would have to constantly struggle amidst scant scoring support from his teammates.

On April 22, the Cardinals gave Lamabe another shot at the big leagues— by dealing him to the Cubs. In return, St. Louis received a couple of other pitching prospects in Pete Mikkelsen and Dave Dowling. Dowling had originally signed with the Cardinals at the same time as Carlton and Briles, but they exposed him to the free agent draft as there was not a roster spot for him at the time. The following day, Brock downed Cincinnati in the first contest of a two-game series with a two-run homer in the tenth to win 4–2. Perhaps the most promising thing on the night, however, was the two scoreless innings thrown by the tender-shouldered Hughes, who reported no stiffness in the wake of the outing. Five days later on April 28, he would receive his 1967 Rookie of the Year award from *The Sporting News* that had been granted at the end of the previous season. Washburn, another pitcher who had been dealing with various arm ailments, showed even more progress by shutting out the Reds the following night 7–0. Flood scored in his thirteenth straight game in the opener, five short of the National League record, and his league-leading batting average stood at .414. Flood himself was battling through a host of ailments, including the lingering pain of his shoulder injury from the previous summer. Trainer Bob Bauman, however, rated Flood right behind Stan Musial as the Cardinals player who, in his recollection, could withstand the most pain.

The Cardinals finished the homestand with a record of 8–2. "The Cardinals are well-spread," was how Pittsburgh pitcher Tom Sisk described the club. "You can't pitch around or through one guy on their team. They don't have a lot of power, but they don't make many mistakes. They run well. They hit the ball well. They move runners around consistently. They just play the game they way it's supposed to be played." Some following the Redbirds were yet concerned about the overall lack of run production by the club. But Gibson, perhaps the person who should have been the most concerned, was not. "They're going to score some runs for me," he said confidently. "It's a long season. Besides, if you're going to have a good year, you've got to win your share of 2–1 games, too." He did indeed on April 26, topping a great game pitched by Bob Veale of the Pirates (who had a record of 3–0 against St. Louis in 1967) by downing Pittsburgh by that very score, the benefactor of solo home runs by Cepeda and McCarver. "Cha Cha" was making good on his promise to hit more balls out of Busch Stadium in 1968, as all four of his round-trippers on the young season had been at home — and his blast that beat the Pirates was his first to exit the right-field portion of the ballpark.

That same night in New York, Mickey Mantle had hit home run number 521 for his career, tying Ted Williams for fourth place all-time. It was his third on the season, and the ball was later retrieved for his possession. Two weeks later, he would take over sole possession of fourth place with a blast off of Sam McDowell of Cleveland, who in his previous start had struck out 16 Oakland batters. Despite Mantle's blast, McDowell struck out 14 Yankees in this contest, as his two consecutive game total of 30 broke the American League record of 28 set by Bob Feller in 1938, and was one short of the 31 posted by Koufax in 1959. After the game, an anonymous donor said that he would give $1,000 to Mantle's foundation for research on Hodgkin's Disease if he could have the ball from number 522. It was retrieved for him, and the donor had it sent to the National Baseball Hall of Fame.

The Cards made a clean sweep of the Pirates by winning the next two days, including the fourteenth straight victory for Briles by a 7–5 score on April 27 as he benefited from five unearned runs, two of which scored on a wild throw from Roberto Clemente that wound up in the seats. Briles' feat made small newsprint, however, for greater events were taking place in the sports world that evening. Tom Phoebus of the Orioles weaved a no-hitter against the Red Sox in Baltimore, saved on a diving play by third baseman Brooks Robinson in the eighth inning. Even more remarkable was the fact that behind the plate for Phoebus was Curt Blefary, making only his fourth appearance in the major leagues as a catcher. And from the boxing ring, Jimmy Ellis would win a 15-round decision over Jerry Quarry in Oakland — and with it came the heavyweight title, the culmination of the eight-man tournament set up the previous summer to fill the championship vacancy left by the conviction of Cassius Clay.

Fortunately for the Redbirds, they were able to miss Bunning in the three games against Pittsburgh, as in the past week the star hurler had become the first pitcher since Cy Young to achieve 1,000 strikeouts in both leagues, shutting out the Dodgers 3–0 for his first win in a Pirates uniform on April 14. The Pittsburgh club was suffering from injuries to key personnel — including Bunning, who was fighting an ankle sprain. And slugger Willie Stargell had strained his knee, being held out of the lineup for much of April. As an invited guest at the Pirates series, the Cardinals hosted left-handed pitcher Jerry Reuss, their first-round draft pick from a year ago, for private workouts at the ballpark. He was currently attending Southern Illinois University, but the plan was for him to join one of the Cardinals' farm teams once the semester was over. It was also during the Pirates series that the Cardinals got their first look at what they called their own Green Monster. The center field wall at Busch Stadium had been painted a deep green, so as to provide a better hitting background for batters.

It was evident that pitching would be the preeminent factor in the 1968 pennant race, and the Cardinals were once again proving that they had plenty of it. And with all the recognition that their strong starting staff had received, the Cardinals' bullpen held a composite ERA of under 1.00 by the end of April. At that time, it was announced that the Cardinals had suddenly reached nearly $2 million in season ticket sales, already breaking the record they had set in 1967. Their success was seen in the ultimate bottom line, the standings:

	W	L	Pct.	GB
St. Louis	13	5	.722	—
San Francisco	10	7	.588	2.5
Los Angeles	9	9	.500	4
Pittsburgh	8	8	.500	4
Cincinnati	8	9	.471	4.5
Philadelphia	8	9	.471	4.5
Chicago	8	10	.444	5
Atlanta	8	10	.444	5
New York	7	9	.438	5
Houston	7	10	.412	5.5

In the American League, the Detroit Tigers (12–5) held a slight lead over Minnesota, Baltimore, and Washington, while the pennant-winning Red Sox, as expected, were simply treading water with an 8–8 record. In just over a couple weeks' time, Kaline would hit his 307th home run to pass Hank Greenberg for the Tigers' club record, as many were beginning to feel that this would finally be the Motor City's year — as well as that of Kaline, devoted to the Tigers organization since signing with them in 1953 and never having experienced a championship.

9. Playing Through the Sorrow

Some men see things the way they are, and ask, "Why?" I prefer to dream things that never were, and ask, "Why not?"
— Robert F. Kennedy, quoting George Bernard Shaw

Gibson allowed no earned runs in going all twelve innings and 179 pitches against the Astros on May 1, getting his second win in a 3–1 decision. Afterwards, he yelped in the locker room as he dipped his sore right elbow into a bucket of ice. Five days later on May 6, he would go 11 innings in beating Seaver and the Mets 2–1. "My arm doesn't hurt half as much as it will tomorrow," he told Russo, "but that's the price you have to pay if you want to be a pitcher ... I had my arm under a heat lamp for twenty minutes before the game, trying to get it loosened up." Despite the affair going two extra frames, he and Seaver were so dominant that the game still barely lasted over two hours, with the first nine being completed in an hour and a half. Brock was among the many who were impressed with the young New York pitcher. "He has good stuff," Brock said of Seaver. "He has to have something to win 16 games as a rookie." Nonetheless the Mets—despite having the best team ERA at 1.70—were in tenth place in the National League. Teams were doing anything to keep the Mets from scoring even a single run, as they feared being shut out on any given night. Evidence of this surfaced on May 1 at Shea Stadium, as Phillies pitcher John Boozer became only the second pitcher in major league history to be ejected from a game for throwing a spitball. Boozer was thrown out of the game by home plate umpire Ed Vargo—in the pre-game warm-ups, no less.

Gibson's performance was followed up by Briles' first loss in 275 days the next night, as the Astros ended his triumphant odyssey with a 4–0 score. "I wasn't even thinking about the streak," he said later. "There's no use building up for a letdown. If you don't keep your feet on the ground, you go crazy. The streak's been a good thing and I hope I win fourteen more before I lose again."

Flood carried a .400 average into May, edged only by Pete Rose of the Reds who was leading the league with a .404 average and who had hit in 21 straight games. Still, runs were still mostly hard-earned for the Cardinals, as the entire offensive load fell on the shoulders of Flood and a couple of other hot-hitting individuals. By early May, the combination of Cepeda, Maris, and Maxvill had gone an aggregate 5 for 69 in the preceding couple of weeks, while Flood, Javier, and McCarver led the way with more impressive numbers. Brock also was struggling, fighting a bad blister on his hand as he would hover around the .200 mark into mid–May (in addition to batting only .115 in the first inning of all the games to date as the Cardinals' leadoff hitter). He did, however, launch the game-winner on May 6 in Gibson's 11-inning epic against Seaver. He tripled to lead off the eleventh, and was then driven home by Cepeda. To help boost the offense, Schoendienst had replaced besieged Maxvill with Schofield in the starting lineup at shortstop on a couple of occasions, as well as Tolan in right field for Maris—the latter of whom was batting .222, as he could not seem to shake the pain in his injured leg. Also on Maris' mind was the fact that he was trying to sell his home in Independence, Missouri, so that he could move his family to Florida. This plan was in preparation for the end of his playing days, as he was figuring to take over the Anheuser-Busch distributorship that August Busch, Jr., had promised him — but as of mid-May, there had been no takers on his home. "I guess houses are selling, but not in the bracket ours is in," Maris said of his $93,000 place in suburban Kansas City.

The talent-laden Cubs had disappointed many with their 8–11 start to the season, and Durocher was once again becoming edgy. He protested a 4–0 loss at Pittsburgh on May 3, as he felt that Pirates manager Larry Shepard had been allowed to make multiple illegal visits to his pitcher during one inning. After the game, a sullen Durocher would not allow his players to speak to the media for the second straight night. Durocher, meanwhile, was also having another problem with "Bill Giles." Another man with that name was the operator of the million-dollar scoreboard at the Astrodome, and Leo felt that the cartoons of visiting players depicted them in a negative light. "I'm surprised that Leo, above all people, would complain about our scoreboard," Giles responded. "You know, Leo and our scoreboard have a lot in common. They're both noisy. They're both animated. They're both unique. They're both expensive. And, in my opinion, they're both good for baseball."

Schoendienst himself would protest a game in San Francisco on May 5, in which a Giants inning was permitted to continue when a throw from McCarver had struck the upright bat of McCovey, sending the ball scurrying away as the runners circled the bases. The Giants would go on to win the game 8–4. McCovey could appear to do no wrong against the Redbirds, as he continued a pace that ended with his hitting .409 against St. Louis in 1967. The Cards' own .400 hitter, Flood, had his mother and several other members of his family present at the games in San Francisco, making the trip from their nearby home in Oakland. Despite the support, the Cards dropped two out of three with the lone victory coming in the middle contest as Torrez got his second win with help from Javier's 1000th career hit. Torrez's victim was Ray Sadecki, long-forgotten in his original Cardinals uniform. The trade with the Giants before the opening of the new Busch Stadium in May 1966 had certainly worked out for the Cardinals in the long run, with Cepeda winning his MVP award in 1967 and Sadecki logging a mediocre 15–13 record for San Francisco since the deal took place. Sadecki's career had faltered shortly after winning twenty games for St. Louis in their championship season of 1964, as his mark tumbled to 6–15 in '65, the original incentive for the Cardinals to put him on the trading block. With San Francisco, he would never regain the promise that made him, as the Pirates pitcher Veale pointed out, one of the first high-paid "bonus babies" of the second half of the century. In the game against Torrez, Sadecki received relief help from former Cardinal Lindy McDaniel, who a few days later would set the National League record for consecutive errorless games with 225, a streak that harkened back to 1964 — although McDaniel, being a relief pitcher, needed to handle only 108 chances during that stretch to set the mark. And in Louisville, Kentucky, that afternoon, Bobby Ussery — despite losing his whip coming around the final turn — became only the third jockey in 94 years to ride back-to-back winners in the Kentucky Derby, bringing the three-year-old Dancer's Image to the wire in two minutes, two and one-fifth seconds. The horse garnered the winner's share of the $165,100 purse, as a record number of bets for the Derby were placed from across the country.

While baseball remained St. Louis's game, no one could ignore the success of the Cardinals' infant brothers, the Blues of the National Hockey League, who were in the process of losing their four straight games to the Canadiens in the league finals. And although the established club handled the expansion team handily, support for the home city was not in small supply. Fans had gotten behind the team ever since they had recorded that first tie in their initial game at the St. Louis Arena against Minnesota in October, while the Cardinals were in the World Series in Boston. The Automobile Club of St. Louis, in fact, had tickets in the Montreal Forum for the first fifty Blues fans who were willing to make the trip north of the border for the series games played there. The series also marked the retirement of Canadiens coach

Hector Blake, better known as "Toe," having completed 15 seasons behind the bench in the Forum. "I don't have any other job in mind," the hockey legend told the press, "but this was my last game as coach." The defeated Blues team was led by a promising young coach named Scotty Bowman, who would ironically take the Canadiens to even more dominant heights in the 1970s, as he had started his career as a scout and minor-league coach in the Montreal organization before taking the job in St. Louis. "This series was far from the walkaway that everyone was predicting for Montreal," said Bowman, despite the 4–0 whitewashing in the games. "I think the Eastern writers are going to have to admit now that we were a lot better team than anyone thought." There was talk after the series that Bowman was immediately heading to Montreal, but he dismissed the notion. "I couldn't even think of it," he said. "There has to be some loyalty in this game." On the ice, the stalwart of the Blues was Hall, the 37-year-old goaltender who endeared himself to the opposition's knowledgeable fans in Montreal with his spectacular saves in Game Four that kept the score a close 3–2 affair. For his efforts, Hall was rewarded with the Conn Smythe Trophy, given annually to the most valuable player in the NHL playoffs—despite the fact that Hall played for the runner-up. The Blues would make it an off-season priority to re-sign Hall, who with his 73 career shutouts ranked third on the all-time list. In addition, the Blues' run through the playoffs enabled Hall to tie the NHL record for playoff appearances with Turk Broda of Toronto. It capped an amazing start for the St. Louis franchise, an assemblage of 23 players from a variety of backgrounds who coalesced quickly and easily under the watchful eye of Bowman. "The first year was budgeted for a loss, but we turned it around to a profit," owner Sid Salomon proudly said, pointing to the windfall that the extra playoff games and a regular-season average of nearly 10,000 fans at the Arena. As for Bowman, he would lead the Blues to the Stanley Cup Finals again in the coming seasons before taking the Canadiens job in 1971. When he finally retired from coaching the champion Detroit Red Wings in 2002, he had won nine Stanley Cups as well as 1,244 games, both NHL records.

The baseball world was still buzzing about the Gibson-Seaver match up from the night before when Cardinals faced Nolan Ryan at Busch Stadium on May 7, the young howitzer of whom they had caught a brief glimpse in spring training. He posted the only Mets win of the series, a 4–1 triumph over Briles who now had lost two in a row after his fantastic win streak. Said Schoendienst simply, "The kid [Ryan] threw harder than anyone than any pitcher I've ever seen." McCarver, despite having caught Gibson (as well as Koufax in Sandy's final All-Star Game), agreed. When Ryan heard this, he was flattered but acknowledged his weaknesses. "Now, I've got to work on my hitting," he remembered. More than 400 players were chosen ahead of Ryan in the 1965 amateur draft, as Ryan attributed his tremendous velocity to the added weight he had put on since high school. "I gained 15 pounds the past spring, and I'm now up to 195 pounds," Ryan said. "I only weighed 150 when I finished high school." His defeat of Briles was only the Cardinals' second loss in twelve games at home to date on the season. Back on April 19 against the Dodgers, Ryan had become only the sixth pitcher in National League history to strike out the side on nine pitches.

Every time someone opened the sports section of the newspaper in 1968, it seemed there was one remarkable pitching feat or another. Perhaps the greatest of all for the year came on May 8, when Jim "Catfish" Hunter threw a perfect game for the A's against the Minnesota Twins. He struck out Rich Reese on a 3–2 pitch to end the game, a high fastball that was well out of the strike zone. When asked about the errant offering, Hunter—only 22 years old, but already having been a two-time All-Star by 1968—reasoned that he was willing to sacrifice the perfect game in order to preserve the no-hitter. Except for Don Larsen's memorable performance for the Yankees in the 1956 World Series, it was the first perfect game in the American League since 1922. Hunter had received his famous nickname when he was six years old, when he got lost from his family for a while in the wilderness of North Carolina. They found him the next day sitting by a creek, quite ably taking care of himself—he was perched next to a string of freshly-caught catfish. When he was eighteen, he shot himself in the foot during a hunting accident. It caused him to miss the entire 1964 season (as he was drafted by the A's that June), and the injury cost him his big toe as well. Hunter had struck out eleven Twins on the evening, including the great Harmon Killebrew three times. In addition, Hunter also drove in three of the four runs that the A's had scored. When he got back to the clubhouse after his perfect outing, Hunter received a phone call from his boss, Finley.

"I just lost $5,000," the owner said.

"Who won it?" Hunter responded.

"You did. I'm tearing up your contract, and giving you one for $5,000 more."

While the National League owners were creating most of the recent news with their efforts on expansion, a new feud erupted between Finley and Ken Harrelson. When the Red Sox came out to play the A's in Oakland for the first time in 1968 in late May, Harrelson noted the mostly-empty stands—and put the blame at the feet of his former boss. "You would think the people would come out with major league baseball here for the first time," Harrelson quipped, "but what was the attendance tonight? 6,875? Yeah, those empty stands did remind me of Kansas City ... things like that happen in Charley's organization. Boy, I felt great when I was released. It was the best thing that ever happened to me." Upon his next visit to Detroit, Harrelson would be greeted by a round of hurled firecrackers from fans in the bleachers at Tiger Stadium, angry with him as one of the culprits who denied the Tigers the '67 pennant. One of the firecrackers hit him in the back of the neck, and reminded sportswriters of the same sort of assault that befell Cardinals left fielder Joe Medwick in the 1934 World Series at the same site.

The headline of the *Post-Dispatch* sports section for May 13 rang a familiar tune:

REDBIRDS' RUN DIET STARVES GIBSON

The pitcher failed to get scoring support once again, falling to the Astros 3–2. Cepeda was now in the midst of a 1-for-23 slump, as Schoendienst would bench him for the first time since he came to the Cardinals in 1966. Tolan, his replacement, was batting only .154 himself. In addition, Edwards was inserted for the sagging McCarver. On that date, Yastrzemski was leading the American League in batting — with only a .296 average, which was that high only after his 5-for-8 performance in a double header that day. A reporter afterwards suggested to him that the end-of-the-year league batting champion might hit below .300. "Don't laugh — it could happen," Yaz responded. When Briles shut out Bunning and the Pirates in Pittsburgh the next night, 1–0, Edwards yelled over to Gibson in the locker room, "Simple instructions, Hoot — All you have to do is pitch a shutout. Simple instructions." Briles' victory put the Cards at an even 7–7 on the road for the year. They went over the .500 mark the next day on another shutout by Carlton, his second in a row. The lone run of the game was scored by Javier, hitting his first homer since his three-run shot in Game Seven of the 1967 World Series. Earlier in the day, Javier had visited an ill six-year-old at Children's Hospital in Pittsburgh. The youngster said to Hoolie, "Why don't you use a heavier bat, and hit a home run for me tonight?" Javier responded, "Well, how about a single instead?" Javier mentioned later that he was thinking about the boy as he rounded the bases on his game-deciding blow. Javier was batting .429 against lefties but only .164 against right-handers (in 1967, he was .323 and .256 respectively). Nonetheless, the diminutive second baseman was currently one of the lone productive forces at the plate, as Cepeda was now 3 for 38, Brock 3 for 30 and McCarver 3 for 32 in the past week.

What could remedy the dearth of runs that was plaguing baseball? The lingering idea of a designated batter for the pitcher still did not sit well with some, including Broeg. "Pinheaded pundits have recommended using a designated pinch-hitter regularly for the pitcher so that, for example, a Stan Musial or Ted Williams might be wheeled up to home plate every day four times, hit and hobble or crawl to first base or beyond." Broeg also pointed out that the famous manager John McGraw of the Giants had made a similar proposition in the early part of the century, only to fall on deaf ears. Other ideas were also being considered in 1968 to increase the offense, such as limiting the size of gloves, shrinking the size of the recognized strike zone, or even increasing the distance from the pitching rubber to home plate. The consensus among major league hitters was that the introduction of the slider to modern pitcher's repertoire had made the biggest impact on the game. Don Drysdale, who was just about to embark on a remarkable period of individual dominance, called contemporary hitters "stupid." "They don't concentrate on their work half as much as the young pitchers do nowadays," he claimed. "If they did, you wouldn't have the situation of the low scores and the low batting averages that you have today." Drysdale was also of the opinion that ridiculous bonuses were being paid to players whom scouts knew little or nothing about, and that not enough teaching of hitting was occurring in the minor leagues. Players, fans, and sportswriters alike respected the traditional mindset of the "Big D," as he was called, as the throwback Drysdale was the lone remaining Dodger in 1968 who had toiled at Ebbets Field in Brooklyn.

The Cardinals were the only team in the National League in 1967 to have a record better than .500 on the road in 1967 with their 52–28 mark. And despite their troubles in hitting the ball, their 8–7 record on the road on May 15 was tops in the game in 1968. In addition, their 12–3 ledger at home was the best in the business as well, keeping them in the top spot in the National League standings:

	W	L	Pct.	GB
St. Louis	20	10	.667	—
San Francisco	17	14	.548	3.5
Atlanta	17	15	.531	4
Chicago	16	17	.485	5.5
Cincinnati	15	16	.484	5.5
Pittsburgh	14	15	.483	5.5
Los Angeles	15	17	.469	6
Philadelphia	14	16	.467	6
New York	13	17	.433	7
Houston	13	17	.433	7

In Milwaukee on that day, the city hosted the first American League game ever to be played there, as the Chicago White Sox confronted the California Angels in the first of the Chicago team's nine planned contests at the location 90 miles north of their home. The game ended after five innings due to rain with an Angels victory, but the 23,000 in attendance enjoyed seeing the major leagues return to their locale. Most in baseball still believed that the act foreshadowed an eventual permanent move to Milwaukee by the White Sox.

Back in the National League, the Redbirds' consistency prompted Pirates manager Larry Shepard to say, "You can't pick a most valuable player on the Cardinals. They have so many good ones. You can't overlook the guy behind the plate [McCarver — even though he, like many, had been struggling with his hitting, being in the midst of an 0-for-16 stretch] because of the way he takes charge, handles the pitcher, and runs the game." The Cardinals recently overwhelmed the Pirates at Forbes Field in Pittsburgh, having gone 36–11 there in the previous 47 games. Upon arriving at their hotel in the Steel City, the players initially thought that some St. Louis-haters had surrounded the establishment, for a police presence was everywhere. The team soon learned, however, that the extra security was for arrival of visiting Governor Romney of Michigan, as Pennsylvania state troopers would be patrolling Romney's floor in the coming days. The Pirates had not scored in their last 25 innings, and were utilizing all techniques possible in breaking the jinx. After the loss to Carlton, they hauled 50 of their most-used bats in a wagon out to the bullpen at Forbes Field. Dumping them on the ground in the middle of the open area, the team ceremoniously poured gasoline on the pile and set the sticks ablaze, hoping to purge whatever vestiges of sickness still lurked within them. Even Clemente could not find his stroke, as he would be batting a measly .213 by the end of the series. The hitting troubles continued the following night — although the tables were turned on the Cards. After 27 impotent innings, the Bucs finally broke through for three runs against Washburn in the third. Veale, the six-foot-six lefthander out of St. Benedict's College in Atchison, Kansas, struck out 13 St. Louis men in posting his own shutout, 3–0, as followers of the major leagues were still puzzled at the death of offensive production around the ballparks. The Pirates were doing their best to manufacture runs, as the aging Maury Wills was able to pick up his tenth stolen base of the season. Dick Simpson went down swinging three times for the Cardinals, as Brock and Washburn were victimized twice each. After the game, Veale told the story of the offer the Cardinals had made to him back in 1958. "The Cardinals gave Ray Sadecki all that big money about the time they looked at me, but all they offered me was a Triple-A contract, a few doughnuts, a couple of bats, and some spikes. I knew Sadecki didn't throw any harder than I did."

There was much relief in the Pittsburgh clubhouse, with the players thinking that the bat-pyre ceremonies had cured the ills having been suffered at the plate. "If we went another game without scoring," Pirates reliever Elroy Face warned, "we were going to burn some of our *hitters*." In the midst of the lack of hitting, Bill Mazeroski was continuing his consistent, sparkling defense at second base for the Bucs. In the following week, he would set the National League record for consecutive games at the position with 392. Russo noted that the Cardinals, despite winning five of their last eight games, had scored a total of just 13 runs in those outings. But Bing Devine predicted that offense all around the major leagues would pick up. "There's the same pattern almost every year," he assured. "The scores get bigger from June 15 to the Fourth of July and they stay big until Labor Day, when the whole thing goes the other way again." Part of the reason, Devine claimed, was not only the warm southerly summer winds that would blow the ball out to left (with home plate in the southwest corner of most ballparks), but that after the spring thaw was complete, infields would harden over the warm summer months as well, causing more would-be ground outs to skip through to the outfield for base hits.

Contrasting the drought of offense in baseball was the furious wave of rain and wind storms that were relentlessly ripping throughout the Midwest in the third week of May 1968, particularly on the 16th. News was released of nearly 100 people having been killed from a fierce funnel cloud that struck in the early hours of the morning in northwest Arkansas (including 34 people in Jonesboro, Arkansas). The National Weather Service announced that 67 tornadoes had been reported in the next 24 hours, including one that touched down at Freeburg, Illinois, twenty miles to the southeast of St. Louis, which killed four people. Meanwhile, the storms of war were still raging on the other side of the world. According to the Associated Press, 562 American soldiers had been killed in Vietnam during the past week, making it the bloodiest seven days for U.S. troops since the beginning of the conflict. The upswing in battle may have been the results of the re-established peace talks, having commenced in Paris a week prior on May 10. And on that evening in Chicago, the music group The Doors played their famous concert at the Chicago Coliseum, which sat in the 1400 block of South Wabash. The historic arena, home of the NBA's Chicago Bulls for one season in 1967, was built from the bricks of the old Libby Prison in Richmond, Virginia, which held Union soldiers during the Civil War. Soon, Denny McLain would be soliciting The Doors for an audition of his keyboard skills. But for the time being, his concentration was on his day job. As Jim Morrison was finishing up his final lyrics at the Coliseum, McLain was putting the finishing touches on his 12–1 win at Washington, which left his record at a perfect 5–0. It also vaulted the Tigers back into first place, which had been temporarily taken over by the Orioles. The Detroit club vowed to not let the top spot escape from their grasp again.

The National League owners, meanwhile, were still attempting to make a final decision on expansion for their circuit. They were trying to move as quickly as possible on the decision, for the prospective National League expansion teams would be at a disadvantage if they could not participate in the amateur draft to be held on June 7 and 8, as the Seattle and Kansas City entries were already planning to do from the American League side. (Ewing Kauffman, the owner of the Kansas City franchise, was already preparing to sign a lease in the coming weeks to have his team play in Municipal Stadium.) However, expansion in the National League was not yet a foregone conclusion, even at this late date. "Don't be too sure that we will expand in 1969," Cubs owner Phil Wrigley advised. "Bob Carpenter of the Phillies isn't the only National Leaguer against expansion. He's only the most adamant one." But on May 27 — after one final session of deliberations that lasted ten hours — the National League owners would vote to add Montreal and San Diego to their circuit for 1969, as the two cities narrowly beat out the other finalists. This was done over the objection of seven United States congressmen, who were opposed to the idea of a major league team north of the border. Milwaukee, vying for a return to big-league baseball after the Braves had left for Atlanta, was dismissed because of the city's proximity to Chicago. "Milwaukee is only 85 to 90 miles away from two major league clubs in Chicago," Giles pointed out. But some, including Veeck, were then wondering why San Diego was approved, which was a similar distance from Los Angeles; and even though it was the same distance from St. Louis to Chicago, the closeness of Dallas to Houston was reported as the dooming factor for the former franchise's hopes — an effort that was reportedly led by Astros owner Roy Hofheinz, who was afraid that another club in Texas would cut into television and radio revenues in Houston. Giles added that the Buffalo group made a quality presentation to the owners, and was "difficult to exclude." Organizers for the Montreal team were counting on playing its games in a local second-rate facility until a planned downtown domed stadium could be built, slated for opening in 1972. The city of Montreal, however, was giving no certainty to Major League Baseball that such a stadium could be built in the near future. In fact, Mayor Jean Drapeau was against the club playing on the existing complex, citing its sub-standard condition as an embarrassment to the city. No professional team had been playing in Montreal, in fact, since the Triple-A Royals had left the International League ten years earlier, leaving the existing city stadium in disrepair. The San Diego team, on the contrary, would play in its new stadium in its very first season, shortly thereafter to be named for local sportswriter Jack Murphy, who was instrumental in lobbying the big leagues for a place in the National League. Once a $10,000,000 entry fee was paid by the two fledgling organizations, both would immediately be eligible to share in the World Series television receipts taken in by the league in 1968. But while the American League approved having two divisions of six teams each in the following year, the Nationals were planning on keeping a straight twelve-team league — an idea that the American League boss Cronin thought was nonsense. "You can't sell a twelfth-place club," he stated. "Who wants a lot of second-division teams?" To which Giles replied simply, "We don't believe in a playoff system because of the history and tradition of baseball." To create a balanced schedule with divisional rivalries, the American League was planning on going to a 156-game schedule for 1969. However, later in June, the Major League Executive Council would decide that both major leagues would continue to play a 162-game schedule, with each to divide into two six-team divisions. Among the most fervent denouncers of the idea of divisional play was the New York Mets, as research had shown that they typically received over half of their home gate revenue only from games with the Cardinals, Giants, and Dodgers—teams which, under the proposed new format, would be placed together in the Western Division, away from the Mets and with fewer games against New York as an out-of-division opponent (the Cardinals in the end, however, would ultimately be placed in the National League Eastern Division with the Mets).

After dropping three straight games at Philadelphia, the Cards got some relief from Jaster, who broke things up on May 20 with another technical shutout over the Dodgers (he allowed no earned runs in a 2–1 win). After throwing 21 pitches in the first inning, he finished the game with only 109. It had been two seasons since Jaster posted his amazing five consecutive shutouts against Los Angeles, but he now looked to resume his dominance. Brock got three hits to finally break out of his slump, but would pull a groin muscle a few days later and need more rest. And when that occurred, once again the team went into offensive hibernation. Washburn and Gilson were the victims the next night, chased for nine runs in just over six innings in a 9–2 loss to Bill Singer and the Dodgers, behind five RBIs from reserve Bob Bailey, who had been hitting .178. Singer, a native of Pomona, California, outside of Los Angeles, now led the National League in strikeouts with 75 with the performance. "The Cardinals still are the strongest-hitting team because they don't have a weak spot from the leadoff man to the ninth man," Singer cautioned to the rest of the league. "The Cardinals are just in a slump. They scored a hundred runs this year before we had fifty. They're still the team to beat." Because of the great movement Singer was getting on his pitches, some hitters around the league were accusing him of putting petroleum jelly on the ball—a modern version of the spitball. It was revealed later, however, that Singer actually used toothpaste instead. "He was running to first base one day," one of his teammates noted, "and the toothpaste tube fell right out of his back pocket."

Gibson did not go for such things, but despite pitching magnificently—better than he ever had in his career to date—he had been, perhaps, the most unlucky hurler in the game. By the end of May, the Cardinals would have won only three of Gibson's first ten starts on the year. On May 17, Gibson's career record against Philadelphia stood at 17–4 heading into that night's contest, but he and the Cards were shut out 1–0 by Woodie Fryman. At that point, Gibson had been the recipient of only three total runs in the past 27 innings he had pitched in his losses. In his next start on the 22nd, he faced in Drysdale the only pitcher in the National League who was currently more effective than him. The tall Dodger overpowered the St. Louis men, beating Gibson 2–0 in a game that lasted an hour and 51 minutes (even though rain had delayed the game twenty minutes in getting it started). It was the third straight shutout for Drysdale in running his overall scoreless-innings streak to 29. Schoendienst was becoming increasingly frustrated with the lack of hitting — particularly *in* clutch situations, and particularly *for* Gibson — and he was starting to be more and more candid on the topic with the press. "You'd think we'd hit a fly ball once in a while, or even hit into a double play to score a run," he griped. "Look at Los Angeles — they've got a utility guy playing second base [Paul Popovich] and he can hit a fly ball when they need one.... There are too many 'guess' hitters in the game now. A good hitter doesn't guess — he looks for a pitch." Hughes faltered in relief of Briles in the eleventh inning the following night and the Cards bowed to Los Angeles again 3–2 (after such a promising rookie campaign in 1967, Hughes went into June 1968 with no wins — although he had only two starts and eight total appearances in recovery from his arm ailment). The loss gave the Cardinals seven defeats in their last eight games since winning the first two games of the series at Pittsburgh on May 14 and 15, and caused them to fall out of first place for the first time since April 21. Continuing their impotence at the plate, the Cardinals had stranded 13 runners by the time Briles had left the game in the eighth inning, and 15 in sum by the end of the game. Now suddenly in the Cards' rear-view mirror were the Cubs, who on the 21st got over the .500 mark for the first time on the year as a result of a 6–5 win at Philadelphia. In the game, Chicago leftfielder Billy Williams set a major league mark for all outfielders by participating in his 695th straight contest.

Gibson would be a victim yet again for another of the league's top throwers in his next start as well, losing a 3–1 decision to Gaylord Perry and the Giants (it was Perry's first win against St. Louis since losing to the Cardinals five straight times in 1967). San Francisco was being led in hitting by the 37-year-old Mays at .277, as the Giants were struggling at the plate as well. Mays hit a two-run homer for the difference in rain-shortened eight innings as Gibson fell to 3–5 (even though he was leading the league in ERA at 1.32). He had not won since May 6, and that victory required 11 innings of work on his part. Gibson entered the sixth inning of this game having pitched 10⅓ total frames of hitless ball, retiring the first fifteen San Francisco batters he faced in addition to finishing his prior 2–0 loss to the Dodgers with 5⅓ innings of no-hit work.

The players felt sorry for all of the pitchers, but especially for Gibson, and approached him from time to time to apologize — but he chased them away angrily, not wanting to hear any excuses. In spite of the setbacks, Gibson was not about to alter the methodology that had made his pitching successful.

Much to his fielders' delight he worked quickly, as Cardinals announcer Jack Buck had once timed him throwing a pitch an average of eight seconds after receiving the ball back from the catcher.

With the hitters struggling, the plethora of Cardinals slump-buster trinkets made their appearances in the clubhouse and on the field. Shannon, who used to pick up the ball and hand it to his pitcher for the warm-up tosses each inning, ceased the practice; Edwards would place his catcher's mask in different strategic positions on the dugout steps, hoping that just the right one would inspire a rally; Washburn, like many players, would never step on the foul line when entering and leaving the playing field; and Maxvill hearkened back to his Gas House Gang predecessors in failing to wash his undershirt in the midst of a hot hitting streak. Gone were Brock's milkshakes and lemon pies prescribed to him by Mr. and Mrs. Hal Woodeshick in 1967, and now he was trying different types of tapes and resins on his bats for a magic formula. Broeg, normally as happy-go-lucky as any of the players, had had enough of the hocus-pocus; he wanted results. "It's time to cut out this monkey business, and get *down* to business," he wrote simply. "That is, it's time for [trainer Bob] Bauman to put on his training room shelf a supply of those magic pills from the past, plainly marked: 'RBIs' ... 'Doubles' ... 'Triples' ... 'Home Runs.'" Perhaps they should have made an effort to acquire Frank Howard, the imposing 6'8" slugger of the Washington Senators—for amidst the scarcity of base hits around the big leagues, Howard had nonetheless just set a record with ten home runs in a week, besting Babe Ruth's and Hank Greenberg's previous mark of nine.

The Drysdale show surfaced again in Houston on May 26, as he promptly executed another shutout, his fourth in a row for a National League record (and his fifth of the season, which accounted for all of his wins). The irony of Drysdale's success was that, at this point, it was largely going unnoticed with the wealth of success being enjoyed by *most* pitchers around the game. Nonetheless, he would ultimately become the unquestioned center of attention on the 31st, as Drysdale became the first National League pitcher to throw five straight scoreless complete games. The fifth was saved for him in the ninth inning, when home plate umpire Harry Wendelstedt called Giants catcher Dick Dietz back to the batter's box after Dietz had thought he had gotten hit by a Drysdale pitch. The bases had been loaded, so the play would have scored a run for San Francisco. Wendelstedt, however, ruled that Dietz did not attempt to get out of the way of the pitch, thus nullifying the play. Also going relatively unnoticed was that, almost three weeks earlier, Drysdale's dominance had been nearly matched in the American League by Luis Tiant of the Cleveland Indians. On May 12, Tiant had shut out Baltimore 4–0 for his fourth straight blanking, a club record. The Orioles would get revenge in beating Tiant just five days later, but his streak was just another piece of evidence that the bats were perishing in both leagues. Some felt that the warm winds of summer would help to start pushing the ball out of the ballparks, but others were convinced that the drought would continue.

After the game, Drysdale's teammates placed a sign above his locker that read, "*Drysdale for president — shoo-in for the California primary.*" This was in reference to the impending visit by the Democratic Party front-runner, Robert F. Kennedy, scheduled to come to California in the coming days. Kennedy would be arriving in California on June 4 to continue his campaign for the presidency, meeting people as he rode through San Francisco's Chinatown neighborhood that afternoon. He was the heavy favorite to take the California primary, and then presumably sweep through the other states en route to the party's nomination at the convention in Chicago in August. Simultaneously in Washington, President Johnson was facing further pressure from various groups to end the high-level bombing campaigns in Vietnam; nonetheless, he refused to yield. "Until the men in Hanoi face the real problems of ending the war, we must stand fast," Johnson said on June 4. "We must stand patiently and hopefully, but with determination, too."

Marichal finished off Briles and the Cardinals on six hits by a 2–1 score on the 29th, as the Cardinals ended May with the worst record in the National League for the month. Shannon, in reflection upon his own poor clutch hitting in the preceding weeks, recalled his remedy. "I must have left three hundred men on base with less than two out," he imagined about the tough stretch of games. "So I decided to forget everything. Judy and I took the kids to a school picnic on Memorial Day. We stayed at the amusement park all day and when we got home, I rushed to the ballpark. I didn't even bother to take batting practice, and on my first swing, I hit a homer." This occurred on the 30th as the Cards beat Sadecki 6–0, before which the Cardinals had gone just 2–11 in their last 13 games. And as the standings showed before the games played that day, the defending champions had dropped down all the way to fourth place. It was their lowest placement in thirteen months, with a record only slightly above .500 and the slimmest of margins separating them from the fifth-place Cubs:

	W	L	Pct.	GB
San Francisco	26	19	.578	—
Atlanta	24	20	.545	1.5
Philadelphia	21	19	.525	2.5
St. Louis	22	21	.512	3
Chicago	23	22	.511	3
Cincinnati	21	21	.500	3.5
Pittsburgh	18	20	.474	4.5
Los Angeles	22	25	.468	5

	W	L	Pct.	GB
Houston	19	24	.442	6
New York	18	23	.439	6

In spite of the disastrous month, the Cardinals were confident in the knowledge that their pitching would sustain them for the rest of the summer, and that sooner or later, their hitters would catch up. Cepeda had been even worse than Shannon, gathering only five RBIs from May 1 to May 26. Only Jaster's win on the 20th and a victory by Carlton over Chris Short and the Phillies on the 24th kept the final two weeks of the month from being winless (distracted, Carlton was also trying desperately that week to get the papers settled to move into his new house in south St. Louis with his wife, Beverly). The following night, they had been shut out by their former teammate, Larry Jackson, after which their nemesis Fryman struck again, beating them 9–3 as all the St. Louis runs came as a result of a throwing error by Phillies' third baseman Dick Allen. That game saw the largest crowd to date on the year at Busch with 42,446 in attendance. Looking for any opponent that would help them shake their batting blues, the Cardinals headed out to Tulsa the next day to play their minor league team. While doing so, they took Wayne Granger off the Tulsa roster and sent Torrez there in his place. Granger had signed with the Cardinals when he turned 21 back in 1965, as he had been attending Springfield College in Massachusetts. One of his first acts as a Cardinal was to hop out of the dugout in his first game, and naively motion for Cepeda to throw him the sacred "Tomato Soup" ball when infield warm-ups were concluded. Cepeda, looking like a medicine man, frantically waved him away until Sisler — the only other man allowed to touch it — appeared. So in learning one of his first lessons of the hidden curriculum in being a Cardinals player, Granger shook his head and returned to the dugout in confusion. Back in early April, Granger had been surprised that he was not originally taken north with the team — but Schoendienst had plans for him. "Actually, Granger probably was farther ahead in spring training than a number of pitchers," the manager pointed out. "But we needed another lefthander [which wound up being Gilson], and we took Torrez because we figured we might need another starter since Dick Hughes had arm trouble."

The Cardinals had batted .263 as a team in their championship year of 1967, but were now at .239 as they entered June of '68 — which was the same average that Brock currently held individually, the man who had torched the Red Sox at a .414 pace in the World Series just eight months earlier. Reasons continued to be offered for the downfall of the bats around the media; was the ball dead? Schoendienst did not think so. "How can the ball be dead when guys like Al Weis and Dal Maxvill hit home runs? You tell me. Maybe the bad weather we're having has something to do with these 1–0, 2–1 games, but it sure isn't any dead ball." Added Flood, who was sailing off into the distance in hitting .333 on June 1, "What else can they do to make it dead?" And Maris, who was the recipient of so many unfair concocted stories about the design of the ball during his record-setting season of 61 home runs in 1961, agreed. "They always gotta say something. What did they say the year I hit my homers? They said there was a rabbit in the ball. Now they say there's no rabbit. Wait'll next year — the scores will go up again, and they'll say the rabbit is back in the ball. Don't they ever think of giving the pitchers some credit?"

The dominant starter to date for St. Louis — at least record-wise — had been Carlton. Just like Hughes and Briles the season before, Carlton was picking up the slack for the Redbirds while the offense was trying to find itself on the days when Gibson and others pitched. In what he called "my best outing of the year," Carlton dominated the Giants 6–0 on May 30 as Sadecki was chased in the first inning on a four-hit outburst by the Cardinals, including homers by Shannon and McCarver. It was only Shannon's second RBI in the past 14 games, but he would go on to ten more in the next five. Jaster as well was another individual who was stepping up after a mediocre 1967 season, as he followed up with a 2–0 shutout against the Mets (on the 31st — the same evening that Drysdale recorded his fifth straight). Jaster had been four outs away from a perfect game when Greg Goosen singled in the eighth inning. He then allowed a lone two-out single to Don Bosch in the ninth as he beat Seaver, even though the Mets used an all-right-handed lineup against him. Jaster, still called "The Creeper" by his teammates, never had a three-ball count over the course of the evening as he looked determined not to be forgotten as a member of the rotation. Jaster's ERA was now actually lower than Gibson's at 0.95, but he did not have enough innings to qualify to be listed among the league leaders. The team was rolling again as Shannon beat the Mets 6–5 with a homer in the tenth inning the next night on June 1. Hoerner got the win, and tied a National League record by recording six straight strikeouts in a relief appearance. He and Gilson both went four strong innings, relieving Washburn who was knocked out in the second and who had actually gone a longer period of time than Gibson in not being victorious, having lost all his decisions since April 30. The Mets' starter was the flamethrower Ryan, who posted seven strikeouts himself to place him in a league-leading tie with Singer's 75. Off the field, the splendid stars of the road trip had been Schofield and Briles, who because of their clothes drew a great deal of snickering applause when they walked into the locker room at Shea Stadium in New York. Schofield was wearing a Nehru jacket with what he described as a "hot pink" shirt and white shoes. Briles, meanwhile, sported a pistachio-green shirt with a green polka-dot tie, a matching jacket, and white shoes as well. A few days later, McCarver would "follow suit" with a Nehru outfit of his own.

Suddenly, the loose, fun-loving Cardinals were back, and things started to break open. On June 2, they won a double header from the Mets to sweep the series. Hughes got his first victory of the year in the nightcap, and Gibson (4–5) finally enjoyed a win in the opener, his first in four weeks, getting a deluge of six runs for his best support of the season. Next came a four-game sweep of Houston in the Astrodome — the first time that had ever happened to the Astros in their indoor park — as the home club had fined their All-Star center fielder Jimmy Wynn $100 for not hustling (Wynn had finished second in the National League in home runs in 1967 with 37). The series began with a 7–2 win for Briles, the most runs that the Cardinals had scored in a month; the series ended with another amazing performance by Gibson, a three-hit shutout (his first of the season) that raised his record to 5–5, thanks to homers by Cepeda (his seventh) and McCarver (his fourth). Astros manager Grady Hatton would be fired twelve days later, as had Gene Mauch of the Phillies three days before Hatton. Suddenly, just as quickly as they had dropped, the Cardinals were now back to ten games over .500 at 31–21, and back in first place with a three-and-a-half game lead over Philadelphia, Atlanta, San Francisco, and Los Angeles, all muddled in a second-place tie. The Cardinals had also won nine in a row, their longest winning streak since 1963. During this streak, Shannon's average climbed from .232 to .266, as he had batted .462 over the first half of the 14-game road trip through which they were working.

But in the midst of the Cards' new-found success during their stay in Houston, the splintered nation had been profoundly shaken once again.

On the night of June 4 in Los Angeles, the astounding Drysdale broke the major league record with his sixth straight shutout, a three-hit, no-walk masterpiece as he struck out eight Pittsburgh hitters in defeating Bunning. He also surpassed Carl Hubbell's National League record of 46⅔ scoreless innings, and he was now only two shy of Walter Johnson's major league record of 56 that was set in 1913 (Drysdale had set the National League mark when he struck out the Pirates' Bill Mazeroski in the second). Drysdale, in his 13th major league season, was now also only three victories shy of 200 for his career. Although winning the Cy Young Award in 1962, only now did Drysdale and others feel that he was finally getting out from under the shadow of his former teammate in Koufax. He had always proven that he was as dependable as anyone, having missed only three scheduled starts over the course of his career.

Drysdale was naturally in a celebratory mood as his teammates showered him with cheers afterwards. As he rode home in his car and listened to the radio, Drysdale was flattered when he heard Robert F. Kennedy praising his feat. Kennedy had been in the midst of grabbing last-minute votes in the California primary election. He had already won the primaries in Indiana,

Nebraska, and South Dakota, and was gaining an impressive amount of political momentum that appeared to be increasing with each passing hour. During the day of June 4, he was relaxing at a beachfront location when his fourth son, David, had decided to take a swim off the California coast. Suddenly, however, the young boy began to be swept away by the surf. His father jumped into the water and saved him, as David had received a harsh lesson about the risky life adventures on which the family seemed to thrive. As the rest of the afternoon and evening wore on, Kennedy and his associates closely monitored the election results that were trickling into their campaign headquarters. As time passed into the nighttime hours, it had been announced that he had amassed an insurmountable lead on Eugene McCarthy, holding a 48 percent to 41 percent edge as the polls closed. A short time later, after midnight on the morning of June 5 at the Ambassador Hotel in Los Angeles, Kennedy gave a brief word of thanks and encouragement to his supporters in the area, over a thousand of whom had crammed into the Embassy Room of the hotel and who had even been celebrating an hour before it was projected that Kennedy had taken the primary from McCarthy. In appearing at the podium, Kennedy boosted their morale even further with his confidence for his chances at the Democratic National Convention in late August. "My thanks to all of you. It's on to Chicago," he said in closing, referring to the site of the convention. "And let's win there." Standing right behind Kennedy was Rosie Grier, his supporter and a defensive tackle for the Los Angeles Rams football team. After his words, Kennedy made his way out of the hotel through the back of the building. He took the same route out of the hotel that he had taken inside only fifteen minutes earlier, a narrow corridor through the kitchen of the hotel's restaurant. As he approached a small room where he was to give a press conference before exiting, a man suddenly jumped out from a side area in which he was hiding and fired eight shots with a .22 caliber revolver, two bullets from which struck Kennedy. One of the bullets hit him with a glancing blow in his shoulder, but the other struck his mastoid bone behind his right ear. He collapsed to the floor immediately, as five other people were also hit by the bullets that sprayed around the room. People back in the Embassy Room — who moments earlier had been cheering wildly — were now wailing with panic, as they could not see what was occurring in the kitchen hallway due to a partition that blocked their view. A speaker went up to the microphone and calmly encouraged the crowd to disperse, which they did. Kneeling by Kennedy's side was his distraught wife, Ethel, who at the time was carrying the couple's eleventh child. Three men instantly jumped on the attacker, including Grier; Rafer Johnson, a former decathlete in the Olympics; and William Berry, a former agent with the Federal Bureau of Investigation who had been traveling with Kennedy as a personal escort. Grier, in fact, had kept other bystanders from maiming the shooter on the spot. Kennedy was conscious for approximately the first ten minutes after the shooting, accepting a rosary that was placed in his left hand as he winked up at a distraught friend. Kennedy was first taken to Central Receiving Hospital, where he was given emergency care as well as the Last Rites from a Catholic priest. He was then moved to Good Samaritan Hospital where he was reported to be in "very critical" condition, but with heart and lungs assessed as "strong" by six doctors as they stabilized him before operating for three and a half hours to remove the bullet from his head.

To the interest of some, Attorney General Ramsey Clark in Washington was quick to assert that there was "no evidence of a conspiracy at this moment" to assassinate Kennedy. Humphrey, one of Kennedy's chief competitors for the Democratic nomination, canceled his appointment to speak to the graduates at the United States Air Force Academy in Colorado Springs. The shooter was soon identified as Sirhan Sirhan, a slight 24-year-old Palestinian man from Jordan who was reported to have brothers living in the area of Pasadena, California. In Sirhan's pocket, officials found keys to a car that was parked in the parking lot of the hotel, and which had belonged to a hotel employee who worked in the kitchen. In addition, they also found in his pocket a copy of a news story in which Kennedy had announced plans to send greater amounts of military support to Israel if he was elected president.

After lying in a coma for over a day at Good Samaritan, Kennedy died at 1:44 A.M. on June 6 at the age of 42. The turmoil of the 1960s did not release its grip on Americans, who in considering the heart-wrenching occurrences of the entire decade including war, race riots, and assassinations, were viewing 1968 as the worst of all.

Sirhan — despite claiming to have no memory of the shooting — would be convicted of first-degree murder on April 17, 1969, and sentenced to death. When California abolished the death penalty in 1972, however, Sirhan's penalty was amended to life in prison. On March 14, 2006, he would be denied parole for the 13th time.

Just three days after the Kennedy shooting, authorities announced that an arrest had been made in the assassination of Martin Luther King, Jr. It was learned that King had been shot by James Earl Ray, a drifter whose attack had come from the open window of the rooming house across the street from the Lorraine Motel in Memphis. Ray was arrested at Heathrow Airport in London, as he was attempting to make his way to Canada. He had been a fugitive even prior to the King shooting, having escaped from the Missouri State Prison in Jefferson City the previous April while serving a twenty-year sentence for the armed robbery of a grocery store back in 1959, a crime for which he was caught by authorities twenty minutes after its commission. Ray had managed to get himself a job at the bakery in the prison, and knowing that a delivery truck arrived to and departed from the bakery each day, it offered him an opportunity to get beyond the walls. A military veteran who had displayed his deadly accuracy with firearms, Ray had also served time at Leavenworth starting in 1955 for forging postal money orders. When he shot King, Ray was reported to have balanced himself on the wall of the bathtub and rested his telescope-equipped .30–06 caliber rifle on the open windowsill. While no one witnessed Ray fire the gun, his fingerprints were found on the rifle, abandoned in a doorway of the rooming house and presumably dropped by Ray as he fled the scene (although it also was later claimed by some authorities that the bullet that killed King did not match the gun). Ray would confess to the killing on March 10, 1969, but would retract his confession only three days later. Nonetheless, upon advice from his attorney Percy Foreman, Ray pleaded guilty to the shooting and was given a 99-year sentence. Vacillating in his own mind between guilt and innocence, Ray then spent his entire life attempting to reverse his plea. Shortly after testifying to the House Select Committee on Assassinations in June 1977, Ray and six other inmates at the Brushy Mountain State Prison in Tennessee managed to escape; he was caught three days later. Upon Ray's death at the age of 70 in 1998, the King family would reveal their belief that he was merely a scapegoat for the crime, placed at the forefront of a massive governmental conspiracy that they claimed included "then President Lyndon Johnson, the Joint Chiefs of Staff, J. Edgar Hoover, several army units, organized crime figures, [and] the owner of a Memphis diner," according to a story by Jack White in *Time* magazine released a month after Ray's death. The previous year, King's son Dexter met with Ray, and sought a new trial for him.

Major league baseball games scheduled for Saturday, June 8, in Washington, New York, and Chicago were canceled, while the starting times of other games were adjusted with respect to Kennedy's funeral, which was to take place in the early afternoon. It was the day, ironically, that Drysdale's streak would come to an end. When Philadelphia's Roberto Pena grounded out to Ken Boyer to start the top of the third inning at Dodger Stadium, Drysdale at that moment surpassed Walter Johnson's major league standard of 56 scoreless turns that had stood for 53 years. He was finally touched for a run in the top of the fifth, as little-known 32-year-old Howie Bedell — making one of only nine plate appearances on the year, and back in the major leagues after a six-year hiatus in the minors — drifted a sacrifice fly to Len Gabrielson in left field to push Tony Taylor across the plate. It would be Bedell's lone RBI on the year (and only the third of his career); and as Drysdale retreated off the mound to wipe his brow, he was swept up by a standing ovation from the crowd of over 50,000 that saw the amazing stretch finally come to a close. Gabrielson's catch actually had tacked on an extra third of an inning to the streak, which expired at 58 and two-thirds rounds of scoreless ball.

Sunday the 9th had been designated by President Johnson as a national day of mourning. The Cardinals players generally were not in favor of playing their double header that day against Cincinnati, but Schoedienst told the press that that club would abide by whatever dictates were handed down by Commissioner Eckert. Some games were going on as scheduled, while others were postponed. "Why should some clubs cancel when others are not?" McCarver asked. "Baseball should act as a group." Many individual statements by certain teams and players would mark the weekend's action.

Briles (7–4) beat the Reds in the single game on Saturday 7–2. Beforehand, however, there was a 45-minute delay in starting the game as the Reds were meeting as a team to discuss two grievances they held with the league: one, that the 7:00 starting time would not be in congruence with the decision that all major league games that day would not commence until Kennedy was buried, and two, that the presence of a double header the following day (Sunday the 9th) precluded them, by league rules, from playing a night game that evening (which preceded the twin bill). Finally, Reds manager Dave Bristol — who himself was taking part in the meeting — was frustrated with its lack of progress and walked out towards the clubhouse exit, inviting at least nine players to come with him so that the game could get underway. Pitcher Jim Maloney grabbed his glove, and told Bristol he was ready to play any position if needed. Then, a handful of the players got up and left the room, much to the scorn of the others. "You guys are wrong, I'm telling you!" pitcher Milt Pappas reportedly yelled to them as they walked away. Pappas was the team's player representative. "There's no sense having a players association if you go out there and play!" The Reds ultimately took the field with the same lineup that had beaten Hal Gilson with Maloney's pitching by a score of 4–2 the day before, as Pappas would be traded by angered Reds officials just two days later. Gilson, Willis, and Granger came to the rescue of Hughes during the game, as he had gotten a rare start from Schoendienst but could barely complete the first inning, experiencing pain in his throwing shoulder once again (the next day, Pete Mikkelson would be recalled from Tulsa to take Hughes' place). Some other games around the league had begun with the funeral not yet concluded, which Eckert ultimately dismissed as acceptable. "Their intentions were proper," the commissioner said of the clubs that played before the burial was complete, going against the original plan. "Nobody could anticipate the long delay [of the memorial service]. The fans were in the ballparks with no certainty of when the funeral would end. The clubs felt it would be unfair to hold off any longer." But in San Francisco, the Mets had refused to even *arrive* at Candlestick Park for their game with the Giants, causing an indefinite postponement. Back at the team hotel, Mets manager Gil Hodges told the players that he was going to spend the day in church, and he advised them to stay out of sight of the media. In their estimation, the

Giants had to refund $80,000 to their ticket buyers when the game was announced as postponed, and they wanted the Mets to pay for it — which the New York club refused to do. A few days later on June 11, Kennedy's former press secretary, Frank Mankiewicz, sent messages of thanks to the Mets for opposing Major League Baseball on the matter of playing that day, as well as specific appreciation for similar gestures shown by individuals such as Hodges, Pappas, Maury Wills, Rusty Staub, and other players who took similar stances. The telegram he sent to the players read, "Please accept my personal admiration for your actions. Senator Kennedy indeed enjoyed competitive sports, but I doubt he would have put box office receipts ahead of national mourning."

Not allowing themselves to be distracted by the dramatics, the Cardinals posted ten runs in the fifth inning of the June 9 game — two short of the club record for an inning — as they came back from an 8–0 deficit to beat the Reds in Cincinnati 10–8. In the big inning, Edwards got the Cardinals' first pinch-hit of the season in twenty tries by the hitting crew. They then swiftly took three out of four in Atlanta, as Gibson (6–5) posted his second straight shutout in beating the Braves for the first time in two years as the Cardinals finished the long road trip with a roaring 13–3 record (after having just completed a 3–7 homestand). The hitting assault on the trip was led by Shannon, who batted .365 throughout its duration. Even so, after Flood's mark of .333, the starters were still mired in averages ranging from .268 (Cepeda) to .227 (Maris), despite the improvement in scoring output in recent days.

At the previous week's amateur draft, the Cardinals had selected 17-year-old outfielder Jim Hairston from Dayton, Ohio, in the first round. The first overall pick in the draft belonged to the Mets, and they selected a high school shortstop named Tim Foli out of Canoga Park, California, who was expected to become a superstar. "He is a fine high school infielder with outstanding power," assessed the Mets general manager, Johnny Murphy.

On June 15, the Cardinals looked for extra relief for the ailing Maris in right field by acquiring outfielder Ron Davis from the Houston Astros for Gilson and Simpson. Davis had batted a modest .212 in 52 games for the Astros, but Schoendienst felt that the move gave him more defensive options at the position with Tolan recently getting more at-bats, but also acquiring many of those at-bats while playing first base. Gilson's place in the bullpen was taken by another left-handed relief pitcher, Mel Nelson, who two years earlier had come back to the St. Louis organization after originally signing with the Cardinals as a power-hitting prospect out of high school back in 1956. The roster changes occurred as the Cards met the Reds back home at Busch Stadium, claiming two out of three with Gibson's third straight shutout in the middle contest as he also struck out a Cardinals season-high 13 to date. It was also one short of his career high, as he had lowered his ERA to 1.29. It was also the shortest game in the National League to that point on the season, with Gibby disposing of Cincinnati in just an hour and 42 minutes. How he *finished* games, however, was what impressed his teammates the most. "He's the best ninth-inning pitcher I've ever seen," Shannon said. "That first man who faces Gibson in the ninth is in trouble; he just won't let that first man get on base." Added Flood, "I know when Hoot is on, because I'm not getting any fly balls out there in center field — it's all strikeouts and ground outs." Suddenly, Drysdale's streak had no sooner ended when St. Louis was now presenting its own man to challenge the mark, with Gibson having posted 38 scoreless innings in a row himself. But more importantly, the June 16 standings had shown that the Redbirds were back on top of the perch after their nightmare month of May, having played .800 ball over the past three weeks:

	W	L	Pct.	GB
St. Louis	38	25	.603	—
San Francisco	34	30	.531	4.5
Atlanta	32	29	.525	5
Los Angeles	34	31	.523	5
Philadelphia	28	28	.500	6.5
Chicago	30	31	.492	7
Cincinnati	29	31	.483	7.5
New York	29	31	.483	7.5
Pittsburgh	27	31	.466	8.5
Houston	23	37	.383	13.5

The Tigers, meanwhile, had won ten out of their last eleven to stretch their lead in the American League to seven and a half games over Baltimore, despite not having star hitter Al Kaline in the lineup since May 25, when he broke his right arm. Shortstop Ray Oyler was batting .146, and even the usually-productive first baseman Norm Cash was only hitting .202, but Mayo Smith's men marched on behind pitching talent that rivaled that of the Cardinals. McLain (11–2) was grabbing the headlines, but was getting plenty of quality help from Earl Wilson, steady relief man John Hiller, and a portly left-hander named Mickey Lolich who had quietly led the American League in shutouts in 1967 with six.

After a poor start, Durocher had been trying to get the Cubs back on track and into the first division. By June 14, they had won five of their last six before dropping two heartbreaking, one-run, extra-inning losses in Atlanta. The next stop on their trip was St. Louis, and the Cubs were counting on their formidable bats — on paper, among the best offensive lineups in the National League — to do some damage against the front-running Cardinals and continue their ascent in the standings. What they found, contrarily, was a championship team with an all-world pitching staff that was rounding into form. First in the showcase was Briles, who had come back to earth with a 7–5 record in 1968 after his remarkable performance the year before. Briles scattered eight Cubs hits with no walks in preserving a 1–0 win, with the St. Louis tally coming on a Tolan home run in the bottom of the fifth. The following inning, McCarver preserved the lead by throwing out a stealing Don Kessinger at third as Briles simultaneously had managed to strike out Ron Santo by having him chase a curveball out of the zone. Chicago lefthander Rich Nye was the victim on the following day, running into an onslaught of nine hits in four innings, including Cepeda's eighth home run of the season. Even more impressive than the Cardinals' bats was Carlton (8–2), as he recorded yet another shutout for the staff, allowing only a leadoff single by Glenn Beckert in the fourth inning for the sole Cubbie safety as Lefty rolled, 4–0. He allowed the count to run full only twice, and kept the Chicago bats scoreless with only 102 pitches. It was also the 1,500th game in a Cardinals uniform for Flood, a mark previously surmounted only by Musial, Schoendienst, Enos Slaughter, Rogers Hornsby, and Marty Marion. Tempers were running short in the visitors' dugout, meanwhile, as Durocher kicked water buckets and slammed clipboards into the wall in frustration of his team's inability to put the bat on the ball effectively.

Leo's last hope in the series was Ferguson Jenkins, who after Gibson's lack of support in the early part of the year had truly become baseball's hard luck story. He would face the mighty Bob on this day, and the result was more of the same for the overmatched batters in the gray and blue uniforms. Whereas one-run games had tilted against him in the previous months, Gibson got on the positive side in the third inning. It was courtesy of a two-out triple by Brock and a subsequent single by Flood, and it held up for the fourth straight shutout on Cubs batters. It was also the fourth in the last five games for Cardinals pitchers, as the man from Omaha held on for a 1–0 final score while his ERA trickled down even further to 1.21. In the 134 innings Gibson had worked on the year to date, he had permitted only 60 hits and 18 earned runs, with 29 walks (including five intentional) and 97 strikeouts. Only Santo had gotten past first base for the Cubs, as he was sent to third on a single by Dick Nen but was left stranded. It was also the fourth blanking in a row for Gibson, and the Cardinals' nineteenth win in their last 24 games had the press murmuring about Gibson's ability to overtake Drysdale's newly-established standard. With Drysdale's streak now over, the sports headlines in Los Angeles were now hovering around the possible acquisition of superstar center Wilt Chamberlain by the NBA's Lakers from the Philadelphia franchise, but Lakers officials refused to confirm that a deal was being negotiated (Chamberlain would in fact be traded to the Lakers for three players and cash on

July 6). A week later, however, Drysdale would once again be the center of attention, as he would surpass Koufax's Dodgers career strikeout record of 2,396. Two starts later on June 26, he would gain the 200th victory of his career, in what would also be the closest he would ever get to a no-hitter — allowing a two-out single in the eighth inning to San Francisco rookie Dave Marshall.

For his part, Jenkins struck out eleven St. Louis batters and permitted even fewer hits than Gibson (four to five). And in his last two complete games of work, Jenkins had allowed one run in 19 innings, only to be saddled with a loss and a no-decision. He would be topped by another hard-luck pitcher in Jim McAndrew of the Mets later in the summer, however, as in July and August McAndrew would lose four straight games with his team being held to *no* runs — a major league record.

The Cubs had now been shut out in four straight games going back through the final game of their visit to Atlanta on June 16, when Joe Torre doubled home Hank Aaron in the bottom of the eleventh inning to waste the ten rounds of shutout ball that Jenkins had pitched that night. When Gibson got Santo to fly out to Tolan in right field to end the series, the Cubs' 46 consecutive scoreless innings set the National League mark for futility. Moving on to Cincinnati, the Cubs finally scored a run for Joe Niekro in the top of the third inning on June 21. With the famine ending at 48 straight frames without a run, they would only tie the major league mark that had been set by the Philadelphia A's in 1906. Ironically, before the game against Gibson, the chalkboard in the visitors' locker room at Busch Stadium had greeted the Cubs when they walked in that day with the message, "NO HITTING THURSDAY." It was a message from Durocher about batting practice not occurring on the field, "but the Cubs took the sign literally," Russo pointed out.

The starting pitching had been so dominant that people were beginning to forget about the talented St. Louis bullpen — but it was desperately needed in the first game of a series against the Braves at Busch, as Willis, Hoerner, and Granger followed up a strong seven-inning start for a 4–3 win for Granger in the 13th inning with Shannon doubling home the speedy Tolan. It was Shannon's 31st RBI, placing him four behind Cepeda for the team lead. In addition to the work of the relief corps, it was assuredly Tolan's night. He had homered in the second inning, and later, in the eleventh, threw out pinch runner Skip Guinn at the plate by stopping a ball in the gap off the bat of Marty Martinez, and whirling his body nearly 360 degrees in making a perfect strike to McCarver. Lum Harris, the Atlanta manager and veteran of 31 years of professional baseball, called it "one of the greatest throws I have ever seen." With Maris fading physically, Tolan was beginning to cement himself as the permanent solution in right field. "I feel strong at bat," Tolan described.

"When we came off the long road trip, I used a lighter bat — Maxvill's. It's 32 ounces, and the one I've been using was 34 ounces. The lighter bat makes me quicker at the plate. When it's hot, your arms get heavy and lazy." He was now the hottest hitter in the lineup, having gone 17 for 43 (a .395 clip) in the course of an 11-game hitting streak.

When Washburn would stymie the Braves the following night 6–1, the Cardinals were now 21–4 in their previous 25 contests and opened up a seven-game lead on their closest competitors, the San Francisco Giants. It was Cepeda's turn to shine at the plate, as his 3-for-4 performance had boosted his batting against Atlanta to .419 for the season (18-for-43) as he and McCarver added home runs to the offensive cause. A doubleheader the following afternoon on Sunday, June 23, saw the biggest regular-season crowd ever at Busch Stadium (49,743), but Briles never recorded an out in being rocked in the first inning for a 5–1 Atlanta decision in the first game. The four runs that the Braves scored in the first included an RBI triple for Hank Aaron, giving him 1,580 runs batted in for his career and jumping him into tenth place on the all-time list, passing Rogers Hornsby. The next day, Aaron would be announced as a starter in upcoming All-Star Game, as he was the only holdover starter from the 1967 contest for the National League.

The newcomer Nelson then came to the rescue of a tired Cardinals starting staff, going all nine innings in the nightcap in salvaging a 3–1 win later in the day. The biggest concern at the end of the afternoon was Javier, as the second baseman had suffered a wide gash on his leg after being spiked on a play at the bag. Even though Javier left the first game of the double header in the seventh inning when the injury occurred, Bauman did not think that the injury would keep him out of the lineup beyond the day. Nelson's endurance and effectiveness was a relatively-unknown commodity upon his arrival in St. Louis, but the results were now in. "I told Mel to go as long as he could today, and he wound up going all the way," pitching coach Muffett marveled afterwards. As Nelson sipped a beer and puffed at a cigar in front of his locker, he was surprised with his complete-game victory. "They told me I threw 102 pitches, but it felt more like 300," he laughed. It was the first time Nelson had won as a starter in the major leagues, with his career dating back to his debut with the Cardinals as a 24-year-old in 1960 before heading to other clubs.

The National League starters for the All-Star Game to be played on July 9 in Houston were announced on June 24, and included the following players:

OF — Hank Aaron, Atlanta
OF — Curt Flood, St. Louis
OF — Pete Rose, Cincinnati

3B — Ron Santo, Chicago
SS — Don Kessinger, Chicago
2B — Tommy Helms, Cincinnati
1B — Willie McCovey, San Francisco
C — Jerry Grote, New York

The balloting was done by players, coaches, and managers around the league, well before the days when fans would have the vote. As the league leader in hitting at .346, Rose had received the most number of selections — 236 out of a possible 258 — while Aaron was chosen despite a .236 batting mark on the season (Aaron, however, was the leading active lifetime hitter in the majors at the time at .316). It was the fourteenth time that Aaron would be going to the Mid-Summer Classic, though he was surprised to find out. "Boy, they must have voted the first day of the season," Aaron said. "I didn't think I had a chance." None of the other Cardinals position players were close to being selected as starters, as even Brock and Cepeda had tallied only eight votes each. The pitchers were yet to be selected (they would be the choice of Schoendienst, manager of the squad as the skipper of the 1967 champion Cardinals), and most were expecting a bevy of St. Louis throwers to be chosen.

An All-Star himself in the past three seasons, 28-year-old slugger Willie Stargell was taking over for an aging Clemente as the main man in the Pittsburgh outfield. Stargell, however, had recently injured himself at Forbes Field, splitting his lip open in making a running catch that crashed him into the ground-level scoreboard at the ballpark. The incident had also left the Pirates star with lingering headaches, as he would miss the series with the Cardinals that took place in St. Louis June 25 and 26. Even without Stargell, the Pirates managed to win two of three from the Cards, as Carlton and Jaster fell victim. But in the middle game, Gibson continued to plow forward as an unstoppable, one-man wrecking crew. Prior to Jaster's loss in the first game of a doubleheader on the 26th, Gibson stalled the Pirates attack on four hits and no walks for his fifth shutout in a row. His own scoreless-inning string now stood at 47, as suddenly he was fewer than twelve away from Drysdale's three-week-old record. Shannon hit his ninth homer in the bottom of the eighth for extra padding on the hot day at Busch, as McCarver felt that Gibby was firing harder in the closing rounds than the initial innings. One of the four Pittsburgh hits was garnered by the leadoff man, Maury Wills, which drove his hitting streak to 24 games — a streak which Jaster would end in the nightcap of the twin bill.

The Cardinals would lose two out of three at Chicago as well to end the month of June, with Flood passing Medwick for seventh place on the club's all-time hit list with 1,590. Medwick, meanwhile — while awaiting his enshrinement into the Hall of Fame later in the summer — was taking great

pride in the fact that he was batting .800 in old-timers' games (he was currently working as a minor league hitting instructor for the Cardinals). A
bright spot in the losing visit to the Windy City was Hughes' return to the
mound, as the sore-shouldered right-hander had not pitched since June 7.
With tornado sirens wailing in the background behind Wrigley Field on multiple occasions, the Cubs turned in their best offensive series of the summer.
Nonetheless, St. Louis was able to still finish with the league's best mark for
the month (22–9), while the Cubs still finished with the league's worst (10–18).
Before the series began, the Cubs had tried to inject some life into their lineup
with the acquisition of outfielder Willie Smith and catcher Gene Oliver in
trades, and by summoning the promising pitcher Bill Stoneman from the
minor leagues. They and the rest of the National League were grasping at
different angles to play against the rolling Cards, who entered July with a lead
that left the rest of circuit bunched in a pursuing pack:

	W	L	Pct.	GB
St. Louis	46	30	.605	—
Atlanta	39	36	.520	6.5
San Francisco	40	37	.519	6.5
Los Angeles	40	38	.513	7
Cincinnati	37	37	.500	8
Pittsburgh	36	36	.500	8
New York	36	38	.486	9
Philadelphia	33	36	.478	9.5
Chicago	33	41	.446	12
Houston	32	43	.427	13.5

And while a few teams were still within striking distance of the Cardinals, nothing would prepare the rest of the National League for the solo storm
that was about to rush over them, coming from a lone man's right arm.

10. Domination

Nothing that has ever been said about Bob Gibson and his talent has ever been overstated. Everybody embellishes, but with Gibson, there is no way to do so outside of the realm of fact.

— Tim McCarver

With the Dodgers struggling to stay above the .500 mark — with no room for faltering — they hosted the Cardinals in Chavez Ravine north of downtown Los Angeles on July 1 for the showdown of the summer. While the Dodgers, Giants, and Braves were still outside of firing range at St. Louis, fans looked at the Gibson-Drysdale match-up that night as not only the best pitching tilt in recent memory, but also a chance to jolt the Redbirds from atop their comfortable position with a landmark win. A shoulder-to-shoulder crowd of over 55,000 squeezed into the five-tier stadium, which in 1968 was only six years old. The yard had received its permanent name after the Angels moved out in 1966, and its attractiveness was already providing for its label as the "Taj Mahal of Baseball." Originally planned to have a capacity of near 90,000, the park took up over 300 acres of real estate and had established itself as a classic pitcher's park in the new age. As the Redbirds took the field, the Dodgers were the only team in Gibson's career that he had not shut out since making his big-league debut against them on April 15, 1959 — a game won by Drysdale, ironically, as Gibson finished up in the 5–0 Dodgers win that day with two innings of scoreless relief in his inaugural with the Cardinals.

The home team wasted no time in defending their own man's record as they halted Hoot's scoreless inning streak at 47 in the very first inning, at which point Gibson had thrown only his twentieth pitch of the night. After Gibson was able to retire Willie Davis and Paul Popovich to start the Dodgers' first turn at bat, Gabrielson singled and was promptly sent to third on another hit by catcher Tom Haller, a ball that grounded through the hole at second, and one which Javier normally fielded. Next was right fielder Ron Fairly, as Gibson started him off with a fastball strike. On the next pitch, Gibson went back to the fastball again, but the twentieth pitch got away from him and skipped towards Edwards, whom Schoendienst said he had chosen for the start over McCarver because Edwards had caught Gibson's last shutout against Pittsburgh on June 26. Edwards was unable to keep the ball in front of him, as it caromed to the backstop for Gibson's third wild pitch of the year. Gabrielson waltzed home from third as the crowd let out a spontaneous, and then more thoughtful, roar. Initially, they were cheering the fact that the home team had taken the lead 1–0, with an extra holler following momentarily for the preservation of Drysdale's record. Then, after a pause of consideration, they recognized Gibson with yet another ovation, along with Drysdale one of the primary figures that was making 1968 the Year of the Pitcher. After an acknowledging tip of the cap, Gibson went back to his main concern of producing a Cardinals win. The streak was over after 47 and two-thirds innings without permitting a run, and in those 47-plus innings, Gibson had allowed a mere 21 hits. His mates made sure that it wound up his evening anyway, as they belted Drysdale for ten hits—all singles—and five runs for a 5–1 triumph, the 135th win in Gibson's career which sent him past Dizzy Dean into second place all alone on the all-time Cardinals victories list behind Jesse Haines' 210. After the game in the locker room, some reporters were hovering around Edwards, trying to focus the blame for the pitching mishap on him. Edwards' teammates, however, quickly came to his aid. Javier, in reference to Haller's single that got by him, said that "I should have kept my glove down ... I was expecting the ball to take an extra hop." When the number-three catcher, Ricketts, was trying to get to his cubicle to take a shower, he said in the direction of Edwards and the mob, "Hey, don't you know where your locker is? Some of us would like to get dressed!" Then entered Gibson into the clubhouse, and even the probing newsman got nervous when the pitcher stormed into the room, threw his glove angrily into his locker, and began to curse out Edwards for missing the ball. Hoot was unable to keep a straight face, however, and when he broke a smile the whole place erupted into laughter. The great showdown with Drysdale had put each pitcher's season record at 10–5, while Gibson's career record against Los Angeles stood only at a surprising 10–16 mark after the win.

It was a springboard for another overpowering stretch by the St. Louis men, as a four-game sweep of the Dodgers was followed up by three straight wins over the Giants in San Francisco as the St. Louis club demolished the West Coast. The offense was provided equally by Flood and Brock, as the outfield mates had each batted .348 (both 16 for 46) during the seven games, while Edwards, Gagliano, Maris, Spiezio, and rookie Floyd Wicker provided clutch hits off the bench in going 6 for 8 in pinch-hitting roles. Wicker, however, was quickly sent back to the club's farm team at Tulsa to make room for Ron Davis, a more experienced player who had been completing military obligations before joining the active roster. As the California writers quizzed each other around the press box, it was the first time in anyone's memory that any club had swept a West Coast trip since the Dodgers and Giants had arrived in the Golden State in 1958. While in Los Angeles, however, Schoendienst had grievances with the conduct of some local fans. He had filed a complaint with the Dodgers executives when a firecracker was thrown into the Cardinals bullpen from the stands, and landed at the feet of Willis while he was warming up. The good news of the trip was highlighted with wins by Briles (10–6), Washburn (6–3), and two out of the bullpen by the impressive rookie Granger (3–0). It was punctuated, however, by Gibson's next performance on July 6 at San Francisco, yet another shutout with a 3–0 suffocation of Herman Franks' men. The loss dealt to Juan Marichal was only his fourth defeat on the year against 15 victories (in facing the Giants in St. Louis on July 17, Franks would thus adjust his rotation so as not to put Marichal up against Gibson, whom Franks was beginning to think was invincible). And Washburn, despite his success off the mound, could not escape the teasing from his fellow players due to his poor hitting. After going 0 for 29 on the season, Ray had found his locker filled with his teammates' bats when he arrived at the clubhouse one morning. Soon after, on July 24, he posted his first hit of the season — and Cepeda and trainer Bauman took special care of the baseball, so that Washburn could keep it for posterity. That same day, another ball would be saved from another game — that used by Chicago White Sox reliever Hoyt Wilhelm, as the pitcher celebrated his 45th birthday by appearing in his 908th major league game, an all-time record. The performance broke the mark of Cy Young, who had set the record back in 1911.

While in San Francisco, a newcomer to the Giants' lineup had caught the eye of the St. Louis coaching staff. A rookie outfielder named Bobby Bonds had struck out twice in going 0 for 4 against Gibson, but his physical talents were readily apparent. Bonds had made his major league debut two weeks earlier against the Dodgers (the day before Drysdale notched his 200th career victory against the Giants), and with his four-year-old son Barry cheering him along near the San Francisco dugout, he hit a grand slam in his third at-bat — making him only the second big-leaguer in history to hit a slam in his first game. The other Giants players were already awed by Bonds' stunning combination of power, running speed, and throwing-arm strength. "That ball was hit about as far as a man can hit it with that wind," said the usual San Francisco power source, McCovey, in reference to the gale-force zephyr that was blowing in from off the bay, beyond left field, when the homer was hit. Bonds, four years removed as a four-sport star at Riverside High School in California, came to the plate in the eighth inning and struck out against Dodgers reliever Mudcat Grant, but still received a standing ovation from the fans at Candlestick Park. Two years earlier, the ballpark was the site of the last Beatles concert in August of 1966, and like Dodger Stadium had come to symbolize the westward movement of the major leagues.

Jaster and Willis combined for another shutout the following day, 2–0, as the Giants were held scoreless in the last 24 innings of the series. The Redbirds headed into the All-Star break with a perfect 7–0 record for July and a ten-game lead on their fading National League competitors, as Gibson's ERA was a staggering 1.06 after his latest masterpiece against San Francisco. It was the largest lead at the break for an NL team since the Brooklyn Dodgers had an eleven-and-a-half game advantage in 1955, the year of the only world championship for the Dodgers while in Brooklyn. Paralleling the Cardinals' success in the National League continued to be the Detroit Tigers in the American, who themselves on the work of a 55–28 record (two games better than St. Louis) carried a nine-and-a-half game lead into the All-Star break with a double header sweep of the A's in Detroit on July 7. It had been longer, in fact, since an American League team led the pack by as many games at the break (in 1947, the Yankees held a twelve-and-a-half game advantage). One of the teams struggling behind the Tigers was the Baltimore Orioles, champions of baseball in 1966 but who had slid to seventh place under manager Hank Bauer in 1967. By the end of the All-Star break, Bauer would be replaced by 38-year-old Earl Weaver, a man who had managed for 11 seasons in the Orioles' minor league system. Bauer was then mentioned as the popular choice to become the first manager of the Kansas City Royals in 1969, but he withheld any immediate plans from the media. At that very moment, the first pieces of earth were being moved for the grand new Jackson County Sports Complex in suburban Kansas City, arriving with a price tag of $43 million to house two stadiums with unprecedented parking availability for 26,000 cars within a short walk to each — one ballpark for the new Royals, as well as a next-door stadium for the Chiefs of the American Football League, as they prepared to merge with the other AFL clubs into the NFL.

The opener in the Tigers' double victory against Oakland was yet another win for the irrepressible McLain, as the Detroit hurler who now had a majors-leading record of 16–2 on the year. Nonetheless, Roger Maris— keeping his eye on the Tigers and the American League race —claimed that the stout left-hander Lolich — not McLain — was the more dangerous pitcher to watch for the rest of the season and into a possible World Series match up.

On July 9, Houston was ready to show off its three-year-old indoor wonder to the world, with the Major League All-Star Game ready to go at the Astrodome. The starting lineups were as follows:

National League	American League
Mays (SF)— CF	Fregosi (CAL)— SS
Flood (STL)— LF	Carew (MIN)— 2B
McCovey (SF)—1B	Yastrzemski (BOS)— CF
Aaron (ATL)— RF	Howard (WAS)— RF
Santo (CHI)— 3B	Horton (DET)— LF
Helms (CIN)— 2B	Killebrew (MIN)—1B
Grote (NY)— C	Freehan (DET)— C
Kessinger (CHI)— SS	B. Robinson (BAL)— 3B
Drysdale (LA)— P	Tiant (CLE)— P

The most noticeable substitution in the National League lineup was Mays, taking the place of Pete Rose, who was recovering from a minor injury. The American Leaguers, meanwhile, spent their first day in Houston examining the bizarre Astrodome in the initial visit for many of them to the weather-proof park. Their starting pitcher, Tiant of the Indians, was becoming famous around baseball as much for his whirling windup as for his effective results. "It's been a good year for me, and for all the pitchers," the Cuban native Tiant exulted in broken English. "I think we're getting smarter." As manager Dick Williams of the Red Sox filled out his selections for the rest of the American League roster, one familiar name was present for one last shining moment. The Yankees legend Mantle was 36 years old, but had already been an All-Star 15 times. At the time of the break, he had posted 11 home runs but was batting only .242, as it was apparent that his career was coming to an end. Williams, in a gesture of respect, chose Mantle for the roster for sentimental reasons. But like Aaron, Mantle felt that another player should have gone in his place. "It has been a big thrill for me every year," Mantle said of All-Star competition. "It always is. But I think the ballplayers who are playing well are the ones who should get to play in the game." As for coming through in key situations like he used to do, Mantle noted that "when I do anything like that anymore, it's an even bigger thrill than it used to be — because I don't do it as often." In October, the Commerce Comet would say goodbye as the game's greatest switch-hitter ever, knocking 536 home runs, over 1,500 RBIs, garnering three MVP awards, and twelve World Series appearances. His timed mark of 3.1 seconds from the batter's box to first base remains unsurpassed today.

Meanwhile, Mantle's former home run wingman in New York, Maris, was discussing his own possible exit from the game. With his public admiration about Lolich and the Tigers, Maris's increased focus on potential postseason opponents fueled speculation that it would be Roger's last year in baseball. "It must be right," he said. "I read it in the newspaper." This statement was in response to a premise recently circulated by New York scribe

Milt Gross, claiming that Maris had already been running an Anheuser-Busch subsidiary in Jacksonville, Florida, which was supposed to be promised to him after retirement from Gussie Busch.

In addition to Javier and Flood, Gibson was an obvious choice for Schoendienst in completing the roster, and he added Carlton as well. Carlton had been struggling of late, winning only twice since June 4. McCarver, his catcher, was not only uninvited to the game but had to spend the break caring for his ill mother back in Memphis. Red would start things with Mr. Dodger, as it was the fifth time in his eight All-Star appearances that Drysdale had gotten the ball to open the game for the Nationals, tying a record for the event held by Lefty Gomez and Robin Roberts. Yet another record was awaiting him as the contest commenced—for if Drysdale could last three innings (the maximum that the starting pitcher was allowed in the All-Star Game), he would set the career mark for innings pitched in All-Star Game play.

Those hoping that the imposing lineups would jolt the second half of the regular-season schedule into an offensive resurgence were disappointed, as the game of stars simply served as a microcosm of the 1968 baseball summer. In a most fitting display for the times, no run would be scored on a safe hit. The National League took a 1–0 lead in the bottom of the first inning as McCovey hit into a double play grounder, scoring Mays unearned from third, as he earlier had gone to second after singling on an errant pickoff throw by Tiant. It was Mays' 23rd hit in All-Star competition, which extended a career record that he already held. (The "Say-Hey" Kid, at 37, appeared to be reaching for the speed of his younger years; a week later in San Francisco, Mays would again plate the only run of the game, beating Houston 1–0 as he scored all the way from first on a single by Jim Ray Hart.) Beyond that lone scoring moment, the game turned into the usual litany of outs seen in most contests that season, ending in the same 1–0 score two hours and ten minutes later despite all the typical All-Star substitutions that took place. Gibson would not take part in the hurlers' feast at the All-Star Game, however, as his manager declined to subject his crown jewel to further extra work. Instead, the pitching load for the Nationals was shared by Drysdale (three innings, giving him the career record), Marichal (two), Carlton (one), Seaver (two), Ron Reed of Atlanta (two-thirds), and rookie Jerry Koosman of the Mets, who threw three strikes to a baffled Yastrzemski for the only batter he faced in ending the game. The American League managed to scrape only three hits off the group, while the Nationals were held to five themselves (Flood had walked in following Mays' hit in the first inning, and later grounded out to California Angels shortstop Jim Fregosi. Javier, meanwhile, entered the game at second base in the ninth inning, and consequently did not bat). Appearing on the mound in the fifth and sixth innings for the Americans was

McLain, who had flown his private jet from Las Vegas to Houston for the event. As soon as he could get out of his uniform and shower, he planned to head back to Vegas. As McLain was bathing, "Sudden Sam" McDowell followed him to the mound in the seventh. He was every bit as intimidating to American League batters during the season as Gibson was in the National. "McDowell has the five best pitches in the league," asserted Fregosi, happy to be his teammate for one day. "He has the best fastball, the best curveball, the best slider, the best changeup, and the best spitball. A smart pitcher? No— he just wants to embarrass them, instead of just getting them out. He wants to strike people out and make them look bad." McDowell would be true to form, as in the midst of allowing a dribbling infield single to Matty Alou, he polished off Haller, Mays, and McCovey easily on strikes.

For his modest services—but still in surpassing most of his peers on the day—Mays became the first two-time winner of the All-Star Game MVP award, having first been granted the honor in 1963. While this particular performance was not outstanding in terms of numbers, Mays had always shone among the brightest in the affair, holding career All-Star Game records for runs (20), triples (3), stolen bases (6) and putouts (51) in addition to his mark of 23 hits. The win gave the Nationals a 21–17 lead all-time in the series with one draw.

On the last day of the All-Star Break (July 10), Eckert officially announced that both major leagues would split into divisional play for 1969. With much discussion and disagreement in the past—with ideas ranging from reconstructing both leagues to simply adding the new clubs to each league's standing list—it appeared to be the path of least resistance, although by no means was there consensus on the move. Many teams that drew a large proportion of their revenues from a small number of teams (such as with the Mets' situation) did not care to make the change, but Eckert's office viewed the situation as needing compliance from both leagues for all of baseball to prosper in the coming decades. The new National League Eastern Division would hold St. Louis, Chicago, Montreal, New York, Philadelphia, and Pittsburgh, while Los Angeles, San Francisco, San Diego, Houston, Cincinnati (ironically), and Atlanta (even more ironically) would call the Western Division home. The geographical distribution made sense to very few, as days were recalled when before the late 1950s, a trip "out west" meant Cincinnati or St. Louis. In counter-point, it was noted by baseball officials that the odd outlay was necessary for the even distribution of the expansion teams—even though on the American League side, strangely enough, Chicago, Minnesota, and Oakland had been placed in the Western Division of that circuit with *three* expansion franchises—the brand-new Kansas City and Seattle entries, as well as the slightly-older California Angels. Gussie Busch was constitutionally opposed to the idea of divisional play, but decided it best to defer to the decision which had been set forth. "Busch, who doesn't like to finish next-best in gin rummy, baseball, brewery sales, or show horses, bunted in the interests of harmony," as Broeg put it.

Divisions or no divisions, it was becoming quite clear which clubs would top the standings in 1968. While the front-running Tigers initially sputtered on the American League side after the intermission, the All-Star break did nothing to cool off Schoendienst's men as the Redbird rampage continued. Opening with a double header against the Astros in St. Louis, Denis Menke's tenth-inning triple gave Houston a 5–4 win, but it was followed by six more victories in a row by the Cardinals. The next day, Menke struck again — not in a manner that would again prevent a Cardinal win, but rather, in precluding another Gibson shutout. With the Cardinals' pitcher working through a bad blister on his index finger, the Astros pushed across a run in the seventh. Rusty Staub touched the plate after circling the bases on a double by Menke, a batted ball that blooped over the head of Shannon at third and in front of the left fielder Brock on a full-count pitch (after Menke had fouled off four pitches). It would be the lone run they would score against the big righthander, with every Cardinal except the pitcher contributing at least one hit (led by Flood's four) for an 8–1 rout. On the defensive side, a boost was given with the return of Maxvill to short, as Schofield had taken his place for the past six games as Dal was dealing with a twisted ankle. What did Bob have to say about the ball that Menke hit? "Well, with eleven pitches, you're going to have to hang one, I think. You're going to throw one out of eleven where you don't want to throw it." Staub, who had finished fifth in the National League in batting in 1967 with a .333 rate, could not believe that Gibson was getting even more improved than he had been in previous years. "Control — that's what makes Gibson better than he ever was before," the red-haired Staub claimed. "Not that he ever had a problem, but before when he was behind, he'd come in with a fastball. You looked for it. Now, he hits the corners with curves and sliders."

Thus, with the Astros' solitary run in the seventh, Gibson had until that point pitched 23 innings before giving up a tally — this after his great streak of 47⅔ scoreless frames had ended in Los Angeles in the first inning on July 1. Therefore, he had allowed no scoring to his opponents in 70 of their last 71 tries against him. After the game in Los Angeles, Schoendienst had halfjokingly said, "Well, now Gib will just have to start over. The way he is pitching, and with the time we've got left, he's still got a crack at six straight shutouts." Gibson, actually, had been unable to shake Menke all season — for back on May 12, it was Menke's two-run single in the seventh that provided the difference in Gibby's 3–2 loss that evening at Busch.

There was one pitcher from the Houston roster whom the Cardinals were fortunate to miss during the series. As the Astros moved on from St.

Louis to play the Reds in Cincinnati in a double header on Sunday the 14th, Don Wilson tied a major-league record in the second game with 18 strikeouts, fanning the phenom Johnny Bench looking to end the game and knot his place in history with Koufax and Bob Feller. Wilson had struck out eight of the first nine batters he faced, and later in the game tied another record with eight straight strikeouts. By the time he had blown the last fastball by Bench, a hard rain was starting to pelt down at Cincinnati's Crosley Field, as Wilson went into double-quick mode to complete the contest. The tremendous performance, however, left Wilson with just a 6–11 mark on the year. "When I've had such a bad record," he reflected, "I'm glad for this because it gives me more confidence." It was yet another anecdote in the ever-growing volume of pitching accomplishments during the year, with the story and characters changing shape every day in the newspapers. And, all one needed to do was glance in the statistics section of the paper for the raw data. For on the 12th, Ken Harrelson had gone 0 for 4 against California, dropping his American League-leading average from .300 down into a tie with the A's Rick Monday at .295. Thus, when the newspapers hit the stands the day before Wilson's performance, *no* .300 hitter — for the first time in the history of the game — was able to be found over in the American League.

Amidst all their success over the past season and a half, the Cardinals of the late 1960s were perhaps no more impressive than in the first half of July 1968. By the 16th, they had won 13 out of the first 14 games of the month, and had gone over one million in home attendance in the fastest time in their history. In addition, they had a record of 37–10 since their low point of late May, when they had lost 11 of 13. The recent bounty of victories put them 28 games above .500, as in the past month and a half they had picked up at least eleven games on every club in the National League (including 17 on the talented San Francisco team). They had now opened up nearly a ten-game lead on the second-place Braves, whose superstar, Aaron, hit his 500th career homer two days earlier off Mike McCormick of the Giants:

	W	L	Pct.	GB
St. Louis	59	31	.656	—
Atlanta	49	40	.551	9.5
Philadelphia	45	41	.523	12
San Francisco	45	45	.500	14
Chicago	44	47	.484	15.5
Cincinnati	42	45	.483	15.5
Pittsburgh	41	47	.466	17
Los Angeles	42	49	.462	17.5
New York	41	49	.456	18
Houston	38	52	.422	21

A resurgent Brock had eclipsed the .400 mark in his past 18 games (36 for 89), in addition to stealing nine bases in the previous week to increase his season total to 23. He still trailed Wills for the league lead by four, mostly due to the batting woes that Lou had encountered through much of the first half of the season. All Cardinals fans were happy to see Brock running again, especially broadcaster Harry Caray — who, when Brock was struck by a pitch from Sadecki on the 16th, hoped that Lou would "steal second, third, and home, and then bunt his next time up and run over him [Sadecki]," feeling that the San Francisco pitcher had thrown at him intentionally. The comment angered the Giants, including manager Franks who filed a complaint with the league office about the comments Caray had made. Brock, however, was taking the pains of a major league season in stride. "Most of my aches are gone now," Brock told the press on July 17 about his season-long battle with a combination of ailments. "I'm in about as good a groove as ever." Nonetheless, Flood remained the only batter in the lineup with an imposing overall average (currently standing in fifth place in the National League batting race, with Matty Alou of the Pirates out in front at .336), as the Cardinals' mediocre 1968 hitting statistics to this point starkly revealed their reliance on the pitching staff:

Batting	AB	H	HR	RBI	Avg.
Flood	371	120	5	42	.323
Brock	374	105	5	23	.281
Shannon	306	83	12	45	.271
Cepeda	333	90	11	46	.270
Javier	324	85	1	30	.263
Maris	135	34	3	16	.252
Tolan	144	36	4	8	.250
Edwards	108	27	2	15	.250
Schofield	72	18	1	6	.250
McCarver	260	63	5	33	.242
Maxvill	248	56	1	9	.226
Gagliano	27	5	0	4	.185
Speizio	38	6	0	2	.158
Ricketts	15	2	0	1	.133

But despite their modest overall numbers, the middle infield tandem of Maxvill (.352) and Javier (.408) was displaying itself as incredibly potent against left-handed pitchers, in addition to the numbers of Shannon (.319), Flood (.316) and Cepeda (.288) versus lefties. The at-bat statistics also pointed to the balance that Schoendienst was achieving in getting Maris and McCarver the rest he had been seeking for them since the start of the season, as Tolan and Edwards had seen significant playing time (Tolan, in particular, had been proving his mettle against lefthanders, for while he did not have the high average against southpaws as did some of his teammates, his consistent contact had led Schoendienst to bat Maris against lefties only six times to date on the year). The plan for this trend of partial platooning was to continue, as the Cardinals had 56 straight games scheduled after the All-Star Break and would need the contributions of all for the pennant drive to be solidified. Players all around the league, in fact, were beginning to complain about the grueling schedule that had been constructed by league officials. It would become yet another issue at the bargaining table for the players association, a large component of which was seeking to do away with doubleheaders as one measure. In light of the torturous itinerary that had been laid out, people following the game figured that Gibson would falter — or at least, slow down — as the summer heat began to take its toll on all the players with the unrelenting schedule (Briles, as one example, claimed to have lost 11 pounds while beating Sadecki and the Giants in the sweltering Busch Stadium heat on July 16). But instead, what happened next was the greatest seasonal pitching performance seen in modern times.

Labor issues such as these were fairly unique to baseball among the professional sports in the late 1960s. However, at about the time when sports thoughts turned to NFL training camps in conjunction with the second half of the baseball season, surprising trouble at the negotiating table was now appearing to threaten the opening of the football season. In mid-July, the NFL players association had voted to strike if certain demands were not satisfied, and the football Cardinals of St. Louis were behind the idea nearly one hundred percent. "In respecting the confidence of each player, we can't give the voting total," Cardinals kicker and team representative Jim Bakken announced. "But I would say it's a pretty good indication of our feeling towards the progress of negotiations." At stake were demands by the players for increased pay to $500 per man for each exhibition game they played, having the minimum league salary increased to $15,000, and an extra $100,000 contributed from each club into the players' pension fund. Despite the vast majority of the 640-member players association voting for approval of a strike, league commissioner Pete Rozelle was confident an agreement could be attained. "I just feel that, in the final analysis, both sides will be responsible enough to reach a satisfactory settlement." One day after Rozelle's statement, however, a telephone poll conducted by the *Knoxville News-Sentinel* reported that 377 out of 394 players surveyed recommended that nobody report for the opening of the training camps. The league-wide player representative from the NFL's rival cousin, the American Football League, guaranteed that their organization would have football in the fall. "Our demands and proposals are based on economics, not emotion," Buffalo quarterback Jack Kemp had said in reference to the name-calling into which many of the NFL bargaining sessions had dissolved. "We also base things on fact, rather than opinion."

Even some key NFL owners, such as Art Rooney of the Pittsburgh Steelers and Art Modell of the Cleveland Browns, were suggesting that the entire 1968 NFL schedule might be wiped off the map. "We have gone as far as we can possibly go," an exasperated Rooney concluded with the latest round of fruitless negotiations. "This is first time anything so serious has come about since I've been connected with the National Football League." In the last round of talks, the owners made concessions on all fronts, but none of the offers were to the liking of the players association. At that point Carroll Rosenbloom, the owner of the Baltimore Colts, officially forwarded the motion that the 1968 season be suspended. Meanwhile, preparing for all contingencies, Vince Lombardi of the champion Green Bay Packers—now a general manager and not coaching for the first time, turning over the field reins to assistant Phil Bengston—announced that St. Norbert's College in Wisconsin would be ready on time to house the rookies that were scheduled to come to camp in the next few days. The turmoil would actually become short-lived, as an agreement was reached on July 15 for the owners to contribute $6 million to the pension over the next two years in addition to an improved, graduated scale for the minimum salary. The veteran players around the league then readied themselves to join the rookies who, like in Green Bay, were already practicing in most camps.

On July 17—as a man named Saddam Hussein had taken the seat as vice chairman of the Revolutionary Council in the nation of Iraq, after his party staged a violent coup—Gibson threw four shutout innings at the Giants before the game was postponed by rain. Earlier in the day, the Cardinals announced the signing of two amateur free agents from the northern California area. One was Gary Marion, a 20-year-old shortstop from San Jose who looked to follow in the footsteps of his uncle, Marty, and hold the shortstop position for St. Louis in the future. The other signee was a third baseman and pitcher from Sacramento named Bob Forsch, whom the Cardinals envisioned as a future star at the hot corner because of his strong bat.

After the postponed game against the Giants, Gibson shut out the Mets 2–0 at Busch Stadium on 13 strikeouts and 144 pitches in his next start on July 21, running his career record against New York to 20–3. Despite the relatively early date on baseball's summer calendar, it was the first time in major league history that a pitcher had shut out eight different teams in one season (leaving only the Dodgers as the remaining team not to be victimized by Gibson). Making his major-league debut opposite Gibson was McAndrew, who needed oxygen treatments in between innings because of the heat. After the game, McAndrew would be returned temporarily to the Mets' Jacksonville farm club, as there was no permanent room for him on the talented New York staff. Next, on July 25, Gibson shut out the Phillies and Chris Short 5–0. With his win over Philadelphia, he had now beaten every National League team in 1968 (he had even accomplished this over his current 11-game winning streak, in fact), as his record — once 4–5 back when he was receiving little run support from his teammates— now stood at 14–5. When Gibby faced the Mets in his next appearance with two out in the fourth inning at Shea Stadium on July 30, he had put together his third extended scoreless-inning streak in only the past two months, with the current one standing at 27⅔. At that point in the game, Ed Charles of New York singled to break up the no-hitter Gibson was authoring (with all his greatness in a Cardinals uniform, a no-hitter was the one achievement Gibson could not seem to attain). Next, Ed Kranepool lined a double to the outfield wall, sending Charles on a sprint to home plate that Gibson rarely had seen occur in front of him in recent memory. And, as usual, it was the only charity he would permit. He shut the Mets out over the final five innings for a 7–1 win, his fifteenth on the year and twelfth in a row, a Cardinals record for one season.

Thus, Kranepool's RBI had ended a 99-inning stretch in June and July of 1968 in which Gibson had permitted two runs. When the game in New York was over, his ERA for the season was at 0.96. "It seemed that every time I delivered a pitch," Gibson would later recall about that stretch of time, "I knew exactly where it was going ... [it was] the most amazing eight weeks of my life."

Not to be outdone or upstaged by anyone, McLain continued his own torrid pace in the American League, being the third-fastest pitcher in history to twenty wins in a season (and the fastest in the post-deadball era) on July 27 as he downed the Orioles 9–0. With a sparkling 20–3 mark, McLain seemed on track to be the first 30-game winner in the majors since Dizzy Dean in 1934. It was the first time he had beaten Baltimore on the year, as the Orioles had dealt him two of his three losses. With McLain's march toward the coveted thirty-win mark, scrutinizers of the statistics wondered how close Gibson could have been coming in the ensuing weeks if his early-season lack of batting support had been different.

During those steaming days of summer, some liked to compare Gibson's rage on the mound to the rage still seen on the streets of American cities. Gibson dismissed these comparisons, as he noted that he wanted to be known "only as a man"— not as a showcase for a racial cause. For as he was overpowering the Phillies during his latest streak on the 25th — and as the 49-year-old Jackie Robinson was recovering from a minor heart attack at his home in Stamford, Connecticut — black militants led by Fred Evans were in the midst of an armed standoff with police in Cleveland, as Evans had been cornered after being charged with trying to illegally obtain firearms. It was a confrontation that came to be known as the Glenville Shootout, as the nation feared a rekindling of the urban riots that had plagued the country over the past year. The situation in Cleveland would subsist until July 28 — four days after Evans surrendered to police — but not before seven people were killed and another fifteen were injured. The Ohio National Guard had been called to the scene by Cleveland mayor Carl Stokes, who was later learned to have given $6,000 to Evans for revitalization of an East Cleveland neighborhood — funds the issuance and spending of which were never accounted for, an act that irreversibly hurt Stokes politically.

As had been Herman Franks' plan, he purposely sat Marichal down for his regular turn in the rotation against Gibson on the 17th, even though the game would be shortened by rain. Franks was of the opinion that even Marichal wasn't going to stop Gibson (and Marichal concurred, claiming that he wanted an "extra day of rest"), so he was held over to face Carlton on the 18th, a 2–0 win for the Giants' right-hander in more stifling St. Louis July heat. Even with the mastery, however, Shannon was quick to point out afterwards that Marichal now held only a 15–15 record against the Cards for his career, the only team in the National League against which he did not have a winning ledger. Nonetheless, with his 17–4 mark for 1968, Marichal himself was on pace for 30 wins if he could maintain the rate he had set. Jaster (7–5) was ineffective on July 19 as the Mets came to town and beat the Birds, 4–2, but the Cardinals would subsequently go on yet another tear, winning seven of their next eight. The only blemish was a 1–0 loss by Briles to Koosman in the second game of a double header on the 21st, the contest that had followed up Gibson's 2–0 blanking of the New York club. That series had also seen the first time all season that Flood had missed an inning, as Schoendienst decided to give him a rest and insert the newly-acquired Ron Davis in center field. In addition, Cepeda sat out his first game of the year on the 20th, prompting his teammates to teasingly refer to him as "El Bencho." Things were not so funny for Orlando two nights later, when he was removed for a pinch hitter (Brock) for the first time in his big-league career while in the midst of a slump. Cepeda pouted on the scene as he stormed back down the dugout steps, kicked the drinking fountain (which then required repair), and flung his helmet down the alley that led to the locker room. Earlier in the game, Cepeda had been booed by the crowd at Busch Stadium for looking extremely bad in striking out. Brock promptly singled and scored the winning run, upon which Cepeda retreated with his comments after the game, and instead acknowledged the wisdom of Schoendienst's move.

After a rain-shortened, eight-inning 2–1 win for Carlton on August 1, the Cardinals were now running away from a demoralized National League, with the distant second-place Braves now needing a telescope to see the leaders. The Cardinals, in going 6–2 on their trip out east, were back to being as

By the late 1960s, Busch Stadium had cemented itself—along with the Gateway Arch—as the centerpiece of downtown St. Louis. (*St. Louis Globe-Democrat* / Archives of the St. Louis Mercantile Library)

loose and easygoing as a team could be. They did not even mind the one-hour delay of their flight in leaving Philadelphia to return to St. Louis, as they entertained themselves in watching Maxvill and Hoerner push Maris around the airport in a wheelchair, while Javier and some of the other players were posing as airport employees and directed confused passengers to gates that did not exist. When Maxvill and Hoerner came to a sharp decline, they spotted several buckets of water left by a janitor at the bottom of a ramp, and sent Roger flying into a splashing crash with him wearing his good clothes. Roger then took what water was left in the buckets and doused McCarver, who had been amusing himself in riding an electric floor mop — years before Tim would receive a similar but not-so-lighthearted bath from football player Deion Sanders, whom McCarver had confronted in a poignant interview he was conducting. The raucous behavior did not calm down by the time the team reached Lambert Airport in St. Louis at three the next morning, as Javier hollered up the aisle to Ricketts in calling him "buck-and-a-quarter" with his .125 batting average. When the players retrieved their luggage from the carousel at the baggage claim, they found Hoerner riding on the conveyor belt, coming through the chute along with the suitcases and sitting cross-legged in a meditative state that broke the team up into laughter once again.

While Brock had regained his stroke with a .350 batting mark for July (and Maxvill had raised his overall mark into the .240s—good enough to place him in the top fifty in the National League, no less), the records of the starting pitchers for the entire season told the story of the team's reliance upon them for their success:

Gibson	15–5
Briles	13–7
Carlton	11–5
Washburn	10–3
Jaster	8–5

Veteran pitcher and former Cardinal Larry Jackson of the Philadelphia Phillies, however, had a warning for the supporting cast of the Cardinals' staff. "Guys like Nelson Briles and Steve Carlton have to be careful that they don't let themselves feel overshadowed too much by Gibson," noted the four-time All-Star, who was with St. Louis for Hoot's first four seasons in the big leagues from 1959 to 1962. "They have to respect Gibson, but continue to be competitive. They have to want to become better pitchers than Gibson, and not just decide to sit back and settle for fifteen victories for themselves. That's why Bob Lemon and Mike Garcia won 20 games for the Cleveland Indians— they respected Bob Feller, but they wanted to become better than he was and make his kind of money." With Gibson deservedly receiving the lion's share of the media attention during the Cardinals' run through the past two months, Washburn was right behind him with seven straight victories during the Cards' high tide. The starters were expecting to easily handle every club, each and every evening out. Things were getting so boring among the Redbirds' relief pitchers, in fact, that Russo told readers, "Don't be surprised if the Cardinal bullpen is stocked soon with such things as a chess set, checkers, a dartboard, and few yo-yos. They might even toss in a television set, horseshoes, and shuffleboard." For laughs, they would sometimes roll a baseball into the cylinder that held the field tarp, and make the skinny rookie Granger crawl into it obstacle-course style and retrieve it.

In Las Vegas, the oddsmakers were giving St. Louis a 7–5 edge against Detroit in a potential World Series match up, as the Cardinals had crafted a 24–6 record in July to pull further away from the field. Gibson, meanwhile, would be named National League Player of the Month for two months in a row, the first time a player ever accomplished the feat.

	W	L	Pct.	GB
St. Louis	71	36	.664	—
Atlanta	56	51	.523	15
Cincinnati	53	49	.520	15.5
Chicago	55	52	.514	16
San Francisco	53	52	.505	17
Pittsburgh	52	54	.491	18.5
Philadelphia	48	56	.462	21.5
New York	49	59	.454	22.5
Los Angeles	47	59	.443	23.5
Houston	45	61	.425	25.5

The most energized team from the rest of the pack was the Cubs, who had suddenly won 10 of their last 14 by the time they welcomed the struggling Dodgers to Wrigley Field for a doubleheader on July 28. The Phillies, meanwhile, had seen the worst free-fall in recent weeks, a drop to seventh place that culminated in their getting no-hit by George Culver of the Reds on July 29. Undaunted by their seemingly-hopeless standing, Chicago fans jammed the friendly confines of Wrigley Field to the tune of 42,000 patrons—the largest gathering the ballpark had seen in twenty years, with a thousand standing-room ticketholders requesting a refund for an inability to see the playing field, and five thousand more who were turned away outside the stadium. The home team rewarded them with a sweep of Los Angeles, slapping a tiring Drysdale for eight runs in the opener behind Joe Niekro—the most scoring that Drysdale had surrendered in two years—while St. Louisan Ken Holtzman struck out ten in shutting out Don Sutton's hitting support in the nightcap. It was a rough day all around for Drysdale, as he collided with Santo while covering first base in the eighth inning of the first game, and Santo's spike gashed Drysdale's right knee which required five stitches to close. The sweep put the Cubs back over the .500 mark with a 52–51 record. And the oddities continued to pile up around baseball during the bizarre summer, as on July 30, Ron Hansen of the Washington Senators turned the first unassisted triple play in the major leagues in 41 years. Hansen's efforts were of little help, however, in the Senators' 10–1 loss to the Indians.

The Cubs continued right on winning, and it didn't matter that the letters "STL" were next on their schedule. The hometown boy, Holtzman, first stopped the Cardinals on August 2 by a 3–0 score, while the bullpen came to the rescue of Jenkins and Bill Hands the following two days for a surprising sweep in Busch Stadium. Cepeda sat out the final two contests, as he continued to struggle at the plate with a batting average that had declined to .257. The Cubs had suddenly jumped to second place, a half-game ahead of the Reds but still a full thirteen from the front-running Redbirds. But despite the wide margin that lay between them, the Chicago men were proving to themselves that they could compete with the league's top club, as Durocher's players were gaining confidence with the passing summer days. The last game of the series was particularly inspiring to the Cubs, as they outlasted the Cardinals in a 13-inning, three-hour and forty-seven minute game in which the winning run was scored by catcher Randy Hundley, as the slow-footed catcher incredibly beat out a bunt single to start the inning. It was also a game in which Gibson was denied his sixteenth win, even though he had labored through eleven of the innings in a heat index that rose above 100 degrees. The Cubs had touched him for twelve hits and five runs, the first major damage any club had placed on him in several months. "Bob spoils people by pitching so many shutouts and one-run games," McCarver explained. "Guys like Ron Santo and Billy Williams and Ernie Banks are being paid $50,000 or more to get hits off pitchers like Gibson, and they're bound to get some. As hot as it was out on that field, a pitcher just can't keep throwing it by them." Chicago had now won six in a row and 23 their last 30, and were looking to build on their success as they continued the road trip to Atlanta and Cincinnati.

Much of the credit for the Cardinals' success had been due to the even-handed nature of Musial in his previous—albeit short—tenure as the general manager. Devine had provided a smooth, seamless transition back into the job, but it was Musial that stuck by the lineup that Schoendienst wanted to put on the field, all while many in the city—including Broeg—doubted that Stan would be an effective front-office man, despite his tremendous ability as a player and even greater personal popularity around St. Louis. But Musial's charisma had triumphed once again, and he was rewarded on August 4 with a permanent piece of recognition at the gates of Busch Stadium. A ten-foot-high, bronze, hand-crafted statue was erected in his honor, sculpted by Carl Mose, a former professor at Washington University in St. Louis, who had worked on the project for over three years. It depicted Stan's patented "peeking around the corner" batting style that terrorized pitchers for over two decades. Before the Cardinals' game against the Cubs that afternoon, Musial was greeted at home plate by his teammates from his first team in St. Louis in 1941, when he was called up from the minors to finish the season with the big league club. Earlier, outside at the stadium entrance at Broadway and Walnut, he gave a short speech as the statue was unveiled. The normally-stoic Musial was so moved by the event that he broke down into slight tears near the end of his remarks. "I want to thank everyone—for my mother and the Musial family—for making me a Cardinal forever," he concluded. The words below the statue read:

HERE STANDS BASEBALL'S PERFECT WARRIOR
HERE STANDS BASEBALL'S PERFECT KNIGHT

And, as usual, he celebrated later that evening by simply playing his harmonica for grateful patrons at Stan and Biggie's.

The unveiling of Musial's statue was followed by a more subtle announcement. It was one which was less expected, yet one that was nearly as emotional for Cardinals fans. It was made official that the 34-year-old Roger Maris was leaving the game at the end of the year, and would take full control (along with his brother Rudy) of the Gainesville distributorship of Anheuser-Busch that Gussie Busch had prepared for him. In batting .269 with 27 RBIs at the time — and starting to split his outfield duties with Tolan and Davis—Maris felt, in consideration of his physical condition, that he could play on for several more years. He was disappointed, however, in the time that he had lost with his family over the past decade, a family that consisted of his wife, Pat, and their six children. Maris acknowledged that, for the seven years he spent in New York with the Yankees, he rarely saw them. In fact, he did not want them living with him in New York, as he feared for their safety with the hate mail he had received for pursuing and ultimately breaking the single-season home run record of Babe Ruth in 1961. His life was completely changed by moving among what he considered "friendlier folks" back in the Midwest. "I don't think any ballplayer could ask for a better place to play than in St. Louis," Maris said. "The fans here have always shown me great respect, and in turn, I have great respect for them." Maris revealed that he had been on the verge of informing the Yankees of his impending retirement two years earlier, but before he could make the announcement, the club had already approved the deal to send him to St. Louis. "I didn't want the press to have anything more to jump on by saying I was quitting because New York got rid of me," Maris added. "I decided to play — and things were good enough last year [1967] and I enjoyed it enough last year to give it one more try." Schoendienst was indeed grateful that he had decided so. "Rog is always ready to play whether he's been out a week, or a night or two," Red praised him. "He's still a fine hitter. He's been a great inspiration to the entire ball club, and a help to some of the younger players. He even helps without saying much, because he's no 'pop-off.'"

After the fumble against the Cubs, the Cardinals resumed command to take three out of four from the Reds in Busch Stadium. The only loss was caused by the overpowering Jim Maloney, who scattered five Cardinals hits with his first complete game in a month and a half in a 5–0 beating of Carlton on August 6, accomplished in just 91 pitches. It was another sultry night at the St. Louis ballpark, and Maloney claimed to have lost twelve pounds during the evening as he darted back to the clubhouse three times to change his undershirt. Ironically, most of the St. Louis hits came via a 3-for-3 night from the modest stick of the shortstop Maxvill. Dal was perhaps inspired by his three-year-old son, Jeff, who entertained the club during batting practice that evening by skillfully utilizing a fungo bat to swat balls he tossed up in the air to himself. One a more serious note, Schoendienst was concerned about the team's dwindling power production, as there had not been a Cardinals home run in ten days—since Carlton himself hit one in his win at Pittsburgh on July 27. To refresh things a bit, Schoendienst planned to give the team leader in home runs and RBIs—Shannon (13–60)—a rare rest, as he would start Gagliano at third base in the next couple of games. Gagliano responded with a key hit in beating the no-hit ace from the previous week, Culver, on the 7th.

Meanwhile, in Pittsburgh, Drysdale (12–10) lost his fourth straight game as he committed two errors in the ninth inning, which led to three unearned runs and a 4–1 Pirates win.

Questions were beginning to rise about the viability of major league baseball in Montreal for 1969, as by August 8, three of the principal financial backers of the expansion franchise had backed out of the deal, threatening its future. Giles, in turn, gave the city one more week to come up the $1.2 million that was in arrears to complete the deal. If that sum could not be generated, the National League would instead grant the new franchise to Milwaukee or Buffalo. A couple of days later, the Montreal coalition was saved when the city announced plans to build a temporary new home for the team in a northern part of the city known as Jarry Park. While the cost of renovating the existing stadium in Jarry Park was not revealed, Mayor Drapeau assured Giles and other baseball officials that the finished product would be up to major league standards. The field at the site currently sat about 3,000 patrons, presently being used only for local Little League and high school games. Drapeau stressed to league officials that Jarry Park was only a temporary solution until the planned domed stadium was ready in downtown Montreal in 1972. On August 14, Giles announced that the National League was officially welcoming Montreal into the family. Three weeks later, the franchise would name Gene Mauch as its first field manager, the man who had been fired earlier in the season by the Philadelphia Phillies.

It was off to Atlanta for the Cardinals on August 9, and it was another ho-hum shutout for Gibson, beating Phil Niekro 1–0 in the series opener (in the locker room afterwards, Bob Tolan yelled over to Gibson, "Don't you ever get tired of getting people out?"). The lone run for the Cardinals was scored in typical fashion as well, as in the third inning Brock singled, stole second, and was driven home on a sharp single to right off the bat of Maris, who was able to handle a low knuckleball from Niekro that caught a good portion of the plate. Gibson had now posted "zeroes" for the opposition in 194 of the 217 innings he had pitched on the year. His latest scoreless affair was the 35th of his career for a new Cardinals mark, and he was one behind Mort Cooper's club record of ten shutouts in a single year. The loss was yet another crushing blow to the pennant hopes of the Braves, who fell 16 games back of the first-place Redbirds. In the Atlanta clubhouse, someone used the word "unreal" to describe Gibson. "Change that to 'unbeatable,'" corrected skipper Lum Harris. "It seems that every time Gibson gets a man on base, he's able to reach back and put something extra on every pitch." Gibby needed the win to stay ahead of Briles by one, however, as Nellie logged his fifteenth victory of the season the following day 7–1, surpassing his tremendous run through 1967. In addition to putting the Cardinals to 36 games over the .500 mark at 76–40 — their highest such point of the season — the night saw some particularly interesting offensive moments, as Cepeda hit his first home run in six weeks (and the Cards' first in a fortnight). Aaron, meanwhile, jumped another spot to ninth on the all-time total base list during the game, passing Honus Wagner with 2,889. Edwards also caught Henry trying to steal, however, ending a string of 17 straight successful stolen base attempts for Aaron. The Cardinals' team ERA had dried up further to 2.34, as opposing managers were left wondering about possible ways to beat Schoendienst's club. Heading into the evening, the Cardinals did not even possess a .300 hitter, as Flood fell below the mark. The short road trip would end with the Cards splitting a four-game set with the Cubs in Wrigley Field, with Gibson and Briles being the victors once again — and this time, Gibson beat the other Niekro brother, Joe. The Chicago newspapers— perhaps in a hopeful tone — were hailing the anniversary of Durocher's miracle in 1951, when he led the Giants to the pennant while being twelve and a half games back in mid-August. Since the Cardinals had beaten the Cubs in a series at the end of June, Chicago had climbed from ninth place all the way to second, sporting a record of 31–14 over that stretch. Unfortunately, they had failed to gain anything on St. Louis, as the Cardinals had gone 30–13 in the same number of days. Bill Hands, the man who was solidifying himself as the Cubs' number-two starter behind Jenkins (as Jenkins was leading the National League in strikeouts with 178), was realistic. "Our primary goal is to finish second," he said in mid-August while holding a strong 14–6 record himself after beating Jaster on the 12th. "But if we can get within shooting range in September — well then, you never know." Durocher, meanwhile, was fighting a legal battle on behalf of one of his other pitchers. Reliever Phil Regan — who was enjoying one of the finest years of his career since coming to the Cubs from the Dodgers back on April 23, along with outfielder Jim Hickman — had been targeted by several National League umpires on suspicion of throwing pitches altered with foreign substances. In a game against the Reds on August 18, umpires Shag Crawford and Chris Pelekoudas would claim to find petroleum jelly inside the rim of Regan's cap, the first time all season that the men in blue had decided to enforce the spitball rule. Durocher appealed to Giles to call off the dogs on the pitcher nicknamed "The Vulture," insisting that Regan simply possessed "tremendous natural movement" on his throws. "In my judgment, Mr. Regan is completely vindicated," Leo would assert on August 21, trying to put the matter to rest himself; but Giles would soon agree anyway, overruling the umpires. The problem was not unique to the Regan or the Cubs' staff, for that matter—at least according to *Sports Illustrated*. "Almost 25 percent of major league pitchers are throwing the spitter," the magazine had estimated back in 1967, "while 100 percent of the major league umpires, unable to enforce the rule, look the other way." Regan, meanwhile, acted innocently enough. "I've got four children, and the oldest one—she's eleven—knows what's going on. She reads about it in the newspaper and sees it on TV. Last night I came home, and I saw that it really affected her. She asked her mother if Daddy was cheating."

Schoendienst was most disappointed in the fact that the managers themselves were not self-policing the spitball, as they all had agreed to do in a meeting before the season. As it became more and more apparent that the umpires were not going to enforce the rule (at least, until the Pelekoudas-Regan incident), Schoendienst considered letting the Cardinals staff practice the illegal pitch under Muffett's supervision. At the very least, there were plans for the St. Louis pitchers to experiment with it when the club toured Japan once again after the season was over. Furthermore, the term "spitball" was loose nomenclature for any altering substance that pitchers were secretly applying to the baseball, such as Vaseline, hair tonic, or even melted throat lozenges. "In other words, we wasted spring training by *not* working on the spitball," Schoendienst would say in September, in reference to the lack of oversight officials were giving to the situation. Going beyond the speculation that *Sports Illustrated* had offered, Red estimated that three-fourths of National League pitchers were currently utilizing it, and pointed to the Giants' Gaylord Perry and the Dodgers' Bill Singer—not Regan—as the most culpable examples. "Perry throws a spitter on 19 out of 20 pitches," Schoendienst claimed. "Singer throws quite a few spitballs, but at least he waits until the right time. He throws it when there are runners on base, or when the big hitters are up. He gets the stuff from the back of his neck—pitchers should be barred from going to any part of their heads with their hands."

When Singer read Schoendienst's comments, he smiled in satisfaction. "I'll be happy to teach them—I could use the extra money," he told a Los Angeles writer.

Jarvis had salvaged the last game for the Braves against Carlton on August 11, as the Cardinal lefthander had been the lone relative disappointment in recent weeks. Carlton, the All-Star, would go only 4–7 in his last eleven decisions by the following week after starting the year 7–1. As Carlyle Pat was grabbing a win for the Braves, Atlanta was making big news off the field that day. Club president William Bartholomay announced that they had signed legendary pitcher Satchel Paige to a contract. Paige was estimated to be approximately 62 years old at the time, but poor record-keeping had kept his true age a mystery. The signing was more of a gesture of respect to Paige than anything substantial, as he needed 158 days to qualify for the Major League pension plan. Ultimately, Paige would even not appear in a contest for Atlanta, but would be officially named a coach before the end of the season, with plans for him to be on the Braves' bench in 1969 to achieve the necessary service time.

The Cardinals had held serve on the week-long trip by going 4–3, which spelled doom for the chasers, for if the Redbirds played only .500 ball for the rest of the way, it would be nearly impossible for them to be caught by any of the pursuers. Shannon perpetuated his offensive climb, his average lifting to .285 combined with a club-leading 68 RBIs, which were nine behind McCovey's league lead. The standings the evening of August 15 looked as follows, after Briles (16–7) shut out the Cubs at Wrigley 8–0 that afternoon as the Redbirds headed home to face the Braves once again:

	W	L	Pct.	GB
St. Louis	78	43	.645	—
Chicago	64	57	.529	14
San Francisco	62	57	.521	15
Cincinnati	59	56	.513	16
Atlanta	61	59	.508	16.5
Pittsburgh	57	63	.475	20.5
Philadelphia	55	63	.466	21.5
New York	56	66	.454	22.5
Los Angeles	53	66	.445	24
Houston	53	68	.438	25

The left field Bleacher Bums at Wrigley Field — the zealots who relentlessly harassed the opposing team's outfielders, drank more than their share of Old Style beer, and sometimes even paid attention to the game — were in their typical form during the Cardinals series, which means they turned it up a notch — and even resorted to hurling missiles at the Redbird flychasers — especially their favorite target in Brock. "They were hitting us with everything," Flood said after the first contest in the series. "Ice cubes, burned-out flashbulbs, fruit, tennis balls, paper cups, and old sandwiches." While Brock and Flood were the main objectives, even the right field stands had gotten into the fray, hitting Ron Davis with a flashlight battery in the back of the neck. Flood retaliated by showing up the next day with a large banner he had painted with his skilled brush, which read "WE'RE STILL # 1." He had tried to tape the sign to Brock's back, but it kept blowing away; so instead, he simply spread it out on the grass in left-center field in full view of the Bums.

Before the game, Gibson — in doing the customary pre-game running that pitchers do — jogged past the Bums while wearing a copy of the same message on a small button that was pinned to the bill of his cap. It was a frank reminder of the standings which, at the end of the day, could not be changed with all the debris the fans in the bleachers would choose to throw. "We broke even with them for the season," Durocher said in self-consolation. "A 9–9 record against a club leading by 14 games isn't bad at all."

Fans in Detroit, meanwhile — where Medwick had received the most famous pelting of objects during the 1934 World Series — were nearly oblivious to Gibson's accomplishments. Their own main man, McLain, had posted a 16–0 record on the road in 1968 when he shut out the Red Sox 4–0 in Fenway Park on August 16 ("I hate Tiger Stadium," he said plainly on August 13. "I want to take advantage of all the other parks. A lot of drives that would be homers in Detroit are outs in other stadiums"). McLain, now a startling 25–3 overall on the year, had beaten Lonborg in the match up for which American League fans had waited all year. Lonborg would never regain his 1967 magic after his off-season skiing accident, as his loss to McLain put his 1968 mark at a nondescript 3–4. "Naturally, I'm thinking about winning 30 games," McLain noted. "It's been on my mind since winning number fifteen, but I'm not losing any sleep over it." But pondering the idea further, he added, "I've got to think about next year, so I don't want to throw my arm out in one season." He was referring to the slight muscle tear that had developed in his pitching shoulder. Nonetheless, McLain said that he was able to control the pain by use of aspirin and pre-game rubdowns. He would, however, lose his next start against the White Sox at Tiger Stadium — resulting from what many felt were his outlandish off-the-field antics. An aspiring keyboard player, McLain had been tooting along with a local band until 4:30 in the morning, and arrived at the ballpark in horrible condition to pitch a baseball game on the humid night in Detroit.

Even with the setback, Tigers second baseman Dick McAuliffe would come to the spiritual rescue the following night. After being hit by Chicago pitcher Tommy John, McAuliffe exchanged words with the hurler as he was walking down to first base. He then sprinted toward the mound and tackled John as the benches cleared, with John screaming in pain as he landed on his pitching shoulder that was laboring with torn ligaments. Les Moss, the interim manager of the White Sox after Eddie Stanky was fired at mid-season, did not appreciate the approach of the Detroit ball club. "If the Tigers are all wound up as tight as that guy [McAuliffe], they're in trouble. That's a joke to charge the mound on a 3–2 pitch to a batter leading off an inning — who's going to throw at the leadoff man?" Seven years later — after a variety of treatments for a variety of ailments in the arm — John would become one of the first pitchers to submit to an experimental type of surgery to permanently fix his problems, in which tendons were taken from his right forearm and transplanted into his left arm as a means of "tightening" the tendons he used in his pitching delivery.

The brashness displayed by the Detroit men had manifested itself in the team's own song, "Sock It to 'Em, Tigers," which, while not a predecessor to the Chicago Bears' "Super Bowl Shuffle" in 1985, was nonetheless much akin to the Cardinals' "El Birdos" album that had been released around the St. Louis area months before.

Gibson's winning streak reached fourteen against the Cubs in front of a Ladies' Day crowd of 33,000 at Wrigley Field on August 14. It then lengthened further to fifteen on August 19 versus the Phillies in Philadelphia, as Washburn had also won his eleventh the evening before against Atlanta, courtesy of a nine-run first inning by the Cardinals against Braves starter Ron Reed that came via seven singles and a lone extra-base hit — a double — by Ron Davis. Before his victory over the Phillies, Gibson had told McCarver that he was not feeling well, but he still managed to hold them to no runs, a 2–0 score, as he tied Cooper's Cardinals record for the most shutouts in a season with ten. He struck out the Philadelphia slugger Dick Allen four times in four at-bats, and was now four consecutive wins away from the major league record of 19, set by Rube Marquard of the Giants in 1912. Russo noted that Gibson's ERA during his win streak was 0.47, while his overall mark for the season was under a run per game at 0.997. "It doesn't matter if Gibson is feeling well or not feeling well," Bill White, the Phillie first baseman and Hoot's former teammate, concluded. "He's not going to be sick if he has to face someone like Juan Marichal, but a lot of pitchers would be." It was his old buddy White who had caused Gibson's only road loss of the year, a tenth-inning hit that plated the only run of the game in a contest in Philly back on May 17.

Among the superlative success of Gibson and the relative success of the remainder of the pitching staff, Dick Hughes had become a "forgotten man," in the words of Russo. His valiant 1967 campaign a distant memory, Hughes' battle with arm troubles caused him to miss much of the Cards' encore ride they were enjoying in 1968. "For a while," Russo wrote in the *Post-Dispatch*, "it looked as if Dick Hughes would wind up with more children than victories this season," pointing to his wife recently having given birth to their second child. But Schoendienst handed him the ball in the last game in Philadelphia on August 21, and the bespectacled hurler finally found his old stuff. He relieved an ineffective Carlton in the fourth inning in saving Lefty from another loss, went five strong frames (including a string of setting down 13 in a row) as his batters overcame a 3–1 deficit, and then handed to the horsehide to Hoerner for the last batter of the game — a strikeout of White — as Hughes gained his second victory of the year in what turned into an 8–3 laugher. Dick had not even pitched at all in ten days, but his apparent healing was important to Schoendienst, giving Red another option for his post-season bag of tricks from the pitching staff. Hughes, in fact, was becoming even more appealing than the struggling Carlton or Jaster, as the latter left-hander dropped his record to 8–10 in losing the series finale to the Phils the following evening.

Back home on August 23, the Cardinals took two out of three from the Pirates. In this series, however, the tables were finally turned on Gibson. On a rare occasion in 1968, he lost the only game of the series for the Cardinals, ending his winning streak at fifteen games (with all fifteen being complete games, including ten shutouts—and comprising nearly three months of the calendar). He was topped in the middle contest by rookie Bob Moose and a host of Pirates relievers in taking a 6–4 loss. Moose had literally just arrived to the Pirates. Serving his country in the Marine Corps Reserves, he had flown separately from the team, on a flight which got into St. Louis in the early hours of Saturday as he scrambled to get to the team's hotel and get a few hours of rest before pitching (Moose had been sent to Camp Lejeune in North Carolina for two weeks of special training duty before coming to St. Louis). The Cardinals' ace took the defeat despite the fact that half of the Pirates' runs were unearned on account of errors by Maxvill (his twentieth of the season) and Cepeda (his fifteenth). Gibson still managed to strike out fifteen Pittsburgh hitters on the 92-degree Saturday afternoon at Busch, which was two shy of the club record that Dean had posted against the Cubs in 1933. Maxvill's boot started the Pirates' rally in the ninth after Stargell—who was wearing glasses in a game for just the second time in his career, in part to atone for the blurred vision he suffered in his collision with the wall in Forbes Field—doubled to lead off the inning. Gibson was beginning to tire, as it was the only inning in which he was unable to post a strikeout on the day. Pittsburgh pushed across two runs to break a four-all tie, as Stargell had busted into Gibson's shutout and four-run lead in the seventh with a three-run slicing shot, just barely getting over the wall in left field. Gibson was, however, also able to secure his first stolen base of the season on the offensive side, while Brock recorded his 37th. Both men, however, still trailed Wills of the Pirates for the league lead in that category. For while the Cardinals shut down Maury's running game in the series, he still topped the circuit with 41 swipes. And even with the fielding mishaps, Gibson's ERA "rose" from 0.99 to 1.07 on the day. Hoerner assured a St. Louis advantage in the series the following afternoon on Sunday, gaining his eleventh save (coupled with six wins—well on to his goal of 20 and eight respectively) to secure Briles' seventeenth triumph 4–2, keeping the Cardinals 35 games over the .500 mark with a record of 83–48.

On August 26—for only the fifth time in history—a record-tying seven shutouts were thrown in the major leagues on a single day, which accounted for almost half of the 16 games played on the date. One could argue that the biggest shut out that day, however, occurred in Chicago. The White Sox were in the process of losing their final game in Milwaukee 3–0 to Earl Wilson and the Tigers, while the Cubs were on the West Coast being blanked by Gaylord Perry and the Giants, 3–0. But in fact, the "Chicago shutout" that day had nothing to do with baseball — but rather, with a collection of people who attempted unsuccessfully to storm an important meeting being held in the Windy City.

That date saw a swarm of many types of people descending on Chicago for opening of the Democratic National Convention, a meeting that was to last four days but that would, in the end, seem much longer with the trouble that ensued. It was 104 years to the day after the same organization had met in Chicago once before, as George McClellan was nominated by the Democrats to attempt to unseat incumbent Republican president Abraham Lincoln in 1864. The 1968 meeting was originally thought to be a celebration for the nomination of Robert F. Kennedy; but with his assassination in June, an extra element of uncertainty was thrown into the upcoming days. A group which called itself the National Mobilization Committee to End the War in Vietnam, organized by a man named David Dellinger, had been calling on people from coast to coast to join a bus trip from New York to Chicago for a mass protest. While the group had been readying itself for the event for months, some speculated that it had received extra inspiration by the violent events unfolding in Czechoslovakia, where on August 20, nearly a quarter-million Soviet and other Warsaw Pact troops had invaded the country with the assistance of 5,000 tanks, in an effort to quell a year-long series of demonstrations for liberation by Czech citizens that came to be known as the Prague Spring. The cost of a round-trip bus ticket from New York to Chicago was $34; if a person could not go, he was encouraged to send the $34 to the organization for another rider to take the person's place. Rumors had been swirling for months about Chicago's inability to keep order during the event, and some within the Democratic Party had suggested that the convention be moved to another city. But Chicago mayor Richard J. Daley refused to allow this to happen, guaranteeing security for attendees. The convention began with welcoming remarks from Daley at the microphone of the International Amphitheatre, as he announced in no uncertain terms that "as long as I am mayor of this city, there's going to be law and order in Chicago." The first major clash between police and demonstrators did not occur until the second-to-last day of the convention on the 28th, as a march commenced from Grant Park to the Conrad-Hilton Hotel (the headquarters for the convention), and to the actual site of the convention at the Amphitheatre, six miles from the hotel. The march was organized even though Daley had expressly forbidden the authorization of any permits for such an action. Hubert Humphrey won the nomination, gaining three times as many votes as the runner-up, McCarthy, according to an unofficial count by the *New York Times*. Original reports also claimed that Humphrey had selected Maine senator Edmund S. Muskie as his choice for his running mate, although the Humphrey camp refused to confirm this announcement. McCarthy had used a fierce anti-war stance as his platform, while Humphrey wished to see the outcomes of the on-going peace talks in Paris before assuming a position on the conflict in Vietnam. President Johnson, meanwhile, was not in attendance at the convention, but was safely tucked away from the protests at his home in Texas, celebrating his 60th birthday on the 27th.

By nightfall of the 27th, the demonstrations started appearing outside the Amphitheatre as draft cards were burned and waved in the air until five in the morning the next day. One of the organizers of the rally, Tom Hayden, suggested that the crowd get some rest by sleeping in nearby Grant Park. Hayden was counting on security to be provided by the handful of convention delegates who had come down from the Hilton to join in the protest. Other guests of the hotel watched from their windows, as little sleep was to be had by anyone with the on-going activity in the park, which was still continuing as the sun was coming up. Some of these delegates—particularly, groups from New York, California, and South Dakota—had actually disrupted portions of the convention proceedings by intermingling their own chants with the words of the various speakers on the platform.

At one point in the evening of the 28th, some of the tear gas used by the Chicago Police Department to disperse the protestors had wafted into the convention hall, causing alarm for the attendees. When Senator Abraham Ribicoff of Connecticut took the microphone, he angered Daley by referring to the alleged "Gestapo tactics in the streets of Chicago." In comparison to the recent conflict in Prague, some were trying to pronounce the city's name as "Czechcago." Soon, many skirmishes were breaking out all over the downtown area, the bloodiest of which occurred at the intersection of Michigan and Balbo where the police charged a line of demonstrators after bottles were hurled at the officers. Nearly 12,000 policemen were on duty over the four days, in addition to 7,500 troops from the U.S. Army, 7,500 troops from the Illinois National Guard (including Cubs pitcher Ken Holtzman), and 1,000 Secret Service agents. The National Guard had set up its base of operations at Soldier Field. With the Bears of the NFL still playing at Wrigley Field at this time (and not moving into Soldier Field until 1971, with the exception of a few exhibition games being played there), the massive lakefront stadium was not only available and large enough to assemble the contingent, but was also a point of interception on the next route the protesters were expected to take.

As the dark of night fell on the 28th, anger had boiled over into a full-fledged fight. When the crowd was ordered to disperse, they did not. And when the mob grew unruly and began threatening the peacekeepers, force was employed simultaneously with honest discernment towards lawbreakers, as well as frolicking randomness towards innocents. "Police and guardsmen used their weapons indiscriminately," wrote James Millstone in a more accusatory tone, covering the scene for the *Post-Dispatch*, "attacking men and women of all ages and sizes and from all walks of life ... police clubbed persons whose only desire was to flee but who could not move quickly enough because of crowds pressing at their backs. National guardsmen released their tear gas at point blank range." Millstone also noted that the legions of media people from around the world — originally on hand to cover the political proceedings of the convention — had captured the chaos occurring in downtown Chicago with their own cameras and pens. "Television lights and police spotlights threw an eerie glare on the scene," he continued, "making it look more unreal than it seemed." Ultimately, a gang of young protesters overtook the fifteenth floor of the Hilton, and used the open room windows as parapets for launching bottle attacks onto the officers below on Michigan Avenue. Authorities were able to locate the origin of the missiles, and did a room-by-room clearing of the floor. They found approximately 50 young people hanging about the hallway, none of whom could authenticate themselves as hotel guests, and they were moved into elevators and ordered to leave the building.

While the convention proceedings strained to continue amidst the confrontation outside in the surrounding blocks, Humphrey was emerging as a clear winner for the nomination — particularly after Senator Edward Kennedy of Massachusetts, the brother of the slain former president and presidential hopeful — declined any interest in the position. By the convention's end, Humphrey's distance from McCarthy was close to 500 delegate votes with a total of 1,761¾ on the first ballot, well beyond the 1,312 he needed for the nomination. Muskie, as expected, was chosen as his running mate. As Humphrey addressed the convention in its final moments, he looked ahead to inauguration day. "No one knows what the situation in Vietnam will be on January 20, 1969," he began. "Every heart in America prays that, by then, we shall have reached a cease-fire in all of Vietnam, and be in serious negotiation toward a durable peace." When Humphrey thanked Johnson for his accomplishments, the statement was greeted with a combination of cheers and derision for the sitting president.

By the end of the convention, nearly 600 arrests had been made, while 119 police officers and 100 demonstrators had been injured. The Cubs were returning home from the West Coast to play the Astros in a series at Wrigley Field, and as the Houston players gazed out their bus windows during the ride from O'Hare Airport to their hotel in downtown Chicago, they were aghast at the debris that had been littered about the city in the previous days' events.

Ultimately, eight men — soon reduced to seven — were brought on trial on conspiracy charges in connection with the uprising; they were soon to become known as the Chicago Seven. They were convicted on February 18, 1970, of violating the Civil Rights Act of 1968 (in crossing state lines for the purpose of inciting a riot), but later had their convictions overturned in an appellate court.

Three hundred miles to the south during the tumultuous days in Chicago, the Cardinals were receiving a dose of their own medicine as August came to a close, with the Mets shutting them out twice in a row in Busch Stadium. Carlton, with his 11–9 record, was acquiring losses that were not entirely his fault. And most recently, he lost 1–0 on the 26th to McAndrew of the Mets, who had been 0–5 entering the contest despite an ERA in the low 2.00s. The next night it was the fireballing Dick Selma who dropped Jaster to 8–11 on the season with a 4–0 whitewashing. Jaster was not able to escape a three-run fourth inning, as an impatient Schoendienst announced after the game that Hughes— now apparently healthy — would take Jaster's spot in the starting rotation at least for the near future. Russo joked in his column about the irony of the 2,200 St. Louis firemen in attendance at the second game. "They didn't have to worry about being called for emergency duty," he assured. "The Cardinals have been so cold at the plate that they couldn't create a spark if they rubbed two bats together." The brief two-game series marked the first time in the Mets' seven-year history that they had held their opponent scoreless throughout an entire set of games in one ballpark. The back-to-back shutouts had put the Cardinals' record for August at a surprising 13–14 after going 46–14 in the preceding two months. To make matters worse, when the Cardinals arrived at their hotel in Pittsburgh at 3:30 in the morning after flying out of St. Louis when the series with the Mets had completed, they found the elevators not working, so they lounged impatiently in the lobby. Schoendienst decided that he desperately needed a shave, so he went into the bathroom off the lobby to do so (in his sleepy state, the razor slipped and he cut his nose). But as usual, the main man stepped to the fore to correct the faltering situation. Gibson (19–6) broke Cooper's team record with his eleventh shutout of the season on the first night in the Steel City, and even broke the Cardinals' 23-inning scoreless string himself with an RBI single in the fourth inning in beating Bob Veale 8–0. Maxvill remarked afterwards that it almost seemed like a "day off" when Hoot pitched, even though he and keystone mate Javier had to field a horde of ground balls. Flood agreed, in thinking that Gibson was most effective when Flood noticed that he was not receiving any fly ball outs. In actuality, however, Gibson believed he had been allowing more balls in the air lately, as he admittedly went to his four-seam (or "rising") fastball into the hotter summer months.

The smoke and dust of the mayhem in Chicago was beginning to settle as the conventioneers, protesters, and National Guardsmen left town, but the wonders of 1968 would never cease. Stability was becoming more rare in most segments of society, as only disorder seemed to reign. Even the business of baseball remained embroiled in the seemingly-endless feud between the Establishment and the New Generation, as Marvin Miller gained nearly unanimous approval from the players association to demand a revised pension plan from the owners before the end of the season. The lone steadiness in American life remained in the National League standings, as the Cardinals—despite their mediocre display during the month—finished August with their lead only slightly shrunken since July, while the Tigers were feeling a warming pursuit from Baltimore and their new manager, Weaver, whom they now led by only six games.

	W	L	Pct.	GB
St. Louis	86	51	.628	—
San Francisco	73	62	.541	12
Cincinnati	71	62	.534	13
Chicago	71	67	.514	15.5
Atlanta	68	69	.496	18
Pittsburgh	65	71	.478	20.5
Houston	64	73	.467	22
Philadelphia	62	73	.459	23
New York	63	76	.453	24
Los Angeles	58	77	.430	27

The Tigers acquired Pirates reliever Elroy Face on the 31st for cash, just moments after he had pitched in an 8–0 win by Pittsburgh over Atlanta. The 802nd appearance tied Walter Johnson's record for the most games pitched in one league, a record which the Pirates—out respect for the fifteen-year veteran of their club—wanted to make sure Face attained before cutting him loose. Both Face and Eddie Mathews, however—the home-run slugging third baseman who was also in his final season, and whom the Tigers had signed in 1967—were thought to be activated too late in the year to join Detroit's World Series roster if the team reached the postseason. Decisions would be needed on others currently on the Tigers' roster if the veterans were to participate in the postseason.

Face joined a Tigers pitching staff whose best record for the month of August belonged to Lolich—not McLain—as the motorcycle-riding left-hander went 6–1 in helping Detroit keep a buffer zone from pursuers. "I play the drums a little," Lolich responded when asked about the colorfulness of his own off-field pursuits in comparison to McLain's—which paled, of course, as McLain (who posted win number 27 on September 1, a game in which he started a triple play) was still playing the organ at local clubs as often as three nights per week.

"But I don't expect any offers from record companies," Lolich said in his humble style.

11. Staying Focused

I always turn to the sports section of the newspaper first. The sports page records people's accomplishments; the front page has nothing but man's failures.
— U.S. Supreme Court chief justice Earl Warren

The eastern swing continued through New York and on to Cincinnati, as at Shea Stadium, Seaver held a perfect game into the eighth inning against the Cards until Cepeda broke it up with a double. It did not prevent Seaver from gaining an ultimate 8–2 win, although Carlton exacted revenge against McAndrew in getting his own shutout five days after the Mets rookie had blanked him, beating New York 2–0 for Lefty's first win in over four weeks. And as Schoendienst had promised, Hughes took the spot of Jaster in the rotation the following night, his first starting assignment in nearly three months. But ironically it was Jaster who picked up his ninth win with two innings of perfect relief after Hughes had pitched six frames of one-run ball.

In Cincinnati, Crosley Field still stood as the home of the Reds on the near west side of town. It was the first major league park to be set electrically ablaze with night baseball in 1935, as Reds owner Powel Crosley proclaimed that a person could read a newspaper in the middle of the night from six blocks away with the glow of the huge frosted moons that hung over the park. From Western Hills to the Kentucky side of the Ohio River and all parts in between in Cincinnati, bright lights of Crosley Field signaled a new age coming to Major League Baseball. Now, the stadium was in its waning days, going the same way as Sportsman's Park in St. Louis as it deferred to a new, multipurpose, circular downtown stadium to open in two years. But for now, the Crosley faithful was privy to the continuance of the artistry set forth in the summer of 1968 by Bob Gibson, as he and the injury-plagued prodigy Gary Nolan of the Reds locked horns in a scoreless tie into the tenth inning on

Labor Day, September 2. Nolan would tire before the Cardinals ace, giving way to veteran reliever Ted Abernathy in the tenth. The initial batter Abernathy faced was Javier, and Hoolie knocked the first pitch he saw over the wall in left, his third homer of the year. It was a rare feat for the second baseman, as he was still hitting considerably better against lefthanders (.364) for the season than against right-handers (.205), of which Abernathy was the latter (the most consistent hitter against both types was Flood, having averages of .305 and .291 against lefties and righties respectively). In the bottom half, Gibson left runners stranded at first and second with two outs as he got pinch hitter Fred Whitfield to fly to Brock in left to end the game, preserving yet another shutout and his twentieth win, 1–0. He joined a select group of Dean, Haines, and Cooper who had posted three twenty-win seasons in a Cardinals uniform. It was also the twenty-seventh scoreless game produced by the St. Louis pitching staff on the year, a new record that surpassed the old team mark set in 1944.

Gibson's ERA had dipped to 0.99 once again, as he raced around the corner of the holiday weekend to the season's home stretch, with people now *really* talking about some serious pitching records falling to his feet.

After splitting the next two contests in Cincinnati, the Cards enjoyed their first open spot on the calendar in 57 days on Thursday, September 5, having played every day since the end of the All-Star break. In that time, they had played 58 games, going 36–22 and lengthening their league lead from ten to thirteen games. Flood spent the free time by finishing his painting of a portrait of the slain Martin Luther King, which he presented to King's grateful widow, Coretta. "Thank you very much for the painting you did of my husband," Mrs. King wrote in a warm-hearted note of gratitude. "My children and I are quite pleased with it, and I intend to hang it in a prominent place in my home as soon as the present remodeling is finished." Other Cardinals players relaxed with a game of golf, while others simply caught up on their sleep. Bristol, the manager of the Reds, did not notice any fatigue among the St. Louis men anyway. "They have momentum going, and when you're going well, you can't wait to come out for the next game." Added Bristol's best player, Pete Rose, "There isn't another team that could go through a tough schedule the way they did, because they can take any player out of their lineup and replace him with a good man."

But the Cards gladly accepted the rest, and headed back to Busch Stadium for a homestand against the Giants and Dodgers, a week in which they could mathematically clinch the National League pennant. Joining them for the games in the ballpark under the arch was their 19-year-old prized catcher-of-the-future, young Ted Simmons, with one year's experience from the University of Michigan and who had been the top hitter in the California League at Modesto with his .329 average, to go along with 27 home runs and 114 RBIs.

Neither Schoendienst nor Devine knew exactly where Simmons would fit into their plans for the remaining month of the regular-season schedule, but they both wanted the rookie to get acclimated to major league life and the handling of a pitching staff at the game's highest level. He had been the club's first-round pick in 1967, the tenth overall selection in the draft. In returning to their home park, the Cardinals not only discovered Simmons there upon arrival, but also a throng of new stadium office workers who were taking postseason ticket orders. Commissioner Eckert had given both the Cardinals and the Tigers permission to start selling World Series seats, with prices the same in both ballparks and not having changed from the 1967 rates: $12 for a box seat, $8 for a grandstand reserved seat, $6 for a pavilion reserved seat (in Detroit), $4 for standing room, and $2 for a spot in the bleachers. While fans were grateful with the news of the stable ticket prices, they were disappointed to learn that the parking lots surrounding Tiger Stadium in Detroit were going to raise their rates during World Series dates.

As American League regular-season play continued there, McLain became the winningest pitcher in the league in 24 years in posting his 28th victory of the year against the Twins, despite allowing the first home run in the career of Graig Nettles. Nettles, just called up from the Twins' farm team in Denver, would go on to hit three more in the following three days against the Tigers. A promising left-handed slugger, he had been leading the Pacific Coast League in home runs at the time of his promotion. An injury to Minnesota star Tony Oliva had opened a roster spot for the 24-year-old, even though Nettles was not sure that he was ready for the big leagues. "I knew I needed this year in the minors," he said. "After all, I hit only .230 in the Southern League last year. I needed more seasoning."

Perhaps the open date threw off their timing, but the Cardinals laid an egg in their return home, dropping a doubleheader to the Giants on the 6th while McLain was putting himself two wins away from the magical mark of 30. The Giants were proving themselves to be a much better club on the road than at home, sporting a 42–30 mark in traveling (the same record the Cardinals held at home) while being barely over the .500 mark at Candlestick Park. The games were mostly inconsequential to the standings at this point, but the St. Louis team nonetheless made Schoendienst furious at their inept play. The Cardinals' infield booted three balls on the afternoon that allowed three runs, including the deciding tally in Gibson's 3–2 loss in the opener. Once again, Marichal shied away from going head-to-head with Gibson, as he instead opted to pitch the second game. Furthermore, Broeg pointed out that Marichal had suspiciously faced Koufax only four times in his career, suggesting that Marichal made an effort to avoid the great Dodgers lefthander as well. As it turned out, the surprising Bobby Bolin outdueled Gibson in getting the first win, while Marichal won an 8–7 decision over Carlton in the later game as Frank Linzy rescued the Dominican from a three-run Cardinals barrage in the bottom of the eighth. Several miscues hurt the Cardinals on the day. One of Gibson's runs was also produced by a Jim Ray Hart single, a one-hop throw by McCarver on Hart's steal of second, and Gibson's wild pitch that sent him to third before a routine grounder to Javier sent him home. The double loss for the Cards kept their magic number for clinching the pennant stuck at nine, and inched Gibby's ERA back up to 1.03. When one of the reporters suggested to Schoendienst that the field had been roughened up by the football Cardinals' exhibition game against the Chicago Bears from the night before, Red would have none of it. His anger was mostly directed at Maxvill, who booted a key ball in the opening loss, and who caused two more unearned runs the following day. "Don't give me that stuff," the old German snarled back. "It's going to get rougher — and I didn't see how it was rough for Hal Lanier [the Giants' shortstop — although ironically (and escaping Red's notice) in the second game, Willie Mays committed two errors in one contest, the first time that had happened in his 17-year career]. If I wasn't with this club — if I was just sitting in the stands— I'd be sick. The way we played, it would make anybody sick." The Cardinals had always described Schoendienst as a "players' manager"— but not meant in the 21st-century, undisciplined meaning of the term, as many modern managers are described that exhibit little or no control over their players; rather, he let his players play, but he also got on their backs when necessary. As in the case of Vince Lombardi, as described by his former guard Jerry Kramer, "He knew when you needed a pat on the back, or a kick in the behind — and he could do both equally well." Washburn got beaten the following evening by Perry, as it was now impossible for the Cardinals to clinch the flag on their current stay in Busch Stadium. Only a run in the bottom of the eleventh inning of the final contest saved the Cards from a four-game sweep, scored by Maxvill courtesy of a Gagliano single after an hour-and-a-half rain delay had halted play. Next, the Dodgers took two out of three, and it was looking like there were cracks in the Redbirds' armor as they had gone only an even 21–21 in their last 42 trips to the field. Gibson's 21st win on the homestand's final day was all that kept the Cards from a Dodgers sweep. Customarily, he threw all nine innings that day, and nine innings was his *average* for his 31 starts to date on the year. "Naturally, there is going to be a letdown," McCarver reassured fans about the team's recent swoon. "You have to build up some false situation in your mind — tell yourself you're only a game ahead, for instance." But in reality, all knew it was just a matter of time; and like Ulysses S. Grant sitting on the outskirts of Vicksburg, Petersburg, or Richmond, the opponents knew that the siege would end soon.

Flood got three hits on the first afternoon against the Giants, while the same day out in California, a man named Andy Messersmith shut out the

Red Sox 4–0 in his first major league start. Several years later, Messersmith and Flood would be mentioned in the same breath in an on-going labor issue that would impact the game forever, despite the fact that the two men would never meet.

While the Cardinals were fumbling around with the Dodgers at home, McLain got victory number 29 in promptly handing Messersmith his first major league *loss* on September 10. The star pitcher smacked a triple to the center field wall to lead off the third inning—Messersmith's last inning of work on the day—as part of the Tigers' offensive attack. The stage was now set for history to be made, as a national television audience would see him go for his 30th win against the A's on the following Saturday, the 14th. Like the fortunate patrons in the stands at Tiger Stadium, those watching on TV at home were treated to one of the best-played baseball games of the year, in addition to the dramatic underpinnings set forth by the Detroit pitcher. Two home runs by the powerful young Reggie Jackson had given Oakland the lead twice, as the 22-year-old was just finishing up his first full season in the major leagues. After Jackson threw a Tigers runner out at the plate, he struck a second time in the top of the sixth with another bomb off his bat to give the A's a 4–3 advantage. The score stood until the bottom of the ninth, as the Tigers put their final chance to work. Kaline was sent in to pinch-hit for McLain, as he walked and was subsequently driven to third by a Mickey Stanley single. When Jim Northrup grounded a ball down to Danny Cater at first, Cater threw wildly home, allowing Kaline to score as Stanley was able to make his way to third. Next up was hometown hero Willie Horton, who drifted a ball over the drawn-in outfield for a hit to give McLain his magical 30th, 5–4. McLain leaped while still inside the dugout when the winning run was scored, and vaulted himself so high that he banged his head on the roof. Recovering, he emerged up the steps arm in arm with Kaline with his cap off, a towel around his neck, and hollering the cry of triumph. With the game over for several minutes, the fans that remained in Tiger Stadium began yelling, "We want Denny! We want Denny!" The pitcher obliged them by appearing from the dugout and giving a wave. The Tigers' shortstop Oyler had asked McLain at the All-Star Break if McLain could win 30 games. "Book it," McLain had said.

Among those in attendance was the majors' last thirty-game winner, Dizzy Dean, who noted the remarkable similarities between the two men. Both wore uniform number 17; both were 24 years old when they performed the thirty-win feat; and both possessed an outpouring of confidence about their craft, which manifested itself in colorful comments for the media men— of which Dean had been one, recently working baseball telecasts for NBC. But on this date, he was just a spectator. Dean had driven from his home in Wiggins, Mississippi—1,000 miles away—to share the event with McLain.

Dean quickly stepped onto the field as soon as the game was over and grabbed McLain's hand. Dean was asked by others on the field who he thought was going to win the probable World Series matchup between the Cardinals and the Tigers—a rematch of Dean's greatest moment in 1934. "I think the 1934 World Series Tigers were a better club," Dean began in his country drawl, "but this club has hustle and they're hungry. If Gibson and McLain pitch the opener, whichever club wins it will take the series."

The team from the Motor City felt it held destiny's favor every bit as much as the Cardinals in 1968. "It seemed like he pitched every day, and won every day," teammate Dick Tracewski said in looking back on McLain's magnificent season.

September 14 was the Tigers' turn in the national spotlight, courtesy of their premier pitcher, and the Cardinals had theirs the following two days. While McLain was capturing the nation's attention, Briles (18–10) had spun an 8–0 shutout of Houston in the Astrodome, paring the magic number down to two. Then, on the 15th, the champagne corks were launched once again for the defending champions. Word came around that the Reds had defeated the Giants 4–0 in San Francisco—meaning that the 7–4 beating that the Cardinals had laid on the Astros had given the Redbirds their second-straight National League pennant, and third in five years. The main benefactor was Carlton, a man desperately in need of a contribution after a rocky second half of the season. Carlton withstood eleven Houston hits to gain the complete-game win, but it was the St. Louis offense that truly carried the day. Flood had five hits in as many trips to the plate with two runs scored, while Brock scored twice himself in logging three safeties, as well as his 55th stolen base of the year in overtaking the league lead from Wills. Cepeda also chipped in with a clutch bases-loaded single. The true man of the hour, however, was Maris. In the third inning after Flood had singled with one out, Roger drove his 275th career home run into the distant right field seats of the Astrodome off Don Wilson. It would be the final regular-season home run in the career of the star from the Great Plains, born just a few weeks before Dean and the Gas House Gang had taken on the Tigers in their first World Series matchup in 1934.

As the Cardinals were waiting in the clubhouse for word on the final score of the Giants-Reds game, they passed the time nervously in any way they could. Many were munching on the spread of fried chicken and baked beans that had been assembled for them; Shannon worked on a crossword puzzle; Edwards, Hoerner, and a few others were playing cards. When the final was read aloud, Edwards flipped over the card table, grabbed the closest bottle of champagne he could find, and toasted the work of his former teammates in Cincinnati from afar. A special platform was set up inside the locker room by St. Louis television stations to interview players on the scene for the folks back home — and when Caray or Buck attempted to bring a new man to the microphone, the subject was awash with bubbly and assaulted with laughter all over again. Undershirts were torn to shreds, as the scene was mostly reduced to a schoolyard game of tag football in the playful celebration. Broeg took part in the euphoria as well, and in all his years of covering the Redbirds, he figured this was the team most assured of overall victory. "Not since the 1931 world champions took the lead the first Saturday of the season and held it throughout," he wrote, "has there been a St. Louis ball club, in this opinion, that was in such complete command of its own destiny."

In clinching the flag on September 15, the Cardinals had not relinquished first place since their doubleheader win at New York on June 2, when Gibson started his win streak in the opener that day. With an open date to enjoy the accomplishment on the 16th, the St. Louis men saw themselves at the top with no more threats:

	W	L	Pct.	GB
St. Louis	86	51	.628	—
San Francisco	73	62	.541	12
Cincinnati	71	62	.534	13
Chicago	71	67	.514	15.5
Atlanta	68	69	.496	18
Pittsburgh	65	71	.478	20.5
Houston	64	73	.467	22
Philadelphia	62	73	.459	23
New York	63	76	.453	24
Los Angeles	58	77	.430	27

With the National League pennant sewn up and the American title soon to follow, a series of oddities, milestones, and astounding achievements would subsequently mark major league baseball in the following week.

Outside of the relatively-unknown commodity of the Tigers in the American League, there appeared to be little that would check the Cardinals in pursuit of their second-straight world championship. Suddenly, however, an unthinkable calamity was revealed that threatened the very occurrence of the World Series — the possibility of an umpires strike. While the Cardinals were relaxing on their travel day from Houston to San Francisco on the 16th, American League president Joe Cronin abruptly fired veteran umpires Bill Valentine and Al Salerno, who respectively had eight and seven years of service in the big leagues, for "activities related to starting an umpires' union." Infuriated by the action, umpires from both leagues threatened a work stoppage immediately. After cooler heads prevailed, however, they agreed to continue working through the regular season and the postseason of 1968. They also, however, formed the Association of Major League Umpires—against the direct orders of Cronin — and assured baseball's executives that they would not take the field in 1969 unless Valentine and Salerno were reinstated. "We will even appeal to Commissioner Eckert," Salerno announced of their plight. "Not for ourselves, but for our brothers in blue. There is going to be an umpires union in the American League, despite our dismissal. It's now time for the umpires in our league to stand up and be counted." Salerno also noted that National League umpires had been organized for several years, and on average made $4,000 more than American Leaguers. Thus, the voice of protest — which had rung out in seemingly every other sector of America in the 1960s — had now found its way even to the arbiters of Major League Baseball.

There were also small concerns about the Cardinals themselves, such as the minor bumps and bruises that had been hampering many of the regular players. In the final two weeks of the season, Schoendienst planned to give extra rest to Maxvill and Shannon in particular, who had missed a combined total of only three games to that point on the year (Javier may have been in need of a break, too, as his wife gave birth to their fifth child on the 18th. He was also requiring regular cortisone shots to alleviate pain in his throwing arm). Brock, Cepeda, and McCarver, on the other hand, asked the manager to *not* remove them from the lineup in an effort to stay sharp, even though Schoendienst wanted the rookie Simmons to start at least one game behind the plate. In another perspective, batting coach Sisler could not understand the anxiety that had set in on some Cardinals followers when the team slumped in recent weeks. "I don't see why writers and other people in this business get panicky when we have a lead of 12 or 15 games," Sisler chided. "Every club is going to have some ups and downs. Just remember, this club never failed to win a really big game or a big series when it had to." To help ease any fears of dullness among the club, Schoendienst also let it be known that all the starters would be back on the field for at least the final four games of the regular season. On the pitching side, the main current concern was over Washburn, who had won only twice in the past seven weeks (despite those two victories being a shutout and a one-run complete game). Carlton appeared to be coming around, but Red knew that Washburn needed to round into consistent form for work in the World Series.

Schoendienst gave him another chance on September 18 against San Francisco, as Washburn (from nearby Washington state) had several family members and friends on hand for his rare appearance in northern California. With a chronic sore shoulder that seemed to come and go with changes in the weather, the softer-throwing Washburn was becoming more and more reliant on a curve which McCarver, Edwards, and Ricketts all testified had become consistently more effective in the passing months. He mixed it in smartly against the Giants in the cool September air off the bay, getting a regular series of strikeouts and ground outs from the bats of the imposing San Francisco lineup. The Giants were coming up and going down so systematically, in fact, that few noticed as the middle innings passed by that he was carrying a no-hitter. He struck out Mays and Dick Dietz to end the seventh, and after two meek ground outs, tempted the rookie Bonds into popping lightly to Cepeda at first to finish the eighth turn at bat for the home team. The small crowd turned over to his side in the ninth, as he downed Ron Hunt on a grounder to Javier and Mays similarly to Shannon at third. Washburn stood on the threshold of baseball history as he faced the intimidating McCovey with one out to go. He laid one out over the plate, and McCovey drove the ball to deep center field. The no-hitter and the shutout looked likely to be lost; but Flood, as he had done so many times in the past eleven years, raced to the gap to run the ball down as Washburn recorded the first no-hit game by a Cardinal since Lon Warneke in 1941.

The Cardinals themselves had not scored until the seventh, when Cepeda was doubled home on a drive by Shannon. The performance gave Washburn a career-high 13 wins, and the dividends were immediate for him, as Devine announced after the game that Washburn — who was imagined to be left unprotected by the Cardinals for the off-season expansion draft — was now suddenly getting a new contract and a pay raise.

The most amazing aspect of Washburn's performance is that it came 24 hours after Gaylord Perry had done the same to the Cardinals, making Washburn's performance the first time consecutive no-hitters had been thrown in the same ballpark (even so, only 4,700 came out to the park for Washburn's gem on the second night). The 1–0 effort the evening before was needed for Perry to even his record at only 14–14 on the season, culminating a frustrating year for the spitballing right-hander had turned 30 just two days earlier. On the Cardinals' roster for the first time that evening was a rookie first baseman named Joe Hague, who at least maintained his sense of humor. "I'd better get back on the plane," Hague said. "This club was doing a lot better without me." It was only the second time in the last fifty years an opposing pitcher had no-hit the Cardinals. In addition, the Cardinals still had not been no-hit at home since 1906 (a mark that stands today). It was also perhaps the only time in 1968 that a great performance by Gibson had been overshadowed by the opposing pitcher. In taking just his second loss since May 28, Gibson had gone the distance once again, striking out ten and making just one mistake, allowing a solo homer to Hunt in the first inning for the only run of the game. It was only Hunt's second homer of the year, as Perry received great defensive help — particularly from first baseman McCovey, known as "Stretch," who roamed to his right and robbed Tolan of two sure hits. With the two masters on the mound, the contest was over before the fans had barely taken their seats. Perry got the royal ride off the field after catching Flood looking on strikes to end the ninth, just over an hour and a half after the game had started. Schoendienst, however, was once again muttering about Perry's spitter. "He was throwing his same old sinker — wet," Red said.

Even in the midst of his own tremendous season, and with the death of bats occurring all around him, Gibson made a surprising prediction. "I don't think I'll ever throw a no-hitter," he speculated. "I make too many mistakes to pitch a no-hitter. Somewhere along the way, I make a mistake and somebody is going to capitalize on it." Ironically, the series ended with Briles being pounded for nine runs and twelve hits in six innings, as the Cardinals lost to the Giants 11–5, only the fourth time all year that the club had allowed double-digit runs to the opposition. Some struggles ensued down the coast, as the Cards were then swept by the Dodgers with losses handed to Willis (2–3), Jaster (9–13), and Gibson (21–9), although Brock was the only regular receiving substantial playing time during the series. It was the final road series of the year, and it left the Cardinals with a slightly-worse away record in 1968 from 1967 (50–31 versus 52–28). They had suddenly dropped 12 of their last 17, which also had precluded themselves from achieving 100 victories on the season. Jaster's defeat marked the debut behind the plate for Simmons, as the talented young catcher got his first hit with a single in the fifth inning after striking out in his initial major league at-bat in the second. In the opener, Willis had pitched four innings of quality ball, relieving a once-again ineffective Carlton, who had permitted seven hits and four runs in not being able to complete two innings of work. The events of the past couple of days had sealed Carlton's fate — for according to Schoendienst, the lefthander had now relinquished his planned Game Three start in the World Series to Washburn, and was relegated to bullpen duty only.

The celebration for Perry in San Francisco paled in comparison to the carnival being launched in Detroit, as the Tigers clinched the American League flag the same day as Perry's no-hitter (the 17th) with a 2–1 win over the Yankees. They had actually clinched it before the game had ended, as a Boston win over the Orioles handled matters before the contest in Detroit had completed. This information was known to Tigers' general manager Jim Campbell, but he instructed the scoreboard operator at Tiger Stadium to keep it off the board and out of public knowledge, for he feared a chaotic scene of fans taking over the field upon the announcement. It occurred as short time later anyway, as the spectators stormed the field and joyously ripped down the screen above the left field wall. This was shortly after the home team scored the winner on a base hit in the bottom of the ninth by Don Wert, as fireworks shot all around Tiger Stadium in a frenzied display. With champagne spraying the Tigers' clubhouse, the celebration quieted down for just a moment, giving owner John Fetzer the chance to say that "this bunch of kids has grown up into men." When he was finished with that comment, Fetzer (oddly enough) was then thrown into the whirlpool by the "men" as the celebration resumed.

Soon after, Woodward Avenue was jammed downtown with cars honking their horns—but unlike in previous scenes in the neighborhood, it was not in anger. Crowds gathered with police in Kennedy Square—but unlike in previous scenes, it was not to rumble. The violent Detroit riots of 1967 seemed to be drifting off into oblivion, as the team had provided the city with a thorough form of catharsis and a healthy way to parade in the streets. With the Tigers offices not having taken ticket orders postmarked before September 23 for World Series games, the Detroit post office found itself awash with customers at the stroke of midnight that evening.

The Mardi Gras atmosphere within the Motor City from the clinching carried over to the field in McLain's next start on the 19th. With the pennant and the 30-win individual season already in the bag, McLain relaxed, got silly, and turned the game with the Yankees into a sideshow. With the Tigers ahead 6–1 in the top of eighth inning with McLain cruising to victory number 31, he wanted to offer a kind gesture to an old friend. After Yankees catcher Jake Gibbs grounded out to open the inning, Mickey Mantle stepped to the plate (Mickey was playing first base on the evening, his knees so sore that he had been relegated to minimizing his running). Suddenly McLain called for a time-out, and summoned his catcher Jim Price to the mound. He told Price to tell Mantle that the next pitch was coming right down the middle of the plate. As he took his position back behind the dish, Price mentioned something to Mantle, at which Mickey spun in a surprised state and glanced out at McLain. McLain went into his wind-up, and the pitch sailed by a stationary Mantle untouched, as McLain beckoned Price to the mound once again. Apparently, Mantle did not believe him. "Tell him I'm serious," McLain said to Price this time. Price returned to his spot behind the plate, and McLain grooved another one. This time Mantle did not pass it up, and exploded with one of his patented destructive swings to propel the ball into the famous right field upper deck at Tiger Stadium. As he came around third base in completing his home-run trot, Mantle and McLain exchanged winks and tips of the caps. Joe Pepitone was next up, and he expected the same treatment as he looked out at the pitcher while holding his bat parallel to the plate, begging for the same offering; what he received instead was a fastball near his head. McLain's actions wound up immaterial on the game itself, as the final score remained 6–2, the twelfth contest in a row in which a Tigers hurler had issued a complete-game performance. Afterwards, not Mantle nor McLain nor Price admitted explicitly to reporters that a set-up had taken place. McLain thought it was a sign of respect, but Gibson disagreed. "My method of showing respect for a guy like Mantle would have been to reach back for something extra with which to blow his ass away," he would comment later.

When the Yankees returned to New York the next day to play the Red Sox, they would meet up with the once bright but long forgotten star pitcher from 1967. Lonborg would enjoy one of his few high points of 1968, as he posted just his third complete game of the season in downing the Bronx Bombers 4–3, giving him only six wins for the year in fourteen decisions. But it was Mantle—carrying over his energy from the curtain call in Detroit— who would bask in the limelight, hitting what would be his 536th and final home run in the major leagues, a two-out solo shot in the third inning that tied the game at one. One week later, Mantle would play his final game at Yankee Stadium against Tiant and the Indians. And, on cue, Mickey would record the only hit on the day for the Yankees, a two-out single in the first inning that preceded Tiant's American League-best ninth shutout of the year, and a Cleveland-record 1.60 ERA to end the season.

Since the Cardinals had clinched the National League flag back on Sunday the 15th, the strange week had culminated with the accomplishment of Cesar Tovar of the Minnesota Twins on Sunday the 22nd. Tovar, a solid but not spectacular player to this point in his career, certainly proved himself versatile on this day. As the Twins game against the Oakland A's got underway, fans thought it was odd that Tovar was on the mound to open the pitching duties that afternoon. The first batter Tovar faced in the first inning was Bert Campaneris; he was able to get the A's shortstop to pop out in foul ground behind third base. Next was Reggie Jackson, batting second in the order as he had often done early in his career. When Jackson took a mammoth empty swing for strike three, the crowd was already on its feet. The situation soon intensified, as Danny Cater walked and was promptly balked to second by a naïve Tovar. Just as quickly as he allowed a runner in scoring position, however, Tovar also got Sal Bando to pop up, ending a scoreless first as the Twins' faithful hollered wildly. They expected him to continue firing at the Oakland batters in the top of the second, but they discovered that Tovar had put on the catcher's gear to take over behind the plate, as Tom Hall assumed the pitching duties. In the third inning, Tovar moved from catcher over to first base, then second base in the next inning, and then to short, third, left field, center, and right, taking a one-inning turn at every position. The strong Twins' pitching to which Tovar contributed held up, as Hall went six more frames and got credit for a 2–1 Minnesota victory. The energetic Tovar had previously set an American League record in 1967 by playing in 164 games.

And to complete the irony of the peculiar past week on the major leagues, it was soon recalled that only one player had ever previously pulled off Tovar's nine-position feat — and it was Campaneris three years earlier, the first man he faced as the pitcher in the first inning. One week later on Sunday the 29th, an embarrassed Finley would fire the manager of his struggling team, Bob Kennedy, and replace him with Hank Bauer.

The only mystery remaining for the St. Louis men and their followers was the extent to which Gibson would permanently dent the record book by the season's end. He would get his last chance in front of the home folks on the 27th; before then, however, more concern emerged as Washburn dropped the opener of a series at Busch against Philadelphia by a 2–1 score, in a strong-yet-unsuccessful encore to his no-hitter in San Francisco. It was the club's fifth loss in a row, the most consecutive defeats for the Redbirds since the 1966 season. It was certainly not a time for slumps, and Schoendienst was not about to allow it to happen. "We'd better give our pitchers a lot of rest between now and the World Series, because it looks as if they have to pitch shutouts to win," Red fumed in decrying the lack of offense that was surfacing once again. The bats would return in the final game with the Phillies, however, as Briles — with help from Hoerner's sixteenth save — broke the slide with a 5–4 win, his nineteenth of the year. Hoerner, cool as always, entered the game with the tying run on third base with two out in the ninth. The left-hander delivered a devastating fastball that made pinch hitter Rick Joseph fly softly to Ron Davis in right to end the game. In Atlanta that night, Mets manager Gil Hodges was recovering from a heart attack that he had suffered the evening before during New York's game with the Braves.

Houston arrived as the last regular-season opponent on the 27th, and as promised, Schoendienst put all the regulars back into the starting lineup to tune up for the World Series. The opener was Gibson's last chance to make his mark on baseball history, finalizing the numbers which would go down as one of the greatest individual pitching seasons ever, regardless of the outcome of the evening's affair. He entered the contest with an ERA of 1.16 — any such performance on the night or better would give him the best single-season mark in modern National League history, currently standing as the 1.22 rate that Grover Cleveland Alexander had crafted in 1915. But also within reach was the modern major league record, held by Walter Johnson and his 1.14 ERA from 1913. Gibson, like Dean and a few other Cardinals pitchers before him, seemed to sense the greater implications of an important ballgame, and reached back for something more on such occasions. He masterfully disposed of the overmatched Houston club, punching eleven strikeouts with his thirteenth shutout of the season, 1–0. He achieved the all-time record with a final ERA of 1.12, and shattered the Cardinals' team mark (1.72) set by Bill Doak in 1914. It was his twentieth win against the Astros in his career and his 22nd victory of the year (a career high to date, and the most by a Cardinal since Dean in 1936). Perhaps most importantly to Gibson and the Cardinals, it reversed a trend that was beginning to resemble his hard-luck first half of the season, as he had lost his last two starts by scores of 3–2 and 1–0. When he returned to his locker after his glorious night's work, Gibson found a stuffed Tiger that had been hanging by a rope, a suggestion of his next victim that was left by a teammate.

Aside from the two-millionth fan to pass through the Busch Stadium turnstiles in 1968, Maris received the most attention in the regular-season finale on the 29th, an afternoon contest with the Astros. The lucky fan received a TV, radio, and free season tickets to the Cardinals game in 1969, while Maris and his family were presented with an electric organ before the game for their new home in Florida, which had been their choice of gift when asked by the Busch family what they would like to have. Roger was looking forward to running the Anheuser-Busch brewery branch in the Sunshine State, but trouble between the family and the company was not far down the road. On August 3, 2001, a jury ordered Anheuser-Busch to pay the Maris family $50 million for improperly taking away the beer distributorship from them, as the company had found a legal loophole in re-acquiring it after Maris's death in 1985. Both sides appealed the verdict, as the Maris family was grabbing for much more at a $139 million asking price.

Washburn had been recognized two nights earlier for his no-hitter on the last road trip, as former Cardinals pitching great Lon Warneke presented him with a plaque at home plate. "Let your next no-hitter be right here next week," the "Arkansas Hummingbird" told Washburn with a smile. In addition to being a top-flight major league pitcher, Warneke also became a big league umpire after his playing days were over after serving in World War II. Warneke had started his career with the Cubs, and ironically on the next afternoon, Jenkins became the first Cubs pitcher since Warneke in 1934 and 1935 to post consecutive twenty-win seasons—even though Jenkins accomplished the feat despite suffering through an amazing nine shutout losses in 1968. In adding to the feel-good stories of the last weekend, old Cardinals reliever Barney Schultz was ordered to be activated by Gussie Busch for the series with Houston—just before the end of the season for the second straight year. Schultz, who entered the big leagues with the Redbirds in 1955 and finished with them ten years later, was put on the roster once again so that he could apply another year towards his player's pension. Schultz had been working as a minor league pitching instructor for the Cardinals when he received the good news, as Mr. Busch had always been loyal to those loyal to him, the brewery, or the baseball organization (often considered one and the same). However, a sad story also pervaded the St. Louis locker room the same weekend, as their beloved team physician, I.C. Middleman, passed away during the previous week. "He had the ability to make every patient, large fee or for free, believe he or she was a special case," Devine said in a testimonial to "Doc." Added his office partner, Dr. Stan London, "The three things Middie lived for were his wife, his son, and the ball club." After Granger permitted three ninth-inning runs in relief of Nelson to lose 3–2 on the 28th, Washburn, Jaster, Willis and Hoerner finished things up in sparkling fashion with an 11–1 pounding of Houston in the season finale, with Washburn gaining his fourteenth triumph. The Cardinals completed the season with a record of 97–65, four and a half games behind their pace from a year ago.

Although one Grover Alexander standard had fallen with Gibson's performance, another remained untouched. On September 28, McLain had an opportunity to log his 32nd win, which would have been the highest total since Alexander had put up 33 victories in 1916. Detroit manager Mayo Smith pulled him in the seventh inning with a 1–0 lead, however, worried about his increasing soreness in his pitching arm. McLain would lead the majors in 1968 with 336 innings pitched, which would be an incredible figure in twenty-first century times and impressive even in the 1960s. The pitcher vociferously objected to being removed from the contest, which many people found interesting—for over the past several months, he often complained about how pitching with a sore arm might shorten his career — the same self-fulfilling prophecy that befell his 30-win counterpart Dean by 1937. Originally, Smith had declared that McLain was to go no more than five innings in the final regular season start, so the manager had considered the two extra frames a gift anyway. On the afternoon McLain was, however, able to break the club record for strikeouts in a season by five, topping the 275 Hal Newhouser had posted in 1946. And his mood swung so quickly, no one in the media noticed him carrying a grudge against anyone. "I've lost so many contact lenses this season," he offered randomly to the press after the game, his eyes looking skyward and his head wagging aimlessly. "I've spent so much time on my hands and knees looking for them, I look like a one-man perpetual crap game." Once again, like Dean, McLain offered out-of-left-field lines that made for good copy.

While the Tigers joined the other clubs around baseball in their struggle to score runs in 1968, anxiety was high on the St. Louis side that the Detroit staff might finish off the Redbird bats for good. In addition to scoring nearly a run fewer per game than in 1967, the Cardinals ended the regular season with a paltry total of 73 home runs—with Cepeda (16) and Shannon (15) the only individuals in double figures—which would nearly be equaled alone by the St. Louis first baseman thirty years later. It was their lowest team total for homers since hitting 64 in 1945, a season in which they had played eight fewer games than in 1968. In addition — while utilizing the same basic starting lineup in 1968 that had taken the field in 1967 — only Maxvill (from .227 to .253) and Shannon (from .245 to .266) had improved their batting averages, as the overall club figure sank from .263 to .249. Nonetheless, the poor team numbers around the National League did not prevent an exciting individual race to the finish, as Pete Rose became the first Cincinnati player to take home the batting title in 30 years with a .335 mark, bettering Matty Alou of Pittsburgh by three points. Rose coasted through a 1-for-3 game on the season's final day after going 5 for 5 the night before (off of Gaylord Perry no less) to stake his lead, as Alou dropped behind with an 0-for-4 perform-ance in his final contest in Chicago. It was rumored that Rose had a friend in the bleachers at Wrigley Field that day, who left the ballpark periodically to send Rose messages by pay phone to the Reds' clubhouse on how Alou was faring. But Rose also drew inspiration from his teammate, second baseman Tommy Helms, who used some tough love on Pete to drive him to excellence. "You're swinging like a girl," Helms hollered at him before Rose's stellar after-noon would take place. "If I see you take four more bad cuts today like you have been recently, I'll throw up four times." Determined to take home the hitting crown, Rose made sure that every at-bat counted. "I've never seen any-one who wanted to win a batting title as much as Pete," his manager, Bris-tol, said. "If I had 25 guys who wanted to win a pennant that much, it'd be a cakewalk."

Yastrzemski, on the contrary, weathered an 0-for-5 final afternoon to win his second straight American League batting title (and third overall) with just a .301 average. His teammate, pitcher Ray Culp, saw his own per-sonal scoreless-innings streak end at 39 when the Yankees scored off him in the first inning, the culmination of just another artifact of moundsmen dom-ination on the season. Just as the sportswriters had warned him back in mid-May, Yastrzemski would indeed be the only AL hitter over .300, and it remains the lowest figure ever to secure a title (Cater finished second with a .290 mark). Flood, with the same .301 average as Yastrzemski, finished a dis-tant fifth in the National League race behind Rose, Matty Alou, Felipe Alou of Atlanta, and Alex Johnson of the Reds. With his sixth .300-plus season, Flood had posted the most singles in the league (160), while his partner Brock added accolades by posting the most doubles (46) and triples (14), in addi-tion to topping the charts in steals with 62. Hoerner, also among the National League leaders, tied for second in saves with 17 behind the mischievous Regan's 25.

The major leagues did not hold exclusivity in the lack of run produc-tion. The leading batter in the Eastern League, Tony Torchi, topped the charts at .294 — and his next closest competitor, Carmen Fanzone, checked in at .270. In Boston, Ken Harrelson — acquired in 1967 as a fill-in for the injured Tony Conigliaro — would lead the majors in RBIs in 1968 with 109. To fur-ther illustrate the overall destruction of hitting around baseball, Rose's .335 average was 38 percent higher than the National League overall mark of .242, while Yastrzemski's .301 average was 31 percent better than the American League's .230. The Oakland A's, in their first year on the West Coast, led the circuit with a .240 team batting average, the lowest ever in the majors for a league leader. The Yankees, meanwhile — with their dynasty of the previous decades growing increasingly distant in the rear-view mirror — had the low-est team batting average since the end of the dead-ball era with a .214 figure.

And Curt Blefary — the Baltimore Orioles' outfielder and stand-in catcher who was in only his fourth game ever behind the plate when he caught Catfish Hunter's perfect game back in May — would become dubiously honored as well, batting .200 for the lowest mark in history in a season by an outfielder who attained 400 or more at-bats.

But the most jaw-dropping stats belonged to Gibson. While most all pitchers dominated in 1968, the distance between which Gibson placed himself and his nearest National League competitors in ERA (1.12 to Bolin of San Francisco's 1.99, and well beyond the National League mark of 3.03), base runners allowed per nine innings (.853 to Seaver's .980), and shutouts (13 to Drysdale's eight) was truly remarkable, even in this anomaly of a season that favored the pitchers. His 13 shutouts were the most in the National League since 1916, while his *highest* ERA for any month during the season was his 1.97 mark in April. Gibson was even tougher on the road than in Busch Stadium, logging a miniscule 0.79 ERA as a visitor. Most amazing, perhaps, was that he managed to post a 2.14 ERA in the nine games that he *lost*— games which, if the Cardinals had posted any offensive effort at all, possibly could have put Gibson near thirty wins himself by season's end.

A record total 339 shutouts were thrown in the major leagues in 1968, with 82 of those being 1–0 scores. Some pointed to improved control by the pitchers as the reason for the lack of scoring, as nearly 400 fewer walks were issued in 1968 than in the previous season. Others noticed the more creative use of the bullpen by managers as a factor, evidenced in one regard by the record 88 appearances in games by Wilbur Wood of the White Sox.

"We have raised the industry standards," Gibson once wrote as an explanation for the supreme dominance of the throwers in 1968. "Pitchers are more capable of this than hitters for the simple reason that the pitcher initiates the exchange between the two."

"Complacent" was a word which more than one writer was using to describe the Cardinals' attitude in the final month of the 1968 season, with their display of too much reliance on the pitching staff, and in particular Gibson. Some complacency could indeed be found in examination of the statistics when he was on the mound. The Cardinals' offense, despite improving for him over the last half of the season, were averaging a full run per game less (2.8 to 3.8) when Gibson started as opposed to the rest of the staff. He had finished 28 of the 34 games he started, and was removed for a pinch hitter in the other six starts (in other words, he was never knocked out of a game in 1968 — a streak he would carry well into the 1969 season). In combing over the numbers from the season, a statistician reasoned that if Gibson received the same run support as the rest of the Cardinals' starting staff (3.8 per game), he would have finished with a record of 24–4; if the team had managed four runs per game for Gibson, the statistician asserted that Gibson's 1968 record would have been 31–2. But in all fairness, the entire Cardinals staff deserved credit for a remarkable performance. Ed Wilks noted in a late-season *Post-Dispatch* article that Washburn, one of the Gibson-obscured hurlers with his sparkling 2.26 ERA on the year, would have won the league title in that category in 31 out of the past 53 seasons. And author William Mead noted that the Redbirds held their opponents to two or fewer runs in more than half their games in 1968, compiling 30 shutouts, 31 one-run games, and 21 two-runs games for a total of 82 contests of such work.

It was a brief window of time in the game that was cherished by the lovers of its defensive aspects. "Although nobody could have predicted the extent to which it would be true," Gibson would later mourn, "it was generally felt that the 1968 season would mark the end of a baseball era, and the game would not be the same thereafter."

*   *   *   *

The irrepressible, enigmatic, 24-year-old McLain was the most unpredictable personality in a major league uniform since Dean, the last man prior to him to win thirty games in a season with a similar self-assuredness which bordered on the unconscionable. Northrup once retold one particular McLain episode to *Sports Illustrated*, a tale which sounded more like Pepper Martin relaying a story about Ol' Diz. "I remember a game when he [McLain] was ahead 3–0 in the ninth. Denny's first pitch was a fastball hit for a home run. His second pitch was a fastball hit for a home run. Then he struck the next three batters out on fastballs. I went to him and said, 'Did it ever occur to you to throw anything but a fastball?' He said, 'Why? When was the last time you saw anyone hit three home runs in a row?'" An aspiring musician on the side, McLain had busied himself in his free time during the winter by giving lessons on the electric organ out of his house for $3.50 an hour. He hailed from an Irish family on Chicago's south side, and had three uncles on the police force that cracked down on vandals during the 1968 Democratic Convention. His father had died when Denny was fifteen, suffering a heart attack while on his way to watch his son play. Now, as a grown man himself, McLain often would not even bother to come to the ballpark on days when he was not pitching, a luxury that the Detroit club was apparently permitting without too much concern. "Tigers management extended McLain more liberties than the Bill of Rights," one writer noted. His south-side White Sox were in fact his first team, signing for a $10,000 bonus in 1962 as he promptly threw a no-hitter in his first minor league game at Harlan, Kentucky. With the White Sox unable to make room for him on their big league roster, the Tigers acquired him off waivers the following spring and he quickly ascended through the Detroit system, using regular bowling in between organ lessons in the winter months which he believed had strengthened his pitching arm.

Long before the days of Dennis Rodman and his antics in the NBA, McLain frequently dyed his hair from blonde to red and then to other colors. And despite his penchant for nightclubs, he was rarely found to be drinking anything besides Pepsi-Cola. McLain was reputed by one Detroit writer, in fact, to have drunk 25 Pepsis once in one day. "My dad used to drink ten or twelve Pepsis a day," he explained. "He'd drink them all day long, and it didn't matter if they were warm or cold. But I was allowed only one a day — that was my limit. He thought that too much Pepsi would ruin my teeth and eat away at my stomach ... after my dad died, I went on a Pepsi binge. With him no longer around to tell me what I couldn't do, I started putting away a dozen a day, just like he had ... by the time I made my major league debut in 1963, I was drinking 15 or 20 bottles a day." Ultimately, the vice president of the Pepsi distributorship in Detroit gave McLain one free case a day, and he told the pitcher that all he had to do was drink it. McLain gladly accepted the soda, and the distributor gladly accepted the advertising. Despite extra sources of income that were appearing for him, however, McLain always seemed to be out of money. "Denny would give you the shirt off his back, but don't let him borrow money from you," his teammate Pat Dobson warned. "You'd never see it again. He was one of those guys, if he made $35,000, he'd spend $45,000; if he had $100, he'd spend $110."

While McLain may have been good for the Pepsi company, his public relations with baseball followers around Detroit left something to be desired. He blasted the fans of the Tigers by saying to the press, "If people go along with us and stay off our backs, we'll win this thing. I don't care if I get booed here for the rest of my life. Detroit is a great town; I like it. I've bought a home and have roots here. But the fans in this town are the worst in the league. If they think we're stupid for playing this game, then how stupid are *they* for watching us?" Denny sometimes relied on the support of the media, who in turn was hardly ever on his side — and perhaps for good reason. When McLain suggested that the Detroit writers were "dampening the spirit" of the ball club, Joe Falls of the *Detroit Free Press* responded, "The Tigers haven't won a pennant for 23 years, which must mean we've had some terrible sports writers around here for 23 years." Interestingly enough, the two Detroit newspapers — the *Free Press* and the *News* — had been on strike for most of 1968, but the radio stations, television outlets, and other newspapers around Michigan were more than happy to pick up on the Dean-like quotes that came from McLain's mouth. Falls, one of the Detroit writers who went to work for another paper during the strike, remembered one such particular story. Signs had been springing up around Detroit suggesting, "McLAIN FOR PRESIDENT!"

"Are you going to run?" Falls asked him, while the team was making a flight on the Tigers' chartered airplane.

"I'm thinking about it," McLain said. With the idea now rolling around in his head, he starting imagining about how he could put his teammates to work for him in his administration.

"Who will be your running mate?"

"Joe Sparma — I've got to get the Italian vote."

"And your secretary of defense?"

"Gates Brown — I've got to get the colored vote, too."

And for the kicker, McLain realized that the presidency would finally give him the kind of money he was seeking from the Tigers, so he gave it some more serious thought before taking a break with a Pepsi.

Even with all of his strange behavior, it was evident that the Tigers organization and fans were willing to put up with McLain's eccentricities — and even his criticism of them — as victories have a tendency to do. McLain had a huge appetite for winning, exemplified on August 29, 1966, when he fired 229 pitches in a game against the Orioles in order to gain the triumph on that day. Detroit had once again gone baseball crazy, sending the Motor City back to the glory days of Hank Greenberg and Charlie Gehringer of the 1930s and '40s. Placemats in Chinese restaurants coast to coast were letting patrons know that 1968 was the "Year of the Tiger," but Detroit baseball followers knew that without ever ordering one plate of sweet-and-sour chicken. After losing the season-opener against the defending pennant-winning Red Sox on April 10, the Tigers ripped off nine wins in a row (with the ninth being McLain's first of his 31 on April 21 — the same day that the Cardinals had received their 1967 championship rings in the ceremony at Busch Stadium), keeping themselves at or near the top of the standings until permanently taking over first place on May 10, when McLain had attained his fifth victory against no defeats in a 12–1 stomping of the Washington Senators. While McLain was racking up the big numbers, the unquestioned leader of the team was Al Kaline, a stabilizing force amidst a team and a city that had dealt with internal pressures all season long. Kaline, only at age 33 but already in his fifteenth major league season, had long yearned for a shot in the World Series. He had grown up in a tough neighborhood of Baltimore in the shadows of one of the city's largest power plants, the main source of employment for his father and the other men of his neighborhood. And often, Kaline would take his own children back to his old surroundings, showing them that his life had not always been easy. He had missed six weeks of the 1967 campaign due to breaking his hand in the Detroit dugout in frustration after a strikeout, obviously a critical factor in the Tigers' inability to catch Boston by the end of the year. In the first week of the regular season in 1968, he had become only the fourth man to play in 2,000 games as a Tiger (Gehringer, Ty Cobb, and Sam Crawford were the others). Later he would find himself on the injury list once again, nursing a broken arm from mid-May to the end of June off

a tight pitch from the A's' Krausse. In addition to his success on the field,
Kaline's many business and charitable interests in Detroit had endeared him
to the people of the city. He was the youngest batting champion in American League history in 1955 when he led the circuit with a .340 clip at the age
of 20, beating Cobb's title in 1907 by just one day's worth of age. He was also
a measure of steadiness, having endured other injuries over the years that
included a broken jaw, broken ribs, a separated shoulder, water on the knee,
and a congenital bone spur in the foot. "I don't want to be run out of the
league on my own stupidity," Kaline had said in 1967, in pointing to his strict
diet and off-season workout regimen. "The pitchers are going to have to do
it. This league is tough enough without making it tougher. Maybe, by taking care of myself, I'll prolong my career an extra year or two." Kaline was
still going strong, having logged a .287 batting average in 327 at-bats in 1968.
And despite being a veritable diplomat of the city, he almost had originally
wound up in another organization. "Detroit wasn't one of my favorite teams,
and Philadelphia and the Cardinals both offered me more money," Kaline
recollected about his younger days to writer Jeff Peek, who covered the Tigers
in Traverse City, Michigan. Kaline remembered getting ready to sign a professional contract out of his home in Baltimore as a high school graduate. "But
money didn't mean anything to me, I just wanted to play. And I thought I
had a chance to play sooner in Detroit. Other than getting married, it was
the best decision I ever made. I love Detroit. It was a big decision for an 18-
year-old, but that's how my dad raised me. I took my time and thought things
out."

While Kaline provided the necessary leadership, it was pitching that had
carried the Tigers in 1968, just as it had the Cardinals and other good teams
around baseball in the drought-stricken pursuit of scoring runs that season.
Like Gibson, McLain had logged 28 complete games among his 41 starts, along
with being credited for six of the staff's 19 shutouts on the year. As with
Kaline, he attributed his endurance to the strict dietary regimen that his wife,
Sharyn (the daughter of former major leaguer Lou Boudreau), had placed
upon him during the season, as well as his incessant wintertime bowling. The
lefthander Lolich (17 wins), Earl Wilson (13), and Joe Sparma (10) also contributed substantial victories in addition to McLain's superb total of 31. All
of the men had a profound respect for their main counterpart in Gibson, but
it was Wilson's quest that was most interesting. When the Tigers had been
knocked out of the pennant on the last day in 1967, Wilson purchased himself a plane ticket to Boston — at that time, not an inexpensive purchase for
a non-superstar in the major leagues — and sat behind home plate for Game
One of the 1967 World Series. "I wanted to see Bob Gibson pitch," Wilson
said as the Tigers and Cardinals met back in spring training of 1968. "That
man showed me more determination and guts than anyone I've ever seen on

the mound. I wanted to find out what made this man click." Wilson had in fact out-pitched McLain and everyone else on the Tigers that season, leading the team in wins (22) and strikeouts (184). It could be argued that Lolich had nearly as quirky a personality as McLain, although of a different style. Lolich's hobbies ranged from slot car racing to bow hunting to riding motorcycles. The son of a milk salesman and parks director from Oregon, Lolich described himself as a "beer-drinker's idol" because of his conspicuous waistline. While most all the fans in Detroit found the lefthander quite charismatic and lovable, McLain never did care much for Lolich. "Lolich had a great arm, but he also had a personality that rubbed people the wrong way, especially me," McLain once told a writer. "Lolich was the kind of guy who could say, 'Good morning,' and piss you off. What bothered me was his petty jealousy. He couldn't stand to see other guys succeed. It seemed to me that Mickey sometimes pulled against the Tigers—and especially the other pitchers. I think that he secretly wished the Tigers would lose every game but the ones he pitched." But it was in McLain, ironically, that the sportswriters saw those characteristics—and to an even higher degree.

Dobson, John Hiller, Jon Warden, Fred Lasher, John Wyatt and Daryl Patterson — while not called upon often — shared the relief load for the Tigers, as all possessed at least two saves to their credit in 1968 with Dobson and Patterson leading the way with just seven each. The Tigers had picked up additional help in the bullpen area in midseason in acquiring 38-year-old veteran Don McMahon from the White Sox as well, a savvy, chunky hurler who himself had led the National League in saves for a stellar Milwaukee Braves team in 1959. Backing up all of the hurlers was (statistically) the best defense in the major leagues with a .984 team fielding percentage (the Cardinals, meanwhile, had managed only to tie for fifth with Cincinnati in the National League with a .978 mark). On the offensive side, Kaline was supported by a surrounding cast that posted meek numbers at the plate, but who always seemed to get the clutch hits. Evidence of this was the fact that the 1968 Tigers won forty games while trailing in the seventh, eighth, or ninth innings. "It wasn't just one guy," remembered Northrup. "[Reserve infielder] Tom Matchick hit a home run off Moe Drabowsky, the only homer hit off Moe all year, and it won a ballgame. Ray Oyler hit one home run, and it won a game. [Another reserve infielder] Tracewski hit a three-run home run in the tenth inning off Sam McDowell to win a game over Cleveland. Those kinds of things happened. It was momentum and attitude. We believed that we could do it, and we did it." While the team batted a paltry .235, it was nonetheless good for fourth in the American League. To prove that their hits counted the most, the Tigers were yet able to top the league in runs per game at just over four. Next to Kaline and Willie Horton (.285), the only hitters with serviceable averages came from a pair of .263s in catcher Bill Freehan and first baseman

Norm Cash, and a .264 mark from Northrup. What the team banked on, however, was a lineup balanced in superb power, with eight of the starters putting up double figures in home runs, led by Horton (36), Freehan and Cash (25 each), Northrup (21), and second baseman Dick McAuliffe (16). In addition, the 185 homers that the Tigers hit as a team were 52 more than the next-closest team in the American League, the Baltimore Orioles. Freehan, the gritty catcher and team leader, had been hit by pitches 24 times in 1968, the most in the majors in one season since 1911. Cash, like Kaline, was a long-standing and much-loved Tiger, as both men were the senior regulars on the Detroit squad with Cash being a month older. Despite being a respected hitter, Cash's only season topping the .300 mark was Maris's magical year of 1961, in which Cash posted superlative numbers with 41 home runs, 132 RBIs, and a league-leading .361 batting average. Cash was also considered the unquestioned ringleader of the off-field fun for the team. McLain remembered one instance in particular in 1965, when Detroit manager Charley Dressen had become fed up with the team's late-night carousing, and angrily informed the club in the locker room that mandatory workouts were going to begin at nine o'clock in the morning. Dressen's announcement—which was intended to curb the partying—was instead met with skepticism about its desired results.

"Charley, it's virtually impossible for me to get to the workout by nine A.M.," Cash told him.

"Why the hell not?" the manager responded.

"Because I'm not done throwing up until ten," Cash answered simply.

To further illustrate just how much scoring had disappeared in major league baseball, Oyler—like Maxvill, having quality defensive skills at shortstop—was permitted to play 111 games even though he squeaked out an embarrassing .135 average. Moving on to the expansion Seattle Pilots and then the California Angels for his final two big league seasons after 1968, Oyler—beginning with the 1968 season—amazingly would close out his career without receiving one intentional walk in his final three campaigns, even though he perpetually batted in the eighth place in the order, just ahead of the pitcher's spot.

But for the 1968 World Series, Mayo Smith had another plan to enhance the offensive output of his team. The reputation of the Cardinals' pitching staff was well-known in the American League, and the manager wanted to maximize his capabilities. Knowing this would not occur with Oyler in the lineup, Smith instead put regular center fielder Mickey Stanley at shortstop for the series. The idea was simple—to allow Kaline an opportunity to bat regularly by giving him the spot in right field, a place he had essentially split with Northrup during the regular season (Northrup appeared in 103 games in right field in 1968, Kaline 70). With the plan, Horton—the biggest liability defensively among the four — would remain in his customary left field position, while Northrup would move to center. Stanley, in essence a Tiger since he was a childhood fan in Grand Rapids, was in his third full season in the major leagues in 1968. He was establishing himself as one of the game's premier center fielders, having made no errors in 304 chances on the season. Because of his athleticism, however, he had been brought in to play short-stop in nine games during the regular season for the first time in his career, in which he had made two miscues in 34 opportunities at the position. The audition had begun the day that McLain was gunning for (but fell short of) victory number 32 in Baltimore on September 23. It was enough of a sam-pling to give Smith the confidence to place him there for the World Series–although Oyler would naturally be inserted back at shortstop, and Stanley back in center, if the Tigers held a lead late in one of the contests. "I'd just be changing one position," Smith reasoned about the idea. "Northrup can play a good center field, so it wouldn't be weakening two positions. This is not a sentimental gesture to get Kaline in the lineup. We're out to win this thing, and by putting an extra bat in the order, we think we can do it." Few in Detroit doubted Smith — who, in the last couple of weeks of the regular season had also toyed with the idea of putting Kaline at third base — as the manager had pulled all the right strings in the summer of 1968. Some in local press, though, were not sure that Stanley was ready for shortstop play in the World Series after only 67 innings of experience. "The Tigers' $40,000-a-year manager is a pretty good pool shooter," Pete Waldmeir of the *Detroit News* granted. "Frankly, I think the move weakens the Tigers. But I don't get paid the $40,000 to write the lineup cards." To a man, the Tiger players were extremely confident that Stanley could do the job.

"Mayo was no great teacher or strategist," McLain would say years later, "but he was a good judge of talent and character. He recognized that, with the players he had, all he had to do was fill out the lineup card every night, and we'd win more games than we lost. And we did." And also winding up his career on the Detroit bench was Eddie Mathews, who unlike Face was indeed made eligible for World Series play. Mathews had appeared in his first World Series eleven years earlier with the Milwaukee Braves.

Among other the intriguing personalities on the 1968 Tigers was pinch hitter Gates Brown, who that season had batted a major league-record .472 in that role. Brown had previously spent two years in the Ohio State Peni-tentiary for a breaking-and-entering conviction, where in 1960 Tigers farm director (and later general manager) Jim Campbell convinced the organiza-tion to give him a contract. He would end his career in 1975 — which was the first full season for another Tigers outfielder, a Detroit kid named Ron LeFlore. LeFlore himself had served time in prison for his role in the Janu-ary 1970 armed robbery of Dee's Bar, a Detroit place across from the Chrysler

Three of the big sluggers in the Cardinals' lineup — Roger Maris, Mike Shannon, and Orlando Cepeda — compare their war clubs before the first game of the 1968 World Series against the Detroit Tigers. (*St. Louis Globe-Democrat* / Archives of the St. Louis Mercantile Library)

Stamping Plant on Mack Avenue to which LeFlore directed his accomplices. It was Brown's conduct after starting his pro career that gave the Tigers the confidence to give LeFlore an opportunity as well. Discovered in 1973 at the Jackson State Prison by then–Tigers manager Billy Martin, LeFlore's athleticism earned him a special tryout with the Tigers, an early parole, and ultimately the Most Valuable Player award in the Florida State League in 1974. He joined the Tigers on August 1 of that year, and would steal 23 bases in his first two months in the big leagues. That same year, Brown — as he did in 1968 — was able to muster the most pinch-hits in the American League. Receiving jeers from spectators due to his checkered past, LeFlore turned to Brown for advice and support during those days, and Gates provided it. "I warned him about associating with his old friends in Detroit," Brown was quoted as saying in LeFlore's autobiography. "I knew they'd come after him, just like they used to come after me whenever I went back to Cleveland. I told him, 'You've got to make a choice — do you want to be messing with them, or do you want to pursue a career?'" In 1976, just as he was beginning that career, LeFlore was struck with devastation again. His younger brother Gerald — whom LeFlore had tried for years to keep off the tough Detroit streets, and out of his older brother's own footsteps — was shot and killed in an east side house on April 23. Throughout the tragedy, however, LeFlore was able to maintain a thirty-game hitting streak that he had perpetuated since the beginning of the season, finally being ended by Baltimore's Tippy Martinez on May 28. In July, LeFlore would lead off for the American League in the All-Star Game, receiving more than two million votes from the fans.

Detroit was not unlike St. Louis, Cincinnati, and other smaller major league cities at the time, in which the fans felt a close kinship to the players and regarded them as true neighbors. The AC Spark Plug Division of General Motors in Detroit, for example, displayed its local pride by announcing that it was donating one hundred baseballs for every home run hit in the World Series — by a Tiger or a Cardinal — to local little league teams. As this type of affinity grew over the 1960s in Detroit, the big gathering place for players and fans alike was the Lindell Athletic Club, or "Lindell A.C." as it was commonly known. Only a few blocks from Tiger Stadium, the A.C. was a place from another era, where superstars could toast a beer with the locals with social class and financial boundaries being temporarily forgotten. Owners Jimmy and Johnny Butsicaris were prominent figures in the Detroit sports community, and enjoyed the prestige that came along with it. Having moved in 1963 from its original location inside the Lindell Hotel, the new spot at 1300 Cass Avenue was, in a sense, the first of the sports bars; while the entertainment did not come from games on big-screen televisions like today, it did arrive each day in the form of fresh sports conversation with anyone sitting nearby. When the Tigers clinched the pennant on September 17, the Butsicaris brothers "closed the cash registers and had the Tigers tend bar and pour drinks for free," according to Susan Whitall of the *Detroit News*. Jimmy Butsicaris had been instrumental in landing LeFlore his tryout with the Tigers, as he had been Billy Martin's best man at his wedding and was always bending Martin's ear about prospects he had uncovered — even behind prison walls. As prosperity passed it by, the doors to the A.C. would close for good in 2002, with its either boarded-up or broken windows on the four-story building now peering down on Cass Avenue.

In attempting to grab a larger portion of the vote in his race for the United States presidency, Hubert Humphrey announced 48 hours before Game One that, if elected, he would immediately suspend all bombing against North Vietnam; the same plan was later pronounced by his opponent, Richard M. Nixon. But political jabs were not only being thrown in Washington — they were audible in the nation's heartland as well. For the night before the series opener in St. Louis, McLain was playing the organ for a crowd in the Gaslight Room bar of the Sheraton-Jefferson Hotel into the early morning hours—even though he was to pitch the next afternoon. Before arriving at the ballpark the same morning as his partying, McLain told a national sports-writer, "I don't want to beat the Cardinals; I want to humiliate them." While McLain had been hooting it up at the Gaslight Room, down the street at the Chase Park Plaza Hotel, Gibson had been enjoying a more low-keyed eve-ning. And if he was the Cardinals' number-one all-time pitcher, then num-ber 1-A was sitting right next to him. Dizzy Dean was in the house, which was more than obvious wherever he decided to show. Tonight, he was pres-ent as a cheerleader. "Detroit's going to hit, but those Tigers aren't going to hit Gibson," Diz proclaimed, just as if he was stepping off the train again in Detroit for the opening of the 1934 World Series, where he was quoted as say-ing, "Where's them Tigers? I could beat them throwin' this-a-way," as he laughed and waved his left (non-throwing) arm. But this was 1968, and it was now another man's turn. "At least their right-handed batters aren't going to hit Gibson," Diz continued. Dean also figured that Lolich would be tougher on the Cards than the headline-grabbing McLain. "Gibson just loves those free swingers like Willie Horton — right, Bob?" Gibby, in his unwavering sto-icism, only cracked a slight smile.

It didn't take long for McLain's inflammatory quote to reach the Cardi-nals' dressing room. "I couldn't ignore what Denny said," Gibson would note years later. "I'm sure he regretted it as soon as it left his mouth. I had noth-ing against him personally. In fact, I kind of admired the way he marketed himself. He understood where the bottom line was in this game. I just didn't think any pitcher could beat me in a World Series. I sure as hell didn't think Denny McLain could do it."

Thus, McLain had awoken the sleeping giant with the big red number 45 on his back, and when Gibson arrived at Busch Stadium to undertake his duty, his irritability was already simmering. Media men who had covered the Cardinals during the past few years knew that it was not a good idea to pester the big right-hander before a game he was pitching — let alone before a World Series opener. Some of the national writers on the scene, in St. Louis for the first time, were somehow oblivious to this notion, however. They instead took the unique opportunity to step over to Gibson's locker less than an hour before gametime. Since that morning, there had been a civil rights march of black activists underway beneath the Gateway Arch, and one reporter rushed over to Gibson — while he was getting into his uniform — to ask him what he thought of it.

"I don't give a f---," Gibson replied, continuing to tie his cleats vigor-ously — and not even looking up. "I've got a ballgame to pitch." In recent days, Gibson and Flood had also been approached by the Black Muslims, who asked for assistance with their cause. Both players refused, believing that the group produced more racial division than unification. The pitcher finished his preparation and trotted out to the field, even a bit more angry than when the suburban Boston coffee shop had left him breakfast-less one year earlier. As the 1968 World Series got underway, the Cardinals were looking to become the only National League team to repeat as world champions since John McGraw's Giants of 1921 and 1922. And according the Broeg, the Cardinals would prevail in the maximum number of contests. "Until someone shows me — a Show-Me guy from Missouri — that Gibson and associates can lose one they've got to win, this choice has to be the Redbirds in seven."

Out on the field, the Tigers were gazing wondrously at the cavernous, modern ballpark in St. Louis. In viewing the far-away outfield walls of Busch Stadium from the visitors' dugout, McLain sent another warning for the St. Louis men. "The Cardinals thought that the Boston park was bad — wait until they get a look at ours. Why, it could be a series of 10-to-9 games. Not that I care — if we won."

For the third time in a row, the Cardinals were going into the World Series as the under-appreciated underdogs— at least in their own minds. It was a warm eighty degrees under partly cloudy skies in St. Louis as the fans piled into Busch for Game One, assembling into what would be the largest crowd to ever watch a sporting event in the state of Missouri. The Cardinals— sporting the exact same lineup as in the 1967 World Series, and for most of the 1968 regular season — took the field in their shining white uniforms with their birds-on-the-bat jerseys, as an overflow mob of 54,692 screamed their support. As in 1967, 1964, and every year that the Redbirds had found themselves in the championship round, Cardinals followers had come into town from out-state Missouri, Arkansas, Mississippi, and beyond, not wanting to miss an opportunity to see baseball's greatest stage. Refusing to be intimidated, however, the Tigers would not strategize like they had in the 1934 World Series against the Cards. In the opener of the Fall Classic that year, Tigers manager Mickey Cochrane withered and used a second-rate pitcher, Alvin Crowder, against Dizzy Dean. Thinking that Dean could not be beaten no matter whom he pitched, Cochrane immediately gave St. Louis a psychological edge. Now, learning from this familiar history and not wanting to make the same mistake, Mayo Smith ran his number-one man out there. Even before a pitch was thrown, experts were anticipating that the Gibson-McLain match-up would become one of the greatest games in postseason history.

12. The Rematch of '34

Obstacles are those frightful things you see when you take your eyes off your goal.

— Henry Ford

The umpires sprinted out to their positions under the warm Missouri sun, as the expanded crew included Tom Gorman, Stan Landes, and Doug Harvey from the National League and Jim Honochick, Bill Kinnamon, and Bill Haller from the American League. Starting quickly, the agitated Gibson struck out seven of the first ten men he faced, and at one point over the first, second, and third innings, he fanned Kaline, Cash, Horton, Northrup, and Freehan in succession. Stanley had interjected a single in the first inning, but was quickly gunned down by McCarver while trying to steal. The Cards had threatened briefly in the bottom of the second when McCarver tripled off McLain with one out, but was left stranded as Shannon and Javier both went down on strikes. McLain missed a chance to help himself in the top of the third, as he bunted foul for strike three, a failed sacrifice that would have moved Don Wert, who had singled, to second.

By the bottom of the fourth, the game was proceeding just as most had imagined — with little offensive punch, and the slightest defensive mistake by either side perhaps tipping the entire balance in favor of the opponent. Maris and McCarver had walked, placing men on first and second with one out. Then Shannon — the Cardinals' clutch RBI man for 1968 — smacked a hard single to left field that Horton bobbled in an attempt to throw out Maris at the plate. Shannon said later that the high, tight fastball would certainly have been called a ball if he had not swung. Maris scored, and on the play, McCarver and Shannon were able to move into second and third respectively on the throw home. Javier then delivered a shattering blow to McLain, driving

332

another hit to right that plated two more runs for a 3–0 lead for Gibson. The protagonist rolled on, and by the time the game reached the Tigers' seventh, Gibson ended the inning by striking out Northrup and Freehan in succession, giving him 13 K's to that point. In the bottom half, Brock slammed a long, two-out, solo homer to the stands for a 4–0 St. Louis advantage, victimizing Dobson who had entered for McLain an inning earlier (McCarver would later speculate that McLain looked like a tired pitcher—from what McCarver presumed to be his overuse during the regular season). Eddie Mathews became Gibson's fourteenth strikeout casualty in the top of the eighth, placing him in reach of yet one more record in the final round.

The Cards were hurried through their turns at-bat in the bottom of the eighth, and when Gibson emerged from the dugout to take the mound in the ninth, a large portion of the crowd at Busch Stadium rose to its feet. Stanley quieted things momentarily with a single to center field, his second hit of the day. But the noise started up again when Kaline struck out, which gave Gibson fifteen for the game and tied Koufax for the all-time single-game record in a World Series. There was now no denying the determined fireballer, as the ear-piercing screams from the stands reached a deafening crescendo when Cash fanned as well, giving Gibby the new mark and topping his career high that he had set only weeks earlier against Pittsburgh. McCarver then quickly hustled out to the mound, simply to let Gibson know what he had accomplished, as the pitcher was unaware of the circumstances (as Gibson would later admit). Even so, Bob merely held his glove out impatiently and muttered something unpleasant to his catcher, at which point McCarver turned and retreated to his position. "I couldn't imagine what all the shouting was about," Gibson told the *New York Daily News* about the cheering. "Then I happened to turn around and look at the scoreboard. I saw something about sixteen strikeouts and a World Series record, and then I knew." Softening only an inch, Gibson took a moment to subtly tip his cap to acknowledge the roaring support that was cascading down from the stands. The last sacrificial lamb was Horton, and he was undone by a devastating breaking ball on a two-strike count that left the Detroit hitter spaghetti-kneed and helpless. It was number seventeen (which also tied Dean's Cardinals record set in the regular season in 1933) and a 4–0 shutout for the toast of St. Louis, as well a 1–0 lead in the series for the home team. When asked what he thought about Gibson breaking his record, Koufax laughed. "Well, there's no way for me to ever get it back," he joked. "I think Bob has put it beyond anyone's reach." As Koufax was getting out of his cab in front of Busch Stadium earlier that day, he had assured the cabbie that the team that won the first game would win the series. In turn, the cabbie spread the prophetic words he had gotten from the great lefthander to all he carted over the course of the day. In speaking years later of the final pitch that left Horton frozen in the batter's box,

McCarver would say, "I can still see that last slider heading right for Horton's ribs, and then breaking over the plate." Out of the 144 pitches that Gibson had thrown on the afternoon, the vast majority (91) were fastballs. In the locker room, the hero spent five minutes on the phone, receiving a congratulatory long-distance call from Hubert Humphrey in Washington.

Despite losing, McLain was relaxed and chatty as usual after the game, and even though he admitted that it was one of his poorer performances of the year, he was nonetheless miffed about being pulled from the game in the top of the sixth. "You don't pitch 336 innings and get yanked out of a ballgame," he squawked with his eyes rolling upwards. He also said that he was not intimidated by the Cardinals' reputation for running speed on the bases, nor were the rest of the Tigers. "Oakland, in our league, has a faster club," he said while calmly sipping another Pepsi. Over in another corner of the locker room, his catcher, Freehan, made a revelation. "McLain hasn't had good velocity on his fastball for a couple of weeks now. He's flipping the ball — he's not throwing it."

It was obvious that the Tigers, in facing Gibson for the first time, were experiencing something unique to anything they had seen in the American League during the regular season. "I've never seen anyone pitch like that before," Kaline confirmed after Game One. "Today, he was the best I've ever seen. If he continues to pitch like that, we can't beat him." Most on the Detroit roster, in fact, could not contain their amazement. "He never wastes a round," Horton added. "He came in throwing as hard to the number nine hitter as to the number three hitter, as hard in the ninth inning as he did in the first." Norm Cash, less apologetic, added a different perspective. "Sure, Gibson pitched a great game. But we helped him. When you're a big swinger — and we've got big swingers — you find yourself overswinging. This is a World Series. You try harder to do things. That's what we did against him." Mathews felt much the same way. "They talk about all the team spirit the Cardinals have, all the team effort ... well, those 17 strikeouts of Gibson — that was a great team effort on *our* part, too."

In response, Gibson simply noted, "I'd *rather* pitch to guys who swing for home runs."

Northrup's simple summary of the afternoon was perhaps the most accurate. "There wasn't any human being alive that could have hit him that day ... I don't think I've ever faced anybody on one given day who could so completely overmatch an entire team of fastball hitters." And, it was a special day for a man with one of the best views in the house — Gibson's shortstop, Maxvill. "I've been playing baseball since I was seven years old," Maxvill said on the Cardinals' side of the wall. "But this was the first time in my life I had chills run up and down my spine."

What did the pitcher say to his catcher when McCarver went to the mound to visit him in the ninth? Apparently, it could not be repeated. "I generally enjoyed McCarver's company," Gibson explained, "but not in my office."

The box score from Game One:

Detroit	0 0 0	0 0 0	0 0 0—0	5	3
St. Louis	0 0 3	0 0 1	0 x—4	6	0

Batting

Detroit	*AB*	*R*	*H*	*RBI*
McAuliffe 2b	4	0	1	0
Stanley ss	4	0	2	0
Kaline rf	4	0	1	0
Cash 1b	4	0	0	0
Horton lf	4	0	0	0
Northrup cf	3	0	0	0
Freehan	2	0	0	0
Wert 3b	2	0	1	0
Mathews ph	1	0	0	0
Tracewski 3b	0	0	0	0
McLain p	1	0	0	0
Matchick ph	1	0	0	0
Dobson p	0	0	0	0
Brown ph	1	0	0	0
McMahon p	0	0	0	0
Totals	31	0	5	0

E: Cash (1), Northrup (1), Freehan (1).
2B: Kaline (1, off Gibson).
CS: Stanley (1, 2nd base by Gibson/McCarver).
Team LOB: 5.

St. Louis	*AB*	*R*	*H*	*RBI*
Brock lf	4	1	1	1
Flood cf	4	0	1	0
Maris rf	3	1	0	0
Cepeda 1b	4	0	0	0
McCarver c	3	1	1	0
Shannon 3b	4	1	2	1
Javier 2b	3	0	1	2
Maxvill ss	2	0	0	0
Gibson p	2	0	0	0
Totals	29	4	6	4

3B: McCarver (1, off McLain).
HR: Brock (1, 7th inning off Dobson 0 on, 2 out).
SH: Gibson (1, off McLain).
SB: Brock (1, 2nd base off McLain/Freehan); Javier (1, 2nd base off McLain/Freehan); Flood (1, 2nd base off Dobson/Freehan).
CS: Javier (1, 2nd base by Dobson/Freehan).
Team LOB: 6.

Pitching

Detroit	IP	H	R	ER	BB	SO	HR
McLain L (0–1)	5	3	3	2	3	3	0
Dobson	2	2	1	1	1	0	1
McMahon	1	1	0	0	0	0	0
St. Louis	IP	H	R	ER	BB	SO	HR
Gibson W (1–0)	9	5	0	0	1	17	0

The Cards had struck a monumental blow, with the two pitching titans having gone head to head in the opening battle with the St. Louis man clearly standing on top. Now, in an effort to keep the momentum going, Schoendienst turned to one of his pleasant younger surprises from the past couple of seasons. Briles, in starting Game Two for the Cardinals, said that he "wasn't so scared" as he had been in starting a World Series game against the Red Sox in 1967. "I was especially nervous the day before I pitched in the series last year," Briles told a reporter. "And I was on pins and needles the morning before I pitched. I think that anyone who says he isn't nervous before pitching in a World Series is fibbing." Briles said he was not concerned by the home-run hitters that filled the Detroit lineup, in light of the fact that the right-hander had given up a club-high 18 longballs during the regular season. The Tigers, on the other hand, were looking to bounce back behind their ever-confident leader in Smith. The date was October 3, and it was the two-year anniversary of Smith's acceptance of a two-year contract agreement to lead the team (two of the Tigers managers from 1966 — Charley Dressen and Bob Swift — had passed away during that year. Swift, in fact — long since fired, and leaving Frank Skaff to finish the second half of the '66 season as manager — would pass on October 17, 1966, two weeks after Smith was given the job). His choice was Mickey Lolich, the meaty lefthander who rode his motorcycle 40 miles each way from his home in the Detroit suburbs every day to his job at Tiger Stadium. Lolich, who had considerable movement on his pitches, threw from the left side only because of a childhood accident in which (ironically) a motorcycle fell on his left shoulder, breaking the collarbone. To rehabilitate the injury, Lolich's parents were told to regularly rotate the arm in a circular motion — a procedure, Mickey was convinced, that readied him for a professional pitching career.

Over in the Cardinals' locker room, meanwhile, Gibson was trying to relax after his incredible performance the previous day, as he worked on a crossword puzzle while sitting in shorts and his sanitary socks in front of his locker. He looked up over in the direction of the newly-acquired Ron Davis, who was seemed exceptionally preoccupied. Schoendienst had just told Davis that he was getting the start over Maris in right field on the afternoon — an order, Gibson sensed, that Davis did not seem to want. "What stands out in my memory is the image of Davis after hearing that he would be in the lineup. Instead of celebrating the opportunity to start a World Series game, he sat solemnly in front of his locker with his head hung low, as if he dreaded the assignment."

The temperature at the starting time of Game Two had dropped considerably from the previous afternoon — down to 60 degrees, and falling throughout the day — as many who had used the Game One temperatures as a gauge found themselves shivering in short-sleeved shirts. In addition to the 130,000 cups of soda and 110,000 cups of beer sold on the day at Busch Stadium according to the *Post-Dispatch*, vendors estimated that a record number of hot coffees were dispensed as well. Shortly after Marty Bronson sang the national anthem, Medwick — fresh off his Hall of Fame induction — threw out the first pitch. And Eugene McCarthy, fresh off his defeat by Humphrey for the Democratic presidential nomination, watched the game from a seat behind home plate. During batting practice, McCarthy — recalling the days in which he played for St. John's College in Minnesota — made his way down to the field as a large collection of photographers followed his every move. McCarthy fancied himself a student of the finer points of the game, and was not seeking out Gibson, McLain, nor one of the other well-known stars — but rather, his object was the inconspicuous Hoerner. The senator had been commissioned by *Life* magazine to write a collection of stories about the series, and had heard that the relief pitcher was one of the major league's wizards in handling a fungo bat. McCarthy thus wanted a first-hand demonstration. It was Hoerner, of course, who made a habit of putting dents in the Astrodome roof with fungo shots whenever the Cards stopped in Houston. Joe obliged the congressman, and sent some long, high, soft fly balls into the outfield. He attempted to launch them in between batting practice hits, but was mostly unsuccessful — causing the batboy Jerry Gibson, and other shaggers to dodge line drives coming their way, while simultaneously watching out for Hoerner's high ones.

It was the Tigers who jumped ahead this time, as in the second inning Horton walloped a long homer halfway up the bleacher seats in left field. The round-tripper traveled way up past the 386-foot sign in the left-center field gap for a 1–0 Detroit advantage. The homer came after a key defensive play by Kaline in right field in the Cardinals' half of the first. With runners on

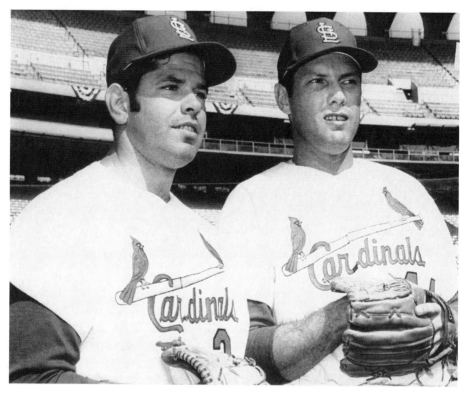

**Pitchers Nelson Briles (left) and Ray Washburn prepare for their starting assign-
ments in the 1968 World Series. (*St. Louis Globe-Democrat* / Archives of the St.
Louis Mercantile Library)**

first and second with one out, Kaline and the rest of the Detroit outfield was
playing Cepeda to pull. Orlando, conversely, hit a slicing shot down the right
field line that required a dead sprint for Kaline to make the catch before the
ball landed in fair territory. Kaline then handled a routine pop fly from Shannon to end the inning, and the initial Redbird threat was thwarted.

The Detroit lead was doubled in the third, when after Wert popped up
to Javier to open the inning, the pitcher, Lolich, launched a blast of his own
off Briles. It would be the only home run in Lolich's 16-year career, coming
on a high fastball that got away from Briles on a 2–2 count. It broke open the
power surge for which Detroit had been looking, and upon which they had
counted for their run support all season long. "The Tiger musclemen
seem to shrink spacious Busch Stadium," Russo admired in his column the
following day. That same power surge made itself readily-known once again
in the sixth, as Cash drove another solo shot out of the park off Briles, part
of a three-run inning that gave Detroit a 5–0 lead. The Cardinals finally

pushed their first run of the day across in the bottom of the sixth, as Brock walked, stole second, moved to third on a Flood single, and went home on a hit by Cepeda. The Tigers squelched any St. Louis spirit for a comeback, however, by replacing the run in the top of the seventh as Northrup grounded into a double play off Willis after Carlton had permitted runners to reach first and third to open the inning. The comfortable lead allowed Smith to implement the second part of his shortstop plan. He inserted the sure-handed Oyler into the game at the position, placed Stanley in his normal position in center field, moved Northrup from center over to left, and took Horton out of the game — giving the Tigers the iron-clad defensive platoon with which they had enjoyed so much success during the summer with their frequent late-game leads.

Like in the 1967 series against the Red Sox, the base-stealing choices of Brock came into question by the opponent later in the game. With the Cardinals trailing 6–1 in the eighth inning, Brock took off for second and stole it successfully, bucking conventional wisdom when a team is down by so many runs. Lolich walked off the mound a few steps towards Brock and said something to him. Afterwards, Lolich's sentiments — though mostly misrepresented — were printed in the papers. "It was definitely for his own self-glory," the pitcher was reported as saying. "He wants to set a record for stolen bases or something. There can't be any other reason [for him to run in that situation] ... sure, I could just disregard him. But when he takes a big lead like that, it's almost an insult." Lolich threw over towards first, but Brock had already taken off for second base, and beat Cash's subsequent throw to Oyler. In the coming days, Lolich would deny making the statements, saying he was taken out of context in only claiming that he did not know why Brock had decided to steal, and that it merely surprised him. He would be left stranded anyway, while control problems would plague Hoerner in the ninth inning. He walked three Tigers hitters that led to two more runs, and the game ended in an 8–1 blowout for Detroit. One of the biggest Detroit cheerleaders on the afternoon was their pinch hitter extraordinaire, Gates Brown. "I enjoy days like this," he said, "just sitting back and watching the guys go around the bases." And interestingly, Lolich was the dominant pitcher that McLain was expected to have been, going the distance in permitting the lone run on six hits while striking out nine Cardinals.

Despite the poor performance by Briles, Schoendienst was planning on bringing him back in the fifth contest in Detroit, where the series now shifted for the next three games.

The box score from Game Two:

Detroit   0 1 1 0 0 3 1 0 2 — 8 13 1
St. Louis   0 0 0 0 0 1 0 0 0 — 1   6 1

Batting

Detroit	AB	R	H	RBI
McAuliffe 2b	5	0	2	2
Stanley ss, cf	5	0	1	0
Kaline rf	5	2	2	0
Cash 1b	5	2	3	1
Horton lf	3	2	2	1
Oyler ss	0	0	0	0
Northrup cf, lf	5	1	1	0
Freehan c	4	0	0	0
Wert 3b	2	0	0	1
Lolich p	4	1	2	2
Totals	38	8	13	7

DP: 1.

E: Stanley (1).

HR: Horton (1, 2nd inning off Briles 0 on, 1 out); Lolich (1, 3rd inning off Briles 0 on, 1 out); Cash (1, 6th inning off Briles 0 on, 0 out).

SH: Oyler (1, off Hoerner).

IBB: Freehan (1, by Hoerner).

Team LOB: 11.

St. Louis	AB	R	H	RBI
Brock lf	3	1	1	0
Javier 2b	4	0	2	0
Flood cf	3	0	1	0
Cepeda 1b	4	0	2	1
Shannon 3b	4	0	0	0
McCarver c	4	0	0	0
Davis rf	4	0	0	0
Maxvill ss	3	0	0	0
Briles p	2	0	0	0
Carlton p	0	0	0	0
Willis p	0	0	0	0
Gagliano ph	1	0	0	0
Hoerner p	0	0	0	0
Totals	32	1	6	1

DP: 2.

E: Shannon (1).

SB: Brock 2 (3, 2nd base off Lolich/Freehan 2).

Team LOB: 6.

Pitching

Detroit	IP	H	R	ER	BB	SO	HR
Lolich W (1–0)	9	6	1	1	2	9	0

St. Louis	IP	H	R	ER	BB	SO	HR
Briles L (0–1)	5	7	4	4	1	2	3
Carlton	1	4	2	2	1	1	0
Willis	2	1	0	0	2	2	0
Hoerner	1	1	2	0	3	1	0

IBB: Hoerner (1, Freehan).

The temperature had now dipped even further, all the way down into the mid-40s as the Cardinals arrived at Tiger Stadium in Detroit for a workout on October 4, the off-day in between the second and third games. Cepeda, looking for some fun, later spent that evening by warming up at the Keyboard Lounge — where the main attraction was not McLain, as one might expect from the name of the establishment, but rather Cepeda's favorite keyboardist in Art Blakely. It was Ray Washburn's turn in Game Three, the starting assignment being his reward for a magnificent second half of the season in recovering from his arm troubles. Schoendienst felt very comfortable using him in the small ballpark in Detroit, as Washburn had allowed half as many home runs (nine) as had Briles during the season. Washburn was optimistic about the prospects of pitching in Detroit. "If you make bad pitches in a big ball-park, the ball will go out of there, too," he pointed out. "The Detroit park looks smaller than it really is because it's double-decked. If you're not pitching well, any park is terrifying." Gibson added that Tiger Stadium was bigger than the Cardinals' previous home in old Busch Stadium at the corner of Grand and Dodier back in St. Louis. Washburn's opponent was Earl Wilson, who like Ray had pitched a no-hitter himself, with Wilson's gem occurring back in 1962 as a member of the Red Sox. While his number of wins had slipped in 1968 (from 22 in 1967 to 13 in '68), he was still considered a reliable veteran for Smith. In addition, Wilson was the top hitter among the Tigers pitchers during the year with a .227 average, having hit an impressive 33 home runs in his career by 1968, the fifth most all-time by a pitcher.

The clock at a bank near Tiger Stadium showed that the temperature had creeped back up slightly to 54 degrees when Wilson offered his first pitch to Brock in Game Three. Lou, undaunted by Lolich's post-game comments in St. Louis, went right back to work as he walked — a base on balls precipitated by third-base umpire Bill Haller calling Wilson for a spitball — and quickly stole second. Flood walked as well in following him, and when the third batter Maris struck out swinging on the third pitch to him, Brock was already heading full-steam for third base. But this time, Freehan was not caught napping. He sprung out of his crouch and threw a perfect strike to a waiting Wert, who put the tag on Brock. Wilson then settled himself down, and made Cepeda ground out harmlessly to end the inning. Over the course of the regular season, the Tigers had strung together overpowering streaks of long-ball hitting. The homer monsters had again been unleashed by Briles two days earlier, and with two out and McAuliffe on first after a single, it was now the "old man's" turn. Kaline grabbed hold of a hanging curve from Washburn, who like Wilson was unable to properly find his grip because of the cold, damp conditions, and added himself to the Detroit power parade as he stroked a two-run homer into the short porch in left field.

Confident the Cardinals could score off Wilson, Schoendienst — while tempted to use Carlton — allowed Washburn to hit for himself in leading off the fifth, primarily because he was still only two runs behind. Washburn went down on strikes, but his mates responded in a hurry. Brock singled and stole second once again on the very first pitch, tying his own World Series record with his third stolen base of the game (in addition to being thrown out at third base in the first inning, Brock had stolen second once again in the third after singling on an infield hit in front of Stanley). With all of his stealing success in the postseason the past two years, it was difficult to believe that Brock did not swipe a single base in the Cardinals' seven-game triumph over the Yankees in 1964. Worried that Brock would try for third once again, Wilson paused nervously for a long time in his stretch as the distracted pitcher then made a weak offering to Flood, who deposited it in the gap for a run-scoring double. Maris then walked to the empty base at first as Dobson made another appearance in relieving Wilson, who had suddenly pulled a muscle in his leg and had to be helped off the field. Cepeda popped out to Freehan, leaving McCarver to bat in a critical turning point of the game. The catcher was looking to make amends for his poor performance against the Red Sox in the 1967 series in which he batted just .125 with two RBIs, and he realized this was an opportunity to make a statement. He responded ably by belting a Wilson fastball far over the right-center wall, giving the Cards a sudden 4–2 lead.

McCarver's shot demoralized the Tigers, although McAuliffe responded with a solo homer off Washburn in the bottom of the fifth to trim the lead back to one. When Washburn walked Horton and Cash with one out in the sixth, Hoerner entered the game unusually early (as Washburn had already thrown 111 pitches), but the Tigers had one of their main left-handed threats— Northrup — up with runners in scoring position. Upon his removal from the game, Washburn took a more understanding stance than McLain did after Game One; he trusted his manager's decision. "In a short series, you have to make every move you can," he said of Schoendienst's hook. It turned out to be the right maneuver, as Hoerner quickly doused the potential rally by retiring both Northrup and Freehan. Then Cepeda — who, like McCarver had struggled in the 1967 postseason with an even-worse .103 mark and one RBI against Boston — delivered on cue with a three-run, line shot home run to left field off Don McMahon, scoring Maris and Flood ahead of him for a 7–3 lead. The ball struck by Cepeda got no more than twenty feet off the ground, leaving the yard before he was even arriving at first base. A couple of steps from home plate, Cha-Cha took a big leap and landed with both feet on the dish, both of his hands slapping those of Flood, as Cepeda hit what he called "the biggest home run of my life." And in the spirit of the superstitious Cardinals, there was no way he was going to break up a hot streak — for Cepeda later announced that he was heading back to the Keyboard Lounge again that night. Hoerner went the rest of the way and held off the Detroit men for the 7–3 final, giving St. Louis a 2–1 lead in the series as he felt much the same about the memorable afternoon as Cepeda.

"This is the happiest day of my life," Hoerner said after the game. "My mother and father were here from Dubuque, Iowa." He had gone nearly four full innings in saving the win, tying his longest stint in his five seasons in the big leagues.

When Brock reached first base in the eighth inning, looking to provide another insurance run, it would become the first time he had been stranded on first by his teammates in the last two World Series.

The box score from Game Three:

```
St. Louis    0 0 0 0 4 0 3 0 0—7  13 0
Detroit      0 0 2 0 1 0 0 0 0—3   4 0
```

Batting

St. Louis	**AB**	**R**	**H**	**RBI**
Brock lf	4	1	3	0
Flood cf	4	2	2	1
Maris rf	3	2	1	0
Cepeda 1b	5	1	1	3
McCarver c	5	1	2	3
Shannon 3b	4	0	2	0
Javier 2b	4	0	1	0
Maxvill ss	4	0	0	0
Washburn p	3	0	0	0
Hoerner p	2	0	1	0
Totals	38	7	13	7

2B: Flood (1, off Wilson); Maris (1, off McMahon).

HR: McCarver (1, 5th inning off Dobson 2 on, 2 out); Cepeda (1, 7th inning off McMahon 2 on, 0 out).

SB: Brock 3 (6, 2nd base off Wilson/Freehan 3).

CS: Brock (1, 3rd base by Wilson/Freehan); McCarver (1, 3rd base by Wilson/Freehan).

Team LOB: 11.

Detroit	**AB**	**R**	**H**	**RBI**
McAuliffe 2b	4	2	2	1
Stanley ss	3	0	0	0
Kaline rf	4	1	1	2
Cash 1b	3	0	0	0
Horton lf	2	0	0	0
Northrup cf	4	0	0	0
Freehan	3	0	0	0
Wert 3b	4	0	0	0
Wilson p	1	0	0	0
Dobson p	0	0	0	0
Matchick ph	1	0	0	0
McMahon p	0	0	0	0
Patterson p	0	0	0	0
Comer ph	1	0	1	0
Hiller p	0	0	0	0
Price ph	1	0	0	0
Totals	31	3	4	3

DP: 2.

HR: Kaline (1, 3rd inning off Washburn 1 on, 2 out); McAuliffe (1, 5th inning off Washburn 0 on, 2 out).

Team LOB: 6.

Pitching

St. Louis	**IP**	**H**	**R**	**ER**	**BB**	**SO**	**HR**
Washburn W (1–0)	5.1	3	3	3	4	3	2
Hoerner S (1)	3.2	1	0	0	1	2	0

Detroit	**IP**	**H**	**R**	**ER**	**BB**	**SO**	**HR**
Wilson L (0–1)	4.1	4	3	3	6	3	0
Dobson	0.2	2	1	1	0	0	1
McMahon	1	3	3	3	0	1	1
Patterson	1	0	0	0	0	0	0
Hiller	2	4	0	0	1	1	0

As dominant as Gibson had been in his record-setting performance in Game One, many of the Tigers—including Kaline—feared that he would be even harder to hit in Tiger Stadium. "We've got a lot of shadows in our park from the third inning on," Kaline revealed. "That's why Gibson will be tougher to hit. He'll be throwing out of the shadows."

The start of Game Four was delayed for more than half an hour by rain, as Gibson passed the time by eating three ice cream cones and working on another crossword puzzle in the locker room, as he listened to Briles give a radio interview on the other side of the room — this time, with no reporter daring to bother Gibson himself. Even so, he endured another evening of attempted distractions the night before. After taping an appearance on *The Bob Hope Show* (to appear on television the following week) and going to dinner with some friends, Gibson went to bed around midnight. In the days before the firewall of privacy was placed around athletes' hotel rooms, he was then awoken at two o'clock that morning with someone pounding on his hotel room door yelling, *"Telegram!"* When Gibson opened the door, no one was to be found. After he had fallen back asleep an hour or so later, the phone rang. The voice on the other end of the line asked, *"Is Denny McLain there?"* When he opened the door again later in the morning, he found the entryway to be decorated with flowers. Flowers are considered bad luck in baseball, as Mickey Cochrane had illustrated at the start of the 1934 World Series, when he refused to accept a wreath from some well-meaning Detroit fans which they had wheeled out to home plate before the first game against the Cardinals (it was a curse that was apparently dismissed by Brock, however, as Lou had recently opened a florist shop in Clayton, Missouri, just outside of St. Louis). With the jocularity only getting Gibson even more focused on his business at hand, apparently the Detroit fans had not learned the lessons of the underhanded coffee shop and hotel in Quincy, Massachusetts, from the previous year.

Additionally, the press in Detroit wanted to hear McLain say that his results against Gibson on this day would be different, even though many were warning Smith against "wasting" McLain in the rematch against the imposing Cardinals hurler. His response was less than satisfying to the locals. "It could be a psychological advantage to pitch in your own park, because it's always nice to pitch in your park," McLain began thoughtfully, scratching his chin and gazing up at the ceiling. "Except that I hate my park — I prefer to pitch on the road."

As McLain began to work with his teammates behind him, it seemed to the Tigers that Brock was always on base — even before the first pitch was made to him. This time, he touched all four bases in the first moment of the game, slamming a homer off Denny on the second pitch to give the Cards and Gibson an immediate 1–0 lead. Still rattled after retiring Flood, McLain then dropped a throw from Cash in covering first base on a grounder by Maris. McCarver and Shannon followed with singles, giving the Cardinals another first-inning run. With two out in the bottom half, the old pro Kaline surprised Gibson with a ringing double to the wall, but Bob escaped the inning unharmed as Cash was called out on strikes. In the third, the St. Louis lead doubled to 4–0 through a wave of hits, highlighted by a triple off the bat of McCarver. Unchecked by the great McLain, the Cardinals' offense was stopped only by nature — for in the middle of the rout that was continuing, a cold downpour hit the Detroit area that closed the contest for another hour and fifteen minutes. Sensing an unrelenting St. Louis onslaught, a large portion of the fans were chanting, *"Rain! Rain! Rain!"* in the hopes that a perpetual storm would cease play permanently for the day, causing a wash-out of the Cardinals runs as well. To take cover, many in the outfield crowd were scrambling towards the large scoreboard in center field that protected a wide swath of seats from the wind-blown elements. Play did eventually resume, however (as the grounds crew — perhaps for the first and only time in baseball history — was booed by the home folks as they pulled the tarpaulin from the field). And when it did, Smith chose to remove McLain with the hope of bringing him back sooner in the series, and instead turned the ball over to Joe Sparma. Sparma, the number-four starter on the staff during the regular season, was a former starting quarterback at Ohio State University. In 1961, he had led the Buckeyes to an undefeated season and the third of four national championships under coach Woody Hayes. Sparma and Lolich were both rumored to be trade-bait at midseason, but strong second halves of the season by both men kept them in Tigers uniforms — especially for Lolich, who won his last five starts of the regular season. McLain, his attitude literally changing with the weather, now started to complain again of stiffness in his pitching shoulder, and claimed that he might be done for the year. He did not join his teammates on the dugout bench, but rather chose to watch the game on a television in the clubhouse.

The entire day was soon becoming a lost cause for Detroit, as only two Tigers reached base after the fourth inning. Gibson would homer in the fourth, the second batter that Sparma faced, becoming the first pitcher to hit two home runs in his World Series career. Brock followed with a triple and another subsequent score, running the tally to 6–0. After they could salvage only a single run on a Northrup homer in the bottom of the fourth, the Tigers began stalling in the hopes of more rain and a postponement, as the home plate umpire Kinnamon constantly found himself going to the mound to break up "meetings" between Sparma and Freehan. The Cardinals, on the other hand, were employing a counter-measure of "hurry-up" tactics — such as with Javier, who took off on a doomed steal for second with the ball still in Sparma's hand. Sparma's successors in Patterson, Lasher, Hiller, and Dobson could do nothing to agitate the weather or stem the St. Louis assault, with the Cards scoring four more times in the eighth to stake a nine-run lead. It was at this point that Brock's choice of running opportunities again raised the ire of his opponents. After he had just cleared the bases with a three-run double to make the score 10–1–his third extra-base hit of the game — Brock stood out on second base with a smirk that Freehan, peering out from behind home plate, did not appreciate. Freehan and the Detroit pitchers knew that they were failing to corral Brock, and the series was quickly becoming a week of frustration for him. Freehan joined Maxvill in being the only hitless regulars so far in the series, with the Tigers catcher currently standing at 0 for 12 and having struck out in eight of those at-bats. After Freehan raised his mask and uttered a few expletives out towards the number 20 in the gray St. Louis uniform, Brock then took off for third and slid in safely, as he tied his record of seven steals in a World Series that he set in 1967 against the Red Sox. Perhaps Brock was thinking that he might not have a chance to tie the record tomorrow in Game Five, provided the Cardinals wrapped up the series that day with a win. Whatever his reasoning, both Brock and the Tigers knew that he was looking at a brush-back pitch the next time he stepped in the batter's box. Lou, however, was unapologetic. "I would not have tried to steal if I didn't have a record to shoot at," he said smugly, acting as if that explanation sufficed. "After all, this could be my last chance, I might never have another chance at a World Series. I owed it to myself." Brock claimed that he didn't hear any derision from Freehan or the Detroit bench — but it would not have mattered to him anyway. "It they did say anything, it wouldn't have been justified," he added.

Ironically, Brock's sometimes casual and risky base running would become a factor in a different manner later in the series.

Gibson permitted no Tigers hits in the fifth, sixth, seventh, and eighth. Cash ended things quietly in the ninth, hitting into a double play that was started and ended by Cepeda. It was Gibson's seventh straight win in the World Series, yet another record as he calmly walked off the mound afterwards, business as usual, as if it was simply a regular-season victory in June. In giving the Cards the most lopsided win in a World Series game in the past eight years, Gibson displayed a new quality never before seen by his pitching coach, Muffett. "It's unbelievable that a guy can pitch so hard four hours after he first warms up," he said in reference to the rain delay not fazing Gibby. "That showed his stamina and desire at their best." On top of all else, Gibson had established another World Series mark on the day by striking out at least ten batters for the fifth time in his career. And Hubert Humphrey, continuing his campaign tour for the presidency, appeared at the Cardinals locker room and congratulated Gibson, who in turn thanked the candidate for his phone call after Game One. Humphrey had viewed the rainy game in dry comfort from a special suite prepared for him, as Commissioner Eckert and baseball immortal Jackie Robinson sat by his side.

The box score from Game Four:

| St. Louis | 2 0 2 2 0 0 0 4 0 — 10 13 0 |
| Detroit | 0 0 0 1 0 0 0 0 0 — 1 5 4 |

Batting

St. Louis	AB	R	H	RBI
Brock lf	5	2	3	4
Flood cf	5	1	1	0
Maris rf	5	1	0	1
Cepeda 1b	4	0	1	0
McCarver c	5	1	3	1
Shannon 3b	5	1	2	2
Javier 2b	4	1	2	0
Maxvill ss	4	1	0	0
Gibson p	3	2	1	2
Totals	40	10	13	10

DP: 1.

2B: Shannon (1, off McLain); Javier (1, off Hiller); Brock (1, off Hiller).

3B: McCarver (2, off McLain); Brock (1, off Sparma).

HR: Brock (2, 1st inning off McLain 0 on, 0 out); Gibson (1,4th inning off Sparma 0 on, 0 out).

SB: Brock (7, 3rd base off Dobson/Freehan).

CS: Cepeda (1, 2nd base by Patterson/Freehan).

Team LOB: 7.

Detroit	AB	R	H	RBI
McAuliffe 2b	4	0	0	0
Stanley ss	4	0	0	0
Kaline rf	4	0	2	0
Cash 1b	4	0	1	0
Horton lf	3	0	0	0
Northrup cf	4	1	1	1
Mathews 3b	2	0	1	0
Freehan c	3	0	0	0
McLain p	1	0	0	0
Sparma p	0	0	0	0
Patterson p	0	0	0	0
Price ph	1	0	0	0
Lasher p	0	0	0	0
Matchick ph	1	0	0	0
Hiller p	0	0	0	0
Dobson p	0	0	0	0
Totals	31	1	5	1

E: Northrup (2), Mathews (1), Freehan (2), McLain (1).

2B: Kaline (2, off Gibson).

HR: Northrup (1, 4th inning off Gibson 0 on, 1 out).
Team LOB: 5.

Pitching

St. Louis	*IP*	*H*	*R*	*ER*	*BB*	*SO*	*HR*
Gibson W (2–0)	9	5	1	1	2	10	1

Detroit	*IP*	*H*	*R*	*ER*	*BB*	*SO*	*HR*
McLain L (0–2)	2.2	6	4	3	1	3	1
Sparma	0.1	2	2	2	0	0	1
Patterson	2	1	0	0	1	0	0
Lasher	2	1	0	0	0	1	0
Hiller	0	2	4	3	2	0	0
Dobson	2	1	0	0	0	0	0

The Cardinals were beginning to look even more impressive than in their 1967 defeat of the Red Sox, and it appeared that Gibson's momentum was accelerating to the point of being indomitable. With a commanding three-games-to-one lead, they were on the verge of wrapping up the title on the road as they had in the previous season, with two games back at home in reserve if needed — as well as Gibson available once again, if needed.

The series had been the first to have television ratings affixed to it, and the showdown between the Cardinals and the Tigers had drawn a 57 percent market share in the broadcast by NBC. It was this large number of people, however, who would next witness one of the more controversial pre-game events in World Series history before Game Five. Jose Feliciano, a blind Puerto Rican jazz singer, had been invited by Tigers radio broadcaster Ernie Harwell to perform the national anthem. As the game was about to begin, Feliciano slowly approached home plate carrying his guitar, with his guide dog Trudy at his side. Feliciano began by picking at a few unrecognizable chords on the guitar, and entered into a choppy, plodding version of the song that was indiscernible to most (although its strangeness would almost be considered the norm in comparison to renditions heard at ballparks today). The distorted version of the anthem caused a coast-to-coast uproar, as the switchboards at the NBC television control room lit up in full fury. It was denounced as an insult to the men currently fighting and dying in Vietnam, and when the song was concluded, Feliciano left the field at Tiger Stadium to a mixture of applause and jeers (the incident reminded many people of the debacle at the 1959 World Series at Comiskey Park in Chicago, when Nat Cole forgot the words to the anthem). When the song was finished, Lolich continued his warm-up tosses in the Tigers' bullpen, the man who was the owner of the Tigers' lone victory of the series in brilliantly bringing the team back in Game Two. Briles was simultaneously loosening up on the Cardinals' side, the choice for Schoendienst just as promised, with the youngster getting a chance to avenge his lackluster outing in the second contest. Schoendienst had considered going back to Carlton, but he figured that Briles was due. Sitting nearby in the bullpen and watching Briles get ready was the rookie Granger, when suddenly Wayne's wife yelled "DUCK!" to the other fans that were sitting in front of her. "This might be his only World Series," Mrs. Granger noted, "and I wanted to get some pictures of him."

Briles began with a desirable edge, as his teammates put him ahead 3–0 in the first inning and looked to make a quick claim for the championship on this day. Once again it was Brock getting under the skin of the Detroit personnel, and for the second day in a row he jumped on the second pitch of the game, this time in doubling, and soon after scoring on another hit from Flood. Flood then showed off his own speed by swiping second before Cepeda cracked his second homer of the series, a tremendous blast to left. It looked as if they were toying with the Tigers, exploding into a three-run first inning to end the series on a painful note for the Detroit men.

Briles had appeared to regain his confidence, breezing along until the fourth when the Tigers struck back. Stanley started things by slashing a triple to right field, a ball that barely touched the foul line and then bounced away from Ron Davis into the corner. Cepeda had claimed that Stanley did not touch first on his way around the bases, as most of the other eyes were on the baseball rattling off the wall. Nevertheless, it looked like Briles might escape unharmed as he next fielded a come-backer off the bat of Kaline, and held Stanley at third while retiring the batter. But another triple by Horton — tying a World Series record for the most three-baggers in an inning — and a single by Northrup closed the gap to 3–2. The Cardinals were starting to figure that they could outscore the Tigers if they had to, however, and they once again turned to their spark plug in the top of the fifth. After Briles led off by striking out, Brock hit his second double of the day and third of the series. Immediately, however, he was involved in the first of two questionable decisions in the coming days by two different Cardinals outfielders that would impact the series significantly. Next up was Javier, and as he had done all season long against lefthanders, he jumped on a mistake by Lolich to push a single through the hole to left field. Brock scampered around third and sped for home, and perhaps finally his overconfidence had gotten the best of him. He attempted to go across home plate standing up, but it was perfectly blocked by Freehan who tagged him out. Meanwhile, Flood — as the next hitter is supposed to do — was there just behind the scene to guide Brock, as Flood was waving his arms frantically downwards in telling Brock to slide. Brock's choice not to slide was doomed with a flawless throw from leftfielder Horton and flawless technique at the plate by Freehan, and the Cardinals' speedster was obviously caught in surprise. Freehan would say after the game that "the umpire [Doug

Harvey] told me that if Brock had slid, he would have been safe." The players in the Cardinals' dugout were noticeably surprised with the strength of Horton's arm, which they had previously only considered to be mediocre. "He's not a Carl Yastrzemski or Reggie Jackson," Tigers assistant coach Tony Cuccinello granted, "but he's a little better than average. He fools a lot of people."

Brock, like Gibson, had been rendering himself almost super-human to the Tigers at this point. But by his interception at home plate, Detroit found new hope for the series, now realizing that the main link in the St. Louis offense could actually be stymied. Lolich battled Briles to keep the score where it was, and when he retired Brock in the seventh by having him meekly ground out to McAuliffe at second, the Tigers finally saw an opportunity to pounce. Lolich, one of the unlikely hitting stars from Game One after being a .114 batter during the regular season, began things with a one-out single to right. A McAuliffe hit and Stanley walk followed, loading the bases for Kaline as Hoerner entered once again. Kaline, the beloved representative of the franchise for so long, now found himself at a rare moment of destiny. It was as if he envisioned his entire postseason career hanging from its proverbial string, the moment for which he had waited his entire life. He was now was determined to prolong the breathing of his beloved Tigers and beloved Detroit. He reached out over the plate, and drove an outside pitch over Javier that skidded on the worn October outfield grass, and the crowd's cheering was already at full throttle when McAuliffe crossed the plate with the go-ahead run behind Lolich's tally. The stands shook with noise again when Cash followed with another hit, scoring Stanley for a 5–3 Tigers lead. Hoerner exited in favor of Willis, but the damage had been done. Mayo Smith, as expected, went to his defensive platoon in the top of the eighth. Lolich cruised until the ninth, when Spiezio (pinch-hitting for Maxvill, who was now 0 for 16 in the series—five away from Gil Hodges' dubious 0-for-21 World Series record in 1952) singled to put runners on first and second with one out. Calmly, Lolich then fooled the seasoned Maris on strikes, and then gleefully got Brock, who in trying to check his swing grounded back to him at the mound to end the game. The men of Detroit would live to play another day.

Once again, Brock felt compelled to come up with an explanation for what he did on the bases, as well as a complaint about the call by Harvey. "I didn't slide because I had the play beaten," he moaned to the writers about the fateful play at the plate, in between chomping on some barbeque ribs that had been brought into the locker room. "My foot was already on top of the plate by the time Freehan got the ball. He didn't catch the ball until after I hit him."

But all an angry Schoendienst could mutter out in response was simply, "I don't know why Brock didn't slide." The series would now head back to

St. Louis, with the Cardinals still confident in running Washburn to the mound — and if necessary, Gibson for a Game Seven.

The box score from Game Five:

St. Louis   3 0 0 0 0 0 0 0 0 — 3 9 0

Detroit   0 0 0 2 0 0 3 0 x — 5 9 1

Batting

St. Louis	**AB**	**R**	**H**	**RBI**
Brock lf	5	1	3	0
Javier 2b	4	0	2	0
Flood cf	4	1	1	1
Cepeda 1b	4	1	1	2
Shannon 3b	4	0	0	0
McCarver c	3	0	1	0
Davis rf	3	0	0	0
Gagliano ph	1	0	0	0
Maxvill ss	3	0	0	0
Spiezio ph	1	0	1	0
Schofield pr	0	0	0	0
Briles p	2	0	0	0
Hoerner p	0	0	0	0
Willis p	0	0	0	0
Maris ph	1	0	0	0
Totals	35	3	9	3

DP: 1.

2B: Brock 2 (3, off Lolich 2).

HR: Cepeda (2, 1st inning off Lolich 1 on, 1 out).

HBP: Briles (1, by Lolich).

SB: Flood (2, 2nd base off Lolich/Freehan).

CS: Brock (2, 2nd base by Lolich/Freehan).

Team LOB: 7.

Detroit	**AB**	**R**	**H**	**RBI**
McAuliffe 2b	4	1	1	0
Stanley ss, cf	3	2	1	0
Kaline rf	4	0	2	2
Cash 1b	2	0	2	2
Horton lf	4	1	1	0
Oyler ss	0	0	0	0
Northrup cf, lf	3	0	1	1
Freehan c	4	0	0	0

Detroit	AB	R	H	RBI
Wert 3b	3	0	0	0
Lolich p	4	1	1	0
Totals	31	5	9	5

E: Cash (2).
3B: Stanley (1, off Briles); Horton (1, off Briles).
SF: Cash (1, off Briles).
IBB: Northrup (1, by Briles).
Team LOB: 7.

Pitching

St. Louis	IP	H	R	ER	BB	SO	HR
Briles	6.1	6	3	3	3	5	0
Hoerner L (0–1)	0	3	2	2	1	0	0
Willis	1.2	0	0	0	0	1	0
Detroit	IP	H	R	ER	BB	SO	HR
Lolich W (2–0)	9	9	3	3	1	8	1

HBP: Lolich (1, Briles).
IBB: Briles (1, Northrup).

During the travel day back to Busch Stadium, Smith — despite seeing his team in the process of a possible comeback — was now faced with a dilemma in deciding upon a starting pitcher for Game Six. Sparma, Wilson, and Dobson were possibilities, but in the end, he decided to hand the ball to his ace. It would be Denny McLain, the supposed sore-arm pitcher who offered his manager an encouraging wink while Smith was conducting a news conference on the off day, suggesting to him that everything was okay. It would be the first time since 1916 that a two-time loser in a seven-game World Series would get the ball on a third occasion. McLain had taken a cortisone shot two days earlier during the last game in Detroit, as he claimed to the papers it was the first time in four years that he had resorted to such a shot to ease the pain. However, he would be quoted later as saying, "Late 1965 was the first time I had a cortisone shot, and it just multiplied from there. In 1968, I probably got a dozen," according to William Mead. He mentioned that he was still sore but feeling better, and was willing to undertake the monumental impending responsibility.

Buoyed by both the return of their main attraction and from their comeback in Game Five, the Tigers soon made the sixth contest a laugher. Getting two runs off Washburn to start things in the second inning as an appetizer, the Detroit bats unloaded for ten runs in the third on seven hits, an assault that tied the one-inning World Series record set by the Philadelphia A's in 1929. McAuliffe, the leadoff hitter in the Tigers' order, reached base with a walk to begin the massacre, and by the time the end of the order was reached in the person of McLain, every man before him had reached base in some form or another. The big blow came off the bat of Northrup, as the home-grown Michigan hero from Breckenridge and Alma College pulled his club out of reach for the day. Washburn, Jaster, Willis, and Hughes all struggled during the inning, one which Schoendienst had been thinking "would never end." It nearly did not—fourteen Tigers hitters came to the plate, and when Northrup drove another ball towards the wall that was mercifully pulled in by Brock, the assault was over. Carlton was next, getting his first work in the series and ironically pitching well over three innings' time, though he permitted a thirteenth Detroit run with Kaline's second homer of the postseason in the fifth.

McLain settled into cruise control thenceforth, gaining his first career World Series victory as the Redbirds mustered a single run to make it a 13–1 final. The Cards' score came in the ninth, when Javier singled home Maris with two out to avoid complete embarrassment. It was a tough couple of days all around for Willis, for while he was in Detroit, his prized six-month-old Schnauzer, Fritz, had wandered away from his St. Louis home.

In the dugout during the game, Lolich — who had earned the nickname of "Lolo" to coincide with his last name, but also in correlation with his low leg drive as he fired the ball home — lobbied Mayo Smith for the pitching duties in Game Seven, provided the series would get that far. The request would be granted, but he would have a tall order on his hands. For even as his club had so completely captured the momentum in the series, Lolich would have to beat the man who had been unbeatable all summer and all autumn, the man who had dissolved bats over the past six months like no pitcher ever had. For even in the new-found enthusiasm that surrounded their efforts, the specter of Bob Gibson hovered menacingly around the Detroit clubhouse as players from both teams went to bed in a struggle to sleep during the night.

The box score from Game Six:

```
Detroit      0 2 10 0 1 0 0 0 0 — 13 12 1
St. Louis    0 0  0 0 0 0 0 0 1 —  1  9 1
```

Batting

Detroit	AB	R	H	RBI
McAuliffe 2b	2	2	0	0
Stanley ss, cf	5	2	1	0
Kaline rf	4	3	3	4
Cash 1b	4	2	3	2
Horton lf	3	2	2	2

Detroit	AB	R	H	RBI
Oyler ss	0	0	0	0
Northrup cf, lf	5	1	2	4
Freehan c	4	0	1	1
Wert 3b	3	1	0	0
McLain p	4	0	0	0
Totals	34	13	12	13

DP: 1.

E: Stanley (2).

2B: Horton (1, off Washburn).

HR: Northrup (2, 3rd inning off Jaster 3 on, 0 out); Kaline (2, 5th inning off Carlton 0 on, 2 out).

SH: McLain (1, off Willis).

HBP: Wert (1, by Willis); Kaline (1, by Granger); Horton (1, by Granger).

IBB: McAuliffe (1, by Willis).

Team LOB: 5.

St. Louis	AB	R	H	RBI
Brock lf	4	0	1	0
Flood cf	4	0	0	0
Maris rf	4	1	2	0
Cepeda 1b	4	0	2	0
McCarver c	4	0	1	0
Shannon 3b	4	0	1	0
Javier 2b	4	0	1	1
Maxvill ss	4	0	0	0
Washburn p	0	0	0	0
Jaster p	0	0	0	0
Willis p	0	0	0	0
Hughes p	0	0	0	0
Ricketts ph	1	0	1	0
Carlton p	0	0	0	0
Tolan ph	1	0	0	0
Granger p	0	0	0	0
Edwards ph	1	0	0	0
Nelson p	0	0	0	0
Totals	35	1	9	1

DP: 3.

E: Brock (1).

Pitching

Detroit	IP	H	R	ER	BB	SO	HR
McLain W (1–2)	9	9	1	1	0	7	0

St. Louis	IP	H	R	ER	BB	SO	HR
Washburn L (1–1)	2	4	5	5	3	3	0
Jaster	0	2	3	3	1	0	1
Willis	0.2	1	4	4	2	0	0
Hughes	0.1	2	0	0	0	0	0
Carlton	3	3	1	1	0	2	1
Granger	2	0	0	0	0	1	0
Nelson	1	0	0	0	0	1	0

HBP: Willis (1, Wert); Granger 2 (2, Kaline, Horton).
IBB: Willis (1, McAuliffe).

As the Tigers took the field for the winner-take-all tilt on October 10, they were as loose for a seventh game as a team could be. The players glanced up at a big sign that they earlier had hung over the lockers. "SOCK IT TO 'EM," it read. Even with Gibson going for the Cardinals in Game Seven, the shellacking that the Tigers' bats put on the rest of the pitching staff lingered in the minds of the entire St. Louis club. "We've had a hell of a year," Mayo Smith said before the final contest, considering the contingency of a loss in the final game. Rhetorically, he was trying to give his players hope in facing the stellar hurler taking the mound in red and white. "This guy is not Superman. He's beatable. But even if we don't win, we've had a hell of a year."

Walking to the dugout from the bullpen area when he had been warming up, Gibson received a standing ovation, rising in waves as he moved along the grandstand, not unlike what Lonborg had received in walking from the Fenway Park bullpen in Boston before Game Seven in 1967.

It was most fitting that the final game of 1968 — the year that had seen such a dismantling of the offensive side of baseball — was a scoreless duel between two great pitchers into the bottom of the sixth. In the second inning, Gibson broke Koufax's one-series record with 32 strikeouts; by the sixth inning, only one Detroit batter had reached base, a fourth-inning infield hit by Stanley. The experts now believed that fate was running its final course of the year, with the seasoned Gibson — a veteran of many World Series contests, and working on a comfortable three days of rest — would ultimately get the best of Lolich, a novice to the postseason and coming back to work after only two off-days. Now, in the bottom half of the sixth, the other half of the Cardinals' machine — the running game — was looking to kick into high gear. Brock made a bold statement by leading off with a sharp single to left, and made a massive turn around first that dared Horton to hurry the ball into second base. Lolich maintained his calm, making sure that he was the most composed man on the field in the heart-pounding scene that was unfolding. The Cardinals' chief jackrabbit was on base, and he focused in on his thieving technique that had served him all season long. McAuliffe, the second baseman on the scene who was peering over at Brock, knew that the mercurial man was about to run. "We'd talked about it, and Mickey knew he had to make Brock make the first move," he said, as told in George Cantor's book *The Tigers of '68*. "He played it perfectly." McAuliffe was an unsung source of steadiness for the Tigers that season, exemplified in part by the fact that he had tied a major league record by not hitting into a double play ground ball while playing in 151 games. Brock took an exceptionally-long lead — daring Lolich to throw over, just as he had in Game Two — and thinking that even if Lolich did try to pick him off, he could beat the second throw of the first baseman Cash to second base. Lolich did, but Lou did not. When Brock took off, Cash calmly moved in towards Lolich to receive the ball more quickly, squared his shoulders towards the second base bag, and fired a perfect strike to Stanley who tagged Brock out. Stanley recorded the next out as well, skillfully snagging a liner off the bat of Javier, and looking as if he had played shortstop his entire life instead of only the past two weeks. His confidence was still running high when Flood dribbled a ball in front of him. Flood beat the play at first, as the Cards had another one of their speedsters on base, still looking to strike the first blow of the game. But Curt, too, was caught off the bag, stuck in purgatory between the bases as Lolich had made yet another perfect pick-off move. Cash fired to McAuliffe this time, who ran Flood back towards first. Lolich had covered first for the vacated Cash, who received the ball from McAuliffe; Flood reversed back and went for second again, thinking he could out-run a Lolich throw and certainly a pursuing Lolich, but once again, Stanley was at the receiving end of the dart that gave him his third putout of the inning, and the end of a once-promising Cardinals threat in the sixth.

Stanley himself would lead things off in the Tigers' seventh, but he was called out as Gibson continued to dominate with his seventh strikeout of the day. It seemed as if it would be a quick inning, as Kaline promptly grounded to Shannon at third for the second out. Cash and Horton, the next batters, turned around a surprised Gibson and suddenly posted back-to-back singles, putting the go-ahead run for Detroit in scoring position. It was particularly uplifting for Horton, who had been 0-for-7 against Gibson to that point. "I just wanted to hit the ball, no matter where it went," he would say later. Coming to the plate now in the key situation was Northrup, a man who despite his heavy hitting in Game Six had never batted higher than .271 in his five years in the major leagues.

Gibson would regret the next pitch for the rest of his life.

"Northrup hit a fastball away — and that's where we try to pitch him, to make him hit the ball to center field," Gibson would say in the locker room about an hour later. "But when I saw Flood looking for the ball, I knew I was in trouble."

Flood initially broke in on the low-flying line shot that came his way, but he appeared to stagger after a few steps. He claimed to have lost sight of the ball amidst the background of white shirts that were bunched among the box seats behind home plate. Realizing that the ball was hit deeper than he had thought, Flood stopped to sprint back in the opposite direction, and lost his footing. The ball flew over his head and sliced away from him as well, falling safely and rolling softly towards the wall as the crowd groaned. The misplay allowed Northrup to head for third with an easy triple, scoring Cash and Horton for a 2–0 Detroit lead. Next was Freehan — having just gotten his first hit of the series in Game Six — who smashed a double to score Northrup and make it 3–0. Wert was intentionally walked, which left Lolich to face Gibson. The Tigers pitcher went down on strikes, but he knew that his true job was to record nine more outs, as now it was the Cardinals who were up against the ropes.

After Cepeda struck out to start the Cardinals' seventh, Flood's counterpart, Northrup, looked as if *he* was now opening the door back up, kicking a ball in the outfield that allowed Shannon to reach. The home crowd's hope was quickly dashed, though, as McCarver and Maris followed with weak pop flies. Gibson angrily went through three Detroit batters quickly in the top of the eighth, and then stood on deck in the bottom half as he watched Gagliano pinch-hit for the struggling Maxvill to start the inning. Gibby casually waved the bat, but he fully expected Schoendienst to look for Tolan, Schofield, or another regular hitter for his place as well. That scenario became more obvious when Gagliano grounded out to Wert at third, as Gibson thought that now, for sure, he would be lifted from the game. He looked back at the dugout, but surprisingly, Red motioned for him to go ahead. "I remain grateful to Schoendienst for sticking with me," Gibson still recalls about that afternoon. He would go down swinging, taking a vicious cut at a Lolich fastball. Next, Brock was able to coax a walk out of the lefthander, but was left stranded when Javier failed to reach on a bunt attempt. The Tigers added another run on the fatigued Gibson in the ninth, a combination of singles by Horton, Northrup, and Wert to make it 4–0. Once again, Lolich made the final out of the inning in popping up to Javier behind second. And once again, Lolich turned and trudged back towards the mound, only three outs away from mending a torn city.

For a final time, Smith shuffled his players to display his own Maginot Line, with once again Oyler taking short, Stanley going to center, and Northrup moving to left. The 1968 season would be the first of four Gold Glove Awards for Stanley in center field, and he jogged out to his normal position with a satisfied smile, knowing that the plan was about to come to full fruition, and that he had done his job at shortstop. He then glanced over at the position to watch Oyler record the first out of the inning, spearing a rocket liner off the bat of Flood. Cepeda next swung anxiously at a bad pitch, and lifted a foul pop-up behind the plate that Freehan fielded easily. Two out. The last hope for the Cardinals was Shannon, the hometown St. Louis boy who would never would quit or back down from a fight. The team's frustration from the past few days was manifested in one swing, as he drove a long home run deep to the seats in left, received by the dwindling audience with light, half-hearted applause. The final curtain came down a moment later, when McCarver followed suit with Cepeda, popping up to his counterpart, Freehan, to secure the championship for the Tigers, leaving the Busch Stadium fans in a stunned glaze while bat boy Jerry Gibson cried in the Cardinals' dugout.

After scoring three runs in the first inning of Game Five, the Cardinals had been shut out by the Tigers in 24 of the last 26 frames.

Lolich leapt into the waiting grasp of his catcher, and wrapped his arms around the back of his neck to hold on for the celebratory ride. A few minutes later, he explained that he jumped into Freehan's arms so that his catcher would not do the same to him — a sort of pre-emptive strike in a sumo match between the two stocky characters. Next over to the scene was Cash, who later would tell the press that Lolich's success was due to the fewer innings he had pitched during the year, logging 220 as Gibson had worn through 305 and had been showing signs of being tired. The team hopped around the infield in festive madness— and the thoughts of some Detroit followers suddenly turned to the 1934 Tigers who had finally been avenged, victims of Dean and the Gas House Gang Cardinals. It was Lolich's third win of the series, and it brought the world championship to Detroit, a city still thirsting not only for athletic victory but for social reconciliation as well. The pitcher would note that, even with his success and national fame from the past week, he still was not getting near the number of endorsement offers that McLain was enjoying. "In fact, I don't even have any kind of job lined up for the winter," Lolich said soon after, back in an era when many major league ballplayers needed to worry about such things— even World Series heroes.

The box score from Game Seven:

| Detroit | 0 0 0 0 0 0 3 0 1—4 8 1 |
| St. Louis | 0 0 0 0 0 0 0 0 1— 1 5 0 |

Batting

Detroit	*AB*	*R*	*H*	*RBI*
McAuliffe 2b	4	0	0	0

Detroit	AB	R	H	RBI
Stanley ss, cf	4	0	1	0
Kaline rf	4	0	0	0
Cash 1b	4	1	1	0
Horton lf	4	1	2	0
Tracewski pr	0	1	0	0
Oyler ss	0	0	0	0
Northrup cf, lf	4	1	2	2
Freehan c	4	0	1	1
Wert 3b	3	0	1	1
Lolich p	4	0	0	0
Totals	**35**	**4**	**8**	**4**

DP: 1.
E: Northrup (3).
2B: Freehan (1, off Gibson).
3B: Northrup (1, off Gibson).
IBB: Wert (1, by Gibson).
Team LOB: 5.

St. Louis	AB	R	H	RBI
Brock lf	3	0	1	0
Javier 2b	4	0	0	0
Flood cf	4	0	2	0
Cepeda 1b	3	0	0	0
Shannon 3b	4	1	1	1
McCarver c	3	0	1	0
Maris rf	3	0	0	0
Maxvill ss	2	0	0	0
Gagliano ph	1	0	0	0
Schofield ss	0	0	0	0
Gibson p	3	0	0	0
Totals	**30**	**1**	**5**	**1**

HR: Shannon (1, 9th inning off Lolich 0 on, 2 out).
SB: Flood (3, 2nd base off Lolich/Freehan).
CS: Brock (3, picked off first by Lolich, 6th inning), Flood (1, picked off first by Lolich, 6th inning)
Team LOB: 5.

Pitching

Detroit	IP	H	R	ER	BB	SO	HR
Lolich W (3–0)	9	5	1	1	3	4	1

St. Louis	IP	H	R	ER	BB	SO	HR
Gibson L (2–1)	9	8	4	4	1	8	0

IBB: Gibson (1, Wert).

It was an evenly-matched, hard-fought series with two formidable teams, a duel which would live for the ages as the final "pure" World Series between the pennant winners of non-divided leagues. The Cardinals as a group were thoughtful and philosophical about the loss. Flood playfully sipped champagne out of a bottle while speaking with reporters, bubbly that had originally been intended for victory — but why let it go to waste? Among the most dejected players in the Cardinals' locker room was Maxvill, who had gone 0-for-22 in the series. Content with his own performance was Brock, however, who the previous year had tied the National League record with 12 hits in the 1967 World Series; with 13 in the 1968 series, he broke that mark and tied the major league record Bobby Richardson set in 1964. And with his seven steals, Brock equaled his own big league record he had established in the 1967 tilt with Boston.

The next day back in Motown, the *Detroit Free Press* headline on the front page read "WE WIN" with pictures of Northrup and Lolich forming exclamation points that surrounded the simple — yet oh-so-important — announcement. "Of course," McLain would later say, "those were still the days when you didn't break into stores or burn squad cars to celebrate a championship." More than ever before, the media attention now focused on McLain's understudy instead of him. "The series changed everything for me," Lolich, who was soon named its Most Valuable Player, would say years later. "It wasn't only about finally getting recognition. It was like I turned over a new leaf in my mind. I knew I was a good pitcher. But I was more confident about being able to challenge hitters. I went after everyone ... all my life, somebody else has been the big star and Lolich has been number two. I figured my day would come." McLain clearly

Mickey Lolich gives a well-deserved toast to himself and his Detroit teammates, moments after he beat the Cardinals for the third and deciding time in Game Seven of the 1968 World Series on October 10 in St. Louis. (*St. Louis Globe-Democrat* / Archives of the St. Louis Mercantile Library)

resented the attention Lolich was now getting, but he still tried to mend the fences with him — at least to a certain degree. A short time later, McLain tried to acknowledge his teammate's accomplishments at a post-season party. "I wouldn't trade twelve Mickey Loliches for one Bob Gibson," he said in a well-meaning spirit. Realizing that it did not come out correctly, he tried again. "I mean, I wouldn't trade one Bob Gibson for twelve Mickey Loliches." Still not having it right, McLain surrendered. "Oh hell," he said, throwing up his hands, "Mickey is damn good."

But the happiest thoughts were for Al Kaline — Mr. Tiger for fifteen years — who like Lolich and Northrup made the most of his first and only World Series, batting .379 with two home runs and eight RBIs to his credit.

*   *   *   *

While another baseball season had ended, the war in Vietnam dragged on indefinitely. It continued to cause rifts in the nation, as during the World Series week 24,000 troops from the Army and Marines were recalled for "involuntary second tours" in the conflict. By this time, over half a million American troops had served in southeast Asia. A new offensive by United States and South Vietnamese troops named Operation Sealords had commenced on the off-day between Games Five and Six of the World Series (October 8) in an area of the Vietnamese theater that came to be known as the Mekong Delta. But by the end of the month, President Johnson — with the country only days away from the election that would proclaim his successor — announced that all bombardment of North Vietnam would cease by the first of November, the result of promising peace negotiations that were taking place in Paris. On November 5, Nixon would win the presidency by just over 500,000 popular votes over Humphrey. Nixon had lost to John F. Kennedy in 1960 by less than 120,000 votes, and now with his defeat of Johnson's stand-in on the Democratic ticket, he had brought to an end to all links to the Kennedy presidential administration. John Kennedy's widow, Jacqueline Bouvier, had married Greek shipping magnate Aristotle Onassis on the Greek island of Skorpios two weeks before the election on October 20, as she herself sought the beginning of a new life. The personal violence endured by the Kennedy family over the past six years had, for some, come to represent the greater communal bloodshed that had dripped forth from many corners of the earth in the 1960s.

But as the decade was nearing its close, it was also a time of human triumph, of hope, and of potential for the future. The day after the Tigers wrapped up their championship, NASA would launch the Apollo 7 rocket, the first of the so-named missions to utilize a manned spacecraft. The crew was charged with providing the earth with its first live television broadcast of a spaceship in orbit, in addition to testing possible lunar module equipment for a future moon landing, a plan which NASA believed would stay on schedule and be only a short time away. Several weeks later on Christmas Eve 1968, Apollo 8 astronauts Bill Anders, Jim Lovell, and Frank Borman would become the first human beings to not only make a complete orbit of the moon, but also to see the earth in its entirety.

But around all of the tumult in American society through the late 1960s, baseball — as it always had, and likely always will — provided a tonic for an ailing nation, and a source of hope with its perennialism of renewal every spring. Detroit had vindicated itself, and with the Tigers returning to the top of the sports world, it was as if the city's sins from the past two summers had been washed away. Harwell, who had peered down upon all of the Detroit's highs and lows from the press box over the past eighteen months, would say, "The greatest moment I've ever known in Detroit was Northrup's triple in Game Seven. It was a great moment because the Tigers were winning a championship that meant so much to the city, while beating the best pitcher I ever saw in Bob Gibson." Detroit had indeed proven how a team and a city could come together.

The Cardinals had also proven something — how a team and a city could *stay* together. Cepeda's "El Birdos" — with their eclectic mix of races, personalities, demeanors, and abilities — modeled a camaraderie, togetherness, and stability that was absent from most other sectors of American life in the 1960s. "I enjoyed the city and my teammates," Cepeda said of his years in St. Louis. "I've never seen a team that had so many different individuals hold the same approach to the game, and to life. I've never seen a group work together so closely."

Epilogue

It's been one of the great rides in the history of sports broadcasting. But the world has changed.

— Mike Shannon

In the clubhouse after the defeat in Game Seven, the Cardinals showered and dressed quickly to catch a flight to Japan for another goodwill tour of games. Before leaving for Lambert Field, they learned that the club had acquired Vada Pinson from the Reds to take the place in right field of the retiring Maris. The Cards had sent two promising youngsters to Cincinnati in Tolan and Granger as payment, consummating a deal that was completed before the expansion draft and subsequent exposure of unprotected players from the various rosters. In addition, the Cardinals on the same day also sent Edwards to the Astros for pitcher Dave Giusti. Three days later, Giusti would be claimed in the expansion draft by the San Diego Padres; in December, the Padres would deal him back to the Cardinals in order to obtain Spiezio, Ron Davis, and two minor leaguers from St. Louis. Giusti would spend only 1969 in a Cardinals uniform before moving on to greater success as a reliever in Pittsburgh. Pinson, unfortunately, would not regain the All-Star level of performance he had enjoyed early in his career. He would have only one mediocre season in a St. Louis uniform while trying to play through a broken leg, while Tolan and Granger would go on to solid careers with Cincinnati and other clubs. Tolan was considered the major part of the deal, and he was finally able to fully display his skills as an everyday player. He would lead the National League in bunt hits in 1969 with 21, and in 1970 would bat .316 with a league-topping 57 stolen bases, edging Brock's total that season of 51. After missing all of 1971 with a torn Achilles tendon, Tolan was named the Comeback Player of the Year in '72 with 42 more steals. His career would soon dissipate, however, as he was also sent to the Padres after a disagreement with the Cincinnati management had led to a suspension. He sustained a serious knee injury while in San Diego, and was never the same player again.

Along with Maris and Tolan, the other conspicuous absence in the Cardinals' everyday lineup in 1969 would be the zesty leader, Cepeda, who was traded in March to the Braves for Joe Torre. Meanwhile, Maris was already enjoying the Florida sun; in hooking on with the Cardinals at the end of his career, Maris would appear in more World Series in the 1960s than any other player.

Gibson beat out Rose in the 1968 National League MVP voting 242 to 205, taking home fourteen first-place votes to Rose's six (Flood, Brock, and Shannon all finished in the top seven in the voting as well). The brilliant young Cincinnati catcher, Johnny Bench, edged Mets pitcher Jerry Koosman as the National League Rookie of the Year by a count of ten votes to nine, despite the fact that Koosman's seven shutouts were the most by a first-year pitcher since 1933 (the 1968 season would also mark the first of ten straight Gold Glove Awards at the catcher's position for Bench.). Over in the American League, Yankees pitcher Stan Bahnsen won the outstanding first-year player award. And even with Lolich's flourishing finish in the World Series, it was still McLain's year in taking the American League hardware. He won the circuit's MVP and Cy Young awards, and even bested Gibson for *The Sporting News'* Pitcher of the Year and Player of the Year awards for all of baseball. In the MVP voting, he secured all twenty first-place votes ahead of the runner-up — his catcher, Freehan — while Horton (fourth) and McAuliffe (seventh) finished in the upper count as well (both Gibson and McLain, understandably, were unanimous winners of the Cy Young awards— it was also the first time that both league's MVP awards went to pitchers). McLain accomplished these feats despite the fact that 1968 had been the third straight year in which he led the major leagues in home runs allowed, permitting a total of 108 over that stretch.

Less than seven days after the 1968 World Series had ended, McLain started a two-week stand playing the organ at the Riviera in Las Vegas, capitalizing to the greatest degree on his on-going fame. The show was recorded live, and an album was produced that was entitled *Denny McLain in Las Vegas* (McLain later joked about the album's lack of popularity to a friend — "If you'd like to hear it, I could sell you a couple thousand copies"). Despite the instant fame and fortune — and even in a decade full of colorful personalities on the playing field — the demise of McLain in the coming years would rank among the saddest in the game. He would claim that the Tigers ruined his arm by forcing him to take repeated cortisone shots and pitch through the pain, as he sat by and watched Lolich reap much of the pitching glory on which McLain had exclusivity during the regular season. The two Tigers pitchers would both make the American League All-Star team in 1969, but became entangled in a personal mess during the All-Star break. McLain had originally indicated to Lolich that he would fly Lolich and his wife back from Washingon — the site of the game — in his private plane. Before leaving, however, McLain told Lolich that he needed to go to Lakeland, Florida, before returning to Detroit, and that Lolich and his wife would have to find their own way back. It was the last straw for Lolich in a strained relationship, as he felt that McLain had simply abandoned them at the airport. McLain would be out of baseball by the end of spring training 1973, in camp with the Atlanta Braves in trying to hang on for one more shot, three years after Commissioner Bowie Kuhn had suspended him until July 1 of the 1970 season for gambling. He was bankrupt, in arrears close to a half-million dollars to several debtors, with no employer willing to take a chance on him.

After trying several business ventures inside and outside of baseball, he was bankrupt again in 1977. Then, in 1984, McClain was sentenced to 23 years in prison on cocaine, extortion, and racketeering charges, stemming from a bag of drugs that had been found in his golf club bag. He served 2½ years before a judge threw out the verdict.

Seemingly then having his life turned around, contrite about his old ways, and ready to give himself back to the people of Detroit as a local radio host, McLain was in trouble once again in 1996. He was indicted on conspiracy, fraud, and theft charges, having been accused in a scheme to raid $2.5 million from the pension fund of the company he had founded with partner Roger Smigiel. This incident occurred eight years after the publication of McLain's supposed tell-all autobiography, *Strikeout* (ironically, both McLain and fellow Tiger Ron LeFlore had chapters in their autobiographies entitled "Wheeling and Dealing"). In 1998, he was sentenced to seven more years in prison. Cutting a deal with prosecutors, McLain pleaded his way out of a longer sentence by doing community service — which consisted of filling up soft drinks at a convenience store in Detroit. He continued to claim he was innocent, although documents had readily proven that he and two conspirators had stolen the $2.5 million from the fund that they had established, naming themselves as the trustees of the fund even though such a move was clearly prohibited by federal law.

Northrup probably summed it up best about his former teammate. "Denny always played by his own rules, and he probably believes he's not guilty of anything ... he's the kind of guy, you'll be at the dinner table with him, and everybody will be there, and he'll take the last piece of pie. When it's all gone, you'll say, 'Hey Denny — how come you took the last piece of pie?' He'll say, 'I didn't take any pie.' And you'll say, 'I saw you eat it.' And he'll say, 'I swear to God, I didn't take the last piece of pie.'" And Northrup's assessment was later backed up by reporter Michael Rosenberg of the *Detroit*

Free Press in 2003. "In 1999, McLain told HBO from prison, 'I didn't do this. I had nothing to do with this. Not one damn thing. I'm here for no reason. Not a (bleep) damned thing? You hear me? No reason at all.' That was two years after he was sentenced."

In fairness, however, not all of the heartbreaks in McLain's life were self-induced. In 1978, a fire destroyed his home in Lakeland, burning his 1968 Cy Young and MVP awards, as well as most of his personal possessions and memorabilia from his major league career. Much more tragically, his oldest daughter, Kristin, would be killed in an automobile accident in 1992.

In the coming years, other sad events would befall several of the Tigers from 1968. Both Oyler and Sparma would die of heart attacks in their forties (Oyler in 1981 and Sparma in 1986). Stanley, the man who took Oyler's position in the World Series, had fond memories of both men, but especially the shortstop. "He never carried a grudge about me replacing him in the series," Stanley said. "He was simply a great guy." Soon after Sparma's passing, Cash — the fun-loving first baseman, and one of the most popular Tigers of all-time — drowned off a Lake Michigan pier on October 12, 1986. But there was also the personal triumph of relief pitcher John Hiller. He would recover from a string of his own heart attacks — the first coming at the age of 27 in 1970 — to resume his baseball career and become the Tigers' all-time leader in games pitched with 545, a mark he still holds to this day.

Happy times continued to greet the portly Lolich later in life, who fittingly went on to open a chain of doughnut shops in the Detroit suburbs of Rochester and Lake Orion, where the amiable pitcher did not consider himself too important to make the doughnuts himself. For until he sold the business in 1998, he often took his own turns at the oven. "What really surprises the customers," Lolich told Kay Houston of the *Detroit News*, "is when they see me coming out of our bakery in the back with flour on my apron. I've heard some of them say, 'By golly, he *really works* here.'" He narrowly missed winning the Cy Young Award in 1971, edged in the voting by Vida Blue of the Oakland A's. To this day, Lolich — long outlasting the more flamboyant McLain — still has more strikeouts than any pitcher in Tigers history.

The pitching-heavy statistics for 1968 would propel several rule changes for the following year, the most notable being that the crest of the pitching mound could be no more than ten inches higher than the playing surface, nearly a 50 percent drop from the 1968 height. Furthermore, it was suggested that the size of the strike zone be shrunken, and that further limitations be put on the size of fielders' gloves. Baseball officials had been clandestinely gathering since the middle of 1968 to consider changes for the following season; in fact, it was revealed that Giles had summoned a secret meeting with National League general managers to generate ideas in which run-scoring could be increased without changing the rules. The conventional assumption was that people wanted to see high-scoring games, as overall National League attendance had dropped in 1968 to a total of 11.7 million. Paul Richards, general manager of the Houston Astros, even suggested moving the pitcher's mound five feet farther away from home plate. The effects were far-reaching, and even Gibson would never again pitch near the 13 shutouts he had posted in 1968 (his career high after that season was five). In addition, the 1968 season would wind up being the only one in Gibson's career in which he would lead the National League in strikeouts; Drysdale, despite his eight overall shutouts and six in a row, would end up winning only 14 total games on the year. After encountering some physical difficulties, Drysdale would retire partly through the 1969 campaign after pitching in only twelve games, not having yet reached his 33rd birthday.

Another place where the Cardinals were seeing changes was in the broadcast booth, always an on-going source of drama with Harry Caray at the microphone. On November 3, 1968, Caray was struck by a car in downtown St. Louis, breaking both of his legs, his nose, and injuring a shoulder. Speculation arose that it had been an intentional hit, in part due to the criticism that Caray had frequently laid on players, the city, and even the Anheuser-Busch brewery and its CEO. "Harry was having problems in St. Louis, and Gussie Busch was aware of the situation," Jack Buck wrote in his autobiography, *That's a Winner!* "Mr. Busch told Harry he was leaving for a trip to Europe and for Harry to keep his mouth shut until he got back and he would take care of the problem. The Cardinals were playing at Wrigley Field, and the *Post-Dispatch* had reported that Caray was in danger of losing his job. Instead of saying nothing as Gussie had told him, Harry interviewed Russo, the newspaper reporter, on the pre-game show and asked him about the story.

"Gussie was on his way to the airport and heard the interview, and said, "That's it." Caray was fired. He would move on to Oakland, while Buck became the main man in the KMOX radio booth for many years to come. Caray lasted one year with A's before becoming the Chicago White Sox announcer in 1970 and moving on to the north side to cover the Cubs in 1982. With the exception of a one-year hiatus in 1975 to do a sports show on national television, Buck remained a fixture in the Cardinals' booth until his death in 2002. Willingly playing second-fiddle to Caray for many years in St. Louis, Buck rose to become one of the more talented, likable, and recognizable voices in the game for decades. "I'm not theatrical," Buck once said. "I'm not an actor or someone who can make it sound better or more promising than it is. But if there *is* something exciting going on — good *or* bad for the Cardinals — then our listeners will know I'll be excited about calling it." Buck was born in Holyoke, Massachusetts, and attended Ohio State University after serving with the Army in Europe during World War II. Wounded just two months before the war ended, he returned to America to complete his studies in Columbus and ultimately landed a job down the street in 1950 calling the games of the Cardinals' farm team in the Ohio city. Three years later, he moved on to assume the broadcasting duties of the Cardinals' other top minor league club in Rochester, New York, before joining Caray at Sportsman's Park the following season.

The exit of Caray from the Cardinals' press box — and the rightful ascension of Buck into the number-one role — was one of many moves that changed the make-up of the organization into the next decade. In 1970, Busch Stadium went to artificial turf, a hallmark of the speedy Cardinals teams in the 1980s that utilized the synthetic grass— patents for the invention of which had been granted to James Faria and Robert Wright, who worked across the river at Monsanto Industries in East St. Louis. Until 1974, the entire dirt infield remained; after that season, the stadium floor was converted further, as only the sliding-pit sections around the bases and the pitcher's mound were left as the dirt areas, similar to what had been done at Candlestick Park in San Francisco.

As the natural grass left Busch Stadium, the Cardinals players from the great teams of the 1960s dispersed as well. Maxvill would continue his solid fielding but light hitting. In 1970, he would set major league records for the fewest hits (80), doubles (5), and total bases (89) for a player who had taken part in 150 or more games. He would nonetheless retire in 1975 with a .973 career fielding mark, the best ever for a shortstop. He and Joe Hoerner would start a travel agency in St. Louis when their playing days were finished, but later Maxvill returned to baseball, coaching for the Mets, Cardinals, and Braves in the late 1970s and early '80s before being named the general manager of the St. Louis club just before the 1985 campaign began. That year, despite being only three years removed from their last World Series championship, the Cardinals were picked for last place in the National League Eastern Division (divisional play had begun in the 1969 season). With a club full of rookies and a relatively-untested bullpen, few of the preseason prognosticators were giving them a chance. When star center fielder Willie McGee returned from an early-season injury in April, a rookie named Vince Coleman convinced Maxvill that he should stay on the roster. He did, and Coleman wound up with a rookie record of 110 steals in helping lead the Redbirds to a pennant.

Running the travel agency for several years after Maxvill went back into baseball, Hoerner died on October 4, 1996. Until the day of his death, he still could not completely bend the tip of his index finger that was injured by the champagne bottle in the midst of the locker room celebration of the Cardinals' 1967 World Series victory in Boston.

Brock would continue to post impressive numbers, including a then-unprecedented 118 stolen bases at the age of 35 in 1974. He was later named the *Sporting News'* 1979 Comeback Player of the Year in the National League, hitting .304 and stealing 21 bases at the age of 40 after dropping his batting mark to a career-low .221 the year before. It was unquestionably Brock's speed and 3,000 hits that gained his entrance to the Hall of Fame in 1985; for at the time of his retirement, Brock had struck out more (1,730) than any man in history, which led many sportswriters to question if he truly was a great leadoff hitter despite his speed. Some claimed that part of Brock's strikeout problem at the plate was his inconsistent choice of bats. Despite disagreement from his coaches and managers over the years, Brock used a variety of lengths and weights with his bats, depending on — as he put it — the particular pitcher that he was facing that day, as Cepeda frequently did. He also had led the National League in errors seven times, the primary reason he stayed in left field for almost his entire career.

Maxvill's partner around the second base bag, Javier, would see his playing days cease in a bizarre coincidence involving similar players. Javier, Bill Mazeroski, and Maury Wills— three of the best infielders of the 1960s— would all end their careers within minutes of each other, being released from three different teams on the same day, October 24, 1972. It would then be Glenn Beckert of the Cubs— not Javier— who would break Mazeroski's five-year string of National League Gold Gloves at second base. Jimy Williams, the long-forgotten minor league shortstop prospect that never was able to supplant Maxvill in St. Louis, would move on to greater heights as a big-league manager, serving with Boston, Toronto, and Houston while being named the 1999 American League Manager of the Year with the Red Sox. In his final stint, he would go 44–44 for the Houston Astros in 2004 when he was replaced by Phil Garner, who in turn led the Astros into the National League Championship Series against the Cardinals.

McCarver would wind up playing in four different decades over his career (1959–1980). From 1978 to 2000, the minor league stadium in his hometown of Memphis bore his name until the new Auto Zone Park was constructed. Maintaining a stellar career in broadcasting, McCarver — the winner of three Emmys— announced his 14th World Series in 2004 when the Cardinals took on the Red Sox once again. He would form a permanent bond with Carlton, who would become a completely different pitcher after 1968, developing a slider that would transform him from a quality starting pitcher to one of the best and most prolific in history. After nearly losing twenty games for the Cardinals in 1970, he won twenty in 1971 for first of what would be six consecutive seasons in doing so. Unfortunately, only the first in the streak would be accomplished in a St. Louis uniform. The lefthander ran into a bitter contract dispute with the club in the winter of 1971–1972, unable to agree to the Cardinals' offer of $55,000, and was thus traded to the Phillies for pitcher Rick

Wise on February 25. Carlton went on to post 46 percent of the Phillies' 59 wins in 1972, an all-time percentage record. His personal total of 27 wins included 15 in a row, and despite the poor team on which he played, he achieved the ERA, strikeout, and victory titles in the National League as well in joining Koufax as the only National League pitchers to ever fan 300 batters in a season to that point. Carlton would also retain a lifelong fondness for his first catcher in McCarver. Their original disagreements in Carlton's first spring training with the Cardinals in 1965 a distant memory, McCarver and Lefty eventually became inseparable, with McCarver serving as Carlton's personal catcher with the Phillies into the 1970s. And in 1980, after Carlton had won his third Cy Young Award, he and McCarver were able to re-live the magic of '67 as the Phillies defeated the Royals in the World Series. Two years later, he would become the first National League pitcher to win a fourth Cy Young in his tenth and final All-Star season, finally emerging out from under the shadow of Bob Gibson once and for all. When he finally retired in 1988, his 4,136 strikeouts were second all-time to Nolan Ryan. Years later, McCarver jokingly suggested that he and Carlton should be buried sixty feet, six inches away from each other when they die — the distance from the pitcher's rubber to home plate.

Washburn, fighting his arm injuries, was traded to the Reds on November 5, 1969. He was exchanged for fellow pitcher George Culver, as the trade comprised half of the National League hurlers who had thrown no-hitters in 1968. Utilizing his degree from Whitworth College, Washburn returned to the Pacific Northwest to teach and coach at Bellevue Community College. Hughes' injury, meanwhile, shortened his career to three years, with 1968 being the last time he would see the major leagues. And Jaster, left unprotected by the Cardinals and picked up by Montreal in the expansion draft, would throw the first big league pitch in Canada on April 14, 1969 — against his old team. Starting the game for the new Montreal Expos, Jaster lasted just over four innings against the Cardinals, allowing seven runs— only two of which were earned. Joining Jaster on the Expos was Wills, another expansion draftee.

Briles would spend two more seasons in a Cardinals uniform before being dealt to the Pittsburgh Pirates in January of 1971, a trade which brought 1966 batting champ Matty Alou to St. Louis. That year, Briles hurled a two-hit shutout for the Pirates in Game Five of the World Series against the Baltimore Orioles, helping Pittsburgh ultimately achieve the world championship in seven games. Also playing with Kansas City, Texas, and Baltimore throughout the remainder of his career, Briles would retire after the 1978 campaign. He would pass away on February 13, 2005, at the age of 62.

Awaiting Gussie Busch in 1969 was one of the most disheartening situations he would ever encounter in baseball, involving one of his players that he loved the most. He always felt that he was generous to his employees, not only in salary, but also in hosting extra events such as picnics for their families, special help during times of need, and other gestures. Thus, he was understandably taken aback by the terse stance of Curt Flood, who had wanted $100,000 before the 1969 season even though Busch offered an increase that would have put him at a healthy (for the time) $90,000. Busch was angered by Flood's attitude, and the center fielder finally settled for $92,000. Broeg could not understand the player's perspective. "The club had helped Flood through personal scrapes," he remembered. "The damage was done. For Busch, the fun [of baseball] had become a funny business." In March of 1969, Busch went on a rant in the Cardinals' spring training locker room, complaining about how ungrateful the players were in these days of riches. After grievances were aired, both Busch and Flood attempted to move on with things. Despite winning his seventh straight Gold Glove that season on defense, however, Flood would hit under .300 for the first time in three years. During that year, in an interview with Howard Cosell, the reporter pointed out to Flood, "You make over $90,000, which isn't exactly slave wages." To which Flood answered, "A well-paid slave is still a slave." Finally, Busch had endured enough. Flood was traded on October 7, 1969, just before the Mets would face the Orioles in that season's World Series with the Cardinals finishing a disappointing fourth in the newly-formed National League East with an 87–75 record. Flood was sent along with McCarver, Hoerner, and Byron Browne to the Phillies for Dick Allen, Cookie Rojas, and Jerry Johnson. While Flood knew that he had certainly shaken some pillars in St. Louis, he was yet stunned by the deal, and did not wish to report to Philadelphia.

Flood requested his "free agency" in the following letter that he sent to Commissioner Bowie Kuhn, who only two weeks earlier had replaced Eckert:

December 24, 1969
Mr. Bowie K. Kuhn
Commissioner of Baseball
680 Fifth Avenue
New York, New York 10019

After twelve years in the Major Leagues, I do not feel I am a piece of property to be bought and sold irrespective of my wishes. I believe that any system which produces that result violates my basic rights as a citizen and is inconsistent with the laws of the United States and of the sovereign States.

It is my desire to play baseball in 1970, and I am capable of playing. I have received a contract offer from the Philadelphia Club, but I believe I have the right to consider offers from other clubs before making any decisions. I, therefore, request that you make known to all Major League Clubs my feelings in this matter, and advise them of my availability for the 1970 season.

Sincerely Yours,
Curt Flood.

Flood's letter also came just a week after the Players Union — by an over-whelming vote of 491–7 — announced that they had discarded a proposal by the owners that would have the clubs add an additional $4.1 million to the pension fund, up from the annual $1 million contribution that was currently being made. It was a stark indication that labor troubles in baseball were far from over as the 1960s came to a close. Maintaining a home in California, Flood returned there to ponder his next move. In studying some documents, he learned that in 1922 Supreme Court justice Oliver Wendell Holmes had ruled that professional baseball was exempt from the antitrust laws; now, Flood was preparing himself to challenge that edict. Flood, with Marvin Miller by his side, repeatedly made their case at federal courthouses in the early winter and spring of 1970 — just as the last segregated public schools of the South were beginning to integrate — to bring a suit against Major League Baseball's reserve clause. Several former ballplayers with much credibility, namely Jackie Robinson and Hank Greenberg, appeared at the proceedings to testify on Flood's behalf. No active players were present, however, as all feared being blacklisted from professional baseball if they spoke publicly. Flood lost his case, and the trials drove him to drink heavily. He fled to Denmark to escape the pressure, and wound up missing the entire 1970 season. Exonerated by the powers in baseball, he came back to the Washington Senators in 1971 under manager Ted Williams (and as a teammate of McLain, interestingly enough, as McLain had been traded there by the Tigers after the 1970 season), but played in only 13 games as he fled once again, this time to the Spanish Mediterranean. The next time he came back to the United States, he was out of money, and out of options. While Flood was away, Baltimore pitcher Dave McNally and Dodgers hurler Andy Messersmith were able to break through the reserve clause, becoming the game's first true "free agents" and in doing so, turning the financial organization of the game on its head forever. Flood spent the next several years painting and doing odd jobs when Charlie Finley hired him as a broadcaster in 1978 to cover the A's in Flood's hometown of Oakland. His name thereafter linked with baseball labor negotiations, Flood spoke to the players union during the strike of 1994, urging them to stay unified. They looked at him as a hero — and later in death, a martyr. Joe Torre called Flood "The Joan of Arc of baseball," initiating the fights for players' benefits which he would never see himself. Flood developed throat cancer in 1996, and died on January 20, 1997.

While he would never know the dominance of 1968 ever again, Bob Gibson would continue to be among the elite pitchers in baseball. He was not knocked out of a game until the Fourth of July, 1969, while pitching against the Cubs in Busch Stadium. He worked his way into the tenth inning with the game tied, but could go no longer as Hoerner relieved him. It was the first time since September 12, 1967, that an opponent's barrage had driven him from the pitcher's mound, a stretch of 53 consecutive games. Even so, Gibson still managed to lead the league in complete games for the only time in his career with 28 — the number he had posted in 1968 — while earning his sixth All-Star Game appearance. And even though his 1.12 ERA in 1968 was the third best all time, Gibson would later claim that he had "physically peaked" six or seven years earlier, long before the Cardinals of the 1960s ever made it to a World Series. As Gibson said on how pitching around baseball had evolved to its dominating stance in 1968, "We had simply become damn good at what we did."

An often-forgotten aspect of Gibson's complete skills was his fielding ability, evidenced in the nine straight Gold Gloves he gathered (1965–1973). He retired in 1975 at the age of 39 as the winningest pitcher in Cardinals history. And at the time, he was only the second pitcher to record 3,000 career strikeouts, leaving baseball with 3,117 (behind only Walter Johnson's 3,509).

Gibson maintained his valued privacy even when his playing days were through. "I might have a phone number for him," McLain once told a writer, "but don't tell him where you got it." Torre, however, who would play with Gibson in St. Louis in the 1970s, remains a close friend of his. "He's mellowed some," the successful Yankees manager once told a magazine in an interview in the late 1990s. "Now he can play in old-timers' games, and not be upset that they're hitting him. When he first started those old-timers' games, he really had a problem with that. I said, 'Gibby, they don't come out here to watch you strike people out!" Gibson still held out bitterness to changes occurring in baseball to favor the hitter — and to what team and league executives still presume to be a more appealing, high-scoring game for the fans. "The rancor between the pitcher and the hitter, which characterized the game in my time and [Babe] Ruth's and [Ty] Cobb's and Musial's, has been legislated out in favor of a kinder, gentler game in which there is more cheap offense for the paying customer," Gibson said. Nonetheless, he maintains that the Cardinals of 1967 and 1968 could play with anyone in contemporary times. "When it came to the intangibles — execution, resourcefulness, sacrifice, and other aspects of the game, we were the equal of any team in modern baseball."

And despite his own self-doubt on the subject, Gibson would indeed post the Cardinals' next no-hitter after Washburn turned the trick in September of 1968. The Pirates would fall victim on August 14, 1971, in the new Three Rivers Stadium in Pittsburgh, as Gibson got Stargell looking on strikes to give Hoot the one honor which had always escaped him.

Schoendienst would be relieved as the St. Louis manager in 1976 by Vern Rapp, ending the longest full-time tenure in the role (twelve years, since 1965) in the history of the club. He returned to manage 57 games for the Cardinals at the end of the 1980 season, all part of a plan to assist Whitey Herzog —

who was to be the permanent new field manager in 1981—so that Herzog could spend that time evaluating players around the league for possible trades. With Red's help (as well as that of Maxvill's in the general manager's post), Whitey was able to craft Cardinals clubs that would win three National League pennants and one world championship in the next decade. Schoendienst would surface again as an interim Cardinals manager in 1990 to guide the team through 67 games, this time *following* Herzog, who was let go, and preceding the five-year stay of Torre as the St. Louis skipper.

When Schoendienst entered the Hall of Fame on July 22, 1989, he concluded simply in his acceptance speech, "I never thought that milk truck ride [from Germantown to St. Louis for the Cardinals tryout in 1942] would eventually lead to Cooperstown and baseball's highest honor." He also let the crowd in on a little personal secret. "Forty-two years ago, I met a dark-haired Irish girl on a Grand Avenue streetcar. She asked me for my autograph. Well, two years later, I signed *her* up." Indeed, over the years Mrs. Mary O'Reilly Schoendienst provided much love to their family of six. Red had been inducted into the Missouri Sports Hall of Fame two years earlier in 1987, while his famous number 2 uniform was retired by the Cardinals. He continues on as a coach for the Redbirds, still hitting infield ground balls with his fungo bat during batting practice in his 65th season in professional baseball.

The relationship between Schoendienst and Gibson remained strong. With the Cardinals battling for the National League's Eastern Division title near the end of the 1974 season, Schoendienst once again allowed a tiring Gibson to finish an important game himself. The manager let his pitcher face the left-handed-hitting Mike Jorgensen of Montreal, with the tying run on base in the eighth inning of a must-win game for the Cardinals. The Cards had ace lefty reliever Al Hrabosky available in the bullpen, but Red let Gibby make one last stand—just like had allowed him to do in Game Seven of the 1968 World Series. Jorgensen hit a long home run, as the Cardinals lost the game and ultimately finish a game and a half behind Pittsburgh for the division title. Gibson would retire after the 1975 season, but he would never forget how Schoendienst remained true to him.

A couple of months into the 1970 season, Mike Shannon was overcome by a severe case of nephritis, a rare kidney disease. He quickly retired from playing, and was given the job of assistant director of promotions and sales for the Cardinals. But the front office was too far away from the dirt and turf and bats for the hard-nosed player, so in 1972, he began what would be a four-decade career behind the microphone as a radio and television announcer for the team. To this day, Shannon gives much credit to Buck, Devine, and KMOX general manager Bob Hyland for their support in developing his broadcasting career, one that may well land him in the Hall of Fame in the role after a solid playing tenure. "I will say that the '67 club didn't have as much talent as the '64 club, but both the '67 and the '68 clubs just never made many mistakes, the kind that can lose ballgames for you," Shannon remembered "Those two were well-balanced, well-oiled machines. When we walked onto the field, hell, we knew we were going to win. That's the attitude any winning ball club takes with them into each and every game, and that's the attitude those '67 and '68 clubs had." Shannon should certainly know, having seen nearly every pitch of Cardinals baseball ever since.

"I was almost like a cheerleader when Gibson pitched in 1968," he added. "I hardly paid any attention at all unless there was a man on first base with less than two outs. Otherwise, all I did was catch the ball from the catcher after strikeouts."

And, on July 17, 1974, Bob Gibson would record his 3,000th strikeout — the same day that Dizzy Dean died.

Appendix:
1967 and 1968 Statistics

1967 Final Standings

National League

	W	L	Pct.	GB
St. Louis	101	56	.627	—
San Francisco	91	71	.562	10.5
Chicago	87	74	.540	14
Cincinnati	87	75	.537	14.5
Philadelphia	82	80	.506	19.5
Pittsburgh	81	81	.500	20.5
Atlanta	77	85	.475	24.5
Los Angeles	73	89	.451	28.5
Houston	69	93	.426	32.5
New York	61	101	.377	40.5

American League

	W	L	Pct.	GB
Boston	92	70	.568	—
Detroit	91	71	.562	1.0
Minnesota	91	71	.562	1.0
Chicago	89	73	.549	3.0
California	84	77	.522	7.5
Washington	76	85	.472	15.5
Baltimore	76	85	.472	15.5
Cleveland	75	87	.463	17.0
New York	72	90	.444	20
Kansas City	62	99	.385	29.5

1967 St. Louis Cardinals Statistics

Batting

	G	AB	R	H	2B	3B	HR	RBI	BB	SO	Avg.	SB
Curt Flood	134	514	68	172	24	1	5	50	37	46	.335	2
Orlando Cepeda	151	563	91	183	37	0	25	111	62	75	.325	11
Lou Brock	159	689	113	206	32	12	21	76	24	109	.299	52
Tim McCarver	138	471	68	139	26	3	14	69	54	32	.295	8
Julian Javier	140	520	68	146	16	3	14	64	25	92	.281	6
Dave Ricketts	52	99	11	27	8	0	1	14	4	7	.273	0
Roger Maris	125	410	64	107	18	7	9	55	52	61	.261	0
Bobby Tolan	110	265	35	67	7	3	6	32	19	43	.253	12
Mike Shannon	130	482	53	118	18	3	12	77	37	89	.245	2
Dal Maxvill	152	476	37	108	14	4	1	41	48	66	.227	0
Alex Johnson	81	175	20	39	9	2	1	12	9	26	.223	6
Phil Gagliano	73	217	20	48	7	0	2	21	19	26	.221	0
Ed Spiezio	55	105	9	22	2	0	3	10	7	18	.210	2
Steve Huntz	3	6	1	1	0	0	0	0	1	2	.167	0
Ed Bressoud	52	67	8	9	1	1	1	1	9	18	.134	0
Ted Savage	9	8	1	1	0	0	0	0	1	3	.125	0
John Romano	24	58	1	7	1	0	0	2	13	15	.121	1
Jimy Williams	1	2	0	0	0	0	0	0	0	1	.000	0

Pitching

	G	ERA	W-L	SV	CG	IP	H	ER	BB	SO
Nelson Briles	49	2.43	14–5	6	4	153	139	42	40	94
Joe Hoerner	57	2.59	4–4	15	0	66	52	19	20	50
Ron Willis	65	2.67	6–5	10	0	81	76	24	43	42
Dick Hughes	37	2.67	16–6	3	12	222	164	66	48	161
Jack Lamabe	23	2.83	3–4	4	1	48	43	15	10	30
Bob Gibson	24	2.98	13–7	0	10	175	151	58	40	147
Steve Carlton	30	2.98	14–9	1	11	193	173	64	62	168
Larry Jaster	34	3.01	9–7	3	2	152	141	51	44	87
Jim Cosman	10	3.16	1–0	0	0	31	21	11	24	11
Mike Torrez	3	3.18	0–1	0	0	6	5	2	1	5
Ray Washburn	27	3.53	10–7	0	3	186	190	73	42	98
Al Jackson	38	3.95	9–4	1	1	107	117	47	29	43
Hal Woodeshick	36	5.18	2–1	2	0	42	41	24	28	20

1967 World Series Batting Statistics

St. Louis Cardinals

	G	AB	R	H	2B	3B	HR	RBI	BB	SO	Avg.	SB
Eddie Bressoud	2	0	0	0	0	0	0	0	0	0	—	0
Nelson Briles	2	3	0	0	0	0	0	0	0	0	.000	0
Lou Brock	7	29	8	12	2	1	1	3	2	3	.414	7
Steve Carlton	1	1	0	0	0	0	0	0	0	0	.000	0

	G	AB	R	H	2B	3B	HR	RBI	BB	SO	Avg.	SB
Orlando Cepeda	7	29	1	3	2	0	0	1	0	4	.103	0
Curt Flood	7	28	2	5	1	0	0	3	3	3	.179	0
Phil Gagliano	1	1	0	0	0	0	0	0	0	0	.000	0
Bob Gibson	3	11	1	1	0	0	1	1	1	2	.091	0
Joe Hoerner	2	0	0	0	0	0	0	0	0	0	—	0
Dick Hughes	2	3	0	0	0	0	0	0	0	3	.000	0
Larry Jaster	1	0	0	0	0	0	0	0	0	0	—	0
Julian Javier	7	25	2	9	3	0	1	4	0	6	.360	0
Jack Lamabe	3	0	0	0	0	0	0	0	0	0	—	0
Roger Maris	7	26	3	10	1	0	1	7	3	1	.385	0
Dal Maxvill	7	19	1	3	0	1	0	1	4	1	.158	0
Tim McCarver	7	24	3	3	1	0	0	2	2	2	.125	0
Dave Ricketts	3	3	0	0	0	0	0	0	0	0	.000	0
Mike Shannon	7	24	3	5	1	0	1	2	1	4	.208	0
Ed Spiezio	1	1	0	0	0	0	0	0	0	0	.000	0
Bobby Tolan	3	2	1	0	0	0	0	0	1	1	.000	0
Ray Washburn	2	0	0	0	0	0	0	0	0	0	—	0
Ron Willis	3	0	0	0	0	0	0	0	0	0	—	0
Hal Woodeshick	1	0	0	0	0	0	0	0	0	0	—	0
Total	7	229	25	51	11	2	5	24	17	30	.223	7

Boston Red Sox

	G	AB	R	H	2B	3B	HR	RBI	BB	SO	Avg.	SB
Jerry Adair	5	16	0	2	0	0	0	1	0	3	.125	1
Mike Andrews	5	13	2	4	0	0	0	1	0	1	.308	0
Gary Bell	3	0	0	0	0	0	0	0	0	0	—	0
Ken Brett	2	0	0	0	0	0	0	0	0	0	—	0
Joe Foy	6	15	2	2	1	0	0	1	1	5	.133	0
Russ Gibson	2	2	0	0	0	0	0	0	0	2	.000	0
Ken Harrelson	4	13	0	1	0	0	0	1	1	3	.077	0
Elston Howard	7	18	0	2	0	0	0	1	1	2	.111	0
Dalton Jones	6	18	2	7	0	0	0	1	1	3	.389	0
Jim Lonborg	3	9	0	0	0	0	0	0	0	7	.000	0
Dave Morehead	2	0	0	0	0	0	0	0	0	0	—	0
Dan Osinski	2	0	0	0	0	0	0	0	0	0	—	0
Rico Petrocelli	7	20	3	4	1	0	2	3	3	8	.200	0
Mike Ryan	1	2	0	0	0	0	0	0	0	1	.000	0
Jose Santiago	3	2	1	1	0	0	1	1	0	1	.500	0
George Scott	7	26	3	6	1	1	0	0	3	6	.231	0
Norm Siebern	3	3	0	1	0	0	0	1	0	0	.333	0
Reggie Smith	7	24	3	6	1	0	2	3	2	2	.250	0
Lee Stange	1	0	0	0	0	0	0	0	0	0	—	0
Jerry Stephenson	1	0	0	0	0	0	0	0	0	0	—	0
Jose Tartabull	7	13	1	2	0	0	0	0	1	2	.154	0
George Thomas	2	2	0	0	0	0	0	0	0	1	.000	0
Gary Waslewski	2	1	0	0	0	0	0	0	0	1	.000	0
John Wyatt	2	0	0	0	0	0	0	0	0	0	—	0
Carl Yastrzemski	7	25	4	10	2	0	3	5	4	1	.400	0
Total	7	222	21	48	6	1	8	19	17	49	.216	1

1967 World Series Pitching Statistics

St. Louis Cardinals

	G	ERA	W-L	SV	CG	IP	H	ER	BB	SO
Bob Gibson	3	1.00	3–0	0	3	27	14	3	5	26
Nelson Briles	2	1.64	1–0	0	1	11	7	2	1	4
Dick Hughes	2	5.00	0–1	0	0	9	9	5	3	7
Steve Carlton	1	0.00	0–1	0	0	6	3	0	2	5
Jack Lamabe	3	6.75	0–1	0	0	3	5	2	0	4
Ray Washburn	2	0.00	0–0	0	0	2	1	0	1	2
Hal Woodeshick	1	0.00	0–0	0	0	1	1	0	0	0
Ron Willis	3	27.00	0–0	0	0	1	2	3	4	1
Joe Hoerner	2	40.50	0–0	0	0	1	4	3	1	0
Larry Jaster	1	0.00	0–0	0	0	0.3	2	0	0	0
Total		2.66	4–3	0	4	61	48	18	17	49

Boston Red Sox

	G	ERA	W-L	SV	CG	IP	H	ER	BB	SO
Jim Lonborg	3	2.62	2–1	0	2	24	14	7	2	11
Jose Santiago	3	5.59	0–2	0	0	10	16	6	3	6
Gary Waslewski	2	2.16	0–0	0	0	8	4	2	2	7
Gary Bell	3	5.06	0–1	1	0	5	8	3	1	1
John Wyatt	2	4.91	1–0	0	0	4	1	2	3	1
Dave Morehead	2	0.00	0–0	0	0	3	0	0	4	3
Lee Stange	1	0.00	0–0	0	0	2	3	0	0	0
Jerry Stephenson	1	9.00	0–0	0	0	2	3	2	1	0
Ken Brett	2	0.00	0–0	0	0	1	0	0	1	1
Dan Osinski	2	6.75	0–0	0	0	1	2	1	0	0
Total		3.39	3–4	1	2	61	51	23	17	30

1968 Final Standings

National League

	W	L	Pct.	GB
St. Louis	97	65	.599	—
San Francisco	88	74	.543	9.0
Chicago	84	78	.519	13.0
Cincinnati	83	79	.512	14.0
Atlanta	81	81	.500	16.0
Pittsburgh	80	82	.494	17.0
Philadelphia	76	86	.469	21.0
Los Angeles	76	86	.469	21.0
New York	73	89	.451	24.0
Houston	72	90	.444	25.0

American League

	W	L	Pct.	GB
Detroit	103	59	.636	—
Baltimore	91	71	.562	12.0
Cleveland	86	75	.534	16.5
Boston	86	76	.531	17.0
New York	83	79	.512	20.0
Oakland	82	80	.506	21.0
Minnesota	79	83	.488	24.0
California	67	95	.414	36.0
Chicago	67	95	.414	36.0
Washington	65	96	.404	37.5

1968 St. Louis Cardinals Statistics

Batting

	G	AB	R	H	2B	3B	HR	RBI	BB	SO	Avg.	SB
Floyd Wicker	5	4	2	2	0	0	0	0	0	0	.500	0
Ted Simmons	2	3	0	1	0	0	0	0	1	1	.333	0
Curt Flood	150	618	71	186	17	4	5	60	33	58	.301	11
Lou Brock	159	660	92	184	46	14	6	51	46	124	.279	62
Mike Shannon	156	576	62	153	29	2	15	79	37	114	.266	1
Julian Javier	139	519	54	135	25	4	4	52	24	61	.260	10
Roger Maris	100	310	25	79	18	2	5	45	24	38	.255	0
Tim McCarver	128	434	35	110	15	6	5	48	26	31	.253	4
Dal Maxvill	151	459	51	116	8	5	1	24	52	71	.253	0
Orlando Cepeda	157	600	71	149	26	2	16	73	43	96	.248	8
John Edwards	85	230	14	55	9	1	3	29	16	20	.239	1
Joe Hague	7	17	2	4	0	0	1	1	2	2	.235	0
Dick Simpson	26	56	11	13	0	0	3	8	8	21	.232	0
Bob Tolan	92	278	28	64	12	1	5	17	13	42	.230	9
Phil Gagliano	53	105	13	24	4	2	0	13	7	12	.229	0
Dick Schofield	69	127	14	28	7	1	1	8	13	31	.220	1
Ron Davis (STL)	33	79	11	14	4	2	0	5	5	17	.177	1
Ed Spiezio	29	51	1	8	0	0	0	2	5	6	.157	1
Dave Ricketts	20	22	1	3	0	0	0	1	0	3	.136	0

Pitching

	G	ERA	W–L	SV	CG	IP	H	ER	BB	SO
Bob Gibson	34	1.12	22–9	0	28	305	198	38	62	268
Pete Mikkelsen	5	1.12	0–0	0	0	16	10	2	7	8
Joe Hoerner	47	1.48	8–2	17	0	49	34	8	12	42
Wayne Granger	34	2.25	4–2	4	0	44	40	11	12	27
Ray Washburn	31	2.26	14–8	0	8	215	191	54	47	124
Mike Torrez	5	2.79	2–1	0	0	19	20	6	12	6
Nelson Briles	33	2.81	19–11	0	13	244	251	76	55	141
Mel Nelson	18	2.91	2–1	1	1	53	49	17	9	16

	G	ERA	W–L	SV	CG	IP	H	ER	BB	SO
Steve Carlton	34	2.99	13–11	0	10	232	214	77	61	162
Ron Willis	48	3.39	2–3	4	0	64	50	24	28	39
Larry Jaster	31	3.50	9–13	0	3	154	153	60	38	70
Dick Hughes	25	3.52	2–2	4	0	64	45	25	21	49

1968 World Series Batting Statistics

St. Louis Cardinals

	G	AB	R	H	2B	3B	HR	RBI	BB	SO	Avg.	SB
Nelson Briles	2	4	0	0	0	0	0	0	0	4	.000	0
Lou Brock	7	28	6	13	3	1	2	5	3	4	.464	7
Steve Carlton	2	0	0	0	0	0	0	0	0	0	—	0
Orlando Cepeda	7	28	2	7	0	0	2	6	2	3	.250	0
Ron Davis	2	7	0	0	0	0	0	0	0	2	.000	0
Johnny Edwards	1	1	0	0	0	0	0	0	0	1	.000	0
Curt Flood	7	28	4	8	1	0	0	2	2	2	.286	3
Phil Gagliano	3	3	0	0	0	0	0	0	0	0	.000	0
Bob Gibson	3	8	2	1	0	0	1	2	1	2	.125	0
Wayne Granger	1	0	0	0	0	0	0	0	0	0	—	0
Joe Hoerner	3	2	0	1	0	0	0	0	0	1	.500	0
Dick Hughes	1	0	0	0	0	0	0	0	0	0	—	0
Larry Jaster	1	0	0	0	0	0	0	0	0	0	—	0
Julian Javier	7	27	1	9	1	0	0	3	3	4	.333	1
Roger Maris	6	19	5	3	1	0	0	1	3	3	.158	0
Dal Maxvill	7	22	1	0	0	0	0	0	3	5	.000	0
Tim McCarver	7	27	3	9	0	2	1	4	3	2	.333	0
Mel Nelson	1	0	0	0	0	0	0	0	0	0	—	0
Dave Ricketts	1	1	0	1	0	0	0	0	0	0	1.000	0
Dick Schofield	2	0	0	0	0	0	0	0	0	0	—	0
Mike Shannon	7	29	3	8	1	0	1	4	1	5	.276	0
Ed Spiezio	1	1	0	1	0	0	0	0	0	0	1.000	0
Bob Tolan	1	1	0	0	0	0	0	0	0	1	.000	0
Ray Washburn	2	3	0	0	0	0	0	0	0	1	.000	0
Ron Willis	3	0	0	0	0	0	0	0	0	0	—	0
Total	7	239	27	61	7	3	7	27	21	40	.255	11

Detroit Tigers

	G	AB	R	H	2B	3B	HR	RBI	BB	SO	Avg.	SB
Gates Brown	1	1	0	0	0	0	0	0	0	0	.000	0
Norm Cash	7	26	5	10	0	0	1	5	3	5	.385	0
Wayne Comer	1	1	0	1	0	0	0	0	0	0	1.000	0
Pat Dobson	3	0	0	0	0	0	0	0	0	0	—	0
Bill Freehan	7	24	0	2	1	0	0	2	4	8	.083	0
John Hiller	2	0	0	0	0	0	0	0	0	0	—	0
Willie Horton	7	23	6	7	1	1	1	3	5	6	.304	0
Al Kaline	7	29	6	11	2	0	2	8	0	7	.379	0

	G	AB	R	H	2B	3B	HR	RBI	BB	SO	Avg.	SB
Fred Lasher	1	0	0	0	0	0	0	0	0	0	—	0
Mickey Lolich	3	12	2	3	0	0	1	2	1	5	.250	0
Tom Matchick	3	3	0	0	0	0	0	0	0	1	.000	0
Eddie Mathews	2	3	0	1	0	0	0	0	1	1	.333	0
Dick McAuliffe	7	27	5	6	0	0	1	3	4	6	.222	0
Denny McLain	3	6	0	0	0	0	0	0	0	4	.000	0
Don McMahon	2	0	0	0	0	0	0	0	0	0	—	0
Jim Northrup	7	28	4	7	0	1	2	8	1	5	.250	0
Ray Oyler	4	0	0	0	0	0	0	0	0	0	—	0
Daryl Patterson	2	0	0	0	0	0	0	0	0	0	—	0
Jim Price	2	2	0	0	0	0	0	0	0	1	.000	0
Joe Sparma	1	0	0	0	0	0	0	0	0	0	—	0
Mickey Stanley	7	28	4	6	0	1	0	0	2	4	.214	0
Dick Tracewski	2	0	1	0	0	0	0	0	0	0	—	0
Don Wert	6	17	1	2	0	0	0	2	6	5	.118	0
Earl Wilson	1	1	0	0	0	0	0	0	0	1	.000	0
Total	7	231	34	56	4	3	8	33	27	59	.242	0

1968 World Series Pitching Statistics

Detroit Tigers

	G	ERA	W-L	SV	CG	IP	H	ER	BB	SO
Mickey Lolich	3	1.67	3–0	0	3	27	20	5	6	21
Denny McLain	3	3.24	1–2	0	1	17	18	6	4	13
Pat Dobson	3	3.86	0–0	0	0	5	5	2	1	0
Earl Wilson	1	6.23	0–1	0	0	4	4	3	6	3
Daryl Patterson	2	0.00	0–0	0	0	3	1	0	1	0
Fred Lasher	1	0.00	0–0	0	0	2.0	1	0	0	1
John Hiller	2	13.50	0–0	0	0	2	6	3	3	1
Don McMahon	2	13.50	0–0	0	0	2	4	3	0	1
Joe Sparma	1	54.00	0–0	0	0	0.3	2	2	0	0
Total		3.48	4–3	0	4	62	61	24	21	40

St. Louis Cardinals

	G	ERA	W-L	SV	CG	IP	H	ER	BB	SO
Bob Gibson	3	1.67	2–1	0	3	27	18	5	4	35
Nelson Briles	2	5.56	0–1	0	0	11	13	7	4	7
Ray Washburn	2	9.82	1–1	0	0	7	7	8	7	6
Joe Hoerner	3	3.86	0–1	1	0	5	5	2	5	3
Ron Willis	3	8.31	0–0	0	0	4	2	4	4	3
Steve Carlton	2	6.75	0–0	0	0	4	7	3	1	3
Wayne Granger	1	0.00	0–0	0	0	2	0	0	1	1
Mel Nelson	1	0.00	0–0	0	0	1	0	0	0	1
Dick Hughes	1	0.00	0–0	0	0	0.3	2	0	0	0
Larry Jaster	1	—	0–0	0	0	0	2	3	1	0
Total		4.65	3–4	1	3	62	56	32	27	59

Bibliography

Broeg, Bob. *Redbirds: A Century of Cardinals' Baseball*. St. Louis: River City, 1988.

Buck, Jack. *That's a Winner!* Champaign, IL: Sagamore, 1997.

Cantor, George. *The Tigers of '68*. Dallas: Taylor Publishing, 1997.

Cope, Myron. "Harry Has His Own Ways." *Sports Illustrated*, 7 October 1968.

Craft, David, and Tom Owens. *Redbirds Revisited*. Chicago: Bonus Books, 1990.

Devine, Bing, with Tom Wheatley. *The Memoirs of Bing Devine: Stealing Lou Brock and Other Brilliant Moves by a Master G.M.* Champaign, IL: Sports Publishing, 2004.

Freese, Mel. *The Glory Years of the St. Louis Cardinals*. St. Louis: Palmerston and Reed, 1999.

Gibson, Bob, and Phil Pepe. *From Ghetto to Glory*. Englewood Cliffs, NJ: Prentice-Hall, 1968.

_____, and L. Wheeler. *Stranger to the Game*. New York: Viking-Penguin, 1994.

Gibson, Jerry. *Big League Batboy*. New York: Random House, 1970.

Halberstam, David. *October 1964*. New York: Villard Books, 1994.

LeFlore, Ron, and Jim Hawkins. *One in a Million*. New York: Warner Books, 1978.

Leggett, W. "Manager of the Moneymen." *Sports Illustrated*, 7 October 1968.

McLain, Denny, and Mike Nahrstedt. *Strikeout: The Story of Denny McLain*. St. Louis: The Sporting News, 1988.

Mead, William B. *Two Spectacular Seasons*. New York: Macmillan, 1990.

Nemec, David, et al. *Twentieth Century Baseball Chronicle*. Montreal: Tormont Publications, 1992.

Reidenbaugh, Lowell. *Take Me Out to the Ball Park*. St. Louis: The Sporting News Publishing, 1987.

Rygelski, Jim. "Lightnin' Len." *St. Louis Cardinals Magazine*, June 1997.

Schoendienst, Red. *Red: A Baseball Life*. Champaign, IL: Sports Publishing, 1998.

Stout, Glenn, and Richard Johnson. *Red Sox Century*. New York: Houghton Mifflin, 2005.

White, Jack E. "Dividing Line: James Earl Ray, Cause Célèbre?" *Time*, 5 May, 1998.

Witcover, Jules. (1997). *The Year the Dream Died: Revisiting 1968 in America*. New York: Warner Books.

In addition to microfilm files from the *St. Louis Post-Dispatch* and the *St. Louis Globe-Democrat* newspapers, the following Internet sites were also utilized for statistics:

Baseball-Reference.com
BaseballLibrary.com
Baseball-Almanac.com
Retrosheet.org

Unless otherwise indicated, all quotations are taken from the St. Louis *Post-Dispatch* and St. Louis *Globe-Democrat* newspapers, and Bob Gibson's autobiographies *From Ghetto to Glory* and *Stranger to the Game.*

Index

387